W9-CYW-762

Insiders' Guide to

THE WORLD'S MOST EXCITING CRUISES

With Personal Reports from Travel Writers on Cruise Getaways

Shirley Linde and Lea Lane

TRAVEL WRITERS
Marty Snyderman, Kim Robertson, Shirley Linde, Anne Kalosh, Gena Reisner, Emily Rosen, D. Rushforth Schild, Bea Tusiani, Vivian Kramer Franke, Ed Kirk, Mark Glass, Catherine M. Senecal, Adele Woodyard, Robert Linde, Lea Lane, Ed Shriver
EDITORIAL ASSISTANTS
Kelly Ann Cole, Ed Shriver

The most complete cruise guide available
* detailed profiles of more than 300 ships
* cruise itineraries around the world
* insiders' tips on successful cruising

HIPPOCRENE BOOKS
New York

Traveling is an unpredictable business, especially cruising. Cruise lines merge, ships are remodeled, itineraries and departure times change. Every effort has been made to ensure the accuracy of the information in this book at press time, but because situations can change, we encourage you to contact the cruise line of your choice or your travel agent to confirm schedules and other information.

Cruise Ports of Call maps in Destination Planner courtesy of Official Airline Guides, a division of Reed Travel Group.

Copyright© 1994 Shirley Linde and Lea Lane.

All rights reserved.

For information, address:
HIPPOCRENE BOOKS, INC.
171 Madison Ave.
New York, NY 10016

Library of Congress Cataloging-in-publication Data

Linde, Shirley.
Insider's guide to the world's most exciting cruises/Shirley Linde and Lea Lane.
p.   cm.
Includes index.
ISBN 0-7818-0258-X
1. Ocean travel. 2.Cruise ships I. Lane, Lea. II. Title. III. Title: World's most exciting cruises.
G550.L54   1994
910.4'5—dc20   94-12404
                                                CIP

Printed in the United States of America

Dedicated to our readers and travelers of the world: Let your travel experience enrich your appreciation of nature, add to your knowledge, and help you build bridges of understanding to other peoples.

CONTENTS

Message from the Authors

Are you a cruise buff, willing to float on anything and go anywhere? Or are you reluctant to get on the water, wary of regimentation, crowded ports and close quarters? Or perhaps you're in between, but ready for an out-of-the-ordinary cruise adventure.

Whichever fits your description, this book is the most comprehensive consumer overview of cruises and ships anywhere. Whether you're new to cruise ships or an old hand, regardless of age, experience or marital status, you'll find something new or exciting.

We give inside information, not just about big, popular cruise ships, but about all types of cruises; we know that many of you enjoy privacy, seek places not yet overrun with tourists, and prefer some adventure on your vacations.

The first section of the *Insiders' Guide to the World's Most Exciting Cruises* will describe the basics of cruise travel, and give you the inside information you need to help you choose and prepare for the most exciting cruise of your life.

In the next section, you'll find specific profiles of more than 300 ships: big, small, basic, deluxe, mainstream, adventure; sailing vessels, freighters, barges, charter vessels, and fascinating, out-of-the-ordinary cruises you won't find in most books.

Armchair travelers will especially enjoy our *Insider Personal Reports*, first-person accounts of memorable cruises written by top travel writers. They will take you along on their exciting voyages from the Seychelles to the Nile, from a first cruise to an adventure deep into Zaire.

We also include a comprehensive *Destination Planner* section, covering over 1,000 cruises voyaging to the most exotic ports of call throughout the world—giving facts on where ships go, and when, as well as information on popular embarkation ports.

You can even order videos of the world's most exciting cruises and cruise destinations, one of the best ways to finalize your choice.

Many people shared their experiences and expertise in creating *Insider's Guide to the World's Most Exciting Cruises*. We wish to thank our editors at Hippocrene, especially George Blagowidow, Michelle Gagne, and Betty Abeles; our editorial assistants Kelly Cole and Edgar Shriver; and our contributing travel writers.

Information came from cruise lines, travel agencies, tour companies, and publications. We especially thank Cruise Line International Association (CLIA) and *OAG Cruise and Shipline Guide, ABC Cruise and Ferry Guide,* (all Reed Publications); Barbara Weiner at Diana Orban Inc.; Robert Scott Milne at *Travelwriter Marketletter*; Donna Green at Surf Song Travel in Tierra Verde, FL; and Harriet Karp at Briarcliff Travel Agency, Briarcliff Manor, NY. And of course, the cruise lines that let us board their ships for first-hand information.

Although we have made every effort to ensure that information was correct at the time of printing, changes in the cruising industry seem to occur as often as the tides. When you find the cruise you are interested in, get last-minute information from the cruise line itself or your travel agent.

Finally, if you have any suggestions or changes, please let us know and we will try to incorporate them into our next edition.

Shirley Linde and Lea Lane

TEN TYPES OF EXCITING CRUISES

Excitement! Something different to everyone. It may be checking out birds hiding in the precipitous crags of the Icelandic island of Heimaey, or riding the rapids down a river on the other side of the world. Or maybe its learning, finally, how to speak Italian.

Whatever you consider exciting, you can find it, or do it, or get to it, on a cruise. But not every cruise is for everybody; like love, it takes the right fit to make magic. *The World's Most Exciting Cruises* is written to help you find a cruise that will match your desires and dreams, and maybe even change your life.

Today, cruises can take you to places you otherwise might not visit, with opportunities for enjoying challenging adventures and meeting fascinating people. For example, you can now travel by boat from the Netherlands to Bulgaria thanks to completion of the Main-Danube Canal linking the Rhine and Danube Rivers — a continuous inland waterway from the North to the Black Seas.

Did you know about a ship you can take into Cuba without getting your passport stamped? How about a ship that lets you go on shore excursions into Russia without a visa? You'll find this kind of up-to-date inside information as you read on.

About 70 percent of the earth is covered by water, and

9

travel by water has always been one of the easiest and fastest ways to get somewhere. But cruising isn't just about getting from Point A to Points B and C. It's about enjoyment.

When passengers noted the amenities of shipboard crossings, and the bracing, exhilarating feeling of traveling on the world's great waterways in comfortable vessels, they started concentrating on the means as well as the end; the journey as well as the destination. And the pleasure cruise was born.

Over the years the ride has gotten smoother and better — and more confusing. The cruise market has tripled every decade since 1970, and now about five million North Americans take cruises every year. New ships are constantly launched, and old ones are continually refurbished and recycled. Competition is fierce, and the cruise passenger is the beneficiary, with better ships, better itineraries, better activities, better value.

If you've resisted cruises, and feel they might be too confining, or too crowded or too organized, or go to the same old places, look again. Today, with a burgeoning fleet of cruise ships, the variety of choices is astounding, and the itineraries offer places most of us didn't know existed. A cruise vacation is no longer just about relaxing, eating, and shopping in port. More and more it is stimulating, enriching, exciting!

Exceptional cruises of all types are available through the year and throughout the world. And even standard mainstream cruises, which a few years ago offered a limited range of predictable pursuits and ports, are spicing up their activities and itineraries in response to today's sophisticated, motivated cruising public. Whether you are interested in a week-long Bermuda cruise, or voyaging to distant ports, such as Viet Nam, where restrictions have recently been lifted, our goal is to point out the full range of the world's cruises and ports of call, provide vivid first-hand cruise experiences, and help you make your future cruises more exciting.

Types of Cruises

When choosing a cruise, if you think in terms of cruise categories, it can help you concentrate on cruises that most parallel your interests and your personality.

Some categories blend with others, such as ecology and adventure. And many cruise lines and ships fit under more than one category, perhaps even offering the elements of all 10 — a surefire exciting cruise. For example, although a ship such as the Sea Goddess may be best known for luxury, it is also an exotic, ecologically-oriented cruise, with lots of lectures and learning. In fact, this reflects the mood of the decade — cruises with environmentally-focused activities, new and interesting itineraries, as well as comfortable quarters.

Think about the categories as you read through the rest of the book.

Adventure/Exploration Cruises

Ericson, Columbus, Magellan, Balboa and other early explorers ventured across uncharted seas on voyages of discovery. The early Polynesians set out on small boats to explore the Pacific. Today many of us still want that feeling of adventure.

Happily, we can still find it. We can cruise the islands off Vancouver or the coast of Malaysia, see the ice floes of McMurdo Sound, and the Southern Cross in the Antarctic sky. (Some 30,000 cruise-passenger days were spent exploring Antarctica last year.)

Adventure cruises — also called exploration or expedition cruises — give you the chance to do, not just view. You can cruise to isolated volcanic islands, then hike to the top of soaring peaks. You can visit primitive tribes and learn their dances, fish in mountain streams, or explore ancient shipwrecks. You can take zodiacs (rubber vessels) from ship to shore to get you in close to observe penguins and seals, crags and grottos.

Too demanding? You can choose "soft" adventure cruises where rough activity is optional, guides do the chores, and you can just enjoy.

Adventure cruising ships usually feature lectures and slide shows. You acquire feelings and understandings that make a port of call — and the voyage to it — more than just a vacation. You may be on a sailing vessel riding with the wind in rarely navigated tropical waters, or on an icebreaker in the polar seas where the summer sun never sets and the only sounds are groaning glaciers and the grunts of walrus. On small vessels you can often help hoist and furl the sails, or haul the anchor.

But unlike earlier explorers, no matter how rugged the terrain, rough the seas, or isolated your destination, you can enjoy the comfort of a well-maintained ship, and often even the luxury of gourmet cuisine and down pillows. (Nightlife however may just be relaxation and conversations with naturalists and fellow passengers who tend to get to bed early to wake up and enjoy the sunrise.)

Typical adventure cruises: The *Columbus Caravelle* explores the headwaters of the Amazon. Biological Journeys focuses on the study of wildlife in Ecuador and the Galapagos, watching whales in Baja California, and diving among the fish and coral of Australia's Great Barrier Reef.

Exotic Cruises

Travelers from different parts of the world may consider different areas exotic: wherever you live, it is the places that are far away — or very different — from you that seem exotic.

Rarely-visited, out-of-the-ordinary, off-the-beaten path destinations are the excitement of exotic cruises, with glamorous itineraries to challenge the imagination.

The world's great, beautiful, strange ports await — and an exotic itinerary can exhilarate even the most jaded traveler. You can voyage to the island of St. Helena, where Napoleon was exiled. Or to Yemen, on the southwest Arabian Coast (which only recently started tolerating tourists). Or Mauritius in the Indian Ocean, or Izmir in Turkey. Or Phuket, Shanghai, Bali, and Ho Chi Minh City in Southeast Asia. Even favorite cruise grounds such as the Caribbean are getting spicier. Sailings now may stop not only in Curacao but also in Cartegena, Columbia. Transits of the Panama Canal, once considered rather exotic in themselves, now often include the nearby San Blas Islands, where you can bargain for colorful fabrics appliqued by Cuna Indians.

Typical exotic cruises: Abercrombie & Kent cruises to China, Galapagos Islands and Indonesia; Renaissance cruises to remote ports in the Chilean fjords, Africa and Indian Ocean islands.

Ecology Cruises

On these environmentally aware cruises — some call them green cruises — you can study, and sometimes even help save, nature.

Longer-than-average shore excursions allow for soft adventure or useful projects, or you can stay awhile to further your interests at the end of your cruise. You can observe nature while whitewater rafting, birdwatching and hiking; study and further knowledge by locating ancient Indian geoglyphs from hot air balloons or recording whale songs; and perhaps perform environmentally helpful assignments such as digging for remnants of lost cities, monitoring water pollution, or rescuing sea turtle eggs.

Cruise staff and guides are especially sensitive to ecology, follow strict codes of ethics in relation to the environment, and make sure that passengers do also. The atmosphere is friendly, and you are encouraged to pitch in. The navigation bridge is often open to passengers, and you may even be able to take the helm. Ship activities and formalized fun are often limited on ecology cruises, but learning experiences abound, and you can find unique opportunities that get you closer to nature.

Typical ecology cruises: Salen Lindblad and Society Expeditions cruises of the Northwest Passage to Greenland, and the British Isles of Scilly.

Activities Cruises

To some, cruising means relaxing on a deck chair with an unopened paperback, but other travelers relish the endless variety of activities available on today's cruises. With so many choices on board and ashore, the hard part is determining just what to do and what to leave out.

Typical shipboard activities include everything from volleyball and basketball to skeet shooting and diving for apples in a pool, from jogging to aerobics, from driving a golf ball off the stern to windsurfing from a fold-out marina.

And you can stretch your mind as well as your muscles. Today, the fastest growing segment of travel and tourism for adults is educational vacation trips, and the cruise world has picked up on the trend. Many ships offer courses on the history, customs, arts and languages of the ports of call. Guest lecturers and exploration leaders can prepare and guide you on field trips focused on geology, astronomy, animal and bird life, botany, volcanology and archaeology.

On-board learning activities may include classes on ballroom or regional island dances, basics of a language, how to carve ice sculpture (such as those that adorn the midnight buffet table), or instruction in scuba, bridge, or stained-glass construction. A learning opportunity has become as much a part of most cruise experiences as a casino. And you can't lose.

Shore activities can include everything from shopping in St. Thomas to horseback riding in Puerto Rico to camel riding in the Arabian desert. There may be opportunity to sail, hike, helicopter, play tennis or golf, and parasail or go hot-air ballooning on shore, or club hopping into the night. Several cruise lines have their own private out-islands where barbecues and beach games are featured. And many cruises have excursions by buses or trains to study the nearby countryside, its culture and activities.

Typical activities cruises: Carnival Cruise Lines has non-stop action on board in the Bahamas, Caribbean and Mexican Riviera. Club Med Cruises, which sail the Mediterranean and Caribbean, are exceptionally sports-oriented — with a stern that opens into a private marina. Classical Cruise Lines focuses on culture and history tours around the Aegean and Black Sea.

Theme Cruises

Specialization or niche marketing has taken over much of the tourism industry — including cruises. Sharing an affinity means exciting opportunities to indulge your interests, or create new ones, on a theme cruise.

Themes can take over the cruise experience or be just a small part of the trip, allowing those who prefer it to stay out of the action. Many ships find the concept a great way to get repeat business when their themes become a tradition.

Theme choices are endless: chocolate fantasy, Scottish Ceilidh (informal evening gatherings), smoke-free, Indonesian cuisine, murder mystery, classical, jazz or country music, bridge, backgammon.

How about wine-and-cheese tasting, health and beauty, soap stars, fantasy, travel photography? Or Cajun cooking, problem-solving, comedy, finance, sports all-stars, religious revivalism, peanut-butter appreciation. These themes, and many more, are available.

Sometimes themes center around the interests of a certain type of passenger, such as singles, seniors, gays, honeymooners, ethnic groups, teachers, hobbyists, or celebrants of school reunions.

Typical theme cruises: Pacquet French Cruises is known for its Music Festival at Sea. Regency Cruises and Royal Caribbean Cruise Line feature jazz cruises, Delta Queen Steamboat Company offers garden themes in spring and foliage in fall along the Mississippi. Clipper offers golf cruises.

Luxury Cruises

Luxury can be excitement in itself, especially if your normal lifestyle is more down to earth. Luxury ships are doubling from year to year, and now account for about 18 percent of the industry's capacity. The luxury category can include large, small, or adventure cruises.

They are usually categorized on the basis of service and spaciousness of cabins and public areas, and crew-to-passenger ratio. It can be a fantasy world of outright hedonism: superior staterooms with floor-to-ceiling windows, whirlpool tubs, refrigerator-bars and VCRs, and suites with verandas and butlers, personal attention, and pampering at every turn. Unlimited caviar and special requests of the finest foods and wines are served in restaurants that rival the world's best, with no assigned time or table. Original art and oriental rugs, top-of-the-line facilities, gala dress-up evenings — all this can be yours, for a price. And the high-end price keeps going up.

Typical luxury cruises: Seabourn Cruise Line, Crystal, and Radisson Diamond have itineraries throughout the world with top amenities.

Family Cruises

Baby boomers are now heads of families, and raring to travel. In 1992, more than 88 million trips were taken by families, and some 40 percent involved children under 18. They seek exciting trips in a safe, comfortable atmosphere.

And cruise lines are responding. Most offer discounts for children, and many provide cabins that accommodate up to five people, or have connecting cabins. Many offer single-parent or family-reunion packages.

Busy parents like to spend quality vacation time with their kids in wholesome, active settings. On a cruise, families can be together where and when they want; and children and parents can also have their own activities. At the end of the day, families can share stories about the fun they had when they were apart.

Children are often offered a camp-like atmosphere, with arts and crafts, ice cream socials, pajama parties and special movies — all supervised. Cartoon characters often roam the ship. Teens have dance lessons, pizza parties and crazy competitions.

There may even be interactive entertainment and computers in special learning environments to keep kids up with their schoolwork. Considering the variation of school terms and vacations, plus the fact that many families take children out of school, this has become as important as playtime.

Typical family cruises: American Family Cruises and Premier Cruise lines (with a tie-in to Florida theme parks) focus on family travel with special menus, babysitting, cartoon characters, supervised play and infant supplies. Norwegian Cruise Line features a circus at sea, where kids learn showstopping skills and then perform them.

Freighter Cruises

If you've got lots of time, a flexible schedule, and not much interest in cruise ship frills and activities, a freighter trip can be one of the most exciting sea voyages. Ports of call can be mixed from the exotic to the commonplace. You can be on board for months at a time, or just sign up for segments that interest you.

Freighter cruises are one of the last ways to really feel like you're getting away from it all. You have loads of time to catch up on reading the Great Books of the Western World, or — perhaps with a laptop — writing one. You can unwind, think, grow a beard, go on a diet, knit a sweater (or two or three), relearn the clarinet, paint pictures of sunsets over the great harbors of the world, or just get your act together. If you love bridge or chess, come with friends of like persuasion and have an endless floating tournament. If you are traveling alone, you can be assured that you will make new friends.

In most cases, freighter accommodations are comfortable and food is hearty (you eat what the crew does, and they need to eat well; all that lifting, you know). Low-key activities center on card games, reading, watching videos, and games like backgammon. Forget the Broadway productions and samba lessons — these are working ships.

Usually only 12 passengers are allowed (more than that, and a doctor has to be on board). All the pros and cons of being in a tight-knit group are here, but the fact that you are all traveling on a rather specialized vessel usually means you probably have something in common with fellow shipmates.

Container ships stay shorter times in port, so if you like to spend time ashore, stick to regular cargo freighters. Be prepared for changes in itinerary and delays — that's part of the excitement.

River and Waterway Cruises

Some of the most exciting cruises in the world are in the calmest waters, hugging the banks of canals and rivers, offering close-up looks at people, customs, flora and fauna. These cruise vessels are usually small and informal, and may make many stops, so you get to know a region at a slower pace, and in more detail.

You can ply the Mississippi on a paddlewheeler accompanied by calliope music, navigate the black waters of the Orinoco, glide by Rhine castles, pass through steamy rainforests along the Congo or visit historic Nanjing on a voyage up China's Yangtze River.

For those who enjoy a really slow pace, barge trips on small waterways can be languid and relaxing, whether along the canals of Burgundy's green vineyards, or cruising by Buddhist temples gleaming gold in the sun. Accommodations and cuisine range widely, but the pace doesn't: it is purposefully slow. Blissful to some, annoying to others, but, paradoxically, an exciting change of pace for people with time and patience.

Typical river and waterway cruises: European Waterways cruises through the rivers and canals of France with great food and wine. Nile cruises travel between Luxor and Aswan and dock by the world's great wonders in Egypt.

Getaway Cruises

If you think excitement comes from taking shorter and more frequent vacations, then you are part of the fastest growing cruise market. Forty percent of today's cruisers opt for long weekends or mid-week getaways, and in the past decade these short cruises have grown by over 300 percent. The shortest of all are "cruises to nowhere," one-or two-night party cruises that sail from and return to a given port with no stops.

On a short getaway, first-time cruisers can test the waters, and stressed out travelers can get a quick fix — with some of the same pampering, dining, activities and ship amenities as on a longer cruise.

On most getaway cruises, activities are non-stop and value is exceptional. Short itineraries are popular to the Bahamas and Mexico, and in Alaska, Hawaii, the Caribbean, and the Mediterranean, and on inland and coastal waterways and rivers.

Some travelers extend the getaway with a pre- or post-cruise package, an ideal way to please everyone: time on the water, and for landlubbers, time to pursue a land-based interest. For example, a visit to Orlando before or after sailing to the Bahamas is ideal for families and for golfers.

Short cruises can also be "pick-me-ups" between longer voyages.

Typical getaway cruises: Maine Windjammers feature short sailing trips along Maine's rocky coast and islands; Dolphin Cruise Line offers three- and four-night cruises from Miami to Nassau and Key West.

CHOOSING THE CRUISE THAT'S BEST FOR YOU

Imagine cruising on a Presidential yacht with its own helipad, watching a lava-fall off the coast of Stromboli in the Aeolian Islands near Sicily, or taking a train excursion into the Canadian Rockies from your ship in Vancouver harbor. Or perhaps learning Russian dances cruising along the Volga River to Moscow.

More and more, cruise ships are multiplying, upgrading, changing, diversifying, and competing to offer everything under the sun and on the seas. Today megaliners with over 2,500 passengers are going "nowhere," and small sailing vessels carrying only 100 guests are traveling anywhere and everywhere in the world. Some ships offer bingo, others head for Borneo. Some do both. Some stop to shop, others drop you off to trek through never-before-visited jungles where you clear your own paths.

So many ships, so many exciting experiences — so little time. With a choice of cruise more important and more difficult than ever, what's the best way to make a selection?

Think about the cruise categories in the previous chapter, and decide which categories interest you the most. Ask yourself the following questions in relation to the ships, to find which cruises have the potential to be the most exciting and satisfying for you. Then read through the *Ship Profiles* section to find ships that match the categories you are interested in.

How much am I willing to spend?

Our ship profiles give a good idea of costs. Divide the price of a cruise by the number of nights afloat and you get an average cost per day. If it is imperative to stay within a budget, concentrate only on ships that can deliver within that budget.

Then you need to decide the type of cabin, amenities, itinerary and other factors that are most important to you.

Cruises probably offer the best value of any vacation. You know what you'll be spending since food and most activities are included. As your floating hotel takes you from port to port, you don't need a car and gas, you don't have to fly from place to place, or have to change hotels, chipping (and tipping) away at your budget. The only extras are tips, drinks, beauty and spa treatments, and shore excursions — and you can control most of these costs. (Some cruises even include tips, drinks and shore excursions.)

Many factors influence what you pay. On **low-cost** cruises, cabins may be small, and the pool may seem not much bigger than a hot tub. But there probably will be non-stop fun including deck games, sports competitions, parties, and informal entertainment into the early hours. Food is often buffet style, and quantity may take precedence over quality.

Mainstream ships charging low prices are often older vessels with basic itineraries. These ships can run as low as $100 a day per passenger double occupancy. Also low-priced are excursion vessels, which usually visit small harbors in exotic ports, but provide modest facilities. The lure here is the itinerary and intimacy. On low-cost adventure cruises, the itinerary may be exciting, but the facilities basic. You may have upper and lower berths and shared toilets ("heads") and showers.

Ships with **middle-range** prices, offer a huge variety of options, from adventure to theme cruises, and attract middle income, middle-aged travelers, and families. **Luxury** ships are often elegant, more formal, with an older, well-off, sophisticated crowd. Prices start at about $200 a day, and can go up to thousands a day. They often make longer trips (up to four months around the world) and dock at exotic ports.

Whether you spend the minimum or the sea's the limit, the next chapter offers many ways to save money.

Where do I want to go?

Do you like beaches, archaeological ruins, 19th century architecture, unexplored jungles, white-water rafting, diving, interesting cultures and customs, rare birds? Do you want to visit unusual, faraway places or familiar favorites?

The most exciting cruises usually emphasize destinations. To find the cruises that will get you where you want to go, check the itineraries that most interest you in our *Ship Profiles* section. Or you could start with our *Destination Planner* section that offers a detailed overview of where in the world ships leave from and go to.

Five ports in seven days may sound exciting, but remember, the more crammed the ship's itinerary, the less time is available in each port. Check to be sure you will have enough time to explore at least the major attractions.

You can also factor in the type of path a ship takes. **Loop cruises** start and end at the same port. **One-way cruises** start at one port and end at another. These cruise paths require flying in and out of different ports, which may mean more expense, but since ships don't have to backtrack, they can travel farther distances in a shorter time and offer more opportunity for far-reaching itineraries. You have the chance to stay in both the original and final ports as long as you want to investigate an area in more depth.

Ships move from one cruising area to another for the season, such as from Alaska in summer to Central America in winter, or from the Caribbean in winter/spring to the Mediterranean in summer/fall. These **repositioning cruises** are good bets for bargains, and are extremely attractive for those with flexible schedules who don't mind traveling off-season. They often stop at infrequently visited ports, and usually offer more days at sea and itineraries combining far-flung parts of the world, such as the Canary and Virgin islands. Airfares are often more expensive and more complicated, but there is a feeling of discovery and adventure just taking an odd run, with an often less-than-full ship.

When looking at itineraries, consider the waters the ship will be plying. If potentially rough open seas are a problem for you, choose a cruise in calmer waters, such as rivers or along coasts, where there is less chance of rolling waves and seasickness.

One-to four-month cruises, such as around South America, around Southeast Asia, or around the world are the queens of itinerary. They include fabulous ports of call, and fabulous prices running to tens of thousands of dollars. But it's not all or nothing. Many passengers book segments on these cruises, usually a minimum of two weeks, and still enjoy top-of-the line service and ambiance.

Freighters can travel for months to ports that are interesting in their own way, and they can also be boarded in segments. They may visit working cities such as Marseilles, France or Galveston, Texas, with gritty, less-than-glamourous ports. And **charters** can go wherever you want. (Check out more information in later chapters, *Traveling by Freighter*, and *Chartering Your Own Boat*.)

How much time do I have?

Whatever your limitations — time, or time of year — a wide choice of exciting cruises is available, so check out the itineraries that fit in with your timing needs.

Seven-day voyages are most popular, and the choices they offer are vast. Thanks to air travel, destinations dense with ports, such as the Mediterranean or Caribbean, the Hawaiian Islands or French Polynesia, can offer an exciting time, even with only a week to cruise.

You can choose a two-to five-day getaway if you don't have

time for a longer excursion. Check air-sea packages that give you discounted or "free" airfare built into the price of the cruise to help keep down travel costs.

Two-to three-week cruises are another popular time span, making it worthwhile to travel to far-flung ports for an exotic cruise. Explore Asia or Australia or the South Pacific. Air travel can bring you to the waters of the world, and places formerly unreachable, and two weeks or more will give you time to explore the area in depth.

What are my special needs?

A cruise can be a disappointment if it doesn't fit your needs. If you're traveling alone, traveling with children, disabled, have a medical problem, or have specific tastes that aren't easily satisfied, make sure a ship meets your requirements. Study our ship profiles carefully. For example, some ships cater to singles, others to couples or families.

If you have a disability, look for a ship with staterooms and deck plans designed for handicapped access, or that allows service animals on board. Some exploration or adventure cruises with limited access and not many luxuries might be a problem. Careful research can assure a good experience.

What size ship do I prefer?

Giant ships are like floating resorts, and offer the most options, deck space, entertainment, activities, and types of passengers. But big ships can also sometimes be crowded, crowd-pleasing, noisy and regimented.

Big ships usually offer meals in two seatings, at specified times and at assigned tables. Big ships also mean you may have to anchor far from shallow harbors and take tenders to port, sometimes with a wait. In fact, big ships must often avoid smaller ports altogether, and miss some of the most interesting shore excursions.

Both big and medium-sized ships tend to be mainstream,

appealing to a wide range of potential passengers. They often have celebrities aboard, and major entertainment.

Smaller ships carry from a few dozen to several hundred passengers, and can more easily slip into small harbors in undeveloped or out-of-the ordinary places — a big plus for adventure travelers. On the down side, they have less space and fewer activities. And if the ratio of staff to passengers is high, you may pay more.

Small adventure or expeditionary ships are outfitted to go to the farthest points on the globe—the most remote islands, the deepest jungle rivers. Some are comfortable, others spartan and informal, and some are small luxury ships with world-class opulence.

Large, medium or small, which is best for a really exciting cruise for you? With the complexity of choice today, you'd have to factor in more than just size.

What about service?

You expect good service on a cruise. Even on an exploration ship, where staff is limited and you might be encouraged to pitch in, you still want to be served with a smile and to have your room cleaned and your towels changed.

Although today many ships have crews from all over the world, check our ship profiles for the crew nationality of each vessel. Just as countries vary widely in their hospitality, the mood of a ship can be reflected by its staff—and its nationality. For example, if you love Italy, consider lines such as Princess Cruises, Costa Cruises, and Carnival Cruise Lines, where most of the dining staff are Italian. Greeks are on staff on Epirotiki Lines, Royal Cruise Line, Sun Line Cruises and Fantasy Cruises. Dutch officers are on Holland America Line; Scandinavians on Renaissance, Norwegian Cruise Line, Royal Caribbean, and Royal Viking Line; British on Cunard and Princess Cruises.

What are my special interests?

Think again of the 10 categories of ships and select a cruise that is consistent with your lifestyle and personality. Do you prefer Las Vegas action or more quiet contemplation, non-stop scheduled activities or freedom to be left alone?

Are you interested in a cruise where you will see unusual animals? Or one that offers the possibility of snorkeling, white-water rafting, birdwatching, hiking, or mountain climbing. Do you like to dress up and dance till dawn? Gamble? Shop? Look at the ship profiles and in the index under different hobbies and activities to find the ships that fit your interests.

How important are the facilities?

The largest ships have facilities matching a grand resort; smaller vessels may offer few or many, but in a scaled-down version. If the ship's environment is important to you, look for and compare number and size of pools, deck areas, restaurants, health clubs, saunas, theaters, night clubs, bars, discos, casinos, library, elevators, sports facilities, shops, meeting areas. Are facilities available for small children? For lap swimmers? For computer hackers?

Does the ship's decor matter? Some ships are polished and proud of their years, and feature wood, brass, and traditional details. Others have plant-filled atriums, glass elevators and modern art. On some vessels decoration is whatever gear is needed for the next day's dive or hike, hung on pegs throughout the cabins.

A ship that shows its years can still be comfortable, especially if it's been recently overhauled, so check our ship profiles not only for the age of the ship, but also for what it offers. Study ship brochures and look carefully at deck plans for an overview.

And short of visiting a ship yourself, the next best thing is looking at a video. See our appendix on Video Resources for a list of videos featuring ships in this book. You can send away for videos of the ships you are most interested in, compare, and make a more knowledgeable choice.

WHAT TO KNOW BEFORE YOU GO

Selecting an Agent

Travel agents receive their commissions from airlines and cruise lines — they are at your service for free (one of the few things in a consumer's life that can actually be as good as it seems). A good agent can cut through the travel hassles and get to the best deals, saving you time and trouble. But make sure you have an agent who will listen to what you want and work hard to get you matched with the best cruise for you — at the best price.

Here are some ways to find a good travel agent:

- Choose the agent the way you would any professional — through recommendations from people they've served.
- Look for an agent's affiliation with travel agent and cruise line associations such as the American Society of Travel Agents (ASTA) or the Cruise Lines International Association (CLIA).
- Seek an agent who asks the right questions — a good sign of later getting the right answers.
- Find an agent who has experience with the places and activities you are interested in.

According to ASTA there are about 32,000 U.S. travel agencies, and over 90 percent of all tours and cruise reservations are booked through their services.

Full service travel agents deal directly with all travel suppliers, including cruise lines, airlines, rental car agencies, and hotels. But the agent you use regularly may or may not know much first-hand about cruises. You may want to compare advice and prices.

"Cruise only" travel agencies, a growing segment of the travel industry, sometimes offer significant discounts when they buy big blocs of tickets from cruise lines and are motivated to meet their quota. That means they are willing to wheel and deal. Some specialty agencies are set up as "clubs" with nominal yearly dues.

For a list of cruise specialists, send a self-addressed, stamped envelope to the National Association of Cruise Only Agencies (NACOA), c/o Consumer, Box 7209, Freeport NY 11520.

Some agencies only sell a few cruise lines and might not be looking out for your individual needs and desires. Ask questions, and hold firm to what you want if you feel pressured.

Get price quotes from more than one travel agent, and emphasize that you are especially interested in cutting costs. Make sure that if the fare drops after you have paid that you will be refunded the difference. Keep an eye on price cuts in the paper, and don't expect agents to volunteer this kind of information unless you make it clear ahead of time that you expect a discount.

For low prices you may also want to try **cruise discounters.** These agents deal in volume and take a lower commission. Although the highest and lowest priced cabins are usually sold out, the rest are generally available through them. Look in the travel sections of newspapers or in the phone book for these discounters. But be sure to know your dates, itinerary, ship and type of cabin, as these businesses offer low-cost booking, but not much more.

Some **tour operators** specialize in cruises, many with an adventure or exotic emphasis. Others charter cruises as part of their overall travel business. Usually these operators are known for a certain type of vessel, a part of the world they are especially familiar with, or wonderful shore excursions and adventures.

Colleges, universities, museums, environmental protection agencies and other **educational and social organizations** may also offer special cruise opportunities. Often these cruises are one-of-a-kind charters, and expensive, but provide top lecturers and naturalists, and fellow passengers who are highly educated and interested in ports of call. Check with major museums and learning institutions for information.

Whomever you work with, check their policies on last-minute cancellation and other business matters. And if possible, talk to previous clients.

Getting a Discount

The cruise industry is a flexible one, and with so many new cruise ships competing, prices are remaining stable — and even dropping. On major cruise lines especially, there is room for negotiation. So before you book, assume that you are going to go on your cruise at a discounted rate. Discounts on identical accommodations can range up to 50 percent. No matter how deluxe your cruise or large your purse, check things out, read the fine print, and you can save big money.

Timing is Everything

For the best discounts, the rule of thumb is to **book a cruise very early, or very late.** Earlybirds who book three to six months ahead not only get savings but also the widest choice of cabins and sailing dates. But if you are willing to risk losing the best room, specific itinerary or date, you can also get deep discounts right before departure. No ship likes to leave with empty staterooms, and they are most willing to bargain just before leaving port. So if you're flexible and willing to take a chance, you may find the best possible deal by taking a cruise that's available at the last minute.

Another way to get a good deal is to **sail off-season.** A Caribbean cruise after Christmas could cost thousands more than one earlier in December, when cruising conditions are about the same. (Also ships and ports are less crowded, and you'll probably get better service.) But if the weather off-season is unpleasant and visibility is impaired, or if the trip is geared to seasonal migrations such as whale-watching, you may find a few weeks make a big difference, and the drop in price is not worth it. Ask about the disadvantages.

Special Deals

Some routes, such as parts of the Caribbean, are currently glutted with ships. Lines competing for passengers are more likely to cut a deal. If you are more interested in the ship than where it is headed, check out popular standard itineraries, and you may be able to get a bargain.

New ships, new routes, third or fourth persons in a cabin, children's discounts, special promotions, discount coupons, twofers—all of these can mean more cruise for your money. Ask about these discounts before you book, as they are usually not volunteered.

Sizeable discounts are offered by most cruise lines booking back-to-back cruises (such as combining two seven-day cruises into a 14-day cruise), or rebooking with a cruise line you have previously sailed with.

The best-known discount is the "fly/cruise" or "air/sea" package, which includes much-reduced or even free airfare available from most major North American cities. Sometimes it is a program with one-way free air, when the ship starts in one port and ends up in another; sometimes it includes roundtrip free air to the point of embarkation and disembarkation. It usually includes transfers between the airport and ship, as well as baggage handling.

How are the cruise lines able to pull this off and still make a profit? Some of the outlay is built into the cost of the cruise for everyone. Larger lines especially, because of their clout, may cut special deals with the airlines. In any case, you should take advantage of this low airfare opportunity. And as the features vary so much, be clear about what, exactly, you will be saving, and what the requirements are.

Also compare costs to see if the low airfare opportunity

beats what you can get on your own. If you don't need air because your departure port is nearby, ask for a credit on the airfare if it is built into the price.

Some lines also offer free insurance that can protect you against sudden cancellation, lost luggage and other problems. Travel agents and cruise lines sell it, at about $50 a ticket, and it's a good idea.

If you can put together a group of friends or colleagues, say about a dozen, you can then ask the cruise line for a group discount, or ask your travel agent to negotiate for you. Or you might consider joining a club dedicated to getting discounts and up-to-the-minute bargains. Among these clubs are Travel Smart, Dobbs Ferry, NY 10522; Trav-L-Tips Cruise & Freighter Assn., P.O. Box 188, Flushing, NY 11358; and World Ocean & Cruise Liner Society, P.O. Box 92, Stamford, CT 06904.

Upgrades

An upgrade is a backdoor way of getting a great discount, and it's amazing how much leeway cruise lines have in offering them. If you think you might qualify for an upgrade, pay for the lowest-cost room possible. Often nicer rooms or suites go for the asking, and you could be upgraded more than one level.

If you are a frequent cruise passenger, cruise lines might reward you with an upgrade. On a honeymoon—first, second, or more? Anniversary? Special occasion—retirement, recovering from an illness? Big birthday? Maybe you've brought others on board. And if you are traveling single, lines might waive some of the single supplement if you give them a reason.

Payments

Before you plunk down any money, go over the fine print in the brochure one last time to check for any hidden costs and so you can ask last-minute questions.

You'll have to pay before you cruise, but usually not until a month or so before you leave; and you reserve with a refundable deposit, usually a few hundred dollars. (If you book at the last minute, you may have to pay everything at once.)

Paying by credit card is a good idea, as the credit card company will stand up for you if you have to cancel. And be sure to know the cancellation policy of the cruise line. Usually you have to put a cancellation in writing, about three months ahead if you want to avoid fees, that can go up to full fare if it's a last-minute cancellation—even for medical reasons. Read the fine print—and get the cancellation insurance.

Choosing a Cabin

When booking your cruise you will also be choosing your cabin or stateroom. (The difference in terms usually refers to the level of accommodation. Stateroom is higher than cabin, deluxe stateroom or suite is higher, owner's suite or penthouse is best of all.) Remember, the most expensive and least expensive accommodations are grabbed first.

A good agent will go over all details of choosing a cabin and show you deck plans to give an overall view of the ship. Depending on the type of cruise you are taking, and your reasons for taking it, a cabin may be major part of your enjoyment or just a place to hang your flippers. Take your time on this decision, as the difference can run into thousands of dollars.

Although some staterooms are becoming more like deluxe hotel rooms, with spacious duplex penthouses offering picture windows, whirlpool baths and verandas, in most cabins space is tight. In fact, vessels that emphasize land activities, adventure expeditions and ecology sometimes have only one type of cabin, considered a place for changing, cleaning up and sleeping.

On the other hand, luxury ships where onboard entertainment is lavish may provide extensive closet space for formal wardrobes. And on ships taking long exotic voyages, when much time is spent in the cabin, large, well-equipped facilities often are available for privacy and comfort.

Paying more for a cabin doesn't necessarily mean getting

more. For example, big stateroom windows may not be worth extra expense if the view is blocked by structures on the deck, or if cruisemates can peer into your room. To avoid this possibility, read the ship's brochure carefully, look at a deck plan, and be aware of variations, even in the same-priced cabins.

Here are some other considerations when choosing a cabin:

Outside or In? Up or Down?

A big moneysaver is skipping a window. First reaction is to dream about seeing moonlight and sunrise on the waves, but if you sleep late, it may be a blessing not to have the morning sun in your face. And even if you like views, how many times will you be looking out to sea? If you want to save money, comfort yourself knowing you can always go on deck.

Generally, the higher in the ship your cabin is, the more expensive it is. But do you need to be so high? With elevators and the health-benefits of climbing stairs, there is no obvious advantage. An inside, low cabin will probably be a bargain.

Size

If you'll be using your cabin for working, reading or entertaining, it may be worth it to get a large one with a sitting area. And if you are a big person, you may feel a bit like Gulliver when you step into a skinny shower, or squeeze into a tiny built-in bench. On some ships, the cost for larger rooms is only about $25 per person.

Check information carefully, as even same-price cabins may differ in size. Remember, if you save money on your cabin, you'll have more to use on shore excursions or shopping. And if you use your room mainly for sleeping and changing, size may not matter much.

Cabin Configurations

Cabins can be small, but give the illusion of space. Beds placed along the wall, built-in cabinets, mirrors, and other design tricks all add to this effect. Some cabins are designed for privacy, with nooks and crannies to retreat behind—

especially valuable in close quarters. Some have large baths with tubs; some, extra closet space.

See if you can get the most practical configuration for your needs. Best is to study plans of the rooms rather than just photos. Videos are a good way, short of visiting the ship, to get a good idea of room size. (See *Video Resources*.)

Bed Configuration

You'll be in bed about a third of your time at sea. How, where, and in what do you want to sleep? Some basic adventure vessels and low-end ships offer upper and lower berths. Most ships offer twin beds, either side by side or in an L configuration. If you prefer a double, queen, or kingsize bed, many ships now offer the option. If there are twin beds, sometimes they can be put together to make things more cozy. This is one very personal element which may be well worth the extra money.

On the other hand, if you are traveling with family or friends, twin beds or bunks may be preferable, and it may be worth it to book a suite with a configuration that can be maximized for privacy, using a cot, or with kids, even sleeping bags.

Noise

People on board congregate into the wee hours, so if you're near theaters, restaurants, jogging tracks, lounges, discos, elevators, stairwells, offices or promenades, you'll hear talking and activity. Also avoid laundries, the kitchen, air conditioning ventilators, and steward stations. If you're aft, you're more likely to hear the engines.

Motion

Any cruise that crosses open seas may sometimes hit rough waters, but advance availability of weather information, ship stabilizers, and preventive medications have eliminated much motion sickness. Lower decks and cabins toward the middle of the ship offer the most stability (and often lower-priced cabins). The aft end often heaves less than the bow in rough seas.

Convenience

Think of your needs when choosing your cabins. If you're with children, it would be convenient to be near the nursery and the laundry; if you like to read, near the library. Athletes might like a cabin near the fitness center, swimmers near the pool, older travelers near the elevator. If easy access is a priority, a quick thought ahead of time may save lots of inconvenience and time throughout the trip.

Booking Ahead

Dining room

Some small informal ships and high-end luxury ones accommodate all passengers in one open seating, but most medium and large ships have two dinner seatings. Remember that older passengers and families tend to eat earlier; party types, singles and sophisticates, later.

Your travel agent can request the dinner seating you prefer when booking, or you can decide when boarding. Ask for specific times of seating before deciding. Breakfast and lunch are often open seating.

You are usually assigned to a table, but can change if you wish. If you're alone, to meet people consider a large table of six or eight, or a table of single passengers only. If you prefer a romantic, private situation, there are often smaller tables for two available if you book early. And don't forget to mention if you prefer the no-smoking section.

Sometimes there are choices of formal and informal dining rooms. Do you want to dress up, or just relax? Keep in mind that informal rooms attract families.

Special Needs

If you prefer a special menu, such as salt-free, low- carbohydrate, vegetarian or kosher, request it when booking your room. Also, if you will be planning any celebrations on board, tell the cruise line in advance so they can prepare and reserve for you, and reconfirm these requests with the maitre d' when you come aboard.

Medical problems? Wheelchairs, oxygen, crutches, special bandages—let the cruise line know about your needs when booking. Also, babysitting and any other child-related needs, such as a crib, should be established when booking.

If you are taking a long cruise and want your mail sent to several ports along the way, set the delivery points ahead with your travel agent. Your mail can be delivered to the ship when you are in port.

Cancellation

When you cancel a cruise more than a month before departure, you can sometimes get a full refund if a doctor verifies that you or a close family member have a sudden medical problem. Other compelling reasons may also allow for a refund.

However, the closer you get to sailing time, the harder it is to get back your money. And if you don't show up because you miss the boat, you are still responsible for payment. To minimize any potential loss, buy trip insurance from your travel agent to cover your losses if you have to cancel.

Paperwork

Exciting cruises and exotic locations mean you'll need not only a passport, but often a visa and/or vaccination certificates. Check as far ahead as possible—preferably a few months before the cruise—so that all papers are in order. And bring along your driver's license and a credit card for additional identification on the cruise.

Contact your public health department as early as possible about vaccinations for your destinations, whether malaria pills are needed, and for other ways to prevent diseases prevalent in the areas you will visit.

If you are going on a long cruise to exotic ports and if you have any medical condition, you might also want to purchase additional medical insurance if your regular policy does not provide adequate coverage.

Pack a copy of your medical record, including blood type,

prescriptions, and any conditions requiring special attention. And be sure your doctor signs prescription slips with the generic name, in case prescriptions have to be replaced where brand names might not be known.

Packing

One of the great advantages of cruising is that you just need to unpack once, so the temptation may be to take lots of changes, and the kinds of clothes that would be too bulky on a land trip. But closet space may be limited, so before packing lay outfits on the bed, from under to outer wear, head to toe, to be sure you take what you need, and no more.

Ships that cruise to expedition or adventure destinations are generally more informal than those with mainstream or around- the-world itineraries. You can find out on-board and on-shore dress codes from ship guidelines, including theme nights, captain's parties or other special festivities.

For daytime, comfortable casualwear is fine on most any cruise. Washable, no-iron clothes are easiest. If your ship has laundry facilities, you may not need as many clothes as you think. One guideline is to bring one outfit for every couple of days on ship; and stretch your wardrobe with mix-and-match.

Except on the most informal ships (where dress is whatever you happen to have that's clean and covers your most private parts), women can use at least one simple long dress or dressy pant suit for evening, which can be accessorized up or down with scarves, belts and jewelry. A sweater or wrap is a must for overactive air-conditioning or breezy nights on deck. Men will want a sports jacket, and a dark suit or dinner jacket if the ship has formal evenings. If you want to participate in a masquerade party, it helps to pack your costume to win a prize for your interpretation of Madonna or a tossed salad or whatever (coordinated couples are often prize winners).

Trekking through jungles, climbing ruins, crossing streams and participating in most adventure excursions require tough clothing. Basic items include backpacks, totes, hats, boots, raingear, windbreakers, sunglasses, sports equipment and swimwear. Bring sealable plastic bags for waterproofing.

As for toiletries and sundries, besides the basics, double up on prescription drugs, eyeglasses and any other necessity.

Other items to consider packing are camera equipment, binoculars, favorite books, tapes and CDs, a laptop computer, diving gear and any needed items you can't purchase on board or in port.

If you'll be docking at undeveloped areas and plan to go it on your own for awhile, pack a simple first-aid kit you can carry in a backpack, including sunscreen, insect repellent, burn medication, bandages, gauze pads, tape, scissors, cotton balls, hydrogen peroxide, a thermometer, pain and fever medication, antacids, antidiarrheal medicine, topical antibiotics, elastic bandage, tweezers and alcohol. For diarrhea, Pepto Bismol is a basic; for constipation, try Metamusil, available in chewable bars. Talk to your doctor for other suggestions.

Don't even think of taking marijuana or other drugs on board with you. Cruises are a time to be free, but not that free. Customs officers use dogs in ports; entire ships have been held in port because of drugs found on a passenger.

And a word of caution: Although it's generally safer on board than almost anywhere you could travel, leave valuables at home. Adventure cruises go to places with wonderful shopping for one-of-a kind native items and jewelry. You can buy as you go.

As with most travel, it's smart to carry travelers checks (keep a record of the checks in a separate place from where you carry them). Even when traveling to exotic ports, money can be changed on board as needed for each destination. Personal checks are usually not cashed.

The amount of money you need depends on the length of the trip, where you're going, and shopping plans. In port you'll need cash for transportation, meals, activities, shopping and tips. Try to figure out what you will need and then bring about a third more than you estimate. (And keep the money you cash in the ship's safe.)

Typical Day

Our *Insider Personal Reports* section offers fascinating first-person glimpses of daily activities on some of the world's most exciting cruises. But while the ships that cover the earth's waters vary from basic vessels to grand ocean liners, some elements are available on almost every cruise. Basic comforts include air conditioning and stabilizers, radio or ship-to-shore telephones if you need to call home, areas to play cards and read, a clinic with a doctor, a pool, dining room and lounges. Most large ships have shops, gambling facilities, exercise equipment and entertainment. And the biggest ships offer facilities comparable to a large resort.

The more informal the cruise, the more likely you are to know your fellow passengers and crew. The cruise director, social staff, waiters, room stewards and purser—who serves as a banker—are the crew members you will most often come in contact with. On big ships, the second night at sea is the traditional time for the captain to host a party where you can meet with him and other officers. And if you are invited to sit at the captain's table at dinner, consider it an honor.

Daily activities on some small vessels may include no more than environmental seminars, advice on skills needed in transversing rough terrain, climbing, or rafting, and lectures on upcoming ports of call. Others add history discussions, cultural awareness and language classes (often taught by the crew in their native language). Informal cruises on small vessels offer hands-on opportunities you can't find on bigger ships. You might get involved coiling the lines of a sailboat, firing a brass cannon at sunset, or playing taps on the ship's bugle.

On mainstream ships, popular activities include aerobics, jogging, shuffleboard, deck tennis and ping pong. You might enjoy card games, first-run movies, videotapes, sports tournaments, reading in the library, investment seminars, arts and

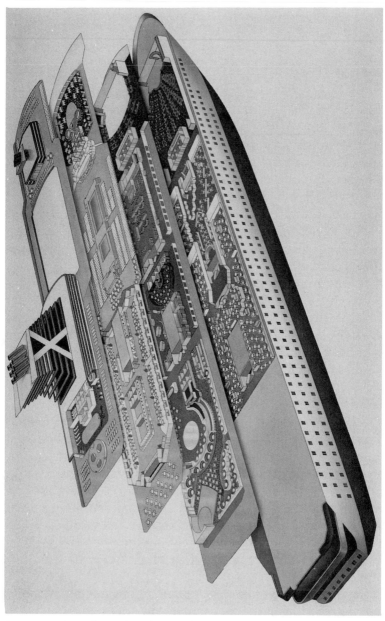

Cutaway view of Zenith, Celebrity Cruises

CUNARD COUNTESS
DAILY PROGRAMME
Based on composite Daily Programme.

THIS MORNING

Coffee and Danish Pastries are served from 7:00 am to 12:00 noon in the Satellite Cafe (5 Deck Aft).
A light breakfast is served in the Satellite Cafe from 8:00 am to 10:00 am.
As an alternative, breakfast is served in the Meridian Restaurant at 7:00 am and 8:45 am.

9:30	Quotations Quiz with a prize for the most correct entry handed in by 3:00 pm at the Purser's office.
10:30	Travel Talk. Where to go, what to see and do and Custom hints, given by your Cruise Director. Showtime Lounge.
11:30	Navigational Bridge Visit. Reservation cards available in the Library.
11:30	Interdenominational Church Service. Theatre.
11:30	Tote On The Ship's Run. Can you guess how far the ship has travelled since leaving port until noon today? Funnel, Starboard Side.
11:30	"Music in the Sun." Indoor/Outdoor Center.

THIS AFTERNOON
Luncheon
A light buffet luncheon is available in the Satellite Cafe between noon and 3:00 pm.
As an alternative, luncheon is served in the Meridian Restaurant at Noon and 1:30 pm.

1:00	An informal meeting of Masons, Rotarians and all Service Club members. Indoor/Outdoor Center.
2:00	Movie in the Theatre.
2:30	The Casino opens for your gaming pleasure. Indoor/Outdoor Center.
2:45	Bridge. Card Room.
2:45	Tennis Tournament. Recreation Deck 8. Golf. Recreation Deck 8.
3:30	Dance Class. Showtime Lounge.
4:00	Afternoon Tea is available. Showtime Lounge.
5:15	Teen Get-Together. Lido Bar.
6:00	BBC World Service News Broadcast. State/Public Rooms & Open Decks.

THIS EVENING
The Captain's Cocktail Party
The Captain and his Officers request the pleasure of your company for cocktails in the Indoor/Outdoor Center.

5:45	Party for guests on Main Sitting followed by dinner in the Meridian Restaurant.
7:45	Party for guests on Late Sitting followed by dinner in the Meridian Restaurant.
8:00	Movie in the Theatre.
9:30	SHOWTIME, presenting Caribbean Calypso & Fancy Dress Ball. Showtime Lounge.
10:00	Movie in the Theatre.
10:00	Dancing to Top Disco Sounds. Indoor/Outdoor Center.
10:00	Casino opens. Indoor/Outdoor Center.
10:30	Repeat of SHOWTIME for passengers on Late Sitting. Showtime Lounge.
12:00	Midnight Buffet. Meridian Restaurant.

)|Carnival.

THE MOST POPULAR CRUISE LINE IN THE WORLD!™

CARNIVAL CAPERS

M.S. ECSTASY		SATURDAY, DAY 7
6:30 AM	Coffee & Danish	Panorama Grill — Lido
7:00 AM – 8:00 PM	Nautica Spa & Gym Opens	Sports Deck Forward
7:00 AM	Walk-A-Mile	Olympic Track — Sun Deck
7:30 AM	Stretch & Relaxation	Aerobics Studio
7:45 AM	Breakfast — Main Sitting	Both Dining Rooms
8:00 AM	Slot Machines Open	Crystal Palace Casino
8:00 AM – 8:00 PM	Nautica Spa Salon Opens	Sports Deck Forward
8:00 – 10:00 AM	Light Deck Breakfast	Panorama Grill — Lido
8:30 AM	Low Impact Aerobics	Aerobics Studio
9:00 AM	Breakfast — Late Sitting	Both Dining Rooms
9:00 AM – 8:00 PM	Galleria Shopping Mall Opens	Atlantic Deck
9:30 AM	Dynaband● Calisthenics	Aerobics Studio
9:30 AM – 8:00 PM	Video Diary Desk Opens	Empress Deck
9:30 AM	Bridge Walk-Through	Meet Portside — Lido Deck
10:00 – 11:00 AM	Coffee, Tea & Bouillon	Panorama Grill — Lido
10:00 AM	Trapshooting	Promenade Deck Aft
10:00 – 11:00 AM	Library is Open	Explorer's Club
10:00 AM	Horse Racing	Blue Sapphire Lounge
10:30 AM	Aqua Aerobics	Verandah Deck Aft
11:00 AM	Photo Gallery Opens	Empress Deck Grand Atrium
11:00 AM	Senior Aerobics	Aerobics Studio
11:30 AM – 2:30 PM	Light Lunch & Salad Bar	Panorama Grill — Lido
11:30 AM – 2:00 PM	Specialty Sandwiches	Lido Deck Poolside
11:50 AM	Captain's Bulletin from the Bridge	
12:00 NOON	Lunch — Main Sitting	Both Dining Rooms
12:00 NOON	Full Casino Opens	Crystal Palace Casino
1:00 PM	Ice Carving Demonstration	Lido Deck Poolside
1:30 PM	Lunch — Main Sitting	Both Dining Rooms
2:00 – 3:00 PM	Library is Open	Explorer's Club
2:00 PM	Trapshooting Tournament	Promenade Deck Aft
2:00 PM	Ping Pong Tournament	Verandah Deck
2:45 PM	Newlywed & Not-So-Newlywed Game	Blue Sapphire Lounge
3:00 PM	Bingo	Blue Sapphire Lounge
4:00 PM	Multi-Impact Aerobics	Aerobics Studio
4:00 – 5:00 PM	Ice Cream & Cookies	Lido Grill — Outside
4:00 – 5:00 PM	Frozen Yogurt	Lido Grill — Inside
4:00 – 5:00 PM	Tea Time	Society Bar
4:30 PM	Masquerade Parade	Blue Sapphire Lounge
5:00 – 6:00 PM	"Fun Ship" Highlight Party (Main)	Metropolis Bar
6:00 PM	"American" Dinner Main Sitting	Both Dining Rooms
7:00 – 8:00 PM	"Fun Ship" Highlight Party (Late)	Metropolis Bar
7:30 – 8:30 PM	Farewell Party for Teens & Jr. Cruisers	Stripes Disco
8:00 PM	"American" Dinner Late Sitting	Both Dining Rooms
9:00 PM	Super Trivia	Blue Sapphire Lounge
9:00 PM	Sweet Music	Society Bar
9:30 PM	Bingo	Blue Sapphire Lounge
9:30 PM	Listen to "Sea Breeze"	Starlight Lounge
9:30 PM	Piano Bar Opens with "Scott"	Neon Bar
9:45 PM	Music Society plays	Chinatown
10:00 PM	Disco Opens with "Jeff"	Stripes Disco
12:30 – 1:30 AM	Quiche & Salad Buffet	Wind Song Dining Room
1:30 – 2:00 AM	Mini Buffet	City Diner — Promenade Deck

DRESS FOR THE EVENING: Casual.   MOVIE: "Regarding Henry" 7:30, 10:00 AM, 12:30, 3:00, 5:30, 8:00, 10:30 PM, 1:00, 3:30 AM

crafts, and dance lessons. Some people join a nonstop bridge or backgammon tournament. The day might also include listening to the band, getting massaged, visiting the bridge or galley, or going to the health club or hairdresser.

When you are in port you can spend most of the day—and

perhaps most of the night—engaging in the activities and tours that get you a glimpse into the world where you have docked, and perhaps a chance to adventure deeper into the environment, participating in local customs with local people.

Back at the ship you may be exhausted from the day's full schedule and just wish to collapse in your cabin. Or maybe your day of relaxing in the ocean air has energized you for a night of fun. You could start out in one of the lounges, with hor d'oeuvres, music and drinks.

Then dinner at sea, a favorite ritual. Later, there may be quiet activities such as lectures and presentations of the next day's shore excursions, or games such as charades or "horse racing." As the evening progresses, adventure vessels may become as still as the sea, but mainstream ships will be swinging, with singers, comedians, magicians—some well-known, some yet undiscovered—or even Broadway musicals or Las Vegas-style revues.

Audience participation will be invited for talent shows or costume parties, opportunity, if you wish, to show off your years of piano training, your shower voice, or your best jokes. Discos may blare rock and pulsate with laser light shows, roulette wheels spin in casinos with croupiers and high rollers, and a midnight buffet lures late-night foodies to admire the bounty as much as devour it. An intimate cabaret may offer a torchy singer or a jazz guitarist to take you into the early morning hours, and there's always a deck chair from which to watch the sunrise.

Romantics may prefer to skip the organized fun and just feel the breeze, listen to the water splash against the ship, and gaze at the stars.

More on Dining

A special joy of cruising is the pleasure of the table: abundant, well-prepared and well-presented food, reflecting the sea, the ship nationality, or the part of the world you are traveling in, all served with grace and attention. Meals are rest stops: a chance to dress up, sit down with fellow passengers, socialize, discuss the day's happenings and life in general, meet new people and reflect on life's pleasures.

No matter which type of cruise you choose, dining will be one of the highlights. Smaller ships often have one seating; larger ones, usually two seatings, and luxury vessels may have open seating and even different class dining rooms, including formal grilles with wine stewards. Most ships provide open- seating breakfasts and lunches in the dining room and by the pool, where snacks and casual meals are also available most of the day.

First seating for dinner (or early, or main seating as other ships might call it) is usually around 6 pm; second, or late, seating around 8 pm. For lunch, meals usually are served from noon to 2 pm; breakfast, 7:30 am and 9 am.

Cruising's reputation for quantity of food is true. Princess Cruises reports that during a typical 10-day cruise, the following items are consumed by passengers: 2,904 pounds of cheese, 36,000 eggs, 500 bottles of champagne, 1,600 bottles of wine, 2,959 cans of beer, 11,120 pounds of meat, 12,200 pounds of fish and lobster, 2,000 pounds of pasta, 21,335 pounds of fresh fruit, 22,355 pounds of vegetables, 1,200 gallons of milk, 1,200 pounds of coffee, 1,900 pounds of sugar, and 87,900 loaves of bread, rolls and breadsticks.

You can consume as much and as often as you wish. If the formal meals aren't enough, most big ships offer round-the-clock room service to get you through those peckish times when you want to nibble. On Royal Caribbean (typical of most large cruise ships) passengers can order a room service breakfast, head to the dining room for a full breakfast, go up on deck for a buffet breakfast, have room service for lunch, go to the dining room for lunch, head back up on deck for a buffet lunch, in the afternoon have sandwiches and ice cream or a hot dog snack, have a room service dinner, eat dinner in the dining room and then catch the midnight buffet. No wonder they say travel is broadening!

But despite the possibility of gluttonous indulgence, ships often provide optional spa menus which you can request

Captain's Farewell Dinner

Black Pearls of the Caspian Sea with Blinis
and Sour Cream

Vodka

Marinated Groenland Lax on Fine Bean Salad
with Fresh Mushroom and Mustard Dill Sauce

Suprême of Tropical Fruits, flavoured with Tia Maria

Consommé Double "Grimaldi"
Cream Soup "Reine Margot"
Chilled Gaspacho

Half Rock Lobster "Thermidor"

Fine Champagne Sherbet "Kir Royal"

Sautéed Mignon of Milk Veal with Morels,
Fresh Cream and Fine Noodles

Fillet of Capon Rôti with Smitane Sauce
and Chamonix Potatoes

Charolais of Tenderloin "Chateaubriand"
with Béarnaise Sauce

Jardinière of Selected Seasonal Vegetables

Chamonix Potatoes, Paillette Potatoes,
Buttered Potatoes

Heart of Lettuce, Iceberg Salad and Escarol with Chives Dressing

Baked Alaska Flambée
Strawberry Mousseline with Meringue
Tarte "Duchesse Anne"
Petit Fours and Praline

Coffee, Sanka, Nescafé, Tea

The Wine Steward will be happy to assist in choosing your wine ahead of time, or order direct from the menu. No longer is it inevitable to put on weight. In fact, with dietary menus combined with on-board workouts, shore excursions and soft-adventure activities, you could come home even lighter than when you boarded.

All Ashore....

Some passengers seem content never to leave the harbor, but one of the exciting aspects of cruising is to get on land: soak up the culture, sample the cuisine, drink the native brew, shop, meet the locals — and even participate in adventure and exploration pursuits.

Some ships spend a few hours in port; others stay in the harbor for several days, acting as floating hotels. Passengers may stay on board or head off for organized or independent adventures.

If the ship is docked, it's easy to get on and off, but if it anchors in the harbor, smaller vessels such as launches, tenders or zodiacs will have to bring passengers to shore. This may mean some waiting, paying special attention to schedule so you don't miss the launch, and some potential problems for disabled passengers.

How can you find out what you want to do when you go ashore? Ask others who have already been. If you haven't brought material with you, check the ship's library, which usually has books about the area visited, information about organized excursions, and walking maps. You may wish to take a guided tour offered by the ship, hire a cab of your own, or simply walk around the port and absorb the local flavor or shop.

Most ships give lectures and multimedia productions on the people, history, flora and fauna of the area. They give detailed descriptions of where the organized tours go. Some even give recommendations for shopping.

Taxis or car services are often waiting for the boats, and "guides" will show up seemingly out of nowhere. They may be good—or just awful. Don't be pressured against your will to hire anyone. Make sure that the guide speaks a language you know, and establish the price before you leave. Write the sum down, and pay at the end of the trip. It might be worth it to join with some like-minded folks and split the cost.

You could also rent a car through an agent and have it waiting at the port, although the paperwork may take up much of your touring time and port reservations made from far away have a way of getting lost. In some situations, bikes or motorscooters are fun alternatives for getting around.

If you like to shop, you can usually walk to an area near the harbor, or hop on a bus and go to an area where the locals shop. Just be sure you're not flashy, and watch out for pick-pockets and bad deals.

How much time will you have in port? This can determine whether you go with a group, sightsee on your own, or just shop around. In some ports, there isn't much choice: take the tour or walk around the harbor. Considering how far you have come, it is generally better to go on a mediocre tour than see nothing much more than warehouses.

If you have a choice of tours and can't make up your mind, find one that features what you can't do or find anywhere else. (And although the cost may be high, later you'll regret not what you paid, but what you didn't do; one of the truisms of travel — and life.)

Organized tours can sometimes be arranged on shore. Tour organizations and the local tourist office can give you maps and information to help you decide what to choose.

Group shore excursions usually leave in vans or buses, and there is inevitable regimentation and a set amount of time allotted for sights. You can visit a specific site, such as the Mayan ruins of Tulum on Mexico's Yucatan coast. Or general ones, such as a drive along the shoreline with a stop for snorkeling, a hike through a rain forest and a drop-off for an afternoon at the market. Night-life tours are often also available. Some guided tours feature shopping, and not much else, and some drop you at stores that offer the organizer a kick-back. Avoid this if you can.

Boat tours of the harbor and shoreline can be a nice way to spend a day. You could rent your own, go on a sightseeing boat, or try a glass-bottom boat or submarine tour to observe underwater life from the comfort of a specialized craft. A sunset sail is a nice option if you are in harbor toward evening.

Aerial tours in helicopters, small planes or hot-air balloons can give you a wonderful overview, especially of places with migrating animals or dramatic terrain. You can fly into the mouths of smoking volcanos, along gorges, over glaciers, up to waterfalls, and along sinuous rivers.

Shore excursions are the highlight of adventure cruising, and ships with a commitment to preserving the environment and an emphasis on learning and doing usually offer exceptional ones. These trips can venture deep into the heart of the area, often in four-wheel drive vehicles, dugout canoes or airboats. You might trade T-shirts for necklaces with a tribe, explore bird nests along a tributary, safari into the bush, or dive to explore wrecks. Then get back to the vessel for dinner, or even more memorable, stay to eat with the locals.

*   *   *

INSIDER TIPS FOR GOING ASHORE:

- Save money by reading ahead and deciding what you want to see.
- For more flexibility, hire a local taxi.
- Pick up a good local guidebook and map to maximize your independence.
- Many ships will pack a picnic basket for shore excursions and will customize it to your tastes.
- Check your library or travel agent for the location of tourist boards of places you are going. Call or write for useful free materials.
- Before sailing into exotic ports, try out the country's food at your home-town restaurants to find the best dishes, learn their names, and get used to the tastes. Restaurants

are also good places to talk to locals who may have friends and family at home who would be willing to meet you in port and show you around.

* * *

INSIDER TIP: HOW TO USE HOTEL BEACHES IN PORTS

- Ask the cruise line ahead of time for a list of their shore excursions. If none seem exciting, you may want to spend the day at a hotel in the port area. For example, if your cruise ship stops in Ocho Rios, Jamaica, you can arrange ahead for a $65 day-pass to Sans Souci Lido (2 miles east) that includes meals, drinks, beach, tennis, windsurfers, hobi cat, glass- bottom boat, hot mineral bath, and — if there's an opening for an appointment — a massage, body scrub, facial and other services at their spa. A day-pass at Grand Lido Negril gets you similar use of beach, tennis and water sports plus two hours around the island on the *Zein*, a gorgeous luxury yacht given by Aristotle Onassis to Princess Grace and Prince Rainier for their honeymoon. For either one, contact the manager for advance arrangements. (No children.)

* * *

Purchasing Rules

Unusual and often inexpensive items fill the ports of the world: hand-made lace in Brazil, straw in the Bahamas, wood carvings in Africa, paintings and sculpture and pottery everywhere. And as ships go farther afield, the temptation to buy increases. As a U.S. citizen you can bring back up to $400 of goods purchased abroad (artworks and antiques excluded), including up to a quart of liquor or wine. Customs will impound any meats, fruits, vegetables, plants and plant products unless accompanied by an import license from a U.S. government agency. And some countries, such as Thailand, have strict rules against taking art or antiques out of the country.

You can send friends and family a gift a day, under $10, —not liquor or tobacco—without having to declare it ($20 from U.S. possessions in the Caribbean and Pacific). To send things from unusual locales is not only cost-effective, but exciting for the recipient.

Tipping

Although a few luxury lines have eliminated tipping, it is a fact of life on most ships, and the staff still depends on it to bolster low wages. On adventure cruises, tipping may mean a collection box set in a main area on the last day of the trip; passengers deposit voluntary and anonymous amounts. On the other end of the scale is the mandatory 15 percent service charges added to the cost of some cruises.

Voluntary tipping is still the norm. Factor in 10 percent of your cruise cost for all combined tips, and if you have any questions, ask the purser, or discuss it with seasoned shipmates. To avoid confusion, guidelines are often explained by the cruise director, or spelled out in printed material. Guidelines assume good service, so if service disappoints, tip what you feel is appropriate.

The industry standard is about $3 per person per day for the dining room waiter, $2 per person per day for the busboy. The room steward cleans your room daily, leaves you towels twice a day, and turns down your bed at night; $3 per person, per day is usual.

Other personnel, such as the musicians, sports staff, maitre'd, wine captain, or bartenders can also be given gratuities for appreciation of service. (Check to see if bar tips are already included with drinks.)

People usually put their tips in an envelope provided by the ship on the last evening of a cruise up to two weeks long. If the cruise is longer, half the gratuity can be given midway, or a part, weekly. (And if you are a generous tipper, it's a good idea to give half midway, even on shorter cruises; it may mean extra-special service.)

Traveling Alone

Being on the water has a way of making even the shyest person warm up. This is especially important for someone traveling on their own.

Whether or not you are interested in finding romance, or just want to make new friends and have a good time, cruising is one of the best ways to succeed. According to CLIA, two out of five people likely to be cruising in the future will be singles. If you're cruising alone, you are not really cruising alone. Even if the ship is not known for being singles-oriented, there will be many people on their own, and many opportunities to meet them.

Often there are special singles parties, sports and games. And the many places with group activities, such as the dining room, health spa, disco, casino, or the deck itself, lend themselves to socializing. Best way to meet people and find like-minded companionship is to participate.

To help things along, at dining assignment, ask to sit at a singles dining table, preferably a large one. And if there is more than one seating, go for the late. It allows for pre-dinner drinks and talk, and transition to after-dinner dancing or the show lounge.

To make the most of the social scene, stay open-minded, move around, join in, stay up late, and attend even corny icebreakers.

You will also make friends with couples. Just remember to pay your own way, despite any protestations; you may quickly lose companions otherwise.

Shipboard accommodations have been a sore point for single cruisers, who are usually forced to pay a supplement. But some lines offer reduced supplements, as little as 15 percent above the double occupancy rate. Many lines provide matchmaking, offering single-share plans for compatible cabinmates. Check before booking, and offer to share. Often no cabinmate will be found, but you'll be given the lower rate.

* * *

INSIDER TIP: DANCING ON THE BARK

- If you like to dance, and you're a single woman, note that some ships provide male partners. The hosts are generally over 45, have outgoing personalities and dancing skills. Most big liners now recruit these social hosts—who get free travel for their unending smiles. Among the lines are Royal Cruise Line, Royal Viking Line, Delta Steamboat Company, Cunard, Regency Cruises, World Explorer, and Holland America Line.

* * *

Traveling With Children

If you seek privacy, escape, romance, indulgence, it is harder with children around. On the other hand, traveling with children gives you the gift of seeing places and experiencing things through their eyes. It can be a time of sharing, bonding, opening up, discovering the world and yourself. And it provides unforgettable memories.

You can choose one of the cruise ships that cater to families, but even if you are on a cruise that does not, you can still all have an exciting time.

Especially on large ships, there are endless activities and choices so that even the most impatient child can keep busy from morning to night. Most ships today have special children and teen areas and activities, especially during holidays and summer. Some have supervised programs, so that if you wish, children can be picked up after breakfast and deposited back in the cabin after dinner. They will have had a day filled with games, nature hikes, scavenger hunts, swimming, and special movies and meals.

However, some small luxury ships do not encourage children; and not all adventure exploration ships, or those that travel to primitive ports where inoculations are required, are right for young children; many do not even accept children under a certain age. But cruises can be a wonderful family experience, and on smaller vessels with adventure activities and ecological ethics, pitching in and being responsible and environmentally aware is a great learning experience.

If you go on shore as a family, remember that shore excursions can be a problem if kids are dragged where they don't want to go. Ideally your itinerary will be of interest to all.

Ship dining can be a time of togetherness for families. Table talk tends to flow easily, even if talk at home may be limited. Your regular waiter can cater to youngsters, even bringing them alternate food such as hot dogs or pizza. Early seatings are best for families. On the other hand, babysitting and supervised activities allow for you to eat with adults only if that is your preference. Staff personnel are usually available to babysit.

On most ships, children under 12 can share a room with two adults for half price, or even free; or consider arranging for adjoining cabins.

Health

With cruise ships of all types now cruising to places never before visited and incorporating activities to stretch your mind and body, you can look forward to a dream vacation. But to head off trouble, and ensure a cruise without nightmarish excitement, there are some precautions you can take.

Large ships usually have hospital facilities, with a doctor, nurses, and supplies of frequently dispensed prescription drugs. Even small ships plying far-flung waters most always have basic medical facilities and a doctor on board. But if you need particular medicines for a known problem, take ample supplies and carry rather than pack them, in case your luggage is lost.

What if a medical emergency strikes? Ships are prepared to have you airlifted by helicopter and flown to the nearest major medical facility.

You may want to look into special health insurance to supplement your regular policy. Check with your insurance broker or your travel agent. Some companies that offer supplementary insurance include: Carefree Travel Insurance, Box 310, 120 Mineola Blvd., Mineola, NY 11501, 516-294-0220; Travel Assistance International, 1133 15th St., NW, Suite 400, Washington DC 20005; 800-821-2828, 202-331-1609; and Travel Guard International, 1145 Clark St., Stevens Point, WI 54481, 800-782-5151, 715-345-0505.

Seasickness

Rough waters may mean seasickness. Although it feels dreadful, a bout of seasickness usually passes within 10 hours. The trouble is, it can return again.

If you're prone to motion sickness or know that rough waters may be ahead, doctors can prescribe a Transderm patch you place behind your ear. This allows medicine to automatically absorb into your skin. Other popular antimotion drugs are Bonine and Dramamine. They should be taken *before* you feel sick. A third solution is a motion sickness shot which keeps you fine for many days.

If you don't like drugs, or the chance of getting drowsy from medicines, you can tough it out by breathing fresh air on deck at the center of the ship, keeping your eye on the horizon and your mind occupied. Ginger in any form and vitamin B6 have also been reported to be effective, as has an acupressure wrist band.

Water Precautions

If you are onshore in "don't-drink-the-water" areas, use normal precautions, such as brushing teeth with bottled or boiled water, avoiding ice and avoiding glasses or utensils washed in unknown water. Close your mouth and eyes while showering, and carry sterile solutions for contact lens cleaning.

Drinking sealed, bottled water is safest. If you must drink the local water, be sure it is boiled for at least 15 minutes. You can also add specific amounts of iodine or bleach, (check with your doctor), then filter it. But it will taste awful.

As for swimming in streams, rivers or lakes on shore excursions, be careful. Harmful microorganisms and parasites may be lurking where you can't see them — especially in tropical and underdeveloped countries. Enjoy the view, but if you want to be absolutely safe, for swimming — or even trailing your hand in the water — stick to the ocean or pool.

Food Precautions

Ships sailing to foreign ports from the United States have unannounced inspections about every six months for food and water sanitation. Good news is that the vast majority of ships sailing from U.S. ports do pass federal sanitary inspection. (Just a few years ago, only about half the ships passed.) Bad news is that about one-sixth still fail.

Ask your travel agent about sanitation scores, or to get your own copy of the latest inspection reports write to: Chief, Vessel Sanitation Program, National Center for Environmental Health, 1015 North America Way, Room 107, Miami, FL 33132.

A couple of decades ago, diarrhea outbreaks on board ship were common, but today they are rare, thanks to higher standards for food storage and preparation. Cruise lines carefully train employees to wash hands and use hygienic habits, and it seems to be working. If you have a problem, see the ship doctor.

Eating on shore? Avoid food carts serving meat or other spoilable food, stick to restaurants or hotel dining rooms, eat only fruit you can peel, avoid raw or undercooked food and large reef-dwelling fish such as grouper, amberjack, sea bass, and barracuda. Also avoid foods with lots of hand preparation, that have been uncovered for long periods, or have custard, mayonnaise, or cream sauces. What does that leave? Simple, hot, well-cooked, peelable foods, especially fresh fruits and vegetables, baked goods and grains, and anything and everything back on the ship.

Diseases

If you're cruising to remote areas of the world, call your

local public health department for latest reports and medical advice for the area you plan to visit. Some of the major problems you may need to be protected against:

- **Malaria.** Especially bad in Central America, parts of Mexico, Haiti, the Dominican Republic, and Southeast Asia. (To lessen mosquito bites, which transmit the disease, wear long- sleeved shirts and long pants. Spray clothes and skin with a permethrin product or DEET or use Avon's Skin-So-Soft bath oil.)

- **Dengue Fever.** Also spread by mosquitos, it's called "Island Fever" in the Caribbean, and causes hemorrhaging and circulatory failure. South America and Southeast Asia are trouble spots.

- **Typhoid.** Fleas, lice and ticks spread this disease, which is especially active in Mexico, Peru, Pakistan and India. High fevers are part of the consequences.

- **Polio.** India has thousands of cases diagnosed every year, and it's an active disease in other parts of the world, including Mexico.

- **AIDS.** Now it's everywhere, and some primitive areas have extremely high rates. Safe sex is a must. Also be careful about blood or blood products; in fact, in a medical emergency it is recommended that you return to the U.S. (or a place where you are sure of the blood supply) or refuse transfusion.

For further disease information check your library, call your public health nurse, or contact: Health Information for International Travel, Superintendent of Documents, Washington DC, 20402; and State Department's Citizen Emergency Center, Washington DC, 202-647-5225.

Safety

Every cruise ship must conduct at least one lifeboat drill early on the cruise, and it is required that you attend. You will put on a life preserver, usually found in your room, and head to your mustering station. The directions are usually on the door or nearby wall. It's also a good idea to memorize the way out of your cabin to the nearest deck in case of fire or any emergency.

While on the ship, keep valuables in a safe, and while in port, act conservatively. Some criminals wait for the ship to come in, so wear a money belt, don't look flashy, stay with others if possible, and stay alert. Don't believe everything you hear, and don't go off in unlicensed vehicles. Watch your cameras, wallets and purses, and leave jewelry on the ship, or at home.

For freshly updated information from the federal government on the safety of a foreign country or city, call the U.S. Department of Transportation Travel Advisory number 800-221-0673.

Just a few precautions can help ensure an exciting, and safe, cruise.

*   *   *

MORE INSIDER TIPS:

- Go to travel agency cruise nights, or take an expert to lunch from a university, museum, zoo, or botanical garden for information.

- Bring a small packable carry-on suitcase for the last night on ship; lines usually collect luggage the night before you disembark.

- Take more film, more lenses and more cameras than you feel you could possibly need. Protect them with lens caps and plastic sealable bags. And be sure to ask about any instructions, dangers or prohibitions in photographing animals or people.

- Except for destinations in Mexico, Canada and some of the Caribbean, you will need a passport, and sometimes a visa. Ask your travel agent and the cruise line in time to get them by mail.

- Keep a record of your passport number, date, place of

issuance and facts about your other documents. They are indispensable if your documents are lost or stolen.

- Leave someone a copy of your itinerary, ship's call letters, ports of call and travel agent's name. Take important phone numbers and addresses.

- Most homeowners policies can be extended to insure cameras, binoculars, computers and other expensive equipment when you travel.

- If you'd like a complimentary cake and a chorus of "Happy Whatever," advise your travel agent in advance— or tell your waiter or maitre'd when you board. You can also arrange for private parties with champagne, canapes, wine and cheese to honor any occasion.

- Some lines offer a discounted package for shipboard weddings, complete with clergy, champagne, wedding cake and a photo album.

- To keep waters unpolluted, the Coast Guard has requested that cruise passengers report any illegal garbage dumping — with specifics, if possible. Watch out for: plastics, such as trash bags, which kill marine life and aren't biodegradable; packing material less than 25 miles from land; food, paper, rags, glass or metal less than 12 miles from land; pulverized materials less than three miles from land.

- If you have hobbies, club or religious associations, or friends of friends, make a connection at the places you visit. This enriches your trip, and can provide you with useful inside information.

- Leave the last day of your vacation for a day of leisure at home to unpack, do laundry, look at mail, read old papers, call friends and reflect on where you've been.

- If you learned something new on your cruise, keep it up when you get home. If you hiked, you can do it on weekends. If you learned about flowers, join a horticultural club. Keep the excitement going.

Follow the Responsible Travelers' Credo:

Make sure where you've been is in the same
state you found it — or better. Take nothing but
images and memories. Leave nothing but
footprints on land and bubbles in water.

SHIP PROFILES

No other consumer travel guide contains as many ship profiles as The *Insider's Guide to the World's Most Exciting Cruises*. We have included giant ocean liners that carry more than 2,000 passengers, and small intimate ships that can go where the big ships can't; we have included luxury liners and budget ships, glamorous formal ships with impeccable service and dive ships with casual live-in-your-shorts atmosphere. We have included tall sailing ships where you can hoist a sail or take the helm, ships with big bands where you can dance on the deck under the stars, ships that cater to families or to art or to tennis or golf or jazz, small environmentally-approved boats that can take you to the face of a glacier or to swim with whales, expeditionary ships to go to the Antarctic or above the Arctic Circle, ships that go to remote villages of seldom-visited islands in the South Pacific, or slow boats that will take you to explore a river.

You can browse through the *Ship Profiles* section to dream about the ships and trips that appeal to you, or you can use the detailed information to help choose a cruise, compare ships and trips, or learn more about a ship you have already booked.

If you have cruised previously, we hope the ship profiles will help you find even more exciting ones. If you have never cruised before, we hope that you find a cruise to fire your imagination and that you experience the special satisfaction in sailing to exotic destinations and learning of the many different peoples and places of our planet earth.

We have inspected many of the ships ourselves; in other cases we have relied on data gathered from travel writers, travel agents, the cruise lines, or others.

Rates are given for the total range of prices of cabins and suites available for a ship. Within that range, rates are lowest for inside smaller staterooms or cabins, higher for outside or larger staterooms, and highest for suites. In-season rates are higher than off-season. Some itineraries are more expensive than others.

A cautionary note: We made every effort to make this book up-to-date right up to the final minutes that we went to press, but cruise lines often change activities and itineraries, and may even change the owners or operators of the ships. And new ships are coming on line as fast as the cruise lines can handle them. In the near future, Princess Lines, Crystal Cruises, Regency, Europe Cruise Line, Royal Viking, and the Delta Queen Steamboat Company each plan to launch new ships; Holland America will launch another sister ship to the Staatendam; Carnival has ordered what is says will be the largest ship ever built; Diamond Cruise is planning another twin-hulled *Radisson*; Royal Caribbean and Celebrity each plan to build a new ship per year through 1997.

Be sure to check with a travel agency or the cruise line to confirm details before you make your final plans!

ABERCROMBIE AND KENT
1520 Kensington Rd., Oak Brook, IL 60521
800-323-7308; 708-954-2944

MV ACTIEF
Built: 1907
Registry: England
Former Name: *Dutch Klipper*
Length: 100 ft.
Beam: 17 ft.
Speed: 8 knots
Officers: British
Crew: 4, British
Passengers: 12. About 90% couples. Guests are mostly from U.S., Australia, and U.K.

MV ACTIEF

Cabins: 7. Three twins, two singles and two suites. All have central
  heating, private bath with shower and hairdryer, window that
  opens. No smoking.
Dining: British with Cordon bleu slant. Single seating for 12.
Facilities: Salon, bar and small library.
Activities: Shore excursions. Bicycles, fishing equipment. Hot air bal-
  looning. Golf on four cruises
Rates: Double occupancy per person from $1,250 to $2,490 including
  transport to and from London.
Itinerary: Three- to six-day cruises of the upper Thames River be-
  tween Windsor and Oxford, with ports of call at Eton, Cliveden,
  Marlow, Hurley, Henley, Sonning, Pangbourne and Shillingford.

MV ANACOLUTHE

Built: Originally a working barge, refurbished in 1991
Registry: France
Length: 210 ft.
Beam: 24 ft.
Speed: 12 knots
Officers: French
Crew: 12, French

Passengers: 51. Singles 10%, couples 75%, families 15%.

Cabins: 26. All cabins are outside with central heating, air-conditioning, private bath with shower and hairdryer; portholes; three have
double bed. No smoking.

Dining: Regional specialties.

Facilities: Piano bar, lounge, library, exercise room, jacuzzi.

Activities: Hot air ballooning.

Rates: Per person double occupancy is $1,990.

Itinerary: Six-night cruises of the Seine and Yonne Rivers from Paris.

MS BASHAN

Built: 1984

Registry: People's Republic of China

Length: 260 ft.

Beam: 52 ft.

Speed: 15 knots

Officers: Chinese

Crew: 112, Chinese

Passengers: 72. Almost all couples over 55.

Cabins: 36. All have air-conditioning, twin beds, private bath with
shower. Eight suites. All cabins and suites have large picture window facing the river.

Dining: Chinese food with limited western menu. Single sitting.

Facilities: Hairdresser, massage, library with many books relevant to
China, lecture hall/cinema, swimming pool, two observation
lounges, laundry service, shops, bar with dance floor and piano
music. Medical facilities with a doctor qualified in western as well
as traditional Chinese medicine.

Activities: Evening lectures and films, show by ship's crew. Excursion
by longboat up the Daning River. Shore excursion to river village
Shibaozhai and to Fengdu ("City of Ghosts").

Rates: Double occupancy per person from $1,250 to $1,900.

Itinerary: Three-night cruises of the Yangtze River from Yichang to
Chongqing.

MS EXPLORER

Built: 1969

Registry: Liberia

Former Names: *Society Explorer; Linblad Explorer*

Length: 238 ft.

Beam: 46 ft.

Speed: 13 knots

Officers: German

Crew: 61, American, German

Passengers: 96

MS EXPLORER

Cabins: 45. All have outside view, individually controlled air- conditioning, private bath with shower, radio. Mostly twin bedded. Two suites with sitting area.

Dining: Continental cuisine, dining room seats 110. One open seating, non-smoking. Lunches are buffet-style.

Facilities: Designed for remote-expedition cruising with ice-strengthened hull and a fleet of zodiac landing craft. Lecture hall, lounge, outdoor pool, gym, sauna, hairdresser, shops, library, laundry. Medical facilities, American doctor.

Activities: Equipment for snorkeling, diving, fishing and water skiing. Nature walks and village visits. In sensitive wildlife sites groups divide into small numbers to avoid disruption of penguins and nesting seabirds. Typical: anchoring in a remote iceberg-surrounded cove to photograph a colony of a thousand or more penguins, view slumbering elephant seals or hike up a hillside for a view. Each program carries a full complement of naturalists, often a wildlife expert, an anthropologist, a botanist and explorer.

Youth Program: Ship is not suited for children.

Access for Disabled: Not suited for disabled travelers.

Rates: Double occupancy per person for 12- to 23-day cruises from $3,490 to $12,490. All shore excursions included in fare.

Itinerary: Twelve- to 23-day cruises to Antarctica with stops at Puerto Montt, Chiloe Island, Chilean Fjords, Puerto Natales (Torres del Paine National Park), Beagle Channel Glaciers, Ushuaia, Drake Passage, Antarctica Expedition Stops, Falkland Islands (Bull Point), Port Stanley (landings based on weather, ice conditions and wildlife.) Twelve- to 20-day Pacific cruises go to Easter Island, Pitcairn Islands, French Polynesia (including Tahiti and Bora Bora), Cook Islands, Samoa, Tonga, Micronesia, Indonesia, Papua New Guinea, Sulawesi, Borneo, Sumatra, Java, Bali, Melanesia, Australia, Solomon Islands, Vanuati and Fiji.

MY HALAS
Built: 1911
Registry: Turkey
Length: 170 ft.
Beam: 28 ft.
Speed: 12 knots
Officers: English, Turkish, Dutch
Crew: 26, English
Passengers: 30. 90% American, 10% English, French, Turkish
Cabins: 15. Comprised of three French double, eight standard twin, two large twin and two suites with 4-poster bed. All outside, air-conditioning, shower.
Dining: Restaurant serves Turkish and international cuisine. Single seating. Fresh fish is a specialty. Meals are also served al fresco on the top deck.
Facilities: Two bars, two motor launches, TV lounge, beauty salon, laundry, exercise equipment, library, masseur.
Activities: Snorkeling equipment. Explore the Byzantine ruins of Gemili or swim in the waters around the boat and on the shores of the islands you visit.
Youth Program:Children below 18 are not allowed on board except for private charters.
Access for Disabled: None.
Rates: Per person double occupancy from $1,200 to $2,100 for three-night cruises and $1,995 to $3,500 for six-night cruises.
Itinerary: Three- or six-nights cruising the Turkish coast (Gocek, Yassicalar Islands, Gemili Island and Domuz Island, a private island once the property of the King of Egypt. The boat travels for 2 or 3 hours each day.

MV L'ABERCROMBIE; MV LAFAYETTE; MV LITOTE
Built: 1979, 1982, 1984
Registry: France
Length: 128 ft.
Beam: 16 ft.
Speed: 8 knots
Officers: French

Crew: 8, British, French, Dutch

Passengers: 20-22. Singles 5-10%, couples 75-90%, families 5-15%.

Cabins: 10-12. All are outside with picture window, air-conditioning, private bath with shower, hairdryer; some with double beds, some with twins. No smoking. (Litote has no air-conditioning).

Dining: Dining room with large windows, meals feature classic dishes of the region.

Facilities: This was once a commercial barge, then refitted into a hotel barge. Salon with bar, library.

Activities: The itinerary and the activities are decided by the passengers. Bicycles, bicycle tours, bus tours. A highlight on the Lafayette is the barge climbing with the assistance of the Arzviller lift, a huge tank on rails that allows the barge to bypass 17 locks, and passage through two tunnels into the mountainous Zorn Valley.

Rates: Per person double occupancy from $1,140 to $3,160.

Itinerary: Three- or six-night cruises along the Burgundy Canal, the Saone, the Rhone au Rhin canal, and through the lakes of the National Park of Lorraine.

MV MARJORIE and MV NAPOLEAN

Built: 1994, 1991

Registry: Great Britain

Length: 129-130 ft.

Beam: 16 ft.

Speed: 8 knots

Officers: British

Crew: 6, British

Passengers: 8-12. Singles 15%; couples 65%; families 20%.

Cabins: 4. All outside, twins and double beds, private bath with shower, individually controlled air-conditioning.

Dining: Dining room with large window. Meals feature classic dishes and wines of the region.

Facilities: Salon with piano, picture window, library.

Activities: The itinerary and the activities are decided by the passengers, and include shore excursions by private minibus, bicycling on the cycling path next to the boat, visits to castles, hot air ballooning.

Rates: Per person double occupancy from $3,350 to $4,200.

Itinerary: Six-night cruises of the Rhone and Danube Rivers.

PRINCESS ELAINE; PRINCESS JEANNIE; PRINCESS SHEENA

Built: 1944

Cabins: 126. All have air-conditioning.

Facilitites: Two restaurants, lounges, gym, laundry service, hairdresser. Medical clinic.

Itinerary: Four-night cruises on Yangtze River.

REMBRANDT

Built: 1937 as cargo vessel
Registry: Netherlands
Former Name: *Zeeuwsche Stroomen*
Length: 130 ft.
Beam: 17 ft.
Speed: 8 knots
Officers: Dutch
Crew: 6, English, Dutch
Passengers: 18. Singles 10%, couples 75%, families 15%.
Cabins: 17. Six doubles, two singles, two suites. All are outside, have
    air-conditioning, private bath with hand shower, hairdryer.
Dining: French kitchen. Single seating for 20.
Facilities: A hotel barge with salon, bar, small library. No smoking.
Activities: Slide shows. Guide for explanations all day on board and
    for shore excursions.
Rates: Double occupancy rate per person is from $1,690 to $2,070.
Itinerary: Six-night cruises of the inland waterways of Belgium and
    Holland from April till October. Ports of call include Amsterdam,
    Haarlem, Delft, Gouda, Willemstad, Alkmaar, Purmerend, Ghent
    and Bruges.

MS SUN BOAT I; II; III

Built: 1986,1990,1993
Registry: Egypt
Length: 138 ft.
Beam: 31-40 ft.
Speed: 18 knots
Officers: Egyptian
Crew: 48-60, Egyptian
Passengers: 40-64. Singles 10%, couples 80%, families 10%.
Cabins: 20-32. All have individually controlled air-conditioning, pri-
    vate bath with shower (some with tub), outside windows overlook-
    ing the Nile. Several suites.
Dining: No smoking in restaurant. Barbecue on deck.
Facilities: Pool, lounge, gift shop and laundry.
Activities: Shore excursions with Egyptologist escort. Lectures.
Rates: Double occupancy per person from $2,035 to $5,045.
Itinerary: Four- to 12-day cruises on the Nile River. Can be combined
    with land tour of Egypt.

ALASKA'S GLACIER BAY TOURS & CRUISES

WILDERNESS EXPLORER

Registry: United States

Length: 112 ft.
Beam: 22 ft.
Speed: 9 knots
Officers: American
Crew: 13, American
Passengers: 40
Cabins: 20. Upper and lower berths, private bath with shower, some
    with picture window.
Dining: Regional cuisine served family style. Lunches to take ashore.
Facilities: Ship serves as a base camp for kayaking and hiking ven-
    tures. Observation lounge. Two-person sea kayak for off-vessel ex-
    cursions.
Rates: Double occupancy per person from $264 to $1,156.
Itinerary: Three- and five-day cruises of Alaska's Glacier Bay National
    Park and Admiralty Island National Monument.

ALASKA SIGHTSEEING/CRUISE WEST

4th & Battery Bldg., Seattle, WA 98121
800-426-7702; 206-441-8687

MV SPIRIT OF ALASKA

Built: 1980
Registry: United States
Former Name: *Pacific NW Explorer*
Length: 143 ft.
Beam: 28 ft.
Speed: 14 knots
Officers: American
Crew: 19, American
Passengers: 82. Usually all couples.
Cabins: 40. Outside cabins, air-conditioned, private bath with shower;
    some with pullman berth. Three suites.
Dining: Casual family-style dining.
Facilities: Observation lounge.
Activities: Whale watching, exploring ports, watching icebergs calv-
    ing from glaciers. Lectures on the cultural and natural history.
Rates: Seven-night cruises from $1,595 to $3,095 double
occupancy per person.
Itinerary: Alaska between Seattle, and Juneau.

MV SPIRIT OF DISCOVERY

Built: 1992
Registry: United States
Former Name: *Columbia*
Length: 166 ft.

Beam: 37 ft.
Speed: 13 knots
Officers: American
Crew: American
Passengers: 82. Almost all couples.
Cabins: 43. All staterooms are outside with a large window. Cabins
   have air-conditioning and private bath with shower. Deluxe cabins
   with bed, TV, VCR, refrigerator; others have two lower berths or
   upper/lower berth. No smoking.
Dining: One sitting, serves fresh seafood.
Facilities: Observation lounge with windows on three sides. The cap-
   tain's wheelhouse is accessible for passengers to visit and learn
   about yachting.
Activities: Visit narrow passageways and stop at small ports. Ship
   will vary its schedule for events such as whale watching or wildlife
   sightings. Vessel size allows cruising close to shorelines.
Rates: From $1,695 to $3,195 per person double occupancy for seven-
   night cruise; $799 to $1,579 for five-night cruise.
Itinerary: Seven-night cruises from Seattle; five-night Pacific Northwest Cruise featuring Vancouver, Victoria, San Juan Islands and La
   Conner; Columbia/Snake River cruises from Portland and Astoria
   to Lewiston/Clarkston.

MV SPIRIT OF GLACIER BAY
Built: 1971
Registry: United States
Former Name: *Glacier Bay Explorer*
Length: 125 ft.
Beam: 28 ft.
Speed: 12 knots
Officers: American
Crew: 14, American
Passengers: 60. Usually all couples.
Cabins: 30. All are air-conditioned, have private bath with shower;
   most with outside view.
Dining: Single open seating.
Facilities: Observation lounge.
Activities: Full day of wildlife and glacier watching at Glacier Bay
   and Tracy Arm National Monument.
Rates: Two-night cruises from $179 to $749.
Itinerary: Glacier Bay and Tracy Arm from Juneau.

MV SPIRIT OF '98
Built: 1984
Registry: United States

Former Names: *Colonial Explorer; Victorian Empress*
Length: 192 ft.
Beam: 40 ft.
Speed: 14 knots
Officers: American
Crew: 21, Canadian
Passengers: 98
Cabins: 49. All are air-conditioned, have private bath with shower.
Dining: Casual family-style dining.
Facilities: Dining room, lounge/bar, gift shop.
Activities: Evening dances, deck sports, up-close viewing of glaciers and wildlife.
Rates: Per person double occupancy rates from $2,095 to $4,295.
Itinerary: Seven-night cruises between Seattle and Juneau with stops at Misty Fjords, Ketchikan, Petersburg, Le Conte Glacier, Sitka and Tracy Arm Fjord.

AMAZON RIVER CRUISES
8700 W. Flagler St., Miami, FL 33174
800-423-2791; 305-227-2266

MV ARCA
Built: 1980
Registry: Peru
Length: 99 ft.
Beam: 23 ft.
Speed: 10 knots
Officers: Peruvian
Crew: 18, Peruvian
Passengers: 37. Singles 10%, couples 90%.
Cabins: 19. Air-conditioned, upper and lower berths, five shared baths with shower.
Facilities: Dining room, lounge.
Activities: Shore excursions to native villages, birdwatching and nature trips.
Rates: Per person double occupancy $365 for three-night; $650 for six-night.
Itinerary: This steel-hulled riverboat makes three- to six-night cruises of the Amazon River.

MV DELFIN and AMAZON CLIPPER
Built: 1982
Registry: Peru
Length: 65 ft.
Beam: 20 ft.

Speed: 11 knots
Officers: Peruvian
Crew: 9, Peruvian
Passengers: 16-20. Singles 20%, couples 80%.
Cabins: 8-10. All are outside with two lower berths, window; shared
   bath facilities. *Amazon Clipper* cabins are air-conditioned; *Delfin* are
   not.
Facilities: Dining room, lounge, bar.
Activities: Launches for fishing and nature trips to remote tributaries
   and lakes. Bilingual naturalist guides.
Rates: Per person double occupancy $350 for three-night, $590 for six-
   night, $815 for five-night cruise.
Itinerary: Two- to six-night adventure expeditions on the Amazon
   River. The *Delfin* goes upriver from Iquitos to the confluence of the
   Ucayali and Maranon Rivers where the Amazon begins, and also
   has a down-river cruise. The *Amazon Clipper* cruises from Manaus
   to mid-Amazon regions.

MV RIO AMAZONAS

Built: 1896 (rebuilt 1981)
Registry: Peru
Former Name: *Arias*
Length: 146 ft.
Beam: 30 ft.
Officers: Peruvian
Crew: 18, Peruvian
Passengers: 44. Singles 10%, couples 90%.
Cabins: 20. Upper deck cabins have private bar, window with river-
   view, two lower beds. Others have three beds. Some cabins air-con-
   ditioned, some are not.
Dining: Buffet-style restaurant.
Facilities: Air-conditioned bars, lounge, shop, library jacuzzi.
Activities: Shore excursions and topical lectures; launches to reach
   more remote villages; jungle walks, birdwatching, piranha fishing.
Rates: From $525 to $1,105 per person double occupancy, shore excur-
   sions included.
Itinerary: Turn-of-the-century riverboat takes passengers on six-night
   exploration cruises of the upper reaches of the Amazon River.

Note: Other trips can be arranged to explore the Amazon by boat during the day and stay in jungle camps at night.

AMERICAN CANADIAN CARIBBEAN LINE
Box 368, Warren, RI 02885

800-556-7450; 401-247-0955

CARIBBEAN PRINCE

Built: 1983
Registry: United States
Length: 160 ft.
Beam: 38 ft.
Speed: 10 knots
Officers: American
Crew: 17, American
Passengers: 80. 15% singles, 85% couples over age 55.
Cabins: 38. Air-conditioned, have private bath with shower. Non-smoking available. More expensive cabins have picture windows, others have portholes.
Dining: All meals served family-style at a single, open seating. Breakfast is buffet. Much fresh seafood. Passengers can help themselves to tea, coffee, lemonade and snacks at any time. Only non-alcoholic drinks are served, but bartender will mix BYOB cocktails.
Facilities: Lounge, library, rec room. Shallow (6 ft.) draft allows access to out-of-the-way places.
Activities: Fishing from the ship and shore (bring your own tackle), snorkeling, sailing, exercise class, water sports, 21-seat glass-bottom boat available free of charge, stern platform from which passengers can swim or sail. A unique bow can be lowered to offload passengers directly onto shore. The Sun Deck has unobstructed circuit of ship; 11 laps equal 1 mile.
Youth Program: Cruise not recommended for children.
Access for Disabled: None.
Rates: Range from $1,622 to $2,569.
Itinerary: In winter, 12-day loops out of Belize City to isolated islands along the coast of Guatemala and Belize, visiting the barrier reef and sailing inland on the Rio Dolce. In spring and fall, cruises to Florida Keys and the Everglades, New Orleans and West Palm Beach. In summer, cruises to Canada via the Hudson River and Erie Canal.

MAYAN PRINCE

Built: 1992
Registry: United States
Length: 169 ft.
Beam: 38 ft.
Speed: 12 knots
Officers: American
Crew: 18, American
Passengers: 96. Mostly seniors.

Cabins: 45. 87% outside. Most cabins have picture window. Twin beds can be converted to doubles. Individually controlled air-conditioning, private bath with shower and hairdryer. Cabins for non-smokers.

Dining: Single seating.

Facilities: Glass-bottom boat. Lounge with informal entertainment, library, meeting room.

Activities: Fishing, snorkeling, exercise workouts. Lectures.

Access for Disabled: None.

Rates: Range per person from $1,188 to $2,599.

Itinerary: In spring, 15-day inland voyage from West Palm Beach, Florida to Warren, Rhode Island via the Intracoastal Waterway. Summer and early fall, 12-day cruises to and from Sanguenay River and Warren, passing through Quebec City, Montreal, Lake Ontario, the Erie Canal, New York Harbor and Long Island Sound. In winter, the Family Islands of the Bahamas, Grenada, St. Thomas, and Antigua; and 12-day Orinoco River explorations.

NEW SHOREHAM II

Built: 1979

Registry: United States

Length: 155 ft.

Beam: 28 ft.

Speed: 10 knots

Officers: American

Crew: 16, American

Passengers: 76. 15% single, 85% couples over age 55.

Cabins: 36. Most are outside. All are air-conditioned and have private bath with shower. More expensive cabins have picture window. Cabins for non-smokers.

Dining: Single seating.

Facilities: Lounge with liquorless bar. Swimming platform folds down from stern. Bow ramp.

Activities: Exercise class, fishing, snorkeling, sailing. Glass-bottom boat.

Youth Program: None.

Access for Disabled: None.

Rates: Range per person double occupancy is from $896 (seven-day cruise) to $1,776 (15-day cruise).

Itinerary: In winter, 12-day loops out of St. Thomas to St. John, Tortola, Virgin Gorda, Beef Island, Jost Van Dyke, Sandy Cay, Norman Island, and Peter Island. Other cruises between Puerto Rico, St. Thomas and Bahamas. In spring and autumn, repositioning cruises between Florida and Warren, Rhode Island. In summer, from Warren through New England and Canada via the Erie Canal.

NIAGARA PRINCE

Built: 1994
Registry: United States
Length: 166 ft.
Beam: 40 ft.
Speed: 12 knots
Officers: American
Crew: 18, American
Passengers: 84
Cabins: 42. All are air-conditioned, have private bath with shower, picture window and sitting area.
Dining: Single open sitting, American cuisine.
Facilities: A riverboat with ocean certification. Lounge with entertainment, library, boutique.
Activities: Exercise classes, watersports.

AMERICAN FAMILY CRUISES

80 South West 8th St., Miami, FL 33130
800-232-0567; 305-358-7325

AMERICAN ADVENTURE

Built: 1963; Rebuilt: 1993
Registry: Italy
Former Name: *CostaRiviera*
Length: 700 ft.
Beam: 94 ft.
Speed: 20 knots
Officers: American
Crew: 654, American
Passengers: 1500, families
Cabins: 476. Appealing to families of all sizes, there are cabins and suites with four to six berths.
Dining: Restaurant has two seatings. Special "kids kuisine" menu, casual attire. Flexible dining allows kids to eat when, where and what they want; parents can dine with their kids or enjoy candlelit dinner for two. Terrace has buffets at breakfast, lunch and dinner, with indoor/outdoor seating. Open 18 hours a day. Pizzeria.
Facilities: Washer/dryer on each cabin deck. Strollers (for shore excursions), cribs on first-come, first-served basis. Babysitting services guaranteed for infants under age 2. Infant supplies available in onboard shop. Nightclub and casino (adults only), show lounge, sports bar, shops, cinema.
Activities: Baseball batting cage, basketball, fitness center, windsurfing simulator.

Youth Program: From ages 2 through teens. Computers and video centers, video production programs that highlight the geography, environment and local cultures of the ship's port calls. There are four separate programs for kids: 2- to 4-year-olds have storytelling, facepainting, treasure hunts, masquerades, campfire roasts; 5 to 7 have games, sports, children's theater night, masquerades, magic and juggling classes; 8 to 12 can participate in a rodeo, donkey polo, rollerblading contests and "hip hop" classes; teenagers have a video arcade, disco, classes in tennis, golf, photography, TV news, computer and can parasail, windsurf or go glacier climbing and wilderness canoeing.

Access for Disabled: None

Rates: Range per seven-day cruise: parents $895 to $2,095; kids: 2-17 years $95 to $395. Special offers: kids free during super value seasons.

Itinerary: Cruises to Nassau, Casa de Campo, Serena Cay, Key West.

AMERICAN PIONEER

Built: 1963; Rebuilt:1994
Registry: Italy
Former Name: *EugeniaCosta*
Length: 713 ft.
Beam: 96 ft.
Speed: 24 knots
Officers: American
Crew: 654, American
Passengers: 1,500. Mostly families.
Cabins: 452. Most are three or four berths; 182 are inside, 230 outside. Four suites. There are 54 cabins and suites with five or six berths.
Dining: Restaurant has two seatings (5:15 and 7:00). Special children's menu, casual attire. Flexible dining allows kids to eat when, where and what they want; parents can dine with their kids or enjoy candlelit dinner for two. Terrace has buffets at breakfast, lunch and dinner, with indoor/outdoor seating. Pizzeria, ice cream parlor, vending machines.
Facilities: Washer/dryer on each cabin deck. Stroller (for shore excursions) and cribs on first-come, first-served basis. Babysitting services guaranteed for infants under age 2. Infant supplies available in onboard shop. Nightclub and casino (adults only), Broadway showroom, sports bar, shops, cinema. Onboard pediatrician.
Activities: Baseball batting cage, basketball, fitness center, windsurfing simulator. Two baseball professionals on each cruise.
Youth Program: From ages 2 through teens. Computers and video centers, video production programs that highlight the geography, environment and local cultures of the ship's port calls. There are four

separate programs: ages 2 to 4 have storytelling, facepainting, treasure hunts, masquerades, campfire roasts; 5 to 7 have games, sports, children's theater night, masquerades, magic and juggling classes; 8 to 12 can participate in a rodeo, donkey polo, rollerblading contests, photography, golf, tennis, and "hip hop" classes; teenagers have a video arcade, disco, TV news, computer and can parasail, windsurf or go glacier climbing, wilderness canoeing and whitewater rafting.

Access for Disabled: None.

Rates: Range per seven-day cruise: parents $895 to $2,095: 2-17 years $95 to $395. Special offers: kids free during super value seasons. Add $200 to adult rate for Alaska.

Itinerary: Beginning in December 1994, *American Pioneer* sets sail from Tampa, visiting Playa del Carmen, Cozumel, Buccaneer Bay (Jamaica), and Grand Caymen. In the summer of 1995, there are seven-day cruises through Alaska out of Vancouver to Ketchikan, Endicott Arm, Juneau, Skagway, Davidson Glacier and Sitka.

AMERICAN HAWAII CRUISES

550 Kearny St., San Francisco, CA 94108
800-765-7000; 800-765-5555; 415-392-9400

SS CONSTITUTION

Built: 1950
Registry: United States
Length: 682 ft.
Beam: 89 ft.
Speed: 20 knots
Officers: American
Crew: 320, American
Passengers: 792. Honeymooners, families, older adults.
Cabins: 383. All cabins have private bath with shower, air-conditioning, radio, TV, phone. Suites with tub, sitting room and refrigerator. Owner's suite with two rooms, two baths and VCR. Most cabins are outside.
Dining: Two dining rooms. Two seatings. American and Hawaiian specialties, fresh local fish and tropical fruits. Poolside buffet. Open seating.
Facilities: Terrace piano bar, poolside bar with big-screen TV, nightclub, Broadway revues, dancing, lounges, movies, meeting facilities, library, self-service laundry, photo shop with personal videotaping, hairdresser, shops, laundry. Medical facilities.
Activities: Dancercise class, water aerobics, two saunas, two outdoor freshwater pools, hula dancing, ukulele lessons, shuffleboard and

SS INDEPENDENCE

ping pong. Four islands with 45 shore excursions, including helicopter sightseeing, submarine rides, deep-sea fishing and a luau.
Theme cruises on humpback whales in February and March, and
big band cruises in May and December.

Youth Program: Activities for children ages 5-16.

Access for Disabled: Ramp access, cabins with wheelchair access.
Travel companion required.

Rates: Double occupancy per person $995 to $3,950.

Itinerary: Three-, four- and seven-day cruises of the Hawaiian Islands.

SS INDEPENDENCE

Built: 1951

Registry: United States

Former Name: *Oceanic Independence*

Length: 682 ft.

Beam: 89 ft.

Speed: 20 knots

Officers: American

Crew: 320, American

Passengers: 728. All ages; many families.

Cabins: 383. About half are outside; each has private bath with
shower, air-conditioning, radio, phone. Suites with tub, refrigerator
and large window. Owner's suite has two rooms, two baths.

Dining: Dining room seats 400, two seatings. American cuisine and island dishes. Poolside buffet, afternoon cookouts.

Facilities: Solarium/spa, two saunas, massage, two pools, library, shops, conference center for 200, beauty salon, lounge, piano bar, nightclub. Medical facilities.

Activities: Movies, showplace performance including Polynesian review, hula dancing, ukulele lessons, deck sports. In-port activities include windsurfing, scuba, tennis, rafting, and cycling 38-mile slope of Mt. Haleakala. Whale watching cruises in February and March.

Youth Programs: Youth center, teen activities.

Access for Disabled: Ramp access. Cabins with wheelchair access. Travel companion required.

Rates: Per person double occupancy from $784 to $3,895. Children with two adults travel free except for holidays.

Itinerary: Three-, four- and seven-day cruises of the Hawaiian Islands.

AQUANAUT CRUISE LINES
241 E. Commercial Blvd., Ft. Lauderdale, FL 33334
800-327-8223; 305-491-0333

MS TROPIC SUN
Built: 1994
Registry: British
Length: 165 ft.
Officers: Austrian
Crew: 35
Passengers: 112

Cabins: All have air-conditioning, private bath with shower, picture windows; two lower beds may be joined to form king-size; upper fold-down berth.

Dining: Dining room and outdoor cafe. Single sitting.

Facilities: Formerly a survey vessel owned by the British government. Lounge for dancing, shows, two whirlpools, audiovisual equipment.

Activities: Shore excursions, watersports, scuba diving on some trips.

Rates: Seven-day cruises per person double occupancy from $1,595 to $2,795, including round trip air from New York.

Itinerary: Mediterranean and Adriatic cruises from Venice, Malta and Genoa.

BALTIC LINE See EUROCRUISES

BERGEN LINE
505 Fifth Ave., New York, NY 10017
800-323-7436; 800-666-2374; 212-986-2711

MS HAROLD JARL; MS KONG OLAV; MS LOFOTEN;

MS NORDNORGE; MS RAGNVALD JARL
Built: 1956-1964
Registry: Norway
Length: 265-270 ft.
Beam: 41-43 ft.
Speed: 16 knots
Officers: Norwegian
Crew: 25, Norwegian
Passengers: 144-220. Passengers also include day-trippers commuting from village to village.
Cabins: Most cabins have private bath with shower; some have wash basin only. Some have lower berths, some have upper and lower.
Dining: Dining room (two seatings) and cafeteria, continental and Norwegian cuisine.
Facilities: Three lounges, bar. These ships are working ships, the lifeline between Norwegian coastal villages that brings supplies and many day-passengers going from one village to another.
Activities: Shore excursions in the stops along the coasts, including one to a Russian village on the border. For many of the excursions, you leave the ship by motorcoach and catch up with it at the next port. You can also transport cars on these ships.
Rates: Per person double occupancy for six- and seven-day cruises from $561 to $1,553.
Itinerary: Six- and seven-day cruises along the Norwegian coast between Bergen and Kirkenes with stops in up to 35 villages along the way. Can be combined into 12-day roundtrip cruise.

KING OF SCANDINAVIA and QUEEN OF SCANDINAVIA
Registry: Denmark
Cabins: There are singles, two, three and four berth cabins.
Dining: Scandinavian buffet for breakfast and dinner; ala carte dinner for high-end cabins.
Rates: Per person $174 to $359.
Itinerary: Three-day minicruises between Oslo and Copenhagen.

MS KONG HARALD; MS NORDLYS; MS RICHARD WITH
Built: 1993; 1994
Registry: Norway

Officers: Norwegian
Crew: 61, Norwegian
Passengers: 490
Cabins: 230. All cabins have private bath with shower; most have picture windows; all have lower berths or sofa beds. Suite is two rooms.
Dining: Dining room with two seatings. Cafeteria open 24 hours. Norwegian specialties.
Facilities: Observation lounge, conference rooms, sauna, gym. Children's playroom. These ships are working ships, the lifeline between Norwegian coastal villages that brings supplies and many day passengers going from one village to another. You can also transport car on these ships.
Activities: Shore excursions in the stops along the coast, including many of the Arctic Circle and one to a Russian village on the border. For many of the excursions, you leave the ship by motorcoach and catch up with it at the next port. Shipboard announcements are made in Norwegian and English.
Rates: Per person double occupancy for six- and seven-day cruises from $561 to $1,553.
Itinerary: Six- and seven-day cruises along the 1,250 mile Norwegian coast between Bergen and Kirkenes, including the North Cape (Europe's northernmost point), with stops in up to 35 ports along the way. Can be combined into 12-day roundtrip cruise.

MS MIDNATSOL; MS NARVIK; MS VESTERAALEN
Built: 1982; 1983
Registry: Norway
Length: 330-340 ft.
Beam: 50 ft.
Speed: 18 knots
Officers: Norwegian
Crew: 40, Norwegian
Passengers: 312-352
Cabins: All cabins have private bath with shower; some have lower berths, some have upper and lower.
Dining: Dining room. Cafeteria open 24 hours per day. Continental and Norwegian cuisine.
Facilities: Lounges, laundry. Medical facility. These ships are working ships, the lifeline between Norwegian coastal villages that brings supplies and many day-passengers going from one village to another. You can also transport cars on the ships.
Activities: Shore excursions in the stops along the coast, including one to a Russian village on the border. For many of the excursions, you leave the ship by motorcoach and catch up with it at the next port.

Rates: Per person double occupancy for six- and seven-day cruises from $1,553 to $4,561.

Itinerary: Six- and seven-day cruises along the Norwegian coast between Bergen and Kirkenes with stops in up to 35 villages along the way. Can be combined into 12-day roundtrip cruise.

MS NORDSTJERNEN

Built: 1956
Registry: Norway
Length: 265 ft.
Beam: 41 ft.
Speed: 16 knots
Officers: Norwegian
Crew: 25, Norwegian
Passengers: 174
Cabins: Most cabins have private bath with shower; some have wash basin only. Some have upper and lower.
Dining: Dining room and cafeteria; continental and Norwegian cuisine.
Facilities: Three lounges. Zodiac fleet.
Activities: Zodiac excursions to view glaciers. Shore excursions in Longyearbyen and fishing villages of Honningsvag with herds of reindeer. Russian folkloric performances.
Rates: Per person double occupancy from $1,208.
Itinerary: Eight-day Arctic cruises roundtrip from Tromso through a series of fjords, villages and glaciers.

BERGEN LINE/ SILJA LINE

MS SILJA EUROPA; SILJA SERENADE; SILJA SYMPHONY; SILJA KARNEVAL

Built: 1993; 1990; 1991; 1985
Length: 669 ft.
Beam: 104 ft.
Speed: 21-23 knots
Passengers: 2,000-3,000
Cabins: 986-1,194. Most cabins have window, some have balconies, some air-conditioned; all have private bath with shower. Several four-person family cabins. Suite with balcony. One deck of cabins for non-smokers.
Dining: Several restaurants, including a gourmet dining room, a seafood restaurant, a supper club, a Tex-Mex, and a Scandinavian smorgasbord. Jackets requested for dinner.
Facilities: Several lounges including show lounge and piano lounge, bars including a wine bar, casino, conference room, hairdresser, cin-

ema, tax-free shop, spa with pool, whirlpools, water slide, steam and sauna, body treatment. Also carries cars.

Youth Program: Playroom. Parents are provided with beepers in case nanny needs to contact them. Teen club.

Access for Disabled: Several cabins for disabled passengers; several allergy-free cabins.

Rates: Per person double occupancy from $88 to $480.

Itinerary: One- and two-night cruises one way or roundtrip from such ports as Helsinki, Stockholm, Turku, Travemunde and Tallinn. Can be combined.

CAPTAIN COOK CRUISES

c/o International Cruise Connections
99 Long Court, Thousand Oaks, CA 91360
800-433-8747; 805-496-0548

MV REEF ESCAPE

Built: 1987
Registry: Australia
Length: 204 ft.
Beam: 43 ft.
Speed: 10 knots
Officers: Australian
Crew: Australian
Passengers: 120
Cabins: Nearly all open directly to outside, air-conditioned; some have queen-sized or twin beds, three rooms have additional sofa bed, two have additional upper berth, some with upper and lower berth.
Dining: Dining is single seating. International and Australian cuisine; fresh seafood.
Facilities: Sauna, spa, pool, shop, piano lounge, conference room shop, library, laundry and ironing facilities.
Activities: Marine biologist and dive instructor on board; glass-bottom boat, snorkeling equipment.
Rates: From $2,785 to $3,280, including airfare from Los Angeles or San Francisco and one night post cruise hotel accommodations.
Itinerary: Three-, four-, and seven-night sailings to the Great Barrier Reef and Australian islands.

CARNIVAL CRUISE LINES

3655 NW 87 Ave., Miami, FL 33178
800-327-9501; 305-599-2600

MS CELEBRATION
Built: 1987
Registry: Liberia
Length: 733 ft.
Beam: 92 ft.
Speed: 21 knots
Officers: Italian
Crew: 670, International
Passengers: 1,486
Cabins: 743. Cabins are air-conditioned and have private bath with shower, radio, TV, phone; 10 suites have tub, whirlpool, sitting area, picture window and balcony.
Dining: Two restaurants, two sittings.
Facilities: Disco, casino, several bars and lounges, hairdresser, shops, meeting room, laundry, self-serve laundromat, library. Medical facilities, doctor and nurse.
Activities: Full array of deck sports and activities. Lido Deck has unobstructed circuit of ship.
Youth Program: Yes
Access for Disabled: Not recommended for wheelchairs.
Rates: Per person double occupancy from $999 to $2,439.
Itinerary: Seven-day cruises of Caribbean from Miami to San Juan, St. Thomas and St. Martin/St. Maarten.

MS ECSTASY; MS FANTASY; MS FASCINATION
Built: 1990; 1991; 1994
Registry: Liberia
Length: 855 ft.
Beam: 105 ft.
Speed: 21 knots
Officers: Italian
Crew: 920, International
Passengers: 2,044-2,600
Cabins: 1,022. Cabins have air-conditioning, TV, radio, phone, private bath with shower. Suites have whirlpool, tub, sitting area, veranda and picture window, some with balcony.
Dining: Two dining rooms, each with two seatings. Grill.
Facilities: Six-story atrium, several bars and lounges, disco, dance lounge, casino, three pools, two saunas, six whirlpools, jogging track, health spa, shops, hairdresser, library, massage, meeting room, laundry. Medical facilities.
Activities: Deck sports, various programs in all-day party action.
Youth Program: Children's playroom, teen center.
Access for Disabled: None
Rates: Per person double occupancy from $459 to $1,319.

Itinerary: Three- and four-day cruises of the Bahamas from Port Canaveral, Florida; and to Bahamas, Key West and Cozumel from Miami. The *Fascination*, entering service in August 1994, cruises Canada from Boston, and the Caribbean from San Juan.

TSS FESTIVALE

Built: 1961
Registry: Bahamas
Former Names: *SA Vaal; Transvaal Castle*
Length: 760 ft.
Beam: 90 ft.
Speed: 22 knots
Officers: Italian
Crew: 580, International
Passengers: 1,146
Cabins: 580. Air-conditioning, TV, radio, phone, private bath with shower. Ten suites with balcony.
Dining: Continental restaurant, seats 700, two sittings. Grill has buffet.
Facilities: Bars, nightclubs, discos, cinema, casino, three pools, sauna, massage, facial and body treatment center, hairdresser, shops, meeting room, laundry. Medical facilities, doctor and nurse.
Activities: Party-oriented ship, aerobics classes, exercise equipment, shuffleboard, ping pong, trapshooting. Walking circuit around ship covers 1 mile in 7 1/2 laps.
Youth Program: Children's playroom, wading pool, teen activities.
Access for Disabled: None
Rates: Per person double occupancy from $999 to $2,439.
Itinerary: Seven-day cruises from San Juan to St. Thomas, St. Martin/St. Maarten, Barbados and Martinique.

TSS FIESTAMARINA

Built: 1956
Registry: Bahamas
Former Names: *Empress of Britain; Carnivale*
Length: 640 ft.
Beam: 87 ft.
Speed: 21 knots
Officers: Italian
Crew: 550, International, Spanish-speaking
Passengers: 950.
Cabins: Air-conditioned, private bath with shower, phone, music, some with queen and king-sized beds; five suites.
Dining: International theme dinners. Latin specialties. Two seatings per meal with passengers assigned to tables. One formal evening.
Facilities: Veranda bar, disco, showplace, lounge, nightclub, casino, li-

brary, three pools, sauna, whirlpool, hairdresser, shops, meeting room, laundry. Medical facilities, doctor and nurse.

Activities: Aerobics, deck sports. Latin music for dancing.

Youth Program: Year-round program of parties, kite flying, arts and crafts. Teen activities. No infants under 4 months.

Access for Disabled: Not recommended for wheelchair-bound persons.

Rates: Three- and four-day cruises per person from $495 to $1,189.

Itinerary: From San Juan or Miami to Caribbean.

MS HOLIDAY

Built: 1985

Registry: Bahamas

Length: 727 ft.

Beam: 92 ft.

Speed: 21 knots

Officers: Italian

Crew: 660, International

Passengers: 1,452

Cabins: 726. Air conditioning, phone, radio, TV, private bath with shower. Ten suites with sitting area, veranda, picture window and whirlpool.

Dining: Two dining rooms.

Facilities: Several lounges and bars, disco, library, casino, three pools, two whirlpools, sauna, hairdresser, shops, laundry, meeting room. Medical facilities.

Activities: Variety of deck activities.

Youth Program: Teen activities.

Access for Disabled: None

Rates: Per person double occupancy from $999 to $2,349.

Itinerary: Seven-day cruises from Miami to Playa del Carmen, Cozumel, Grand Cayman and Ocho Rios.

MS JUBILEE

Built: 1986

Registry: Liberia

Length: 733 ft.

Beam: 92 ft.

Speed: 21 knots

Officers: Italian

Crew: 670, International

Passengers: 1,486

Cabins: 743. Air-conditioned, phone, radio, TV, private bath with shower. Ten suites with balconies.

Dining: Two main dining rooms, bar and grill.

Facilities: Disco, casino, several lounges and bars, show lounge seats

1,000, library, three outdoor pools, two whirlpools, sauna, massage, hairdresser, shops, meeting room, laundry. Medical facilities. Activities: Deck activities, aerobics, jogging track.
Youth Program: Yes
Access for Disabled: None
Rates: Per person double occupancy from $999 to $2,439.
Itinerary: Seven-day cruises of the Mexican Riviera from Los Angeles.

SENSATION

Built: 1993
Registry: Panama
Length: 855 ft.
Beam: 118 ft.
Speed: 21 knots
Officers: Italian
Crew: 1,300, International
Passengers: 2,600
Cabins: 1,025. Staterooms include individually controlled air- conditioning, TV, music and telephone; 54 suites.
Dining: Two dining rooms.
Facilities: Ship contains ultraviolet lighting and sound effects, casino, 10 lounges, three outdoor pools. Medical facilities, doctor on board.
Activities: Deck sports, gym, full activities.
Youth Program: Children's playroom. Teen center. Wading pool.
Rates: From $1,149 to $2,479 double occupancy rates per person. Rates include air transportation from major cities throughout North America.
Itinerary: Seven-day cruises from Miami to Nassau, San Juan, St. Thomas, Cozumel, Grand Cayman and Jamaica.

MS TROPICALE

Built: 1981
Registry: Liberia
Length: 660 ft.
Beam: 85 ft.
Speed: 22 knots
Officers: Italian
Crew: 550, International
Passengers: 1022
Cabins: 511. All have private bath with shower, phone, TV. Veranda suites have sitting area, fridge, tub and private verandas. Most outside cabins have large window.
Dining: Two dining rooms, two sittings.
Facilities: Five bars, four entertainment lounges, casino, disco, two outdoor swimming pools, library, piano bar, sauna, massage, facial

and body treatment center, gift shop, hairdresser, full-service laundry, self-serve laundromat. Medical facilities.

Activities: Deck sports, aerobics, exercise equipment, small circuit for jogging.

Youth Program: Children's playroom, wading pool and teen programs.

Access for Disabled: Not recommended for wheelchair-bound persons.

Rates: Per person double occupancy from $999 to $3,699.

Itinerary: Seven-, 10- and 11-day cruises of the Caribbean departing from San Juan to St. Thomas, Guadeloupe, Grenada, La Guaira/Caracus and Aruba. Seven-day cruises from Tampa year-round beginning October 1994 to Grand Cayman and Cozumel.

CELEBRITY CRUISES

5200 Blue Lagoon Drive, Miami, FL 33126
800-437-3111; 305-262-6677

MV HORIZON

Built: 1990
Registry: Liberia
Length: 682 ft.
Beam: 95 ft.
Speed: 21 knots
Officers: Greek
Crew: 642, International
Passengers: 1,354
Cabins: 677. All cabins have air-conditioning, private bath with shower, TV, radio and phone. Two Presidential suites with separate living room, walk-in closet and marble bathroom with whirlpool tub; 18 suites with sitting area, marble bath with whirlpool, hairdryer and butler service. Outside cabins with picture window.

Dining: Two rooms; two seatings. Cafe for breakfast, lunch and afternoon tea. Two formal evenings each cruise.

Facilities: Show lounge, club with cabaret bands, piano lounge, jazz and big band music, casino, health club, sauna, massage, whirlpools, two outdoor pools, laundry/dry cleaning, barber/beauty salon, shops, library. Medical facilities with doctor and nurse.

Activities: Lectures, putting green, shuffleboard, trap shooting, ping pong, dance and snorkeling lessons, fitness program. Five laps around Marina Deck equal one mile.

Youth Program: Children's playroom and teen activities, including theatre production during holiday cruises. Children's menu.

Access for Disabled: Ramp access; five cabins with wheelchair access. Travel companion required. Provide own collapsible wheelchair.

Wheelchair passengers cannot be accommodated at every port.
Rates: From $895 to $3,520 (airfare included) for Caribbean cruises;
$975 to $3,095 (cruise only) to Bermuda. Children under age 2
travel free.
Itinerary: In summer, seven-night cruises from New York to Hamilton
and St. George, Bermuda. During winter, five- and seven-night
cruises out of San Juan to Martinique, Barbados, St. Lucia, Antigua
and St. Thomas.

SS MERIDIAN
Built: 1963
Registry: Bahamas
Former Name: *Galileo*
Length: 700 ft.
Beam: 94 ft.
Speed: 24 knots
Officers: Greek
Crew: 580, International
Passengers: 1,106
Cabins: 553. All have air-conditioning, private bath with shower,
phone, radio. Some with TV, skylights, sitting area, tub, floor-to-
ceiling windows.
Dining: Two seatings. Dining room (international cuisine) seats 644;
Marina Cafe (continental cuisine) seats 460.
Facilities: Showroom with Broadway-style entertainment, disco, danc-
ing, two lounges, bars, cinema, casino, health club, sauna, massage,
two outdoor pools, three whirlpools, hairdresser, shops. Medical fa-
cilities.
Activities: Shuffleboard, ping pong, putting green, skeet and trap
shooting, jogging track, lectures.
Youth Program: Playroom. Teen activities on holiday cruises include
theatrical production, navigation instruction and kite flying.
Access for Disabled: Nine cabins, ramp access, travel companion required.
Rates: From $745 to $2,695 for Bermuda (cruise only); $1,695 to $4,795
for Caribbean (air included). Children under two travel free.
Itinerary: Six- to 11-day cruises of the Caribbean and Bermuda. In
summer, seven-night loops out of New York or Ft. Lauderdale to
Bermuda. In winter, 10- and 11-night cruises from San Juan or Ft.
Lauderdale to Aruba, Venezuela, Barbados, St. Lucia, Martinique,
St. Maarten, St. Thomas, St. John, Curacoa, Grenada, San Blas Is-
lands.

MV ZENITH
Built: 1991

MV ZENITH

Registry: Liberia
Length: 682 ft.
Beam: 95 ft.
Speed: 21 knots
Officers: Greek
Crew: 657, International
Passengers: 1,374
Cabins: 687. All staterooms with air-conditioning, private bath with shower, TV, radio, phone. Some cabins with tub; some with floor-to-ceiling window. Suites with sitting area, marble bathroom with whirlpool tub. Two Royal Suites with separate living room and walk-in closet.
Dining: Two seatings. Dining room (continental cuisine) seats 856. Cafe seats 700 for breakfast and lunch buffet.
Facilities: Celebrity show lounge, nightclub with cabaret bands, bar with piano music, disco, casino, spa, two outdoor pools, sauna, whirlpool, massage, hairdresser, shops, laundry, dry cleaning, library, meeting room. Medical facilities.
Activities: Exercise classes, jogging track, ping pong, shuffleboard, trap shooting, dance and snorkeling lessons.
Youth Program: Seasonal teen activities; children's playroom.
Access for Disabled: Five outside cabins. Travel companion required.

Rates: From $1,145 to $3,320 (air included).
Itinerary: All year long, seven-day cruises of the Caribbean leaving
   from Ft. Lauderdale to San Juan, St. Maarten, St. Thomas, Nassau,
   Ocho Rios, Grand Cayman and Key West.

CLASSICAL CRUISES
132 E. 70th St., New York, NY 10021
800-252-7745; 212-794-3200; In Canada 800-245-7746

MV AURORA I and II
Built: 1991
Registry: Bahamas
Length: 270 ft.
Beam: 49 ft.
Speed: 14 knots
Officers: Greek
Crew: 40, Greek, Filipino, American, European
Passengers: 80; 10% single, 90% couples.
Cabins: 44. All are outside, with phone, TV, VCR, radio, sitting area, re-
   frigerator, bathroom with tub, climate control. Most have two pic-
   ture windows; others have portholes. One suite.
Dining: Restaurant has ocean views, accommodates all passengers at
   a single open seating. Continental cuisine.
Facilities: Health club, one swimming pool, jacuzzi, Sun Deck with un-
   obstructed circuit for fitness walks, two bars, exercise room, lecture
   hall, library, lounge with dancing, computer room, boutique, hairdresser. Hospital.
Activities: Launches and zodiacs enable access to small ports. Lectures. Study cruises with Smithsonian Institute.
Youth Program: Traveling with children under 12 is discouraged.
Access for Disabled: Wheelchair-bound passengers are discouraged
   from taking Classical cruises because physical exertion is often required.
Rates: Per person double occupancy from $2,095 to $7,745.
Itinerary: Five- to 14-day cruises to Alaska, Antarctica, Mexico and
   Central America with Panama Canal crossing. Six- to 14-day
   cruises to southeast Asia, Egypt, Mediterranean, Spain, France,
   England, Scotland, Ireland and West Africa (including Morocco, Ca-
   nary Islands, Mauritania, Senegal and Gambia).

CLASSIC SAIL
P.O. Box 459, Madison, NJ 07940
201-966-1684

RICHARD ROBBINS

Built: 1902
Registry: United States
Length: 60 ft.
Beam: 18 ft.
Speed: Sails up to 9 knots plus diesel power
Crew: American
Passengers: 18. No children under age 16 allowed, unless booking entire vessel.
Cabins: 9. Seven have double beds, two have bunk beds; all outside. Shared head.
Dining: Meals served family-style in main cabin or on deck.
Facilities: Originally a classic Delaware Bay oyster dredger. Rowboat for exploring. There is a cat on board.
Activities: You may help crew or take the helm.
Access for Disabled: No.
Rates: Per person from $175 to $275.
Itinerary: The schooner makes one- to three-night sails from Greenwich, New Jersey up Hudson River to Stony Point, Bannerman's Island, and Bear Mountain, or down river to New York City and Sandy Hook.

CLIPPER CRUISE LINE

7711 Bonhomme Ave., St. Louis, MO 63105
800-325-0010; 314-727-2929

MV NANTUCKET CLIPPER

Built: 1984
Registry: United States
Length: 207 ft.
Beam: 37 ft.
Speed: 11 knots
Officers: American
Crew: 37, American
Passengers: 102. Mostly couples over age 55.
Cabins: 51. All cabins are outside, air-conditioned, have two lower beds, private bath with shower, radio; some have pullmans and can accommodate a third person.
Dining: Single open seating. American cuisine with regional specialties.
Facilities: Lounge lined with windows, library. Promenade Deck has an unobstructed circuit of the ship. No shops, no casino, no disco, no bingo. No medical facilities.
Activities: Lecturers, including local experts relevant to the cruises,

MV NANTUCKET CLIPPER

either cultural or adventure. Shore excursions. Snorkeling equipment and instruction. No organized activities on board. Zodiac landing craft for adventure cruises. Golf cruises up the Intracoastal Waterway provide individual and group instruction, videos, play at port courses (greens fees and cart rentals included).

Youth Program: None

Access for Disabled: No provisions for the disabled.

Rates: Per person double occupancy from $1,700 to $3,050.

Itinerary: Seven- and eight-day cruises in the Virgin Islands; eight- and 12-day cruises of the Intracoastal Waterway from Jacksonville; eight-day cruise of the Chesapeake Bay; a 15-day Civil War cruise from Jacksonville to Washington DC; eight- and 15-day cruises of the St. Lawrence Seaway and Thousand Islands; a 15-day cruise of Canada's Bay of Fundy and coastal Maine; a 12-day art cruise from Baltimore to Boston; an eight-day and 11-day autumn cruise on the Chesapeake Bay and Hudson River.

MS WORLD DISCOVERER

Built: 1974

Registry: Liberia

Length: 285 ft.

Beam: 50 ft.

Speed: 12 knots

Officers: European

Crew: 75, International

Passengers: 138. Almost all couples over 55.

MS WORLD DISCOVERER

Cabins: 71. All cabins are outside, air-conditioned, have lower beds, private bath with shower, radio, phone; some single, some double. Three suites.

Dining: Single seating. American cuisine with regional specialties.

Facilities: Ice-hardened double-hulled hull. Three bars, lounges, observation lounge lined with windows, cinema/lecture hall, library, gift shop, hairdresser, laundry, gym, sauna, solarium, swimming pool. A doctor on call.

Activities: Naturalist lecturers on board, including local experts. Zodiac landing craft for shore excursions. Equipment for diving, fishing, snorkeling, waterskiing, windsurfing. No organized activities on board.

Rates: Per person double occupancy for 11-to 15-day cruises from $2,250 to $7,465; for 16- to 22-day cruises from $4,865 to $11,865.

Itinerary: Eleven- and 12-day naturalist cruises of Alaska and British Columbia; 11- and 13-day cruises of the Bering Strait, Russian Far East and above the Arctic Circle; 15- to 22-day cruises of Antarctica, the Falklands and Chilean Fjords; a 19-day cruise of the western coast of South America; 18-to 21-day cruises of French Polynesia, Pitcairn and Easter Island.

MV YORKTOWN CLIPPER
Built: 1988
Registry: United States

Length: 251 ft.
Beam: 43 ft.
Speed: 13 knots
Officers: American
Crew: 57, American
Passengers: 138. Mostly couples over age 55.
Cabins: 69. All cabins are outside, air-conditioned, have two lower beds, private bath with shower, radio; some have pullmans and can accommodate a third person.
Dining: Single seating. American cuisine with regional specialties.
Facilities: Lounge/entertainment center lined with windows. Doctor on call whenever the ship sails beyond the easy reach of U.S. ports.
Activities: Lectures on board, including local experts relevant to the cruise themes. Promenade Deck has as unobstructed circuit of the ship. Free snorkeling equipment and instruction. Shore excursions. No organized activities on board.
Youth Program: None
Access for Disabled: No facilities provided.
Rates: Per person double occupancy for six- to eight-day cruises $2,050 to $2,950; for 11- to 15-day cruises from $2,250 to $7,465.
Itinerary: Eleven-day cruises of the Caribbean and the Orinoco River; a 14-day cruise of Costa Rica, the San Blas Islands and the Panama Canal; an 11-day cruise of Mexico's Sea of Cortez; eight-day cruises of Alaska, eight-day cruises of Pacific Northwest; eight- and 11-day cruises of the Columbia River and British Columbia; six-day cruises of California.

CLUB MED

40 West 57th St., New York, NY 10019
800-258-2633; 800-453-7447

SV CLUB MED I and II

Built: 1990, 1992
Registry: Bahamas
Length: 617 ft.
Beam: 66 ft.
Speed: 13 knots. Five-mast sailing vessel with computer-operated sails plus diesel engines.
Officers: International
Crew: 190, International
Passengers: 386-392. Almost totally couples.
Cabins: 193-196. All outside with phone, TV, radio, fridge, honor bar, private bath with shower and hairdryer. Two suites.
Dining: Two restaurants, open seating; one is buffet style; the other

more formal. Continental cuisine.

Facilities: Three bars and lounges, cabaret nightclub, theater, casino, two pools, sauna, fitness center, massage, hairdresser, shops, laundry, meeting room, piano bar, disco. Medical facilities.

Activities: Sailing, windsurfing, sunfish sailboats, scuba, snorkeling and water skiing off a stern swimming platform that lowers into the ocean. Two zodiac dive boats. Exercise classes, bridge lessons, classical music concerts. Both top decks have unobstructed circuits for fitness walks.

Youth Program: Children under 12 are not allowed.

Access for Disabled: No provisions for wheelchairs.

Rates: Per person for three- and four-day cruises from $600 to $970; seven-day cruises from $1,400 to $2,240, including tips. In addition to the cruise fare, passengers are required to join Club Med by paying a $30 initiation fee and an annual membership fee of $50.

Itinerary: From September through May, Club Med I sails out of Martinique on seven-day loops to the Virgin Islands o the Grenadines or other Caribbean islands. Summer in the Mediterranean. Club Med II makes three-, four-, and seven-day cruises of New Caledonia, southeast Asia and South Pacific Islands.

COASTAL CRUISES
P.O. Box 798, Camden, ME 04843
800-992-2218; 207-236-2750

SV MARY DAY
Built: 1962
Registry: United States
Length: 90 ft.
Beam: 24 ft.
Speed: 8 knots, depending on wind
Officers: American
Crew: 5, American
Passengers: 28
Cabins: 15. Upper and lower berths, keg with water for washing, shared bath facilities.
Dining: Family style.
Facilities: Main salon.
Activities: Shore excursions, lobster bakes.
Rates: Per person double occupancy $575.
Itinerary: Six-day cruises of the coast of Maine.

COMMODORE CRUISE LINE

800 Douglas Rd., Coral Gables, FL 33134

800-237-5361; 800-538-1000; 305-529-3000

SS ENCHANTED SEAS

Built: 1957

Registry: Panama

Former Names: *Queen of Bermuda; Liberte; Canada Star; Volendam; Brasil*

Length: 617 ft.

Beam: 84 ft.

Speed: 18 knots

Officers: European/American

Crew: 350, International

Passengers: 736

Cabins: 369. All have private bath with shower, radio, air conditioning, phone, TV. A few suites and double beds available; some with picture window and sitting area. Rooms for nonsmokers.

Dining: Dining room seats 375. Two seatings. Grill seats 175.

Facilities: Lounge with piano and dancing to top-40 music, disco, theater, showroom presents Broadway productions, casino, fitness room, two outdoor pools, jacuzzi, whirlpool, sauna, shops, hairdresser, library, conference facilities, laundry. Medical facilities.

Activities: Jogging track, shuffleboard, ping pong.

Youth Program: Youth center, teen activities during holidays.

Access for Disabled: Ramp access; travel companion required.

Rates: Double occupancy per person from $1,045 to $1,895.

COMPAGNIE DES ISLES DU PONANT

c/o Worldwide Cruise

400 SE 12th St., Ft. Lauderdale, FL 33316

800-881-8484; 305-463-1922

LE PONANT

Built: 1991

Registry: French Polynesia

Length: 288 ft.

Beam: 39 ft.

Speed: 14 knots

Officer: French

Crew: 30, European

Passengers: 64

Cabins: 34. All cabins have air-conditioning, private bath with shower, hairdryer, phone, radio, picture window.

Dining: French and continental cuisine.

Facilities: A three-masted yacht. Main salon.
Activities: Shore excursions, shore-based entertainment, exercise classes, watersports.
Rates: Per person double occupancy from $2,280 to $3,810.
Itinerary: Six-day cruises of the Caribbean and the Mediterranean departing from Guadeloupe and Nice.

CORAL BAY CRUISES
17 Fort Royal Isle, Ft. Lauderdale, FL 33308
800-433-7262; 305-563-1711

MY CORAL STAR
Built: 1955
Registry: British Virgin Islands
Former Name: *Global Star*
Length: 115 ft.
Beam: 22 ft.
Speed: 13 knots
Officers: American
Crew: 10, American, Bahamian, Jamaican
Passengers: 16
Cabins: 9. Three staterooms have queen-size beds and private bath; two cabins have private baths and bunk beds (lower is full-size); four cabins have bunk beds and share a bathroom. All have individually controlled air-conditioning.
Dining: Meals served family-style in main salon or as buffet on deck. American and island cuisine.
Facilities: Main salon with TV, VCR, and tape library. Air compressor for scuba tanks. Small launches.
Activities: On cruises to whale mating and calving grounds passengers watch, swim or snorkel with humpback whales. (This is one of the only places in the world where it is legal to swim with whales; no scuba allowed). On diving cruises passengers snorkel and scuba. On dolphin cruises they swim with dolphins. On wilderness excursions passengers investigate iguanas of Mayaguana and Allen Cay, the 50,000 flamingos of Great Inagua, and beachcomb various uninhabited cays. Windsurfers and sunfish sailboats are available to sail from the floating watersports platform. Slide show presentations by whale specialists or other naturalists.
Rates: Per person double occupancy from $1,395 to $1,595.
Itinerary: Eight-day cruises from Georgetown, Exumas in the Bahamas to Conception Island, Rum Cay and San Salvador for diving. From Freeport to the Little Bahama Bank for encounters with dolphins. From Great Exuma or Grand Turk for wilderness excursion

cruises. The whale cruise goes to the Silverbank area of the Bahamas between Grand Turk and the Dominican Republic.

COSTA CRUISE LINES
World Trade Center, 80 SW 8th St., Miami, FL 33130-3097
800-462-6782; 305-358-7325

MV COSTAALLEGRA
Built: 1992
Registry: Italy
Former Name: *Alexandra*
Length: 613 ft.
Beam: 84 ft.
Speed: 22 knots
Officers: Italian
Crew: Italian, International
Passengers: 804
Cabins: 402. Air-conditioned, phone, TV, radio, private bath with shower, hairdryer; 13 suites.
Dining: Restaurant with Italian-accented continental cuisine. Indoor/outdoor cafe for informal breakfast and lunch.
Facilities: Three-deck atrium with waterfall. Bars, lounges, showroom, ballroom, casino, swimming pool, three whirlpools, solarium, hairdresser, meeting center, laundry. Spa with greenhouse, salt water therapy, facials and body wraps, Roman bath, workout equipment. Medical facilities.
Activities: Deck sports. Shore excursions include beach parties, golf, tennis, helicopter tours.
Youth Program: Year-round, age 5 and up. Italian lessons, teen program.
Access for Disabled: Eight cabins feature wider access doors and special bath facilities.
Rates: Seven-day cruises from $795 to $3,995 double occupancy per person; 10- and 11-day Mediterranean cruises, $2,995 to $12,995.
Itinerary: In summer, Black Sea cruises to Bulgaria, Turkey, Greece, Egypt and to Scandinavia. In winter, seven-day cruises from San Juan to St. Maarten, St. Lucia, Barbados, St. Thomas, St. John and Dominican Republic.

MS COSTACLASSICA
Built: 1992
Registry: Italian
Length: 723 ft.
Beam: 98 ft.
Speed: 20 knots

Officers: Italian
Crew: 650
Passengers: 1,300. Almost all couples over 55.
Cabins: 654. Staterooms, hairdryer, TV. Suites can sleep up to four.
Dining: Main dining room with two sittings, strolling musicians. A pi-
    azza Viennese cafe serves cappuccino, croissants, aperitifs and
    high tea; open-air cafe serves pizza. Buffet on upper deck with in-
    door and outdoor seating for breakfast and lunch.
Facilities: Shopping promenade of boutiques and shops, showroom ac-
    commodates 600 guests in tiered-amphitheater style, Observatory
    on the ship's top deck offers a panoramic view, fitness center,
    steam and sauna, whirlpools, Roman bath, massage, water therapy,
    beauty parlor, swimming pool. A television shows current movies
    and CNN news. Doctor on board.
Activities: Deck sports. Shore excursions.
Youth Program: Wading pool, playroom. Italian lessons. Teen pro-
    gram.
Access for Disabled: Six cabins accommodate wheelchairs.
Rates: For seven- and eight-day Caribbean cruises, from $795 to
    $3,395. For seven-day Mediterranean cruises, from $2,295 to $6,165
    including airfare from most gateway cities.
Itinerary: Seven-day Western Mediterranean cruises out of Genoa, sail-
    ing to Naples, Palermo, Tunis, Ibiza, Palma de Mallorca and Bar-
    celona. Southern Caribbean itinerary from San Juan.

MS COSTAMARINA

Built: 1969
Registry: Italy
Former Name: *Axel Jonson*
Length: 572 ft.
Beam: 84 ft.
Speed: 20 knots
Officers: Italian
Crew: 385, Italian/International
Passengers: 770
Cabins: 386. All have air-conditioning, private bath with shower, ra-
    dio, TV, phone. Some have double bed, some two lower beds, some
    upper and lower berths.
Dining: Two seatings. Continental cuisine. Two formal evenings.
Facilities: Lounge, showroom, casino, nightclub, boutique, duty-free
    shops, gym, outdoor pool, solarium, hairdresser, laundry, sauna,
    three jacuzzis, massage. Medical facility.
Activities: Jogging track, ping pong, shuffleboard, skeet shooting,
    dance and Italian lessons.
Youth Program: Children's playroom.

Rates: Double occupancy per person $2,990 to $5,490.

Itinerary: Ten- and 11-day cruises of the Mediterranean in summer; South America and Anarctica November through May.

COSTAROMANTICA

Built: 1993

Registry: Italy

Length: 719 ft.

Beam: 98 ft.

Speed: 21 knots

Officers: Italian

Crew: 650

Passengers: 1,350

Cabins: 678. All have phone, TV, private bath with shower and hair-dryer. Of 34 suites, 10 have verandas and 6 have floor-to-ceiling windows, whirlpool baths, separate shower, sitting area with mini-bar and accommodate four-six passengers.

Dining: Dining room seats 756, features two movable panels creating a different ambience for theme dinner each evening. Indoor/out-door cafe located aft under a canvas canopy is for breakfasts and lunch buffets.

Facilities: Meeting and conference center accommodating up to 150 people, two smaller rooms for groups of up to 30 each. Theater, disco, library, lounge with teak dance floor and live entertainment, pool bar with dancing, ballroom, casino, pizzeria, shopping prome-nade. Spa with floor-to-ceiling windows, jogging/fitness track, steam and sauna rooms, jacuzzi, massage, hairdresser. Doctor on board.

Activities: Deck sports. Shore excursions include beach parties, golf, tennis, helicopter tours.

Youth Program: Teen center; children's playroom. Italian lessons.

Access for Disabled: Six staterooms available.

Rates: Seven-day cruises from $795 to $2,995; 10- to 11-day holiday cruises from $1,095 to $4,590.

Itinerary: Seven-day Caribbean itinerary from Miami to Ocho Rios, Cancun, Cozumel and Grand Cayman; or to San Juan, St. Thomas, St. John, Serena Cay, Casa de Campo and Nassau. Ten-day holiday cruise from Miami to St. Maarten, St. Lucia, Antigua, St. Thomas, St. John, Serena Cay, Casa de Campo. Seven-day cruises in Mediter-ranean.

DAPHNE

Built: 1956

Registry: Liberia

Former Name: *Port of Melbourne*

Length: 532 ft.
Beam: 74 ft.
Speed: 21 knots
Officers: Italian
Crew: 250, Italian, European
Passengers: 422. Singles 5%, couples 90%, families 5%.
Cabins: 212. Air-conditioned, twin beds, private bath with shower, radio, TV, phone; most are outside. There are 27 suites.
Dining: Restaurant, buffets.
Facilities: Lounge, showrooms, bar, disco, casino, outdoor pool, sauna, two whirlpools, shops, laundry, library. Medical facilities.
Activities: Deck sports, exercise equipment.
Youth Program: Yes
Access for Disabled: Not recommended.
Rates: Double occupancy per person from $1,260 to $44,080.
Itinerary: An 86-day cruise of the Orient, southeast Asia and Indian Ocean (available in segments), and seven- to 14-day cruises of the Mediterranean and Scandinavia.

ENRICOCOSTA
Built: 1950
Registry: Italy
Former Name: *Provance*
Length: 579 ft.
Beam: 73 ft.
Speed: 18 knots
Officers: Italian
Crew: 300, Italian, International
Passengers: 726. Singles 20%, couples 65%, families 15%.
Cabins: All have private bath with shower; some with sitting area, balcony, picture window.
Dining: Restaurant with international and Italian cuisine.
Facilities: Theater, lounges and bars, three outdoor pools, hairdresser, shops, chapel.
Activities: No casino, gym, or library. Shore excursions.
Youth Program: Children and teen programs, age 5 and up.
Access for Disabled: Several cabins are wheelchair accessible.
Rates: Double occupancy per person from $1,070 to $2,840.
Itinerary: Seven- and 11-day cruises of Scandinavia, departing from Amsterdam.

EUGENIOCOSTA
Built: 1966
Registry: Italy
Length: 713 ft.

Beam: 96 ft.
Speed: 27 knots
Officers: Italian
Crew: 475, Italian
Passengers: 1,100
Cabins: 579. All have air-conditioning, private bath with shower, some
    have radio, phone and TV. Some have two lower beds, some have
    upper and lower. Six suites.
Dining: Two seatings.
Facilities: Lounges, nightclub, boutique, duty-free shops, three out-
    door pools, jacuzzi, sauna, gym, hairdresser, laundry, massage.
    Medical facility.
Youth Program: Nursery, children's playroom.
Itinerary: Mediterranean.

CROWN DIVING CORPORATION

157 E. Port Rd., Riviera Beach, FL 33404
800-245-3467

MS CROWN DIVER and CROWN ISLANDER

Built: 1968, 1963
Registry: Panama
Length: 131 ft.
Beam: 26 ft.
Speed: 8-17 knots
Officers: International
Crew: 7, International
Passengers: 33; 32
Cabins: 12. Cabins for one to four people, have air-conditioning, pri-
    vate bath with shower, window.
Dining: Buffet dinners in lounge or on deck.
Facilities: A casual live-aboard ship for dive vacations. Lounge, li-
    brary, gift shop, dive platforms with twin ladders. Film processing
    on board. On board store with photo and dive accessories.
Activities: Snorkeling, scuba diving, waterskiing, windsurfing, fish-
    ing. Certification and specialty courses. Wall-diving is available in
    Caicos, free diving and swimming with bottlenosed dolphins in the
    Bahamas.
Youth Program: None.
Access for Disabled: None.
Rates: Per person double occupancy from $499 for three-night trip to
    $1,349 for seven-night trip, including use of tank, weights, weight
    belt and unlimited air fills.
Itinerary: Three-, four- and seven-night dive trip of Bahamas from

Nassau and seven-night dive trip of Turks and Caicos.

CRUCEROS AUSTRALIS See ODESSAMERICA

CRYSTAL CRUISES
2121 Avenue of the Stars, Los Angeles, CA 90067
800- 446-6645; 310-785-9300

MS CRYSTAL HARMONY
Built: 1990
Registry: Bahamas
Length: 791 ft.
Beam: 97 ft.
Speed: 22 knots
Officers: Norwegian, Japanese
Crew: 505, International
Passengers: 960
Cabins: 480. Staterooms with air-conditioning, sitting area, combination tub/shower, hairdryer, 9-channel TV, VCR, 5-channel radio, phone. Most with private veranda. Penthouse suites with dining area, complimentary-stocked wet bar, living room, king-size bed, marble baths with jacuzzi tub, vanity desk, daily hors d'oeuvres service and butler. Crystal Penthouses measure 948 square feet, 492 square feet and 360 square feet. Cabins for nonsmokers.
Dining: Crystal Dining Room seats 550; Kyoto Restaurant (Japanese cuisine) seats 80; Prego (Italian cuisine) seats 60. Indoor/outdoor cafe for breakfast and lunch alternative.
Facilities: Ocean-view spa, saunas, steam rooms, massage, two swimming pools (one for laps and the other with a swim-up bar), two whirlpools, seven bars, six entertainment lounges, casino, cinema, disco, library, piano bar, smoking room, video-game room, arcade of boutiques, beauty salon/barber, full-service laundry and dry cleaning, self-service laundry room, video-camera rentals, translation equipment for meetings.
Activities: Exercise classes, paddle tennis, shuffleboard, skeet shooting, computerized golf simulator, ping pong. Promenade Deck offers an unobstructed circuit for fitness walks.
Youth Program: Only if 10 or more children booked on a sailing.
Access for Disabled: Four outside cabins with wheelchair access. Passengers must provide their own small traveling wheelchairs.
Rates: Per person from $2,670 to $21,825. Children under 12 are half-fare when traveling with two full-paying adults.
Itinerary: Ten- to 21-day transcanal cruises between Acapulco and

Fort Lauderdale, Fort Lauderdale and Los Angeles, San Juan and Los Angeles. Ten-day cruises between New York and Montreal during the fall, stopping at Newport, Boston, Bar Harbor, Halifax, Charlottetown and Quebec City, and one- to two-day cruises of the Gulf of St. Lawrence and the Saguenay River. Twelve- to 14-day cruises with stops in Amsterdam, Copenhagen, Oslo, Dublin, Waterford, St. Petersburg, Haifa, Venice and Cannes. Pacific/Orient cruise with stops in Honolulu, Lahina, Bora Bora, Rarotonga, Bay of Islands and Auckland.

CTC CRUISE LINES See ODESSAMERICA

CUNARD LINE
555 Fifth Ave., New York, NY 10017
800-221-4770

MV CUNARD COUNTESS
Built: 1976
Registry: Bahamas
Length: 536 ft.
Beam: 74 ft.
Speed: 18 knots
Officers: British
Crew: 350, British, International
Passengers: 750
Cabins: 398. Cabins are small, but convert into sitting rooms for use during the day, air-conditioning, radio, phone. Deluxe staterooms have sofa or armchairs, bathtub, TV, VCR and refrigerator.
Dining: Dining room seats 400. Two seatings, assigned tables. Two formal evenings each week. Menus feature local specialties.
Facilities: Four bars, indoor/outdoor nightclub, three entertainment lounges, two outdoor whirlpools, swimming pool, casino, cinema, disco, library, piano bar, shops, beauty salon/barber, gym, sauna, massage, full-service laundry. Doctor on call.
Activities: Boat Deck for walking, basketball, golf driving, paddle tennis, ping pong, volleyball, shuffleboard, exercise classes, dancing classes. Country music theme cruises.
Youth Program: During holidays or in summer. Children's wading pool.
Access for Disabled: Not all public areas are accessible to wheelchairs. Portable wheelchair is required.
Rates: Three- to four-days from $725 to $1,735 and six- to eight-day cruises from $845 to $3,525 per person double occupancy, with free

or low-cost round-trip air transportation between 100 North American gateway cities and the ship.

Itinerary: Three- to eight-day cruises out of San Juan that call in St. Maarten, Guadeloupe, Grenada, St. Lucia, St. Kitts and St. Thomas or at Tortola, Antigua, Martinique, Barbados and St. Thomas.

CUNARD CROWN DYNASTY

Built: 1993
Registry: Panama
Length: 537 ft.
Beam: 74 ft.
Speed: 18 knots
Officers: Scandinavian
Crew: 320, Filipino
Passengers: 900

Cabins: 400. Air-conditioning, TV, phone. Deluxe cabins with sitting area, large window and refrigerator. Connecting cabins available. 12 suites with bay window or balcony.

Dining: Dining room features windows on three sides. Cafe has indoor/outdoor informal buffets for breakfast and lunch.

Facilities: Nightclub, library, casino, pool bar, outdoor pool, three whirlpools, fitness spa, sauna, massage, aerobics, beauty salon, shopping arcade. Medical facilities.

Activities: Jazz combos, Broadway-style shows, dancing.

Youth Program: Teen centers. Programs if more than 15 children on board.

Access for Disabled: Two outside and two inside cabins. Cabins with wheelchair access, wide bathroom doors.

Rates: Double occupancy per person from $1,195 to $4,825 for seven-day cruises.

Itinerary: Seven- through 14-day cruises of the Caribbean (including Mexican ports); Panama Canal; seven- to 12-day cruise of Alaska.

CUNARD CROWN JEWEL

Built: 1992
Registry: Panama
Length: 537 ft.
Beam: 74 ft.
Speed: 18 knots
Officers: European
Crew: 300, Filipino
Passengers: 820

Cabins: 410. Air-conditioned staterooms with two lower berths (which convert to doubles), TV, radio, phone. Suites have double bed, sitting area and refrigerator, some with private balconies.

Dining: Nouvelle, oriental and haute cuisine served in the formal dining room. Indoor/outdoor cafe for casual buffet breakfast and lunch.

Facilities: Nightclub, casino, lounge, fitness center, aerobics, two saunas, two steam rooms, massage, facials, hairdresser, outdoor pool, jogging deck, game room, shops, dry cleaning, laundry, library. Medical facilities.

Activities: Jazz combos, variety show, shuffleboard, paddle tennis, ping pong, skeet shooting, snorkeling instruction.

Youth Program: Children's counselors on a seasonal basis.

Access for Disabled: Two outside and two inside cabins with wheelchair access, wide bathroom doors. Travel companion required.

Rates: Three- and four-day cruises from $725 to $1,735, and six- and eight-day cruises from $845 to $3,525 with free or low-cost roundtrip air transportation between gateway cities and the ship.

Itinerary: Three- to eight-day cruises of the Caribbean from Ft. Lauderdale to Puerto Plata, St. Thomas, San Juan, Nassau, Freeport, Abaco, Ocho Rios, Grand Caymen, Tortola, Cozumel, Cancun, Key West.

MV CUNARD CROWN MONARCH

Built: 1990

Registry: Panama

Length: 494 ft.

Beam: 69 ft.

Speed: 18 knots

Officers: Filipino

Crew: 190, International

Passengers: 530

Cabins: 265. Air-conditioning, TV, radio, phone, some with tub and picture window. Ten suites with veranda, walk-in closet, whirlpool bath, sitting area and bar. Standard cabins have double beds.

Dining: Nouvelle, oriental and haute cuisine served in the formal Palm dining room. The Ocean Terrace for casual buffet breakfast and lunch.

Facilities: Nightclub, casino, exercise classes, health spa and gym, outdoor pool, jogging deck, two saunas and whirlpools, massage, hairdresser, shops, dry cleaning, laundry, library. Medical facilities.

Activities: Paddle tennis, ping pong, skeet shooting, snorkeling instruction.

Youth Program: Counselors available for children on a seasonal basis.

Access for Disabled: One deluxe stateroom, two standard outside staterooms, one suite and one mini-suite are wheelchair accessible.

Rates: Four-day cruises from $1,885 to $3,250; nine- to 14-day cruises from $1,695 to $7,635; 28-day cruises from $3,995 to $10,315 per person double occupancy. Discount for passengers over age 55.

Itinerary: Nine- to 14-day cruises of Australia, New Zeland, Coral Sea, South Pacific, Solomon Islands and New Guinea from Sydney or Cairns. A four-day Hunter Valley Wine Cruise and seven-day Melbourne Cup cruise. From Singapore, Hong Kong, or Darwin, 14-day cruises to the Java Seas, Indonesia and Asia.

CUNARD PRINCESS

Built: 1977

Registry: Bahamas

Length: 536 ft.

Beam: 75 ft.

Speed: 18 knots

Officers: International

Crew: 350, International

Passengers: 750. Mostly British and American, with some Germans. Most are 50 and over.

Cabins: 400. Standard rooms furnished with twin beds, phone, air-conditioning, radio. Most have two lower berths; a few have an upper berth for the second person; some have space for a third person. Deluxe staterooms with twin beds, armchairs, tub, TV and refrigerator.

Dining: Dining Room seats 400. Two seatings for dinner. Cafe features outdoor buffet breakfasts, lunches and snacks.

Facilities: Pool, sauna, whirlpool, gym, jogging track, hairdresser, shops, library, classes, lectures and workshops, conference facilities, laundry, cinema, indoor/outdoor center for dancing, theater in-the-round. Medical facilities.

Activities: Paddle tennis, driving range, ping pong, shuffleboard, exercise classes, lectures.

Access for Disabled: Limited wheelchair accessibility. Travel companion required.

Rates: Double occupancy per person for 10- to 14-days from $2,785 to $8,075 with free or low-cost round-trip air between gateway cities and the ship.

Itinerary: Seven- through 15-day cruises of the Mediterranean, Canary Islands, Black Sea and Morocco.

RMS QUEEN ELIZABETH 2

Built: 1969

Registry: England

Length: 963 ft.

Beam: 105 ft.

Speed: 32 knots

Officers: British

Crew: 1,000, International

Passengers: 1,870

Cabins: 932. Staterooms with individual temperature control, radio, 20-channel TV, phone. Luxury cabins with VCR and veranda. Split-level suites with jacuzzi. Prices for suites cover as many as four passengers and are therefore more economical than paying for two luxury cabins for a family of four.

Dining: Passengers are assigned to one of four restaurants (each offering a different level of quality and service). The gourmet Queen's Grill and Princess Grill are elegant, single-seating restaurants for occupants of suites and ultra-deluxe cabins. The single-seating Columbia Restaurant is for the occupants of the deluxe and higher-priced outside cabins. All others are served in two seatings in the Mauritania Restaurant. Early dinner for children. Two formal evenings each week. The wine cellar stocks more than 20,000 bottles of wine.

Facilities: Shopping arcade with major stores, IBM computer learning center, four swimming pools, six bars, five entertainment lounges, casino, chapel/synagogue, cinema, disco, board room, library, piano bar, men's formal rental shop, hairdresser, full-service laundry, dry cleaning, self-serve laundromat, ironing room, two fitness centers that include health and beauty programs for men and women, whirlpools, massage, jogging track (3.5 laps equals 1 mile). Kennels for dogs on transatlantic cruise. Hospital staffed by doctors and nurses.

Activities: Putting green, golf driving range, paddle tennis, ping pong, shuffleboard, tetherball, trap shooting, volleyball, numerous lectures and seminars, classical music concerts, fashion shows, lectures by celebrity experts, dance contests, talent contests, costume party, computer courses, extensive exercise and fitness program. Pool is covered at night for dancing on deck.

Youth Program: Children's playroom, nursery run by professional nannies, teen center; programs offered all year.

Access for Disabled: A few cabins have been equipped with wide doors, low-threshold ledges and special bathrooms. Wheelchairs may not be carried aboard tenders, so wheelchair-bound passengers may not be able to see all the ports on the itinerary.

Rates: Per diem from $202 to $1,334. Suites from $2,422 to $4,155. For cruises from $425 to $189,590.

Itinerary: Transatlantic crossings between New York and Southampton, England. Cruise to the Caribbean from New York and other eastcoast cities. Cruises through the Panama Canal to Bermuda, along the east coast of Canada, and European itineraries. Annual four-month circumnavigation of the globe, with stops at 37 ports on six continents.

MS SAGAFJORD

Built: 1965

Registry: Bahamas

Length: 620 ft.

Beam: 80 ft.

Speed: 20 knots

Officers: Norwegian

Crew: 352, European

Passengers: 588. Mostly late-fifties and up.

Cabins: 338. All rooms equipped with air-conditioning, TV, radio, phone. Most have picture windows. Some deluxe cabins with king-size beds, sitting room and private terrace. Some suites have TV, VCR, refrigerator.

Dining: Restaurant seats 588. One seating for dinner. Passengers may eat at any time between 7 PM and 9 PM. Every evening is at least semiformal. Cafe for casual breakfast and lunch. International cuisine, regional specialties.

Facilities: Golden Door spa, sauna, massage, ballroom, indoor and outdoor pools, whirlpool, four bars, three entertainment lounges, casino, cabaret, cinema, library, hairdresser, full-service laundry, dry cleaning, self-service laundromat/ironing room. Promenade Deck for fitness walks (seven laps to a mile). Doctor on call.

Activities: Golf driving, shuffleboard, ping pong, trap shooting, lectures, dance classes, gentleman hosts for dancing, video-taped golf lessons, computer learning center, personal fitness program, jazz band, concert pianist or operatic duo, light musical review. Theme cruises: big band, classical music, soap opera, natural history.

Youth Program: Program available with five or more children on board.

Access for Disabled: Travel wheelchairs needed. Most doorways, restrooms and spa not accessible. Tenders cannot be used.

Rates: Ten- to 20-day cruises from $2,730 to $21,720 double occupancy per person, including airfare.

Itinerary: In January, a 108-day world cruise from Ft. Lauderdale that visits 34 ports in South America, Antarctica, Africa and the Orient. Ten-day cruise from Ft. Lauderdale to Bermuda and Freeport. In summer, 10- to 14-day cruises of Alaska from Vancouver. Autumn and winter include New England/Labrador itineraries between Montreal and Ft. Lauderdale and Caribbean cruises out of Ft. Lauderdale.

MS VISTAFJORD

Built: 1973

Registry: Bahamas
Length: 628 ft.
Beam: 82 ft.
Speed: 20 knots
Officers: Norwegian
Crew: 379, International
Passengers: 695
Cabins: 404. Air-conditioning, radio, phone. Suites and some deluxe
rooms have verandas. Deluxe staterooms may include king-size
bed, sitting room, refrigerator, VCR. Adjoining luxury suites may
be converted to two-room apartments.
Dining: One seating for dinner. International cuisine, regional specialties from ports of call.
Facilities: Golden Door Spa, sauna, massage, whirlpools, exercise
classes, indoor and outdoor pool, library, hairdresser, boutique,
two orchestras, cabaret-style entertainment, three lounges, casino,
full-service laundry, self-service laundromat/ironing room, dry
cleaning. Promenade Deck is used as the jogging track. Medical facilities.
Activities: Golf driving, shuffleboard, ping pong, trap shooting, lecture series. Gentlemen hosts for dancing. Theme cruises: murder
mystery, classical music opera, natural history, theater.
Youth Program: Program available when five or more children are on
board.
Access for Disabled: Cabins with wheelchair access, but most doorways and restrooms not accessible. Tenders cannot be used.
Rates: Eleven- to 21-day cruises from $2,910 to $27,110 per person double occupancy.
Itinerary: Fifteen-day Amazon/Caribbean cruises between Ft. Lauderdale and Manaus. Thirteen- to 21-day cruises of the Holy Land, the
Mediterranean and Black Sea, the Baltic, Ireland, Scotland, Scandi-
navia, Greenland and Ireland. A 14-day cruise of Morocco and the
Canary Islands. Other cruises between Los Angeles and Papeete,
from Ft. Lauderdale to the Caribbean, transcanal, and between Ft.
Lauderdale and Tenerife.

SEA GODDESS I and II

Built: 1984; 1985
Registry: Norway
Length: 344 ft.
Beam: 40 ft.
Speed: 15 knots
Officers: Norwegian
Crew: 89, International
Passengers: 116

Cabins: 58. All cabins are outside and include twin or queen-sized bed, private bath with tub, shower and hairdryer, air-conditioning, TV, VCR, radio, phone and sitting room. Adjacent rooms may be purchased to form a two-room suite.

Dining: Open seating for dinner. Two formal evenings each week. Passengers tend to dress elegantly at all evenings. Outdoor cafe for casual breakfast and lunch.

Facilities: Gym, sauna, massage, individualized fitness programs, swimming pool, three bars, two entertainment lounges, casino, greenhouse, library, piano bar, shops, hairdresser, full-service laundry, dry cleaning. Promenade has an unobstructed circuit of the ship. Doctor on call.

Activities: Skeet shooting; windsurfing, snorkeling, sailing, waterskiing off the stern swimming platform; on-shore clubs for tennis, golf; special-interest cruises; pianist or dance trio in piano bar, local entertainment from ports of call, passengers may visit casinos or nightclubs in ports.

Youth Program: None.

Access for Disabled: Passengers in wheelchairs may not board launches, preventing them from going ashore.

Rates: Cruises range from $3,900 to $10,500 per person. Transatlantic cruises are less expensive.

Itinerary: Winter in the Caribbean out of St. Thomas to St. John, St. Martin/St. Maarten, St. Barts, Antigua, Virgin Gorda and Jost Van Dyke. Occasionally, seven-day cruises between St. Thomas and Barbados visiting Mustique, St. Lucia, Martinique, Antigua, St. Martin/St. Maarten (or St. Barts) and Jost Van Dyke (or Virgin Gorda). In spring and summer, Europe, Java Seas and the Orient.

CUNARD EUROPAMERICA RIVER CRUISES

555 5th Ave., New York, NY 10017
800-528-6273; 800-226-1666; 800-221-4770; 212-880-7500

MV DANUBE PRINCESS

Built: 1983
Registry: Germany
Length: 364 ft.
Beam: 50 ft.
Speed: 10 knots
Officers: Austrian, German
Crew: 75, Austrian, German
Passengers: 185
Cabins: 95. All equipped with private shower, air-conditioning, TV, VCR, radio, phone; hairdryer available on request. Most cabins

have outside picture window.

Dining: Window-lined dining room seats 200. Single seating. International cuisine with local specialties.

Facilities: Large lounge with turn-of-the-century furnishings and nightly entertainment by local artists and ship's orchestra, massage, sauna, whirlpool, heated outdoor pool, sightseeing tours, boutique, library, hairdresser, laundry. Medical facilities.

Activities: Sightseeing tours to historic cities, medieval castles, gothic churches and countryside of seven countries from Germany to Romania. Chamber music, dancing, local entertainment such as Hungarian gypsy bands or flamenco dancers.

Rates: $1,435 to $2,495 double occupancy per person.

Itinerary: Seven-day cruises from Munich, Germany (port of Passau) to Austria, Hungary and Slovakia; 10- and 11- day cruises of the Black Sea.

MS DRESDEN
Built: 1991
Registry: Germany
Length: 304 ft.
Beam: 35 ft.
Speed: 15 knots
Officers: European
Crew: 47. German
Passengers: 110.
Cabins: 56. Picture windows for river views, air conditioning, private bath with shower, phone, radio, hairdryer available upon request, minibar and TV.
Dining: Single-seating dining. International cuisine and local specialties.
Facilities: Massage, sauna, whirlpools, heated swimming pool. Medical facility.
Activities: Shore excursions in German and Czech Republic ports, including Meissen, Bad Schandau, and Duin. Chamber music, local bands and dancers.
Rates: From $1,595 to $2,495 per person.
Itinerary: Seven-day cruises along the Elbe River from Hamburg or Dresden to Meissen, Prague and Wittenberg.

MS MOZART
Built: 1987
Registry: Austria
Length: 396 ft.
Beam: 74 ft.
Speed: 7 knots

Officers: International
Crew: 80, International
Passengers: 212. Singles 5%, couples 95%.
Cabins: 104. Air-conditioned staterooms with private bath and
    shower, radio, phone, hairdryer, minibar. All except four are out-
    side. Sixteen cabins are non-smoking. Cabins have one queen-size
    bed or two sofa beds. Two standard cabins can be combined to cre-
    ate a double suite.
Dining: Dining room has single sittings, cocktail attire for the Cap-
    tain's cocktail and dinner. Cafe for casual meals.
Facilities: Lounge with orchestra music, indoor pool, outdoor pool,
    whirlpool, sauna, gym, solarium, massage, shops, hairdresser, con-
    ference facilities, library, piano bar, laundry, dry cleaning, bou-
    tique. Medical facilities.
Activities: Jogging on sun deck, wine-tastings, gypsy feasts,
    weisswurst parties. Shore excursions to castles, cathedrals, vine-
    yards, towns and old villages.
Rates: From $1,685 to $2,885 per person.
Itinerary: Seven-day cruises from Vienna to Slovakia, Hungary and
    Germany along the Danube.

MV PRINCESSE DE PROVENCE

Built: 1992
Registry: Germany
Length: 363 ft.
Beam: 37 ft.
Speed: 13 knots
Officers: German
Crew: 71, European
Passengers: 135
Cabins: 71. Cabins outside, picture window for river view, air-condi-
    tioned, private bath with shower, radio, phone; hairdryer available
    upon request.
Dining: Dining room seats 148, single seating. International cuisine
    with local specialties.
Facilities: Lounge with local entertainment, hairdresser, boutique,
    laundry, library. Medical facilities.
Activities: Shore excursions to French towns and villages along the
    Rhone, including vineyards of Burgundy.
Rates: From $1,595 to $2,495 double occupancy per person.
Itinerary: Seven-day cruises round-trip from Lyon up the Saone river
    and down the Rhone river to Vienne, Macon, Arles and Avignon.

MV PRUSSIAN PRINCESS

Built: 1991

Registry: Germany
Length: 363 ft.
Beam: 37 ft.
Speed: 13 knots
Officers: Austrian, German
Crew: 71, Austrian, German
Passengers: 135
Cabins: Cabins with picture window for river view, private bath with shower, air-conditioning, TV, radio, phone, hairdryer upon request. Four cabins have upper berths.
Dining: Dining room seats 144, single seating. International cuisine with local specialties.
Facilities: Lounge and two bars featuring entertainment, hairdresser, boutique, library, laundry. Medical facilities.
Activities: Shore excursions to villages and towns along river and canal waterways.
Rates: From $1,595 to $2,495 double occupancy per person.
Itinerary: Seven-day cruises of the Rhine and Main Rivers and the Main-Danube Canal; between Amsterdam and Basel; round-trip from Frankfurt or Amsterdam through German, Belgian and Dutch canals.

DELTA QUEEN STEAMBOAT COMPANY
Robin Street Wharf, New Orleans, LA 70130
800-543-7637; 504-0631

DELTA QUEEN
Built: 1926
Registry: United States
Length: 285 ft.
Beam: 58 ft.
Speed: 9 knots, powered by stern paddlewheel
Officers: American
Crew: 75, American
Passengers: 176
Cabins: 88. All have air-conditioning, private bath with shower, some with brass bed, stained glass and antiques, outside view for river watching, two with tub. Suites have large windows and sitting area.
Dining: Two sittings. American cuisine with creole and southern specialties, such as catfish, gumbo and etouffee.
Facilities: Authentic river steamboat, designated a National Historic Landmark. Piano bar, lounge, library, exercise room, jacuzzi.
Activities: Jazz, big band, cabaret shows in the lounges. Jogging around deck. Kite flying. Calliope concerts. Riverlorians on board

for lectures on American heritage, river history and steamboat tales. Shore excursions. Theme cruises include spring gardens of southern plantations, fall foliage on northern rivers, and a cruise to Cincinnati and Louisville during the Kentucky Derby.

Youth Program: None

Access for Disabled: Limited wheelchair access. Traveling companion required.

Rates: Per person double occupancy from $790 to $7,070.

Itinerary: One- to 12-night cruises of the Mississippi River and tributaries. From New Orleans cruises go north to view antebellum homes, or south through marshland to the mouth of the Mississippi River, or on the Atchafalaya River to Louisiana Cajun country. Other cruises go between St. Louis and St. Paul, and on the Ohio, Tennessee, Arkansas and Cumberland Rivers. One cruise is a steamboat race between the *Mississippi Queen* and the *Delta Queen* from New Orleans to St. Louis. Cruises can be combined.

MISSISSIPPI QUEEN

Built: 1976

Registry: United States

Length: 382 ft.

Beam: 68 ft.

Speed: 9 knots, powered by stern paddlewheel

Officers: American

Crew: 165, American

Passengers: 436. Mostly couples over 55.

Cabins: 204. All are air-conditioned, have private bath with shower, phone, radio; some with brass bed, sitting area, picture window and veranda overlooking the river.

Dining: Dining room seats 220, two sittings. American cuisine with authentic southern dishes.

Facilities: Gym, pool, whirlpool, theater, library, hairdresser, boutique, lounge in stern with view of giant paddlewheel in action, gift shop, laundry.

Activities: Jazz, ragtime, big band, cabaret shows in the lounges. Jogging around deck. Kite flying. Shuffleboard, calliope concerts, cooking demonstrations, singalongs. Riverlorians on board for lectures on American heritage, river history and steamboats tales. Shore excursions. Theme cruises include baseball, Civil War, gardens of southern plantations, fall foliage on the northern rivers, big band cruises with well known vocalists, and a cruise to Cincinnati during the Kentucky Derby.

Youth Program: None.

Access for Disabled: Ramp access, cabins with wheelchair access. Travel companions required.

Rates: Double occupancy rate per person in $790 to $7,070.
Itinerary: Two- to seven-day cruises on the Mississippi River and
tributaries. From New Orleans cruises go north to view antebellum
homes and Civil War sites, or south through marshland to the
mouth of the Mississippi River, or on the Atchafalaya River to Louisiana Cajun country. Other cruises go between St. Louis and St.
Paul, and on the Ohio, Tennessee, Arkansas and Cumberland Rivers. One cruise is a steamboat race between the *Mississippi Queen*
and the *Delta Queen* from New Orleans to St. Louis. Cruises can be
combined.
Note: The *American Queen* is scheduled for delivery in 1995.

DIAMOND CRUISE
600 Corporate Dr., Ft. Lauderdale, FL 33334
800-333-3333; 402-498-5072

SSC RADISSON DIAMOND
Built: 1992. The first major cruise ship to utilize the submerged twin-
hull principle, called SWATH (small waterplane area twin hull). En-
gines are in the hulls beneath the water line so engine noise and
vibration are greatly minimized. Stabilizer fins on the front and
back of each submerged hull reduces pitching and heaving.
Registry: Finland
Length: 420 ft.
Beam: 103 ft.
Speed: 14 knots
Officers: Finnish, Italian
Crew: 192, International
Passengers: 350. Mostly North American.
Cabins: 177. Of these, 121 have a balcony and 54 have a sitting room.
All cabins feature an ocean view and have TV, VCR, complimentary bar, refrigerator, sitting area, shower and bathtub, queen-size
beds (half can be converted to twin beds), hairdryer, individual
temperature control and direct-dial phone. Two owner suites fea-
ture a king-size bed, whirlpool tub, separate shower, balcony and
large bay window.
Dining: The dining room has open seating—eat when you want,
where you want. Homemade breads, homemade ice cream, fresh-
ground coffee. The grill, seating 60, serves four meals a day in a casual atmosphere and features northern Italian specialty dishes, with
violin and accordion music in the evening.
Facilities: Five-story garden atrium, outdoor swimming pool, lounge
with dancing and cabaret shows, stage on pool deck for outdoor entertainment, fitness equipment, outdoor jogging track, steam

rooms, saunas, jacuzzi, massages and herbal wraps, boutique, laundry, dry cleaning, casino, book and videotape library; business center with state-of-the-art audio-visual equipment, publishing facilities and personal computer hook-ups. Medical facilities with doctor and nurse.

Activities: Golf driving range with nets and putting green, occasional lectures on topics of educational and cultural interests, dancing. Retractable marina between the hulls creates shelter for snorkeling, sailing and windsurfing. Island excursions.

Youth Program: None

Access for Disabled: Two wheelchair-designed staterooms. Elevator doors are 39.97" in width. Outside decks can be reached without assistance.

Rates: Per person $1,595 to $5,495. No tipping.

Itinerary: Seven-night cruises in Mediterranean to Spain, France, Italy, Malta, Monaco, Greece and Turkey. In the Caribbean, three- to seven-night cruises to San Juan, Barbados, Bequia, Grenada, Martinique, St. Kitts, St. Barts, St. Maarten, St. Thomas, Iles de Saintes, Antigua, Virgin Gorda, Nassau, the Abacos and St. Lucia. A transPanama 10-night cruise calls at Ft. Lauderdale, Key West, Playa del Carmen, Cozumel, Grand Cayman, San Andres Island and Puerto Caldera.

DIAMOND CRUISES/ SWEDISH AMERICAN CRUISES

MS RADISSON KUNGSHOLM

Delivery: 1995

Length: 492 ft.

Beam: 69 ft.

Speed: 17 knots

Officers: European

Crew: 134, International

Passengers: 232

Cabins: 116. Two-room suites; have air-conditioning, private bath with shower, radio, TV, VCR, two phones. Some have veranda.

Dining: Dining room and cafe.

Facilities: Show lounge, piano bar, casino, cinema, business center, massage. Medical facility. Decompression chamber for divers. Helipad.

Itinerary: The Mediterranean.

DIRIGO CRUISES
39 Waterside Lane, Clinton, CT 06413
800-845-5520; 203-669-7068

CUAN LAW and LAMMER LAW
Built: 1978, 1983
Registry: British Virgin Islands, Chile
Length: 105 ft.
Beam: 42 ft.
Speed: Sail power.
Officers: American
Crew: 5, American, Chilean
Passengers: 18
Cabins: 9. All staterooms are outside with twin or double bed (no bunks), air-conditioning, private bath and shower.
Dining: International cuisine served on deck.
Facilities: Sailing trimaran with main salon.
Activities: Diving and sailing. Scuba diving compressors, tanks, weight belts, snorkels, fins and masks are free. Regulators, BC's, cameras are available for rent. Two professional naturalists on board for briefings on ecology, animal and bird life.
Rates: $1,290 for *Cuan Law*, $1,950 for *Lammer Law*.
Itinerary: Six-night cruises of British Virgin Islands from Tortola (*Cuan Law*), and the Galapagos Islands from San Cristobal (*Lammer Law*).

SOREN LARSON
Built: 1949
Registry: Great Britain
Length: 105 ft.
Beam: 25 ft.
Speed: Sail power.
Officers: British
Crew: 10, British
Passengers: 18.
Cabins: 9. Washbasin in cabin, shared head and shower. No portholes.
Dining: Family style, mostly served on deck. Casual attire.
Activities: Hands-on sail training.
Rates: From $1,050 to $2,100 for nine- to 26-day cruises; $9,443 per person for 83-day cruises.

HARVEY GAMAGE
Built: 1973
Registry: United States
Length: 95 ft.
Beam: 24 ft.
Speed: Sail power.

Crew: 7. (Young men and women are accepted on the ship to live and work with the crew in a program which provides knowledge of seamanship and navigational skills; $975 per month).

Passengers: 32

Cabins: 17. Toilet facilities and showers are shared.

Dining: Meals are family style in main saloon or buffet on deck; occasional picnic ashore.

Facilities: No bar.

Activities: Passengers are welcome to help sail the ship, beachcombing, snorkeling; scuba diving trips can be arranged, small sailboats. One "Nature Expedition" with naturalist and daily lectures. Some "men only" cruises.

Rates: From $645 to $999 per person for six-night cruises. The transatlantic passages begin at $845.

Itinerary: In winter, seven-day cruises from St. Thomas with calls in the British and American Virgin Islands including St. John, Jost Van Dyke, Tortola, Virgin Gorda and Norman Islands. Navigational passages from Annapolis to Bermuda and Bermuda to St. Thomas include a complete course in celestial navigation, study materials and instruments supplied. In summer, there are three-night family cruises from Boston to Marblehead, Salem, Provincetown and Gloucester. Children have the opportunity to watch, learn and share the excitement of sailing. In fall, seven-day trips in Long Island and Block Island Sound with stops at Newport, Nantucket and Block Island. Individual passages on other sailing vessels from 68 to 140 ft., 8 to 37 passengers, are also available from Dirigo Cruises with itineraries in Maine, Connecticut, the Great Lakes, Caribbean, the Galapagos and South Pacific.

DOLPHIN CRUISE LINE

901 South American Way, Miami, FL 33132

800-222-1003; 305-358-2111

SS DOLPHIN IV

Built: 1956

Registry: Panama

Former Name: *Ithaca*

Length: 501 ft.

Beam: 65 ft.

Speed: 17 knots

Officers: Greek

Crew: 285, International

Passengers: 588. Singles 20%, couples 70%, families, 10%.

Cabins: 294. All have air-conditioning, private bath with shower, radio, phone. Suites have picture window.

Dining: Two seatings. Formal evenings.

Facilities: Swimming pool, four bars, two entertainment lounges, casino, disco, small library, gift shop, hairdresser. The Boat Deck has an unobstructed circuit of the ship. Doctor on call.

Activities: Variety shows, masquerade parties, dance classes, aerobics, ping pong, shuffleboard, skeet shooting, movies.

Youth Program: Children's playroom. Youth programs during summer and holidays with kite-flying, Yogi bear and Flintstone characters on board, educational programs about ports of call.

Access for Disabled: Passengers confined to wheelchairs must be accompanied by an adult companion.

Rates: Cruises range from $255 to $815 per person.

Itinerary: Three- and four-night cruises out of Miami to Nassau. On the four-night cruises, the ship also docks at Key West.

Itinerary: Nine- to 10-day cruises in Caribbean; 11- to 18-day cruises in the South Pacific, and an 83-day sail from Panama to Easter Island and Tahiti. Ten-day to three week navigation workshop to and from the West Indies stopping at Bermuda to learn navigation skills or prepare for deep water sailing.

SS OCEANBREEZE

Built: 1955

Registry: Liberia

Former Names: *Azure Seas; Calypso; Southern Cross; Monarch Star*

Length: 604 ft.

Beam: 78 ft.

Speed: 20 knots

Officers: Greek

Crew: 310, International

Passengers: 776

Cabins: 384. All have private bath with shower, air-conditioning, radio, phone. Twelve suites with sitting area, TV, picture window.

Dining: Restaurant with two seatings, international cuisine. On-deck buffets.

Facilities: Three lounges with entertainment, showroom, casino, small disco, meeting room, library, outdoor pool, exercise room, sauna, shops. Medical facilities.

Activities: Aerobics, shuffleboard, ping pong, snorkeling instructions.

Youth Program: Children's playroom.

Access for Disabled: Not recommended because of steep stairs and narrow hallways.

Rates: Double occupancy per person from $995 to $2,545.

Itinerary: Seven- and eight-night cruises of the Caribbean, including Central and South American ports, departing from Aruba.

SS SEABREEZE
   Built:1958
   Registry: Panama
   Former Names: *Starship Royale; Royale Frederico*
   Length: 605 ft.
   Beam: 79 ft.
   Speed: 21 knots
   Officers: Greek
   Crew: 400, International
   Passengers: 842. Singles 10%, couples 70%, families 20%.
   Cabins: 423. All have air-conditioning, radio, phone, private bath with
      shower; some with tub. Suites have picture window. Some cabins
      will sleep five.
   Dining: Dining room has two sittings. Buffet lunches on deck.
   Facilities: Swimming pool, three whirlpools, gym, massage, five bars,
      four entertainment lounges, casino, cinema, disco, piano bar,
      shops, beauty/barber, full-service laundry, dry cleaning. Daphne
      Deck has an unobstructed circuit for fitness walks and jogging, 6
      laps equal 1 mile. Doctor on call.
   Activities: Aerobics, basketball, golf driving, ping pong, scuba and
      snorkeling lessons, shuffleboard, skeet shooting.
   Youth Program: Children's playroom. Youth programs during holi-
      days or in summer.
   Access for Disabled: Cabin bathroom doorways are 20" wide. Passen-
      gers confined to a wheelchair must be accompanied by an adult.
   Rates: Cruises range from $635 to $1,755 per person double occupancy.
   Itinerary: Seven-night cruises from Miami to Nassau, San Juan, St.
      John and St. Thomas or to Grand Cayman, Montego Bay, Playa del
      Carmen and Cozumel. Seven-day cruises of the Caribbean, includ-
      ing Central and South American ports.

DOLPHIN HELLAS CRUISES
   26 6th St., Stamford, CT 06905
   800-473-3239; 203-973-0111

MV AEGEAN DOLPHIN
   Built: 1973
   Registry: Greece
   Former Name: *Narcis*
   Length: 462 ft.
   Beam: 66 ft.
   Speed: 20 knots
   Officers: Greek
   Crew: 175, Greek

Passengers: 558. Singles, 15%, couples 70%, families 15%.
Cabins: 291. Air-conditioning, phone, hairdryer. Two suites with sitting area, queen bed and window. Cabins for nonsmokers.
Dining: Restaurant seats 340.
Facilities: Several lounges and bars, disco, casino, gym, masseuse, outdoor pool, sauna, hairdresser, cinema, boutique, library, laundry. Hospital with doctor.
Activities: Paddle tennis, ping pong.
Rates: Double occupancy per person from $535 to $2,390.
Itinerary: Three-, four- and seven-day cruises of the Greek Isles and Turkey from Piraeus to Mykonos, Heraklion, Santorini, Rhodes, Kusadasi, Patmos.

ECOVENTURA SA
c\o Galapagos Network, 7200 Corporate Center Dr., Miami, FL 33126
800-633-7972; 305-592-2294

MV CORINTHIAN
ReBuilt:1967
Registry: Ecuador
Length: 195 ft.
Beam: 40 ft.
Speed: 15 knots
Officers: Ecuadorian
Crew: 24, Ecuadorian
Passengers: 48
Cabins: 24. All are outside, have air-conditioning, private bath with shower, picture window; cabins for non-smokers.
Facilities: Formerly a research vessel in Alaska. Lounge, gym, jacuzzi. Medical facilities. Heliport.
Activities: Lectures on natural history, shore excursions, snorkeling.
Rates: Per person double occupancy from $400 to $1,300.
Itinerary: Three-, four- and seven-night cruises of the Galapagos Islands.
Note: Eight-passenger sailing vessels with crew are also available for seven-day cruises.

MS ERIC; MS FLAMINGO; MS LETTY
Built: 1990, 1991, 1993
Registry: Ecuador
Length: 83 ft.
Beam: 24 ft.
Speed: 10 knots
Officers: Ecuadorian
Crew: 10, Ecuadorian

Passengers: 20
Cabins: 10. All have individually controlled air-conditioning, private
   bath with shower, two twin beds or double bed; cabins for non-
   smokers.
Dining: International and Ecuadorian cuisine.
Facilities: Each is a motor yacht. Lounge, conference room.
Activities: Scuba, snorkeling.
Rates: Per person double occupancy $600 to $1,650.
Itinerary: Three- to seven-day cruises of the Galapagos Islands from
   San Cristobal.

EPIROTIKI LINES
551 Fifth Ave., New York, NY 10176
800-221-2470; 212-599-1750

MTS JASON
Built: 1967
Registry: Greece
Former Name: *Eros*
Length: 333 ft.
Beam: 52 ft.
Speed: 18 knots
Officers: Greek
Crew: 120, Greek
Passengers: 278. Singles 20%, couples 80%, families 20%.
Cabins: 139. All have air-conditioning, radio, phone, private bath with
   shower; some with tub/shower. Most are outside.
Dining: Dining room with picture windows. Two sittings. Interna-
   tional cuisine with Greek specialties.
Facilities: Lounge and bar, nightclub, casino, swimming pool, library,
   hairdresser, shops, laundry. Medical facilities.
Activities: Aerobics, games.
Rates: Double occupancy per person from $1,290 to $2,600.
Itinerary: Seven-day cruises of the eastern Mediterranean, departing
   from Piraeus, Greece.

MV NEPTUNE
Built: 1985
Registry: Greece
Former Name: *Meteor*
Length: 286 ft.
Beam: 45 ft.
Speed: 14 knots
Officers: Greek
Crew: 97, Greek

Passengers: 184

Cabins: 93. All have air-conditioning, private bath with shower or tub. Some have convertible sofa and lower bed, some have upper and lower.

Dining: Two sittings.

Facilities: Lounge, casino, boutique, duty-free shops, outdoor pool, solarium, hairdresser, laundry, massage.

Itinerary: Greek islands.

MTS ODYSSEUS

Built: 1962

Registry: Greece

Former Name: *Aqua Marine*

Length: 450 ft.

Beam: 19 ft.

Speed: 16 knots

Officers: Greek

Crew: 190, Greek, International

Passengers: 454. Singles 5%, couples 90%, families 5%.

Cabins: 226. All have air-conditioning, private bath with tub or shower, radio, phone; some with sitting area.

Dining: Two sittings.

Facilities: Show lounge, cinema, casino, gym, outdoor pool, sauna, massage, library. Medical facilities.

Activities: Deck activities, guest lecturers.

Rates: Double occupancy per person from $2,230 to $4,570.

Itinerary: Fourteen-day cruises of the Mediterranean departing from Venice, Italy.

MV ORPHEUS

Built: 1969, rebuilt 1987

Registry: Greece

Length: 264 ft.

Beam: 50 ft.

Speed: 14 knots

Officers: Greek

Crew: 110, Greek

Passengers: 288

Cabins: 166. All have air-conditioning, radio, phone, private bath with shower or tub. Most have two lowers, some with upper and lower. Eight suites.

Dining: Greek and international cuisine. Open single seating. No smoking. Buffet-style meals are in the tavern, and more formal luncheon and dinner in the restaurant. Two dressy nights.

Facilities: Lounge with dancing, two bars, shops, casino, library, boutique, outdoor pool, hairdresser, laundry. Medical facility.

Activities: Very little traditional cruise entertainment. Lectures. Shore excursions to sites of early civilization. Greek night by crew. Special interest cruises on ornithology, marine biology, volcanology and astronomy.

Access for Disabled: Not accessible.

Rates: Fourteen-day cruises from $3,590 to $7,935 per person double occupancy. Rates include airfare from gateway cities, two night hotel accommodation, most shore excursions and all gratuities.

Itinerary: Cruises in the West and East Mediterranean, Red Sea, Aegean through the Bosphorus into the Black Sea, mostly of two week's duration. Two one-week cruises can also be linked with adjacent itineraries to form two, three, or four week holidays.

MTS PALLAS ATHENA

Built: 1952

Registry: Greece

Former Names: *CarlaCosta; Prinuss Carle; Flandre*

Length: 596 ft.

Beam: 80 ft.

Speed: 19 knots

Officers: Greek

Crew: 370. Greek

Passengers: 746

Cabins: 385. All have air-conditioning, sitting area, radio, bath with shower; some with tub. Suites.

Dining: Dining room with two sittings, continental cuisine. Outdoor cafe. Pizza and ice cream parlor.

Facilities: Lounges and bars, casino, fitness center, library, two outdoor pools, sauna, hairdresser, shops, laundry. Medical facilities.

Activities: Deck sports, exercise classes, dance lessons.

Rates: Double occupancy per person from $1,290 to $4,570.

Itinerary: Seven- and 14-day cruises of the Mediterranean.

TSS STAR TEXAS

Built: 1962

Registry: Bahamas

Former Names: *Empress of Canada; Mardi Gras*

Length: 650 ft.

Beam: 87 ft.

Speed: 21 knots

Officers: Italian

Crew: 550, International

Passengers: 906

Cabins: 457. All cabins have air-conditioning, private bath with

shower, TV, radio, phone. Six suites have sitting area and tub.
Dining: Two sittings.
Facilities: Disco, ballroom, casino, three pools, two saunas, hairdresser, shops, meeting facilities.
Activities: Gambling cruise.
Youth Program: None.
Access for Disabled: None.
Itinerary: One-night cruise out of Galveston.

MS TRITON
Built: 1971
Registry: Greece
Former Names: *Sunward II, Cunard Adventurer*
Length: 492 ft.
Beam: 70 ft.
Speed: 16 knots
Officers: Greek
Crew: 315, Greek, International
Passengers: 676
Cabins: 340. All have air-conditioning, phone, radio, private bath with shower; some with sitting area, tub.
Dining: Two sittings.
Facilities: Lounges and bars, theater, casino, outdoor pool, sauna, gym, jogging track, massage, hairdresser, shops, laundry. Medical facilities.
Activities: Exercise classes, deck sports, dance lessons.
Rates: Double occupancy per person from $555 to $1,485.
Itinerary: Three- and four-day cruises of the Mediterranean departing from Piraeus, Greece.

MV WORLD RENAISSANCE
Built: 1966
Registry: Greece
Former Name: *Renaissance*
Length: 493 ft.
Beam: 69 ft.
Speed: 18 knots
Officers: Greek
Crew: 205, Greek, International
Passengers: 536. Singles 15%, couples 80%, families 5%.
Cabins: 268. All have air-conditioning, radio, phone, private bathroom with shower, TV on request. Suites have sitting area.
Dining: Two sittings.
Facilities: Show lounge, cinema, casino, gym, library, hairdresser. Medical facilities.

Activities: Sports, guest lecturers.

Rates: Double occupancy per person from $1,840 to $7,350.

Itinerary: Twelve- to 14-day cruises of the Mediterranean departing from Piraeus, Greece; 14-day cruises of the Caribbean.

ETOILE DE CHAMPAGNE
89 Broad St., Boston, MA 02110
800-280-1492; 617-426-1776

ETOILE DE CHAMPAGNE
Built: 1979
Registry: Netherlands
Length: 300 ft.
Beam: 16 ft.
Speed: 8 knots
Officers: International
Crew: 6, Dutch
Passengers: 12. Almost all couples.
Cabins: 7. Owner's Suite has sitting area. All include air-conditioning, split bathroom with separate shower and two sinks.
Dining: French cuisine, regional specialties and wines.
Facilities: Originally built as a transport barge it has a dining room that doubles as a dance floor, three large salons, library, main lounge with piano, cocktail lounge and observation lounge.
Activities: Minibus accompanies barge for daily shore excursions with driver/tour guide. Available for shopping and other special requests, golfing. Bicycles on board. Ballooning in France can be arranged for an additional fee.
Youth Program: No children accepted under age 14 unless boat is chartered.
Access for Disabled: One suite is wheelchair accessible.
Rates: From $2,940 to $3,350 per person double occupancy.
Itinerary: Springtime in Holland Cruise from Weesp to Ouderkerk. Chablis Cruise along the River Yonne through Burgundy. Twelve-day trip through southern Holland, Belgium and France ending in Paris. In winter, the Etoile is used as a waterside restaurant in Blokzijl, Holland.

EUROCRUISES/ BALTIC LINE
303 West 13th St., New York, NY
800-688-3876; 800-323-7436; 212-691-2099

MS ANNA KARENINA
Built: 1980

Registry: Russia
Former Name: *Braemar*
Length: 478 ft.
Beam: 83 ft.
Speed: 21 knots
Officers: Russian
Crew: Russian, Swedish
Passengers: 1,090
Cabins: 464. Some have two lower beds, some have berths. All have
    private bath with shower. Some have TV.
Dining: Continental cuisine. Two restaurants.
Facilities: Show lounge, disco, conference rooms, indoor pool, sauna,
    gym, duty-free shop. Doctor on board. Also carries 500 cars on car
    deck.
Activities: Shore excursions at all ports.
Rates: From $335 to $2,110 double occupancy rate per person.
Itinerary: Five- to seven-day cruises (visa-free) from Stockholm, Swe-
    den or Kiel, Germany to St. Petersburg, Russia and five-day cruises
    from Nynashamn to St. Petersburg.

MS BALTIC CLIPPER
Built: 1989
Registry: Finland
Officers: Finnish
Crew: Finnish
Passengers: 300
Cabins: Cabins have two lower berths, private bath with shower, hair-
    dryer, TV, telephone. Suites and some staterooms have refrigerator.
Dining: Restaurant with panoramic view.
Facilities: Lounge, bars, duty-free shop.
Activities: Nightly entertainment, dancing. Shore visits.
Rates: Per person double occupancy from $780 to $4,095.
Itinerary: Six- and 13-day polar cruises of the North Cape and Norwe-
    gian fjords from Gothenburg, Sweden.

M/S ILICH
Built: 1973
Registry: Russia
Former Name: *Bore I*
Length: 422 ft.
Beam: 74 ft.
Speed: 22 knots
Officers: Russian
Crew: Russian, Swedish
Passengers: 360

Cabins: 180. All have air-conditioning; some have private bath with shower; others have washbasin only. Either two lower beds or upper and lower berths. Some four-berth cabins. Suites have bedroom with double bed.

Dining: Two restaurants. Continental cuisine.

Facilities: Several bars and lounges, show salon, nightclub, casino, gym and pool. Also carries cars. Doctor on board.

Activities: City tours on excursions or on your own, including Russian circus and ballet. Crew show, Russian language lessons.

Rates: From $340 to $1,095 double occupancy per person.

Itinerary: Four- to six-day cruises (visa-free) between Stockholm, Sweden and St. Petersburg, Russia.

MS KONSTANTIN SIMONOV

Built: 1982

Registry: Russia

Length: 450 ft.

Beam: 68 ft.

Speed: 18 knots

Officers: Russian

Crew: 160, Finnish, Russian

Passengers: 492

Cabins: 106. Renovated cabins have lower berths; others have upper and lower berths. Suites have bedroom, living room, TV. All cabins have full facilities, phone, radio, some also have refrigerator and television.

Dining: Several restaurants. Continental cuisine.

Facilities: Pool, nightclub, sauna, massage, hairdresser, shops, meeting room. Medical facilities.

Activities: Disco, music salon with entertainment.

Youth Program: None

Access for Disabled: None

Rates: Per person double occupancy from $170 to $1,020 for four days, $445 to $2,910 for eight days.

Itinerary: Four-day cruises (visa-free) between Helsinki, Finland and St. Petersburg, Russia. Seven-and eight-day cruise to the Canary Islands and Morocco from Spain.

EUROCRUISES/ EUROPE CRUISE LINE

RHINE PRINCESS

Built: Reconstructed 1992

Length: 273 ft.

Beam: 36 ft.

Officers: European

Crew: European

Passengers: 120

Cabins: 60. All are outside, have individually controlled air-conditioning and heating, private bath with shower or tub, hairdryer, TV, radio, direct-dial telephone. Adjoining cabins can be converted to
large suite. Choice of twin or double beds.

Dining: Dining room with single seating, picture windows. Dutch and
German theme dinners.

Facilities: Main salon with bar, dance floor, picture windows; separate
non-smoking lounge, swimming pool, whirlpool, sauna, gift shop,
meeting facilities with audiovisual equipment.

Activities: Musical entertainment nightly. Shore excursions to old
towns and villages in Holland and Germany along the Rhine and
Moselle Rivers. Wine-tasting events.

Rates: For three-day cruise from $445 to $1,180 per person double occupancy; seven-day cruises from $1,035 to $1,995.

Itinerary: Three- to seven-day cruises from Amsterdam, Basle, Arnheim, Cologne and Mainz,; three- and five-day cruises from Cologne to Mainz on the Rhine and Moselle Rivers.

EUROCRUISES/ FRED OLSEN LINES

M/S BLACK PRINCE

Built: 1966

Registry: Norway

Length: 465 ft.

Beam: 71 ft.

Speed: 19 knot

Officers: Norwegian

Crew: 200

Passengers: 450

Cabins: Singles to family size, air-conditioned, private bath with
shower. Connecting rooms can make up a suite. Bed may be a fixed
bed, a folding sofabed, a pullman bed which folds away against
the wall or lower bed and upper berth.

Dining: Two main restaurants, both non-smoking, a third for alfresco
dining; two seatings, International cuisine with Norwegian specialties. Open-air dining area for buffet lunch.

Facilities: Casino, piano lounge, bars, hairdresser, shop, library, marina park, outdoor pool, gym, laundry and ironing facilities. Medical facilities, doctor and nurse on board.

Activities: Passengers can swim from marina park at stern. Art
classes, board game tournaments, golf at courses en route, special
interest talks and demonstrations by experts on gardening, bridge

and ballroom dancing.

Access for Disabled: Several cabins for physically handicapped; lifts to all public decks; must be accompanied by an able-bodied companion.

Rates: From $1,390 to $5,510 double occupancy per person (12- to 17-nights), $3,125 to $7,025 double occupancy per person (23-nights).

Itinerary: Twelve- to 23-night cruises from England to Canary Islands and Agadir; Canary Islands and Tangier; Iberia and Mediterranean; Norwegian Fjords and North Cape; Norway, North Cape and Svalbard; round Britain.

EUROCRUISES/ FRITIDSKRYSS
MS FUNCHAL
Built: 1961

Registry: Portugal

Length: 500 ft.

Beam: 63 ft.

Speed: 18 knots

Officers: Portuguese

Crew: 160, Swedish

Passengers: 424

Cabins: 217. All cabins have a shower and toilet.

Dining: Two dining rooms.

Facilities: Several lounges and bars, library, hairdresser, tax-free shop, pool and sauna.

Activities: Trap shooting, singalongs.

Rates: From $2,960 to $5,490 double occupancy per person.

Itinerary: Twelve- to 18-day roundtrip cruises from Gothenburg, Sweden to Amsterdam, Rouen, Falmouth, Southampton, London; to Geiranger, Honnigsvag, Tromso, Molde, Nordfjord, Bergen, Lysefjord; to Torshavn, Reykjavik, Akureyri, Spitzbergen, Longyearbyen, Honningsvag, Trondheim, Geiranger; or to Zeebrugge, O'Porte, Sevilla, Tangier, Lisbon, and St. Malo.

EUROCRUISES/ GOTA CANAL STEAMSHIP COMPANY
MS DIANA; MS WILHELM THAM; MS JUNO
Built: 1931; 1874; 1912

Registry: Sweden

Length: 105 ft.

Beam: 23 ft.

Speed: 10 knots

Officers: Swedish
Crew: Swedish
Passengers: 60. Usually all couples.
Cabins: Turn-of-the century steamer with small cabins, upper and lower
berths; all with windows and sink. Shower and WC are shared.
Dining: Window-walled dining room. Traditional cuisine plus daily
Swedish smorgasbord including salmon, sherried herring, caviar-
stuffed eggs, reindeer meat, cloudberry jam and flat breads.
Facilities: Library.
Activities: Walking, jogging or bicycling along the canal path. Shore
excursions on 13 stops.
Rates: From $715 to $1,777 double occupancy per person.
Itinerary: Three- to six-day cruises of Gota Canal between Stockholm
and Goteburg with port calls among the following: Gripsholm,
Mariefred, Stegeborg, Mem, Soderkoping, Norsholm, Berg,
Borensberg, Motala, Vadstena, Forsvik, Toreboda, Lyrestad, Sjo-
torp, Lacko, Lodose, Hajstorp, Lilla Edet, Vanersborg, Tatorp,
Karlsborg, Borenshult, Berg, Snovelstorp, Soderkoping, Taxinge,
Motala and Trollhattan.

EUROCRUISES/KRISTINA CRUISES
MS KRISTINA REGINA
Built: 1960
Registry: Finland
Former Names: *Bore; Borea*
Length: 328 ft.
Beam: 49 ft.
Speed: 15 knots
Officers: Finnish
Crew: 60, Finnish
Passengers: 220. Singles, 10%; couples 75%; families, 20%.
Cabins: 145. All have air-conditioning, private bath with shower, ra-
dio, internal phone; some have large windows, queen-sized beds,
minibars. Five allergy-free cabins. Connecting cabins available
Dining: Two dining rooms, cafe. Single seating. Continental cuisine
with Finnish specialties. Casual dress.
Facilities: Four bars, casino, lounge with dance floor meeting room,
saunas (no pool), shop, hairdresser, laundry. Nurse.
Activities: Lectures. Dancing. Theme cruises: Hans Christian Ander-
son and Danish fairy tales; Viking lore. Folkloric entertainment.
Shore excursions with English-speaking guides.
Youth Program: Playroom.
Access for Disabled: Not wheelchair accessible.

Rates: Double occupancy per person from $1,685 to $8,885, including most shore excursions.

Itinerary: From five-to 15-day cruises of Scandinavia between between Helsinki or Copenhagen and of Baltic State with port calls in Poland, Latvia, Estonia and Russia.

EUROCRUISES/ NORTHWESTERN RIVER SHIPPING COMPANY

M/V SERGEI KIROV and MV ALEXEI SURKOV

Built: 1988
Registry: Russia
Length: 414 ft.
Speed: 15 knots
Officers: International
Crew: Russian
Passengers: 280. Nearly all couples.
Cabins: 136. All cabins are outside, air-conditioned, with private bath and shower. Suites.
Dining: Two dining rooms.
Facilities: Lounges, massage, sauna, hairdresser, boutique, drug store, liquor store, library, laundry. Medical facility, doctor on board.
Activities: City tours and village visits along river route.
Rates: From $2,947 to $4,897 double occupancy per person.
Itinerary: Four-day cruises from St. Petersburg to Moscow with port calls at Kizhi, Goritsy, Yaroslavl, Uglich; 10- or 11-day and 13- and 14-day cruises from St. Petersburg to Moscow.

EUROCRUISES/ SMYRIL

MF NORRONA

Built: 1973
Registry: Denmark
Speed: 22 knots
Passengers: 1,050
Cabins: 62. Cabins have lower beds or upper lower berths, have air-conditioning, private bath with shower.
Dining: Restaurant serves Scandinavian smorgasbord. Also a cafeteria.
Facilities: Lounges, bars, duty-free shop. Capacity for 300 cars.
Activities: Viewing fjords. Shore visits.
Rates: Per person double occupancy from $180 to $661.
Itinerary: Seven-day cruises of the North Atlantic between Iceland, Denmark and Norway.

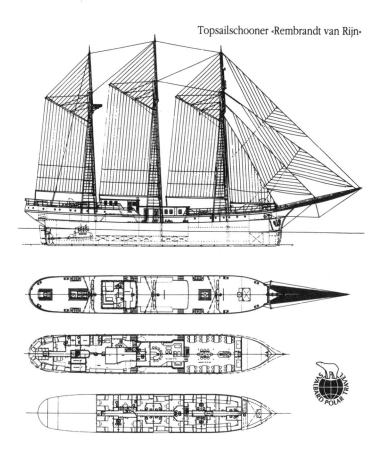

Topsailschooner «Rembrandt van Rijn»

REMBRANDT VAN RIJN

EUROCRUISES/SVALBARD POLAR TRAVEL
MS POLARSTAR
Built: 1948
Registry: Norway
Length: 152 ft.
Beam: 26 ft.
Officers: Norwegian
Crew: Norwegian
Passengers: 25
Cabins: Each cabin has washbasin, but showers and toilets are commu-

nal.

Dining: Mostly buffet. Expedition-type service.

Facilities: This polar expedition ship was built for ice, formerly was expedition, patrol and rescue ship for the Norwegian Polar Institute.

Activities: Inflatable boat landings on glaciers and ice floes; emphasis on the nature and the history of the land, searching for polar bears, walrus and whales, and looking for relics of the old days of exploration and whaling.

Rates: Per person double occupancy from $3,290 to $3,502, including airfare from Tromso.

Itinerary: Eight-day cruises from Longyearbyen to far reaches of Arctic; itinerary adjusted to ice-conditions.

REMBRANDT VAN RIJN

ReBuilt: 1992

Registry: Netherlands

Length: 390 ft.

Beam: 34 ft.

Speed: 9-11 knots. Uses sail or engine power depending on time, wind and weather.

Crew: 8

Passengers: 36

Cabins: 17. All with private bath and shower.

Dining: Dining room for 48 persons. Scandinavian cuisine with buffets.

Facilities: Restored three-masted Dutch schooner with bow propeller for tight maneuvering. Lounge with bar. Heating and air-conditioning.

Activities: Sightseeing in Longyearbyen, daily lectures, guides for tours ashore. Zodiacs for landings and cruising islands, fjords and glaciers around the rim of the North Pole. Visits to research stations, graves of polar explorers, and to Russian mining community of Barentsburg.

Rates: From $1,840 to $2,225. Rates include flights from Tromso to ship, land excursions.

Itinerary: Three-night sailings from Longyearbyen to the rim of the North Pole, including the coastline of "The Seven Icebergs", Spitsbergen (the starting point in races to the North Pole), Moffen Island to see walrus, northern coast of Svalbard. Route and landing-sites depend on weather and ice conditions.

EUROPEAN WATERWAYS/ BARGE FRANCE

140 E. 56th St., New York, NY 10022

800-438-4748; 212-688-9538

ANJODI; LA JOIE DE VIVRE; LA REINE PEDAUQUE
Built: 1984, 1982, 1991
Registry: France
Length: 98-128 ft.
Beam: 16 ft.
Speed: 5 knots
Officer: French
Crew: 4-6, French, English
Passengers: 10-12
Cabins: 5-6. Twin or double beds, private bath with shower (some with tub), air-conditioning and heating, large opening windows.
Dining: Traditional and Provencale cuisine served in the dining salon with regional specialties. Wine-tasting of regional wines.
Facilities: Salon with TV, video, and stereo, library. *La Joie de Vivre* has a swimming pool.
Activities: Walking or bicycling along towpath. Minibuses accompany the barge for shore excursions to villages, museums, cathedrals and vineyards. Golf, tennis, horseback riding and hot air ballooning are optional.
Access for Disabled: *La Reine Pedauque* has an elevator lift.
Rates: Per person from $1,590 to $2,965. Shore excursions included.
Itinerary: Six-night cruises of rivers and canals of France. Other barges—the *Berendina, Hirondelle, Lady A, Meanderer,* and *Nymphea*—are also available for four to six passengers.

STELLA
Built: 1984
Registry: France
Length: 102 ft.
Beam: 16 ft.
Speed: 5 knots
Officers: French
Crew: French, English
Passengers: 8
Cabins: 4. Twin cabins, private bath with shower.
Dining: Dining room serves French cuisine, with local specialties in the Alsace area that blends German and French.
Facilities: Main salon is social area.
Activities: Art cruise, tulip cruise. Shore excursions to Baccarat and other crystal works. Bicycles on board to use on towpath.
Rates: Per person from $1,990 to $2,490. Shore excursions included.
Itinerary: Six-night cruises between Amsterdam and Brussels during spring tulip season; otherwise the canals of Alsace-Lorraine in France.

MV VERTROUWEN

Built: 1931
Length: 117 ft.
Beam: 16 ft.
Speed: 10 knots
Crew: 5
Passengers: 8
Cabins: 4. Two twin cabins and two double cabins with central heating. Private bath with shower. Windows, one opens.
Dining: Traditional Scottish cuisine with freshly caught salmon, sea trout, crab and lobster. Scotch beef, pheasant and partridge served in season.
Facilities: Salon, dining room, library.
Activities: Fish for brown trout or salmon. Excursions ashore in ship's bus with guide. Theme cruises: golf and landscape painting.
Rates: Per person $1,990. Rates include all excursions and fees except green fees for golfers.
Itinerary: Waterways of Scotland including the Caledonian Canal, Loch Ness and other lochs.

FAIRSTAR CRUISES See P&O FAIRSTAR CRUISES

FANTASY CRUISES

5200 Blue Lagoon Dr., Miami, FL 33126
800-437-3111

SS AMERIKANIS

Built: 1952
Registry: Panama
Former Name: *Kenya Castle*
Length: 576 ft.
Beam: 74 ft.
Speed: 16 knots
Officers: Greek
Crew: 400, International
Passengers: 617
Cabins: 310. Cabins have TV, phone, private bath with shower; those on the Sun and Boat decks have picture windows. 54 mini-suites have sitting area.
Dining: Two restaurants, two dinner seatings; international menu.
Facilities: Five bars, four entertainment lounges, casino, ballroom, cinema, disco, library, gift shop, hairdresser, gym, two pools, jogging track, full-service laundry. Doctor on call.

Activities: Putting green, shuffleboard, skeet shooting, exercise
classes, ping pong.
Youth Program: Children's playroom, preteen youth program.
Access for Disabled: Not recommended for wheelchair-bound passen-
gers.
Rates: Per person from $199 to $1,549. Passengers over 65 sharing a
cabin with a full-fare companion pay 50% of the double-occupancy
rate. For each child under 12 sharing a cabin with two full-fare
adults, the fare is $57 a day. Children under two travel free.
Itinerary: From Miami, two- and five-night cruises to Nassau, or Key
West, Playa del Carmen and Cozumel. Seven-night loops from San
Juan to St. Thomas, Guadeloupe, Antigua, Martinique and St.
Maarten.

SS BRITANIS
Built: 1932
Registry: Panama
Former Names: *Monterey; Matsonia; Lurline*
Length: 638 ft.
Beam: 82 ft.
Speed: 20 knots
Officers: Greek
Crew: 532, International
Passengers: 926. Singles, 10%, couples 90%, families, 0%.
Cabins: 463. Air-conditioning, phone, shower, some with tub. Eight
suites with picture window.
Dining: Restaurant with two dinner seatings.
Facilities: Disco, lounge, bar, cinema, ballroom, library, gym, outdoor
pool, casino, beauty salon/barber, laundry, massage, shops, sauna,
Promenade Deck with circuit of ship (nine laps to a mile); six laps
around Boat Deck equal 1 mile. Medical facilities.
Activities: Shuffleboard, golf putting, table tennis, trap shooting, exer-
cise classes.
Youth Program: Youth programs during holidays and in summer.
Access for Disabled: Not recommended for wheelchair-bound passen-
gers.
Rates: Cruises from $259 to $1,749 per person double occupancy. Chil-
dren under 12 traveling with two full-fare adults are $40 per day.
Children under 2 travel free.
Itinerary: Two-nights from Miami to Nassau; five-nights from Miami
to Key West, Playa del Carmen, Cozumel; three-nights from Miami
to Key West, Nassau; seven-nights from Miami to Nassau, Ocho
Rios, Grand Cayman, Playa del Carmen, Cozumel. In September
and October, circumnavigate South America, transiting the Panama
Canal.

FIESTAMARINA CRUISES See CARNIVAL CRUISE LINES

FRED OLSEN LINES See EUROCRUISES

FRENCH COUNTRY WATERWAYS
P.O. Box 2195, Duxbury, MA 02331
800-222-1236; 617-934-2454

MV ESPRIT; MV HORIZON II; MV NENUPHAR
Built: 1979, 1984, 1986
Registry: France
Length: 128 ft.
Beam: 17 ft.
Speed: 6-10 knots
Officers: French, English
Crew: 6-7
Passengers: 12-18. Passengers must be at least 18 years old, except for families or groups who charter an entire barge. Singles 5%, couples 80%, families 15%.
Cabins: 6-9. Both doubles and twins, individually controlled air-conditioning, private bath with shower. Suites include hairdryer.
Dining: French cuisine, fresh produce from local markets en route, regional specialties and wines produced in the cruise regions.
Facilities: Lounge, library, complimentary bar. No smoking.
Activities: Shore excursions via private motorcoach to castles, historic towns and vineyards for wine tasting; hot air balloon flight, walking along towpaths, bicycles.
Rates: From $2,275 to $2,975 double occupancy per person, including shore excursions and wines.
Itinerary: Six-night cruises on the Marne River from Meaux to Reims (Esprit); on the River Saone and the Canal du Centre from Dijon to St. Leger-sur-Dheune (Horizon II); and on the northern section of the Canal de Bourgogne from Venarey-les-Laumes to Tonnerre (Nenuphar).

MV LIBERTE
Built: 1910
Registry: France
Length: 100 ft.
Beam: 16 ft.
Speed: 6 knots
Officers: French, English

Crew: 4

Passengers: 8. Passengers must be at least 18 years old except for families or groups who charter an entire barge.

Cabins: 4. One double and two twins, individually controlled air-conditioning, private bath with shower. One suite.

Dining: French cuisine, fresh produce from local markets en route, regional specialties and wines produced in the cruise regions.

Facilities: Lounge, library, complimentary bar. No smoking.

Activities: Shore excursions via private motorcoach to castles, historic towns and vineyards for wine tasting, hot air balloon flight, walking along towpaths, bicycles.

Rates: Double occupancy per person from $2,275 to $2,775.

Itinerary: Six-night cruises on the Canal du Nivernais in western Burgundy and the Yonne River from Joigny to Clamecy.

FRENCH CRUISE LINES See KD RIVER CRUISES OF EUROPE

GT CORP CRUISES

1239 39th St., Brooklyn, NY 11218

800-828-7970; 718-934-4100

MS RUSS

Built: 1987

Registry: Russian

Length: 425 ft.

Beam: 55 ft.

Speed: 25 km/hr

Officers: Russian

Crew: Russian

Passengers: 332

Cabins: All are outside, with individually controlled air-conditioning, and windows, and have private bath with shower. Single, twin, triple and quad accommodations.

Dining: Russian and continental cuisine, and regional specialties including Russian caviar, tea, wines, vodka.

Facilities: Lounge, music salon, boutique, theater, hairdresser, laundry, solarium. Medical facilities, physician on board.

Activities: Shipboard entertainment, dancing, guest lecturer, aerobics, Russian language courses. Shore excursions by private motorcoach with English-speaking guides to areas not available to those from the West in recent years. Visits to kremlins, churches, museums, palaces, market places and to talk to the Russian people about their ex-

periences in Glasnost, Perestroyka and the new democracy.
Rates: From $699 to $1,599 per person double occupancy, including excursions.
Itinerary: A 14-day Russian Waterways cruise along canals, lakes and
rivers connecting Moscow and St. Petersburg, and a 14-day Moscow to Rostov cruise on the Moscow Canal, Volga, Svir and Neva
Rivers.

GALAPAGOS CRUISES

Adventure Associates, 13150 Coit Rd., Dallas, TX 75240
800-527-2500; 214-907-0414

MS FLOTEL ORELLANA

Built: 1976
Registry: Ecuador
Former Name: *Flotel Francisco*
Length: 154 ft.
Beam: 24 ft.
Speed: 7 knots
Officers: Ecuadorian
Crew: 15, Ecuadorian
Passengers: 48. Singles 20%, couples 89%.
Cabins: 22. Twenty double berth cabins and two quadruple-berth cab-
ins. Private bath with shower. Cabins for non-smokers.
Dining: Dining rooms serve local and international cuisine. Barbecue-
style lunch at camps.
Facilities: This three-deck, flat-bottomed boat has bar, library, lounge,
conference center. Medical facilities.
Activities: Informal ship with an emphasis on nature, ecotourism and
educational tours. Naturalist guides, hikes in the jungle conducted
by natives, fishing, birdwatching, visits to Cuyabeno River by dugout canoe. Optional overnight at rustic camp in Pacuya. Informal
clothing at all times, rubber boots, bottled water and rain ponchos
are provided.
Rates: Four- and five-nights from $642 to $616 double occupancy per
person. Bus ride from airport and three-hour dugout canoe ride to
floatel are included.
Itinerary: Ecuador's northwestern corner of Amazonia, the lower
Aguarico in the Cuyabeno Wildlife Reserve to communities of Co-
fan and Quichua Indians. This region's tourism is controlled by
Ecuadorian Foundation for Conservation and Sustainable Develop-
ment dedicated to research and the protection of the Ecuadorian
Amazon basin resources.

ISABELA II
Built: 1989
Registry: Ecuador
Length: 166 ft.
Beam: 38 ft.
Speed: 12 knots
Officers: Ecuadorian
Crew: 27, Ecuadorian
Passengers: 40. Singles 20%; couples 80%; passengers should be in
   good health.
Cabins: 20. All outside twin cabins with air-conditioning, private bath
   with shower. Four cabins have double beds.
Dining: International cuisine with Ecuadorian specialties.
Facilities: Salon, bar.
Activities: Two multilingual naturalist guides, small panga craft for
   landings; all parties are accompanied by guides of the National
   Park Service. Masks, snorkels and flippers are available to rent on
   board. Passengers should wear long sleeved shirts and very infor-
   mal clothes for jungle walks. Wildlife watching.
Rates: Double occupancy per person from $1,960 to $2,380.
Itinerary: Seven-night cruises of the Galapagos Islands.

MV SANTA CRUZ
Built: 1980
Registry: Ecuador
Length: 230 ft.
Beam: 87 ft.
Speed: 14 knots
Officers: Ecuadorian
Crew: 48, Ecuadorian
Passengers: 90. Nearly all the passengers are couples.
Cabins: All are air-conditioned with outside views, private bathroom
   and shower; single, twin and triple cabins; cabins for non-smokers.
Dining: Dining room with single seating, serves continental and local
   cuisine.
Facilities: Lounges and observation decks, cocktail lounge and bar,
   boutique. Medical facilities.
Activities: Fleet of pangas to take guests ashore for interaction with
   Galapagos mammals and birds. Island tours for small groups are
   led by naturalists who give lectures in the evening and slide shows
   to brief passengers on the following day's schedule. Parties are accompanied by guides of the National Park Service. Flippers, masks
   and snorkels are available to rent on board. Terrain is rough so passengers should be in good physical condition and have informal
   clothes.

Rates: Three- and four-night cruise from $585 to $1,120 and seven-
   night cruise from $1,190 to $1,960 double occupancy per person.
Itinerary: Three-, four- and seven-night cruises of the Galapagos Islands.

GALAPAGOS YACHT CRUISES
c/o Galapagos Inc.
7800 Red Road, South Miami, FL 33143
800-327-9854; 305-665-0841

ALBATROS II; CRUZ DEL SUR; DORADO; ESTRELLA; PODEROSO II
Built: 1989-1993
Registry: Ecuador
Length: 75-80 ft.
Beam: 21-23 ft.
Speed: 9 knots
Officers: Ecuadorian
Crew: 7, Ecuadorian
Passengers: 12-16
Cabins: 6-8. All are double cabins, have private bath with shower and
   air-conditioning.
Dining: Fresh caught fish and other seafood, fresh vegetables and
   fruits grown in the islands.
Facilities: Dining-lounge area.
Activities: Land excursions with naturalist guides; swimming, fishing,
   snorkeling, diving. Diving equipment: two zodiacs, weight belts,
   two compressors, Nikono cameras with electronic flash for rent.
Rates: Seven-night cruises from $1,300 to $1,879. Smaller yachts are
   also available for $600 to $1,300 per person.
Itinerary: From San Cristobal to stops including Islas Lobos, Punta
   Pitt, Punta Suarez, Gardener, Cormorant, Puerto Ayora, Darwin
   Station, Bartholome, Sullivan, Islas Plazas, Cerro Brujo, Barranco,
   Baltra, Bachas, Rabida, Puerto Egas, Sullivan, Espanola, Floreana,
   Hood Island, the Highlands, Seymour, Santa Fe and Leon Dormido.

MV GALAPAGOS EXPLORER
Built: 1957
Registry: Ecuador
Former Name: *Attica*
Length: 314 ft.
Beam: 41 ft.
Speed: 16 knots
Officers: Ecuadorian

Crew: 70, Ecuadorian

Passengers: 100. Singles 5%, couples 85%, families 10%. Children under age 7 are not permitted on board. It is recommended that passengers be in good physical condition as some trails are difficult to traverse.

Cabins: 53. All cabins are outside, have air-conditioning, private bath with shower, radio. Five suites.

Dining: Meals served in dining room or buffet style on deck; international and Ecuadorian specialties served. Dress for dinner is casual.

Facilities: Swimming pool, solarium, conference room, two bars, boutique, library. Medical facilities.

Activities: Six naturalist guides aboard lead daily shore excursions and nightly briefings; snorkeling equipment.

Access for Disabled: Disabled persons may have problems negotiating the difficult trails.

Rates: Three-night cruises $850 per person double occupancy; four-night cruises $1,130; combination seven-night cruises $1,880.

Itinerary: Three- to seven-night cruises of the Galapagos Islands.

YOLITA

Registry: Ecuador

Length: 53 ft.

Beam: 17 ft.

Speed: 8 knots

Officers: Ecuadorian

Crew: 4, Ecuadorian

Passengers: 12

Cabins: Six double cabins with private sink and toilet, air-conditioned, shared shower.

Dining: Fresh caught fish and other seafood, fresh vegetables and fruits grown in the islands.

Facilities: Dining-lounge area.

Activities: Land excursions, swimming, fishing, snorkeling, diving. Diving equipment: two zodiacs, weight belts, two compressors, Nikono cameras with electronic flash for rent at $100 per week. Naturalist guide.

Rates: Seven-night cruises from $900.

Itinerary: From San Cristobal to Islas Lobos, Espanola, Punta Suarez, Gardener, Darwin Station, North Seymour, Baltra, Bachas, Rabida, Puerto Egas, Bartholome, Sullivan, Islas Plazas, Santa Fe, Santa Cruz.

GREEK ISLANDS CRUISE CENTER/ ATTIKA CRUISES

50 Post Rd. W., Westport, CT 06880
800-341-3030; 203-226-7911

MTS ARCADIA
Built:
Registry: Greek
Length: 350 ft.
Beam: 54 ft.
Speed: 15 knots
Officers: Greek
Crew: Greek
Passengers: 280
Cabins: 139. All are air conditioned.
Dining: Dining room seats 200.
Facilities: Two lounges, casino, library, gym, sauna, pool, duty free shop, hairdresser. Medical facilities.
Activities: Shore excursions
Rates: For three- and four-night cruises from $540 to $1,160 per person.
Itinerary: Three- and four-day cruises to Aegean islands and Turkey with port calls at Piraeus, MyKonos, Kusadasi, Patmos, Rhodes, Heraklion, Santorini.

GREEK ISLANDS CRUISE CENTER/ VIKING STAR CRUISES

MY VIKING STAR
Registry: Greece
Length: 118 ft.
Beam: 29 ft.
Speed: 10 knots
Crew: 8
Passengers: 30
Cabins: 14. All are outside, have air-conditioning and heating, private bath with shower. Cabins have two lower berths or upper and lower berth. Some cabins can be modified to accept families of three and four persons.
Activities: Cruise 4-5 hours daily; the rest of the time is spent on islands for exploration, shopping, swimming, beaches and nightlife.
Rates: From $1,195 to $1,345 per person double occupancy. Monthly cruise for single travelers with emphasis on nightlife, no single supplement charged.
Itinerary: Seven nights cruising the Aegean from Athens to Mykonos,

Santorini, and the Cyclades.

HAVANA CRUISES

c/o Caribic Vacations, White Sands Beach PO, Montego Bay, Jamaica W.I.

809-952-4469; 809-952-5013

MV SANTIAGO DE CUBA

Built: 1966
Registry: Bahamas
Former Name: *Scandinavian Song*
Length: 457 ft.
Officers: European
Crew: International
Passengers: 350
Cabins: 150. All have air-conditioning, private bath. Some cabins have two lower beds, some upper and lower berths. Five suites with separate sitting area.
Dining: Dining room seats 362 with single seating.
Facilities: Main salon with bar, show lounge, disco, casino, pool, hairdresser, massage, duty free shops including on-site manufactured Cuban cigars. Medical facilities with doctor and nurse on board. Direct dial telephone system to all countries.
Activities: Cuban music and shows. Shore excursions to towns and villages in Cuba.
Rates: For six-day cruise from $776 to $1,136 per person double occupancy; for seven-day cruise from $905 to $1,325.
Itinerary: Six- and seven-day cruises from Havana or Santiago; however passengers can also begin or end cruises in Montego Bay, Jamaica or in Cozumel. Other stops include Cayo Largo, Cienfuegos, and Casilda, Cuba. A passport or other identification is required, but passports are not stamped by the Cuban authorities.
Note: A 120-passengers overnight ferry, the *Caribbean Queen* of CQ Lines, also can be taken to Cuba, leaving from Port Antonio or Ocho Rios, Jamaica to Santiago de Cuba. There are reclining lounge seats, but no cabins. A package tour includes one or two night hotel accommodations and shore excursions, at $219 and $275 per person double occupancy. Contacts: In Kingston, Jamaica 809-976-2151; 809-929-7865 or 6368.

HEBRIDEAN ISLAND CRUISES

c/o Elegant Vacations
800-648-1136; 516-747-8880

MV HEBRIDEAN PRINCESS

Built: 1964
Registry: Scotland
Former Name: *Columbia*
Length: 235 ft.
Beam: 46 ft.
Speed: 14 knots
Officers: British
Crew: 35, British
Passengers: 50. Mostly British, one third singles, two thirds couples.
Cabins: Originally built as passenger ferry, the ship was redesigned to resemble a country house hotel. Staterooms range from two-room suites with private bath to inside singles with shared facilities. All cabins include TV, radio.
Dining: Restaurant serves local specialties.
Facilities: Lounge, library, conservatory, speed boat, gift shop, video library.
Activities: Clay shooting, fishing. Shore excursions, visits to fishing communities, castles and churches. Local guides and lecturers. The ship can carry private cars, allowing guests to disembark with their vehicles to explore for themselves.
Rates: Seven- and 14-night cruises from $1,625 to $12,545, including shore tours.
Itinerary: Visits lochs, estuaries and islands of the Inner and Outer Hebrides on Scotland's west coast such as Iona, Rhum, Muck and Eigg, Lewis, Skye, Staffa and the Orkney Islands. Most departures are from Oban with a coach connection from Glasgow.

HOLLAND AMERICA LINE

300 Elliott Ave. W, Seattle, WA 98119
800-426-0327; 800-544-0443; 206-281-3555

MS MAASDAM

Built: 1993
Registry: Netherlands Antilles
Length: 720 ft.
Beam: 101 ft.
Speed: 21 knots
Officers: Dutch
Crew: Indonesian, Filipino
Passengers: 1,266
Cabins: 633. Each of 149 suites and deluxe staterooms has a private veranda, VCR, whirlpool bath and minibar. All staterooms are equipped with sofa, hairdryer, individually controlled air-condi-

tioning, phone, music system and TV. Beds are convertible from queen-size to two singles. 52 staterooms have connecting doors.

Dining: Dining room seats 657 on two levels connected by a pair of grand curved staircases. Two private dining areas, each seating 44. Cafe offers espresso and cappucino for informal coffee breaks. Separate restaurant features buffet for casual dining at breakfast and lunch.

Facilities: A two-deck, 600 seat show lounge features Broadway-style entertainment, three-deck grand atrium features monumental glass sculpture. Theater, fitness center, hairdresser, massage, sauna, steam rooms, outdoor swimming pool, two deck tennis courts, piano bar, observation lounge overlooking the bow, casino, laundry, dry cleaning, self-service laundry. Infirmary staffed by a physician and three nurses.

Activities: Exercise classes, deck and pool games, dance lessons, golf putting, paddle and deck tennis, shuffleboard, skeet shooting. Cruises of 10 days or longer have a Goren bridge lecturer on board. Alaska cruises feature an on-board naturalist. Show by Indonesian and Filipino crew featuring songs and dances from their homelands.

Youth Programs: Full-time youth counselor on board.

Access for Disabled: Six staterooms are equipped to accommodate wheelchair passengers. All public rooms, restroom facilities and elevators are accessible to wheelchairs. Service animals are permitted on board. Arrange for quarantine papers and port clearance through travel agent.

Rates: Seven-day cruises from $1,495 to $5,995; 11-day cruises from $4,125; 16-day cruises from $4,560 to $25,340. Children under 12, sharing a cabin with one adult, are charged half the single- occupancy rate. Children under 2 (in Alaska) or under 3 (in the Caribbean) sail free if sharing a cabin with two adults. Single staterooms available. Guaranteed share available for non-smoking single guests willing to share.

Itinerary: Nine- and 10-day cruises of Caribbean from Ft. Lauderdale. In summer, seven-day cruises of Alaska. In fall, 62-day cruise to the South Pacific, Australia and New Zealand, with 16- to 19-day segments available. New sister ship *Ryndam* will sail from Ft. Lauderdale in 1995.

MS NIEUW AMSTERDAM and MS NOORDAM
Built: 1983, 1984
Registry: Netherlands Antilles
Length: 704 ft.
Beam: 90 ft.
Speed: 19 knots

MS NIEUW AMSTERDAM

Officers: Dutch
Crew: 542, Indonesian
Passengers: 1,214. Mostly couples.
Cabins: 605. All have private bath with shower, air-conditioning, TV, radio, phone. Suites have picture window.
Dining: Dining room seats 722. The 325-seat Lido restaurant features an extensive buffet for casual dining at breakfast and lunch.
Facilities: Several lounges and clubs, theater, casino, outdoor pool, two saunas, whirlpool, jogging track, hairdresser, massage, facials, shops, laundry, dry cleaning, coin-operated washing machines and dryers, as well as ironing boards and irons, are available in laundry rooms, library, meeting room, computer room. Two-deck showroom. Crows Nest nightclub atop the ship directly above the bridge. Promenade Deck has an unobstructed circuit of the ship; 5 laps equal 1 mile. Infirmary staffed by a physician and three nurses.
Activities: Exercise classes, fitness center, deck and pool games, dance lessons, golf putting, paddle tennis, ping pong, shuffleboard, skeet shooting. Cruises of 10 days or longer have a Goren bridge lecturer on board. Alaska cruises feature an on-board naturalist. Show by crew featuring songs and dances from their homelands.
Youth Program: Full-time youth counselor on board. Wading pool.

Access for Disabled: All public rooms and elevators are accessible to wheelchairs. Public restroom facilities for the handicapped.

Rates: Double occupancy per person from $1,660 to $6,890. Children under 12, sharing a cabin with one adult, are charged half the single-occupancy rate. Children under 2 (in Alaska) or under 3 (in the Caribbean) sail free if sharing a cabin with two adults. Single staterooms available. Guaranteed share available for non-smoking single guests willing to share.

Itinerary: *Noordam* makes seven-to 14-day cruises from Ft. Lauderdale to Caribbean and seven- to 14-day cruises to Alaska. *Nieuw Amsterdam* makes seven- and 11-day cruises from Tampa to Key West, Playa del Carmen, Cozumel, Ocho Rios and Georgetown, Grand Caymen and seven- and 14-day cruises of Alaska.

SS ROTTERDAM
Built: 1959
Registry: Netherlands Antilles
Length: 748 ft.
Beam: 94 ft.
Speed: 19 knots
Officers: Dutch
Crew: 603, Indonesian
Passengers: 1,075. Mostly couples.
Cabins: 575. All have private bath and shower, air-conditioning, TV, radio, phone. Twelve suites with picture window and living area.
Dining: The 275-seat Lido restaurant features buffet for casual breakfast and lunch. Two dining rooms seat 276 and 462 passengers respectively; two seatings.
Facilities: Theater, ballroom, library, seven lounges, two-deck 500-seat showroom, smoking room, nightclub, casino, indoor and outdoor pools, fitness center, jogging track, hairdresser, shops, laundry, dry cleaning, coin-operated washing machines, dryers, ironing boards, meeting room, computer room. Infirmary staffed by a physician and three nurses.
Activities: A deck encircles Upper Promenade Deck for running and walking. Exercise classes, deck and pool games, dance lessons, golf putting, paddle and deck tennis, shuffleboard, skeet shooting. Cruises of 10 days or longer have a Goren bridge lecturer on board. Alaska cruises feature an on-board naturalist. Show by Indonesian and Filipino crew featuring songs and dances from their homelands.
Youth Programs: Full-time youth counselor on board. Children's playroom.
Access for Disabled: All public rooms and elevators are accessible to wheelchairs. Service animals are permitted on board.

Rates: Double occupancy per person from $3,390 to $6,240. Seven-day Alaska cruises from $1,095 to $3,895. Children under 12 sharing a cabin with one adult are charged half the single-occupancy rate. Children under 2 (in Alaska) or under 3 (in the Caribbean) sail free with two adults. Single staterooms available. Guaranteed share available for non-smoking single guest willing to share.

Itinerary: Cruises of 17-days from Newport News (15 days from Ft. Lauderdale) to Puerto Rico, Virgin Islands, Bonaire, Curacao, Venezuala, St. Lucia and St. Kitts. In summer, seven-day cruises of Alaska.

MS STATENDAM

Built: 1993

Registry: Bahamas

Length: 720 ft.

Beam: 90 ft.

Speed: 20 knots

Officers: Dutch

Crew: 604, Indonesian, Filipino

Passengers: 1,266

Cabins: 633. All have private bath with shower, air-conditioning, TV, phone, twin beds that convert to queen-size; some with whirlpool, minibar, refrigerator, picture window and private balcony. 28 suites.

Dining: Dining room seats 700 on two levels connected by a pair of curved staircases. Two private dining areas, each seating 44. Lido restaurant features buffet for casual dining at breakfast and lunch.

Facilities: Three-deck atrium has an escalator for access to staterooms. Two-deck 600-seat show lounge features Broadway-style entertainment, a theater is used for lectures, meetings, religious services, and films. Library, fitness center, hairdresser, massage, sauna, steam rooms, outdoor swimming pool, piano bar, casino, observation lounge and nightclub overlooking the bow, laundry, dry cleaning (coin-operated washing machines, dryers, ironing boards and irons available), computer room. Infirmary staffed by a physician and three nurses.

Activities: Exercise classes, deck and pool games, dance lessons, golf putting, paddle and deck tennis, shuffleboard, skeet shooting. Cruises of 10 days or longer have a Goren bridge lecturer on board. Show by crew featuring songs and dances from their homelands. On the Sports Deck, a specially surfaced jogging track encircles the stack.

Youth Program: Full-time youth counselor on board.

Access for Disabled: Six staterooms are equipped for the handicapped. All public rooms and elevators are accessible to wheelchairs.

Rates: Double occupancy per person from $2,410 to $7,290. Children under 12 sharing a cabin with adult are charged half the single-occupancy rate. Children under 3 (in the Caribbean) sail free if sharing a cabin with two adults. Single staterooms are available. Guaranteed share available for non-smoking single guests willing to share. No tipping.

Itinerary: In winter, from Ft. Lauderdale 10 to 14 day cruises to St. Maarten, St. Lucia, Barbados, Dominica, Virgin Islands and Bahamas or Curacao, Venezuela, Grenada, Martinique Virgin Islands and Bahamas. In summer, cruises of the Mediterranean and Black Sea, Scandinavia and Russia, and the British Isles. In January, the *Statendam* embarks on a World Cruise for 98 days with segments ranging from 14 to 34 days.

MS WESTERDAM

Built: 1986

Registry: Netherlands Antilles

Former Name: *MV Homeric*

Length: 798 ft.

Beam: 95 ft.

Speed: 22 knots

Officers: Dutch

Crew: 620, Indonesian, Filipino

Passengers: 1,494

Cabins: 753. All have private bath with shower, air- conditioning, TV, music, phone, and most have a sitting area with a convertible couch. Five suites.

Dining: The dining room seats 882. Casual dining is available at the 250-seat Lido Restaurant on Upper Promenade Deck (buffet) and in the 238-seat Veranda Restaurant adjacent to the pool.

Facilities: Theater, library, meeting room, audiovisual facilities, 800-seat two-deck show lounge, duty free shops, nightclub, piano bar, saunas and massage rooms, fitness center, beauty salon/barber, 2 swimming pools, jogging track, laundry, dry cleaning, coin-operated washing machines and dryers, as well as ironing boards and irons, are available in laundry. Infirmary staffed by a physician and three nurses.

Activities: Exercise classes, deck and pool games, dance lessons, golf putting, paddle and deck tennis, shuffleboard, skeet shooting. Cruises of 10 days or longer have a Goren bridge lecturer on board. All Alaska cruises feature an on-board naturalist. Show by Indonesian and Filipino crew featuring songs and dances from their homelands.

Youth Program: Full-time youth counselor on board all ships.

Access for Disabled: Four staterooms are equipped for the handicapped. All public rooms and elevators are accessible to wheel-chairs. Public restroom facilities for the handicapped. All stateroom doors are 25" wide. Bathrooms in staterooms, except those specifically equipped for the handicapped, are not wheelchair accessible due to a 5" sill and 22" doorway. Service animals are permitted on board. Arrange for quarantine papers and port clearance through travel agent.

Rates: Double occupancy per person from $1,695 to $4,595. Children under 12 sharing a cabin with one adult are charged half the single-occupancy rate. Children under (in Alaska) or under 3 (in the Caribbean) sail free if sharing a cabin with two adults. Discounts as high as 35% for early booking. Single staterooms available. Guaranteed share available for non-smoking single guests willing to share.

Itinerary: In fall/winter/spring, 7- and 14-day cruises of the Caribbean from Ft. Lauderdale. In summer, seven-day cruises of Alaska.

INLAND VOYAGES
c/o McGrepor Travel, 112 Prospect St., Stamford, CT 06901
800-786-5311; 203-978-5010

LUCIOLE
Built: 1984
Registry: France
Length: 100 ft.
Beam: 17 ft.
Officers: Belgian, French
Crew: 6, British, French
Passengers: 14
Cabins: 8. Six double or twin-bedded cabins, two with single berths. All air-conditioned, with private bath with shower.
Dining: Serves local produce.
Facilities: Converted from cargo barge to hotel barge.
Activities: Excursions by private bus to chateaux, medieval towns, and vineyards; bicycles on board, strolling beside the barge towing path. Hot air balloon flights available.
Rates: Per person double occupancy $2,490, includes bus for local excursions and transfers between Paris and the barge.
Itinerary: Six nights on the Canal de Bourgogne or on the Nivernais from Montbard.

INTERCRUISE
800-447-5667; 212-221-0006

MS LA PALMA
Built: 1978
Registry: Greece
Length: 492 ft.
Officers: Greek
Passengers: 648. Mostly European.
Cabins: 324. Private baths
Facilities: Casino, pool, gym, nudist deck.
Rates: For three to seven days $593 to $2,375.
Itinerary: From Venice to Greece and Turkey.

IVARAN LINES
111 Pavonia Avenue, Jersey City, NJ 07310
800-451-1639; 201-798-5656.

MV AMERICANA
Built: 1988
Registry: Norway
Length: 578 ft.
Beam: 85 ft.
Speed: 20 knots
Officers: Norwegian
Crew: 53, Norwegian/American
Passengers: 88
Cabins: 52. MV Americana is a modern working cargo vessel. A standard, double stateroom measures 258 sq.ft. and includes a sitting area, stocked minibar/refrigerator, TV/VCR, phone, private bathroom (outside double cabins and suites also have a tub). More than 1/3 of the staterooms are singles with upper berth and are available at a reduced rate. Eight deluxe suites have separate sleeping and sitting area, and four of these have private verandas. The two owners' suites occupy the width of the superstructure.
Dining: Outdoor bar/grill. Breakfast and lunch are served buffet-style. Dinner features continental cuisine and Norwegian specialties. All passengers can be accommodated at a single seating, and there is no assigned seating. On certain nights, a suit and tie are required; on other nights, neat, casual attire is fine. A tuxedo is not required.
Facilities: Lounge, bar, library, pool, whirlpool, health club, sauna, gift shop, slot machines, hairdresser, massage. Medical facilities with physician and nurse.

Activities: Light entertainment, shore excursions in many ports-of-call, but not all. Shuttle buses in some ports from the ship to the downtown areas. Informal lectures, ping pong, shuffleboard. Open-bridge policy, except when the ship is loading and unloading freight in port. Pianist entertains nightly in the lounge. In South America, local dance troupes are brought on board and samba dancing is taught. There are 10 days at sea, but one can fly to South America and come aboard there.

Youth Program: None

Access for Disabled: None

Rates: For 17- to 23-day cruise from New Jersey or Miami, per person from $3,880 to $6,800. For 46-day, round-trip including airfare and two nights in hotel, per person from $6,900 to $13,800. Shorter segments are available.

Itinerary: From New York or New Jersey to Baltimore, Norfolk, Savannah, Miami, Puerto Cabello, La Guaira, Rio de Janeiro, Santos, Buenos Aires, Montevedeo, Rio Grande de Sul, Istajai, Ilheus or Salvador, Fortaleza.

KD RIVER CRUISES OF EUROPE

170 Hamilton Ave., White Plains, NY 10601
800-346-6525; 800-858-8587; 212-724-2116

MS ARLENE and MS NORMANDIE

Built: 1986, 1989

Registry: France

Length: 300 ft.

Beam: 35 ft.

Speed: 13 knots

Officers: French

Crew: 20-22, International

Passengers: 104. Five percent singles; 85% couples; 5% families.

Cabins: All are outside with TV, individual climate control, hairdryer, radio, shower, large window, phones.

Dining: Serves French cuisine. Single seating at all meals. Jacket and tie customary for dinner.

Facilities: Lounge with nightly musical entertainment, boutique, laundry.

Activities: Shore excursions.

Rates: Five- and eight-day cruises from $1,575 to $1,995 per person double occupancy.

Itinerary: Inland waterways of France, on the Rhone and Saone Rivers (*Arlene*) and the Seine (*Normandie*).

AUSTRIA; BRITANNIA; DEUTSCHLAND; EUROPA; HEIN-RICH HEINE; ITALIA

Built: 1971, 1960, 1991
Registry: Germany
Length: 290-361 ft.
Beam: 38 ft.
Speed: 20 knots
Officers: German
Crew: 48-54, German, International
Passengers: 104-184
Cabins: 50-92. All are outside with air-conditioning, have sofa bed or berths, private bath with shower, radio, phone. *Britannia, Deutschland* and *Heinrich Heine* have suites.
Dining: Two dining rooms. Both serve continental cuisine and have single seating.
Facilities: Observation/entertainment lounge, sauna, solarium, boutique, laundry. *Britannia* and *Deutschland* have heated outdoor pool. *Heinrich Heine* has indoor pool.
Activities: Guided tours on shore excursions. One cruise is eight day wine seminar.
Rates: Three- and four-day cruises from $245 to $1,925 per person double occupancy. For eight-day cruises: $1,400 to $2,675.
Itinerary: Cruises along the Rhine, Moselle and Main Rivers. The *Heinrich Heine* does eight-day cruises on the Rhine, Main and Danube Canal.

MS CLARA SCHUMANN and MS THEODOR FONTANE

Built: 1991
Registry: Germany
Length: 312 ft.
Beam: 36 ft.
Speed: 20 knots
Officers: German
Crew: 39, German, International
Passengers: 128
Cabins: 62. All cabins are outside, one or two windows; air-conditioning, shower, WC, radio, TV, phone, convert into sitting rooms by day. Most have twin beds, three have three beds.
Dining: Dining room seats 128 and serves continental cuisine. Single seating. Breakfast and lunch are buffet style.
Facilities: Observation lounge accommodates 128, sauna, boutique, laundry.
Activities: Shore excursions. The two boats use pump jets to propel and steer instead of propellers and rudders and have a draft of only 3 ft., allowing access to areas too shallow for most ships to

navigate.

Rates: Three- to seven-days from $425 to $1,455 double occupancy per person.

Itinerary: River Elbe, including regions of Saxony and Prussia.

KIRIACOULIS LINES

757 Deep Valley Dr., Rolling Hills Estates, CA 90274
800-367-1789; 310-554-3551

MV DEMETRA K.

Built: 1992
Length: 120 ft.
Beam: 22 ft.
Speed: 10 knots
Crew: 10
Passengers: 49
Cabins: 23. Twin-bedded cabins and three-bedded cabins with private bath and shower, air-conditioning, radio, TV, VCR.
Facilities: Water skiing, speed boat, windsurfing.
Activities: Shore excursions to beaches, fishing villages, archeological sites.
Rates: From $790 to $1,330 per person for seven-day cruise.
Itinerary: Seven-day cruises through the Greek Isles.

KRISTINA CRUISES See EUROCRUISES

MAINE WINDJAMMERS

Box 482, Rockland, ME 04841
800-648-4544; 207-594-8007

AMERICAN EAGLE

Built: 1931; rebuilt 1986
Registry: United States
Length: 92 ft.
Beam: 24 ft.
Speed: Sail plus auxiliary power.
Crew: American
Passengers: 22-28. Half couples and half singles.
Cabins: 11. The cabins have side-by-side or upper-lower bunks, opening windows, cold-water washbasin. Common heads and hot showers. No smoking below deck.
Dining: Meals served family style in dining salon or as buffet on deck. Local cuisine with fresh produce, real maple syrup, fresh fish,

baked goods from galley woodstove.
Facilities: Traditional two-masted gaff-rigged coastal schooner, designated a National Historic Landmark. Main cabin for socializing aft. Bring soft luggage only, casual clothes, foul-weather gear. Two handbuilt rowboats for exploring.
Activities: You may help crew or take the helm. Lobster bake on shore, exploring islands and coves. Singing around wood-burning potbelly stove in main cabin in evening, or bring an instrument. No radios allowed unless with earphones. Special cruises: Great Schooner Race in July, Gloucester Schooner Race or Woodenboat Sail in September, Swans Island Music Festival with an afternoon concert on the schooner and folk music concert ashore.
Youth Program: Minimum age for passengers is 16. Special three-day family cruises include children 10 or older.
Access for Disabled: Not recommended.
Rates: Per person double occupancy from $375 to $645.
Itinerary: Three- to seven-day sails from Rockland, Maine to Penobscot Bay and various coastal islands and small towns such as Mt. Desert Island, Pemaquid, Monhegan, Boothbay; sometimes to Boston.

HERITAGE
Built: 1983
Registry: United States
Length: 94 ft.
Beam: 24 ft.
Speed: Sail power.
Crew: 6. American
Passengers: 33
Cabins: 16. The cabins have two bunks, cold-water washbasin. Common heads and hot showers on deck level. No smoking.
Dining: Meals served family style in main salon or as buffet on deck.
Facilities: Traditional two-masted gaff-rigged coastal schooner. Bring soft luggage only for easy storage, casual clothes and foul-weather gear. Two 18 ft. rowing sailing wherries for exploring harbors.
Activities: The itinerary and the activities are decided by the weather. You may help crew or take the helm if you wish. Lobster bakes on shore, exploring islands and coves.
Youth Program: Minimum age for passengers is 16.
Access for Disabled: Not recommended.
Rates: Per person double occupancy from $585 to $645.
Itinerary: Seven-day cruises from Rockland, Maine to various islands, including Mount Desert Island.

ISAAC H. EVENS
Built: 1886, rebuilt 1973
Registry: United States
Length: 94 ft.
Beam: 24 ft.
Speed: Sail power
Crew: American
Passengers: 22
Cabins: 11. The cabins have side-by-side or upper-lower bunks, opening windows, coldwater washbasin. Shared heads and hot showers. No smoking below deck.
Dining: Meals served family style in dining salon or as buffet on deck.
Facilities: Traditional two-masted gaff-rigged coastal schooner, formerly an oyster-fisherman. Bring soft luggage only, casual clothes, foul-weather gear. Small powered yawl boat for tender; two rowboats for exploring.
Activities: The itinerary and the activities are decided by the weather. You may help crew or take the helm if you wish. Lobster bake on shore, exploring islands and coves. Singing around wood-burning potbelly stove in main cabin in evening, or bring an instrument. No radios allowed unless with earphones. Special cruises:·Great Schooner Race in July with some 20 vessels under sail, Swans Island Music Festival with an afternoon concert on the schooner and folk music concert ashore.
Youth Program: Minimum age for passengers is 16. Special three-day family cruises include children 10 or older.
Access for Disabled: Not recommended.
Rates: Per person double occupancy from $585 to $645.
Itinerary: Three- to seven-day sails from Rockland, Maine to various coastal islands and small towns such as Stonington, Frenchboro, and Burnt Coat Harbor. No set schedule.

MAJESTY CRUISE LINE
901 South American Way, Miami, FL 33132
800-532-7788; 305-358-5122

MV ROYAL MAJESTY
Built: 1992
Registry: Panama
Length: 568 ft.
Beam: 91 ft.
Speed: 20 knots
Officers: Greek
Crew: 500, International

Passengers: 1056
Cabins: 528. All have air-conditioning, TV, music, phone, private bath
   with shower and hairdryer, ironing boards. Suites (16) have minibar, queen-size bed, picture windows. Cabins for nonsmokers.
Dining: Non-smoking dining room, outdoor cafe, pizza/ice cream par-
   lor.
Facilities: Fitness center, Princess Deck jogging track, swimming pool,
   two whirlpools, showroom, three bars, casino, disco, meeting
   room, conference room, library, shops, beauty salon.
Activities: Shore excursions, karaoke, classical guitar concerts, local
   folk groups.
Youth Program: Children's playroom and splash pool.
Access for Disabled: Four staterooms equipped for the disabled.
Rates: Double occupancy per person from $489 to $1,499, including
   air from gateway cities.
Itinerary: Three- and four-night cruises out of Miami seven-day to
   Nassau. On four-night cruises, the ship also docks at Key West. Sail-
   ings from Boston to Bermuda.

MARINE EXPEDITIONS
13 Hazelton Ave., Toronto, M5R1E2 Canada
800-387-1387; 416-964-2569

AKADEMIK IOFFE
Built: 1987
Registry: Russia
Length: 383 ft.
Beam: 59 ft.
Speed: 14 knots
Officers: Russian
Crew: 51, Canadian, American
Passengers: 75
Cabins: 40. All cabins are outside, most with private bath, some with
   bed and sofa bed or bunk beds and shared bath facilities. Three
   suites have bed and sofa bed, living area; ensuite facilities. Cabins
   for non-smokers.
Dining: Dining room seats 104, single open seating. Meals served fam-
   ily style, mostly North American cuisine.
Facilities: Two lounges with TV, VCR and player piano, library/confer-
   ence room, exercise equipment, four zodiacs, meterology rooms,
   four laboratories, sauna, laundry. Open bridge policy, 24 hours.
   Medical facility, doctor on board.
Activities: This ship is used by the Russian Academy of Sciences as
   their expedition ship and research vessel and is being used for the

first time for cruising available to the public. The zodiacs are used for shore excursions and to approach icebergs. Lectures and seminars by naturalists on board who also guide shore excursions. The cruise will also visit working research stations and be joined by local experts.

Rates: Per person double occupancy from $2,995 to $6,195. Fees include airfare from five U.S. and Canada gateway cities and shore excursions. No tipping.

Itinerary: Eight-day cruises from Ushuaia in Argentinian Patagonia to the Antarctic and the Shetland Islands.

MARQUEST/TRANSOCEAN CRUISE LINES

101 Columbia, Suite 150, Laguna Beach, CA 92656
1-800-221-3254; 800-510-7110; 714-362-2080.

MV COLUMBUS CARAVELLE

Built: 1990
Registry: Bahamas
Former Name: Sally Caravelle
Length: 380 ft.
Beam: 56 ft.
Speed: 15 knots
Officers: Ukranian
Crew: 120, European
Passengers: 250. Singles, 20%; couples to 55, 30%; couples over 55, 50%.
Cabins: 170. Including 78 single cabins without rate supplement. All cabins with shower, TV, radio, telephone, minibar, hairdryer. Eight suites have balconies and bathtubs with whirlpools.
Dining: One sitting. International cuisine.
Facilities: Lounge seats 170, piano bar seats 70, conference center seats 250. Ten zodiacs, two saunas with jacuzzi, swimming pool, boutique, hairdresser, laundry, library. Hospital facility staffed by doctor.
Activities: The Columbus Caravelle is fully equipped for polar regions, capable of withstanding 32-inch ice floes. Whether it is cruising in icy climes or the tropics, there are experts in natural history, geology, oceanography, ornithology, culture and exploration. Dress is casual during the day. Evening is in accord with personal preferences, generally jackets for men. Festive attire recommended for Captain's Dinner. Expedition parka and Wellington boots provided. Amazon features zodiac exploration and hikes in rainforests, visits to Indian villages.
Youth Program: None.

Access for Disabled: Specially adapted cabins.

Rates: Iceland and Greenland 12- to 16-day cruises from $4,800 to $9,470. 14-night cruises to Antarctica or Chilean fjords range from $4,190 to $7,270. Amazon rates: $2,740 to $6,900. No single supplement. Early-booking incentives from $500 to $1,000.

Itinerary: In spring the ship cruises the entire Brazilian coastline and the entire Amazon to Iquito, Peru; in summer, the Baltic Sea, British Isles, Canadian Maritimes, Iceland/Greenland, Scottish Isles, Spitsbergen and Iceland; in fall from Nassau to the West Indies, French Guiana and Brazil; in winter, the Chilean Fjords and Antarctic.

MV LEV TOLSTOI

Built: 1981
Registry: Ukraine
Length: 449 ft.
Beam: 68 ft.
Officers: Ukrainian
Passengers: 250. Almost all German.
Itinerary: Mediterranean, Suez Canal, Thailand, Java.

MS MODAVIA

Built: 1980
Registry: Ukraine
Length: 380 ft.
Width: 56 ft.
Passengers: 160
Cabins: 80. All outside, air-conditioning, private bath, radio.
Dining: Single seating
Facilities: Lounge, pool, gym, sauna.
Rates: $3,485 to $4,580, including air from New York and three nights in hotel.
Itinerary: Eight-night cruises on Dunube River.

MS ODESSA

Built: 1974
Registry: Ukraine
Former Name: *Copenhagen*
Length: 440 ft.
Width: 70 ft.
Speed: 19 knots
Officers: Russian
Crew: 250, Russian
Passengers: 450. Mostly European.
Cabins: 241. All cabins are outside with air-conditioning, telephone, radio, window, twin beds and TV for video programs. Three suites.

Cabins for non-smokers.

Dining: Two sittings.

Facilities: Salons, restaurant, bars, casino, theater, boutique, hair-dresser, theater, shops, library, heated outdoor pool, sauna, small gym and laundry. Medical facilities.

Activities: Shore excursions to seldom-visited destinations, deck games, Russian dances, shuffleboard and skeet shooting.

Rates: For 18- to 23-night segments from $4,132 to $5,672 per person double occupancy. Full cruise of 60-nights from $11,802 to $21,392.

Itinerary: Around the southern extremities of South America, then continues through the South Pacific visiting islands of Polynesia.

MELANESIAN TOURIST SERVICE
NIUGINI EXPLORATION CRUISES
302 W. Grand Ave., El Segundo, CA 90245
800-776-0370; 310-785-0370

CORAL PRINCESS
Built: 1988
Registry: Papau New Guinea
Length: 35 meters
Beam: 15 meters
Speed: 12 knots
Crew: 8
Passengers: 54
Cabins: 27. Cabins have individually controlled air-conditioning, private bath with shower, choice of single or double beds. Some interconnecting doors for families.

Dining: Buffet style featuring local seafood and fresh fruits.

Facilities: A catamaran-style yacht. Two lounges, jacuzzi.

Activities: Glass-bottom boat for viewing coral. Zodiac for diving, dive equipment for hire, instructor. Snorkeling and fishing equipment. Boat typically cruises three to four hours per day, then has shore excursions to islands for beachcombing, swimming, reef exploration, and barbecue. Marine biologist on board provides programs on the reef, rain forest and mangrove environments. Casual clothes.

Rates: Per person double occupancy from $896 to $1,188.

Itinerary: Three-night cruises of the Great Barrier Reef of Australia and the islands and coastline between Cairns and Townsville, with stops at Dunk Island and Orpheus Island.

MELANESIAN DISCOVERER
Built: 1988

Registry: Papau New Guinea
Length: 117 ft.
Beam: 43 ft.
Speed: 16 knots
Officers: New Guinea
Crew: 16, New Guinea
Passengers: 35-54. Singles 5%, couples 95%.
Cabins: 21. Cabins have individually controlled air-conditioning, phone, music system, TV, private bath with shower. All except two have large windows. Four suites with queen-size beds; one four-bunk cabin.
Dining: Restaurant on main deck serves alacarte and buffet, one sitting.
Facilities: The ship is a shallow-draft catamaran for easy maneuverability among islands. Observation lounge with player piano and local entertainment, dive and gift shops, library with 300 books and 60 hours of videos on Papau New Guinea, laundry. Business services available. Helipad on roof. The ship is self-contained with desalinators and other expeditionary equipment for up to 30 days.
Activities: Two aluminum speedboats and four zodiacs depart from stern of the ship to explore beaches and villages and for diving. Naturalist on board lectures on Papau New Guinea culture and wildlife and accompanies shore excursions. Cultural performances by villagers. Optional diving (visibility 200 ft., certified dive master on board, dive gear available to rent). The itinerary and the activities are decided by the weather. Casual clothes.
Rates: Per person double occupancy from $980 to $2,650.
Itinerary: Four-, five- and seven-night cruises of the Melanesian islands along the north coast of Papau New Guinea, including the Trobriand Islands and the Sepik River. Four- to five-night river cruises encompass the lower Sepik (Bongi people) and the middle Sepik (Iatmal people). In January a special expedition explores the furthest reaches of the upper Sepik to its headwaters at the Iran Java border. The itinerary is based mostly on old trading routes, called the Kula Trading Circle. All trips are expeditionary and are subject to change according to weather and cultural events, such as sing-sings, tribal ceremonies and dances.

MIR TESEN RIVER CRUISES
PO Box 1396, Salt Lake City, UT 84157
800-878-7742; 801-269-8612

MS LEONID KRASIN
Built: 1988

Registry: Russia
Length: 424 ft.
Beam: 54 ft.
Speed: 26 knots
Officers: Russian
Crew: 75, Russian
Passengers: 260
Cabins: 161. All cabins are outside, have air-conditioning, private bath
    with shower, radio, picture window. Cabins for non-smokers.
Dining: International and regional cuisine.
Facilities: Lounge, sauna, massage, jogging track, hairdresser, shops,
    florist, laundry. Medical facilities.
Activities: Emphasis on Russian culture. Shore excursions.
Rates: Per person double occupancy from $616 to $1,166.
Itinerary: Ten- and 11-day cruises between St. Petersburg, Moscow
    and Volgograd, Russia.

MS SAINT PETERSBURG
Built: 1975
Registry: Russia
Former Name: *Vladimir Ilyich*
Length: 424 ft.
Beam: 54 ft.
Speed: 26 knots
Officers: Russian
Crew: 75, Russian
Passengers: 200
Cabins: 170. All cabins are outside, have air-conditioning, private bath
    with shower, radio, picture window. Cabins for non-smokers.
Dining: International and regional cuisine.
Facilities: Lounge, sauna, massage, jogging track, hairdresser, shops.
    Medical facilities.
Activities: Shore excursions.
Rates: Per person double occupancy from $616 to $1,060.
Itinerary: Seven- and 14-day river cruises from St. Petersburg, Russia.

NABILA NILE CRUISES
Nagar Tours, 605 Market St., San Francisco, CA 94105
800-443-6453; 415-979-0160

MS OUEEN OF SHEBA; RAMSES OF EGYPT: RAMSES OF THE NILE: QUEEN NABILA I & III
Built: 1984-1991
Registry: Egypt

Length: 52-71 meters
Beam: 9-13 meters
Speed: 13 knots
Officers: Egyptian
Crew: 60-70, Egyptian
Passengers: 154.
Cabins: 36-78. All suites. They have individually controlled aircondi-
    tioning, picture window, private bath with shower and hairdryer,
    sitting area, phone, radio.
Dining: Single seating.
Facilities: Lounge, outdoor pool, boutique, laundry. Telephone service,
    even on shore, not reliable.
Activities: Shore excursions, including visits to temples. Casual cloth-
    ing, no formal nights.
Rates: Per cabins (for one, two or three) from $740 to $2,190.
Itinerary: Four- and six-night cruises of the Nile from Luxor or Aswan.

NATHANIAL BOWDITCH
Box 459, Warren, ME 04864
800-288-4098; 207-273-4062

NATHANIAL BOWDITCH
Built: 1922, rebuilt 1973
Registry: United States
Length: 82 ft.
Speed: Sail plus diesel power
Crew: American
Passengers: 24
Cabins: 11. Cabins have running water, but heads and showers are
    shared. Some double bed berths, some single pullman berths.
Dining: Meals served family style in dining salon or on deck.
Facilities: A gaff-rigged topsail schooner originally built for racing,
    then used as a coastal patrol boat during World War II. Bring soft
    luggage only, casual clothes, foul-weather gear.
Activities: The itinerary and the activities are decided by the weather.
    You may help crew or take the helm if you wish. Lobster and clam
    cookout on shore. Rowboats available. Some cruises involve whale
    watching and schooner races.
Youth Program: None. Not recommended for children under age 8.
Access for Disabled: No.
Rates: Per person from $300 to $645.
Itinerary: Three-, four- and six-day sails from Rockland, Maine
    through Bay waters of mid-coast Maine, including Frenchman,
    Blue Hill and Penobscot.

NEKTON DIVING CRUISES

1057 SE 17th St., Ft. Lauderdale, FL 33316
800-899-6753; 305-463-9324

NEKTON PILOT

Built: 1993
Registry: United States
Length: 78 ft.
Beam: 40 ft.
Speed: 14 knots
Officers: American
Crew: 10, American
Passengers: 34
Cabins: 17. All are outside, have air-conditioning, private bath with
    shower, picture window, two twins or one queen-size bed.
Facilities: Double-hulled dive vessel with new SWATH design.
    Lounge, two bars, elevated dive platform, jacuzzi, photo lab, two
    tenders, library. Medical facilities.
Activities: Shore excursions, snorkeling, scuba with certification.
    Tanks and weight belts supplied. Other equipment, including un-
    derwater camera, for rent. Special cruises for singles and families.
Rates: Per person double occupancy from $1,350 to $1,495.
Itinerary: Seven-day cruises of the Bahamas from Ft. Lauderdale to
    Andros, Exuma, Bimini, Abacos and Cay Salbank.

NILE CRUISES HILTON

c/o Misr Tours
800-223-4978

MS ISIS and MS OSIRIS

Built: 1962
Registry: Egypt
Length: 232 ft.
Beam: 36 ft.
Speed: 9 knots
Officers: Egyptian
Crew: 100. Egyptian
Passengers: 124. About 8% singles, 85% couples, 5% families.
Cabins: 48. All suites. They have air-conditioning, private bath with
    shower and hairdryer, phone.
Dining: Single seating. International and Egyptian cuisine.
Facilities: Lounge, outdoor pool, shops, hairdresser, laundry. Medical
    service.
Activities: Shore excursions, including visits to temples.

Rates: From $1,100 to $3,000.
Itinerary: Three- and six-night cruises of the Nile between Luxor and
Aswan.

MS NEPHTIS
Built: 1990
Registry: Egypt
Officers: Egyptian
Crew: 100. Egyptian
Passengers: 144
Cabins: 60. All have air-conditioning, private bath with shower,
phone. Two suites, eight connecting rooms.
Dining: International and Egyptian cuisine.
Facilities: Lounge, disco, pool, jacuzzi, disco.
Activities: Shore excursions, including visits to temples.
Rates: From $1,100 to $3,000.
Itinerary: Three- and six-night cruises of the Nile between Luxor and
Aswan.

NINA CRUISE LINE
747 Deep Valley Dr., Rolling Hill Estates, CA 90274
800-367-1789; 310-544-3551

MS ITALIA
Built: 1994
Registry: Italy
Length: 528 ft.
Beam: 69 ft.
Speed: 22 knots
Officers: Italian
Crew: Italian
Passengers: 500
Cabins: 260. All have private bath with shower and bidet, TV, phone,
air-conditioning, minibar; many with double beds, some with
berths and some with sofa beds; 38 suites with jacuzzi.
Dining: Dining room has single seating. Pizza parlor.
Facilities: Party lounge, meeting center, casino, library, four bars, bou-
tiques, hairdresser, laundry/ironing, swimming pool. Doctors and
nurses on board.
Activities: Shore excursions by motorcoach, films.
Rates: Four- and five-day cruises from $875 to $2,260.
Itinerary: From Rome to Capri, Sorrento, Livorno, Bastia, or to
Palermo, Agrigento, Malta and Catania.

MS DREAMWARD

NOBLE CALEDONIA See SPECIAL EXPEDITIONS

NORTHWESTERN RIVER SHIPPING COMPANY See EUROCRUISES

NORWEGIAN CRUISE LINE
95 Merrick Way, Coral Gables, FL 33134
800-327-7030; 305-445-0866

SS DREAMWARD
Built: 1992
Registry: Bahamas
Length: 624 ft.
Beam: 94 ft.
Speed: 21 knots
Officers: Norwegian
Crew: 483, International
Passengers: 1,246
Cabins: 623. All have individually controlled air-conditioning, radio, TV with movies, phone, private bath with shower and hairdryer. Most have sitting area and picture window. Some suites have pri-

vate balconies. Adjoining suites can be combined.

Dining: Three main dining rooms seat 256, 190 and 282, two seatings. Cafe seats 76.

Facilities: Piano bar, observation lounge also functions as a disco, sports bar features a wall of multiple TV's with video-taped and live sports activities, main show lounge, spa, casino, hairdresser, laundry, conference center, exercise equipment, jogging track, library, two pools, twin jacuzzis. Medical facilities.

Activities: Basketball, deck sports, snorkeling, golf, tennis, volleyball, football and baseball. Theme cruises that feature sports stars, top entertainers.

Youth Program: Year-round for 6-8, 9-12 and 13-17. During summer and holidays, program extended to 3-5. Playroom, teen center. Circus at Sea, cartoon characters on board.

Access for Disabled: Six cabins with wheelchair access. Several cabins with features for hearing-impaired.

Rates: Double occupancy per person from $1,199 to $3,139. Some include airfare from major North American gateways.

Itinerary: November through April, seven-day, round-trip cruises from Ft. Lauderdale to Grand Cayman, Playa del Carmen, Cozumel, Cancun, NCL's private island (Bahamas). In November-December, seven-day round-trip cruises from Ft. Lauderdale to St. John, St. Thomas, San Juan and NCL's private island (Bahamas). May through October, seven-day round-trip cruises from New York to St. George's and Hamilton, Bermuda.

SS NORWAY

Built: 1960

Registry: Bahamas

Former Name: *SS France*

Length: 1,035 ft.

Beam: 110 ft.

Speed: 18 knots

Officers: Norwegian

Crew: 900, International

Passengers: 2,022

Cabins: 1,039. All staterooms have individually controlled air-conditioning, private bath with shower, TV, radio, phone. Each owner's suite has a wrap-around balcony, living room, bedroom, dressing room and jacuzzi. Some suites have a separate living room and bedroom in addition to the master bedroom. Most Penthouse suites have private balconies.

Dining: Two dining rooms accommodate 528 and 724; two seatings. Outdoor restaurant for informal breakfast and lunch. Extra charge for supper club.

Facilities: The ship is 10 blocks long and 11 stories high. There is an International Deck lined with sidewalk cafes, bars and boutiques, a 6,000 sq.ft. spa with fitness center, 14 rooms for massage, reflexology, herbal treatment, hydrotherapy, thermal body wraps, two saunas, two steam rooms, jacuzzi, an indoor pool for water exercise, two outside pools, Olympic Deck jogging track, seven bars, six entertainment lounges, ballroom, cabaret, casino, disco, ice-cream parlor, library, piano bar, theater, hairdresser, full-service laundry, dry cleaning. Medical facilities.

Activities: Broadway shows, jazz, exercise classes, dancing, basketball, golf driving and putting, paddleball, ping pong, shuffleboard, skeet shooting, snorkeling classes and excursions, volleyball. Theme cruises: Jazz, big band, country music, hockey, volleyball, ski, tennis and basketball.

Youth Program: Children's playroom. Kids' and teens' (ages 6-17) programs are offered all year, including a circus at sea in which kids learn circus routines. Program for younger children during summer and holidays. Universal Studio theme cruise in summer with movie characters, lectures.

Access for Disabled: Ten cabins designed for wheelchair passengers. The *Norway's* size forces it to anchor offshore at ports of call, meaning that passengers must be ferried ashore in tenders. Passengers must provide their own small collapsible wheelchairs.

Rates: Double occupancy per person for seven-day cruise from $999 to $4,329, including airfare. Ten- and 11-day cruise from $1,859 to $9,105, including airfare.

Itinerary: Year-round, seven-day round-trip voyages from Miami to St. Maarten, St. Martin, St. Thomas, St. John and NCL's private island in the Bahamas. In December, 10- and 11-day round-trip cruises from Miami to St. John, St. Thomas, Antigua, Barbados, St. Lucia, Martinique and St. Maarten.

MS SEAWARD

Built: 1988
Registry: Bahamas
Length: 700 ft.
Beam: 96 ft.
Speed: 20 knots
Officers: Norwegian
Crew: 630, International
Passengers: 1,534. The majority are couples in their late 40's and 50's. There are also honeymooners, young families with children and a scattering of singles.
Cabins: 763. All with individually controlled air-conditioning, private bath with shower and hairdryer, radio, TV, phone. Six suites with

separate sitting area, tub, refrigerator.

Dining: Mid-ship dining room accommodates 372; aft dining room accommodates 476. Two seatings. Indoor/outdoor cafes for casual breakfast and lunch. Extra-cost gourmet restaurant.

Facilities: A two-story entrance hall with cascading waterfall, cabaret lounge, fitness center, massage, sauna, two swimming pools, two whirlpools, six bars, five entertainment lounges, casino, disco, piano bar, shops, hairdresser, library, full-service laundry, dry cleaning. Promenade Deck has an unobstructed circuit of the ship; 4 laps equal 1 mile. Medical facilities, two doctors, two nurses.

Activities: Exercise classes, dancing, basketball, golf driving, ping pong, shuffleboard, skeet shooting, snorkeling lessons and excursions, volleyball. Theme cruises on golf and tennis.

Youth Program: Programs for ages 6-17 offered all year and include Circus at Sea, in which kids learn circus routines. Programs for ages 3-5 during summer and holidays.

Access for Disabled: Certain cabins are equipped to accommodate disabled passengers. They must provide their own small collapsible wheelchairs.

Rates: Double occupancy per person from $689 to $1,499, including airfare from most North American gateways.

Itinerary: Three-day loops from Miami to Great Stirrup Cay and Nassau in the Bahamas. A four-day Mexico cruise departs from Miami to Key West, Cancun and Cozumel.

MS SOUTHWARD

Built: 1971
Registry: Bahamas
Length: 536 ft.
Beam: 75 ft.
Speed: 16 knots
Officers: Norwegian
Crew: 320, International
Passengers: 752. Singles 42%, other 58%.
Cabins: 377. All have individually controlled air-conditioning, radio, phone, private bath with shower. Ten suites have sitting area, fridge and tub. Outside cabins have portholes rather than windows.

Dining: Dining room accommodates 420 and has two seatings. Informal breakfast/ lunch on the Beach Deck.

Facilities: Exercise equipment, sauna, massage, swimming pool, four bars, three entertainment lounges, casino, cinema, library, shopping arcade, disco, hairdresser, full-service laundry. The Boat Deck has an unobstructed circuit of the ship for fitness walks. Medical facilities, doctor, nurse.

Activities: Exercise classes, dancing, skeet shooting, ping pong, basketball, shuffleboard, snorkeling lessons and excursions.

Youth Program: Children's playroom. Youth program during holidays and in summer, including Circus at Sea.

Access for Disabled: No specially equipped cabins. Passengers must provide own collapsible wheelchairs.

Rates: Double occupancy per person from $499 to $929, including airfare from most major North American gateways.

Itinerary: Year-round three- and four-day cruises from Los Angeles to Catalina Island, San Diego and Ensenada.

MS STARWARD

Built: 1968

Registry: Bahamas

Length: 525 ft.

Beam: 75 ft.

Speed: 16 knots

Officers: Norwegian

Crew: 315, International

Passengers: 758

Cabins: 381. All have individually controlled air-conditioning, private bath with shower, radio, phone. Seven suites. The lowest-priced cabins are small outside rooms that have upper and lower berths.

Dining: Windows on the Sea Restaurant seats 438. Two seatings. Cafe on the Boat Deck offers informal breakfast and lunch.

Facilities: Main show lounge, cinema, shopping arcade, casino, library, two outdoor pools, fitness center with massage and sauna, hairdresser, full-service laundry. On the top deck, a large glass pyramid, closed on three sides, covers bar/lounge and one of the pools. Medical facilities with doctor and nurse.

Activities: Exercise classes, basketball, volleyball, ping pong, shuffleboard, skeet shooting, scuba and snorkeling lessons and excursions.

Youth Program: Children's playroom. Youth programs during holidays and in summer, including Circus at Sea.

Access for Disabled: No cabins are specially equipped. Passengers must provide own collapsible wheelchairs.

Rates: Five- to seven-day cruises from $899 to $2,179; nine-day cruises from $1,295 to $2,595; 12-day cruises from $1,689 to $3,895. All include airfare from most major North American gateways.

Itinerary: Five- to seven-day round-trip voyages from San Juan to St. Kitts, Grenada, Tobago, St. Lucia, St. Barts, St. John and St. Thomas. In December, 12-day holiday trans Panama Canal cruise from Los Angeles to Acapulco, Caldera, Balboa, Cartagena and San Juan. In April, nine-day, round-trip cruise from San Juan to Tobago, Grenada, St. Lucia, Guadeloupe, St. Kitts, St. Barts, St. John and St. Thomas.

SS WINDWARD
Built: 1993
Registry: Bahamas
Length: 624 ft.
Beam: 94 ft.
Speed: 21 knots
Officers: Norwegian
Crew: 483, International
Passengers: 1,246
Cabins: All have individual thermostat controls, TV, radio, phone, private bath and shower and hairdryer. Some have sitting area and picture window. 101 suites.
Dining: Four dining rooms. Two seatings for dinner, open seating for breakfast and lunch.
Facilities: Piano bar, observation lounge/disco, sports bar, show lounge, hairdresser, casino, conference center, exercise equipment, jogging track on Promenade Deck, library, two pools, jacuzzis, shopping arcade. Medical facilities.
Activities: Aerobics, basketball, deck sports. Bike cruises in Caribbean in winter and spring.
Youth Program: Children's playroom. Teen center. Programs year-round for ages 6-8, 9-12 and 13-17. During summer and holiday periods program is extended to include ages 3-5. Circus at Sea program, cartoon characters on board.
Access for Disabled: Some cabins especially designed for hearing-impaired.
Rates: Double occupancy per person from $699 to $4,995. Some include airfare from major North American gateways.
Itinerary: From October to April, seven-day cruises from San Juan to Barbados, Martinique, St. Maarten, Antigua, St. Thomas, Aruba, Curacao, Tortola, Virgin Gorda, St. John. May through September, seven-day Alaska cruises from Vancouver. April and September, a 14-day trans Canal repositioning cruise from San Juan to Los Angeles, stopping at Aruba, Cartagena, Caldera, Acapulco, Zihuatanejo/Ixtapa and Puerto Vallarta. In May, eight-day repositioning cruise from Los Angeles to Vancouver with stop in San Francisco. In September, six-day cruise from Vancouver to Los Angeles with cruising of Puget Sound and Columbia River.

OBEROI NILE CRUISES
800-562-3764

SHEHRAYAR and SHEHRAZAD
Built: 1983, 1984

Registry: Germany
Length: 232 ft.
Speed: 15 knots
Officers: Egyptian
Crew: 102. Egyptian
Passengers: 152.
Cabins: 71. Shower, radio, phone and air-conditioning; TV on request.
Cabins for non-smokers.
Facilities: Restaurant, disco, plunge pool, hairdresser, shops, library laundry. Medical facilities.
Itinerary: Sister ships cruising the Nile on four- and six-day cruises between Luxor and Aswan, Egypt.
Rates: Double occupancy per person from $798 to $1,596.

OCEANIC CRUISES
5757 W. Century Blvd., Los Angeles, CA 90045
800-545-5778; 310-215-0191

OCEANIC GRACE
Built: 1989
Registry: Japan
Length: 336 ft.
Beam: 50 ft.
Speed: 19 knots
Officers: Japanese
Crew: Japanese
Passengers: 120. Some from the West; the rest Japanese. Age range from 20's to 70's.
Cabins: 60. All are outside, have a picture window, hairdryer, climate control, TV, radio, VCR, phone, minibar, separate sitting area. Each has two twin or one queen-sized bed, some shower, some tub.
Dining: Dining room offers a traditional Japanese cuisine as well as Continental dishes, emphasizes fresh ingredients from ports on route. Open seating; passengers dine on their own schedule. Two formal nights.
Facilities: Main lounge with nighttime entertainment and dancing, piano bar, library, hairdresser, gym with professional trainer, shops, laundry, dry cleaning, meeting room, jogging track, massage, sauna, pool, jacuzzi. Medical facilities.
Activities: The ship carries motor launches and zodiacs for scuba and coastline expeditions, two Boston Whalers for fishing and shore excursions. Windsurfers, dinghy, canoe. Dive and water sports instructors. Tea ceremonies, flower arranging. On Festival Cruise visitors become participants in local festivals.

Youth Program: None. Children under 12 not accepted for passage.
Access for Disabled: One cabin available. Need own wheelchair and
   companion.
Rates: For two- to six-night cruises $800 to $2,500; for seven- to 10-
   nights $2,450 to $5,000. On cruises of seven nights or longer, airfare
   included. Tips included.
Itinerary: Two- to 10-night cruises of Japan's western coastline; the Inland Sea along Japan's subtropical Pacific coastline; along the coast
   of Asia with stops at Eastern Russian, Korea, and mainland China.

ODESSAMERICA
170 Old Country Rd., Mineola, NY 11501
800-221-3254; 516-747-8880

MS ANDROPOV; MS CHICHERIN; MS LENIN; MS GLUSHKOV
Built: 1987, 1988
Registry: Russia, Ukraine
Length: 390 ft.
Beam: 51 ft.
Speed: 15 knots
Officers: Russian, Ukrainian
Crew: 150, Russian, Ukrainian
Passengers: 280-300
Cabins: All staterooms are outside with individually controlled air-
   conditioning, private bath with shower, and refrigerator. There are
   single, double and quad cabins and suites.
Dining: Continental cuisine and Russian specialties of the surround-
   ing regions.
Facilities: These are sister ships. Each has two lounges, boutique, mu-
   sic salon, theater, hairdresser, solarium.
Activities: Dancing, aerobics. Local guest lecturers discuss Russia's
   history, culture and its struggles to convert to a market economy.
   Russian language courses, Russian entertainment. Shore excursions to villages and towns by private motorcoach.
Youth Program: None
Access for Disabled: None
Rates: From $599 to $2,399 per person double occupancy. Rates include shore excursions.
Itinerary: The *Andropov, Chicherin,* and *Lenin* make eight-night cruises
   of rivers, lakes and canals connecting Moscow and St. Petersburg,
   plus three-night stay in Moscow and two-night stay in St. Petersburg where passengers can stay aboard the boat while sightseeing
   the two cities. The *Glushkov* makes seven- and 14-day cruises between Kiev and Odessa and Sevastopal along the Dnieper River,

the Danube delta, and to the Black Sea.

MV AZERBAYDZHAN and MV BELORUSSIYA

Built: 1975, 1974
Registry: Ukraine
Length: 515 ft.
Beam: 73 ft.
Speed: 20 knots
Officers: Ukranian
Crew: 250, Ukranian
Passengers: 550. Nearly all European.
Cabins: 231. All have air-conditioning, private bath with tub or
    shower, radio, some with phone, TV, picture window. Some cabins
    with two lower beds, many with upper and lower berths; doubles
    and quads. Four suites.
Dining: Two restaurants. Single seating. Ukrainian specialties.
Facilities: Five bars, music salon, casino, library, disco, cinema, out-
    door pool, sauna, gym, hairdresser, shops, laundry. Medical facili-
    ties.
Activities: Deck sports. Exercise classes. Cabaret shows. Russian tea
    ceremony.
Youth Program: Children's programs on holidays only.
Access for Disabled: No.
Rates: Double occupancy per person on a typical 10-night cruise for
    two lower berths would be from $1,495 to $2,300. Rates for Euro-
    pean cruises include airfare from London.
Itinerary: The Azerbayhzhan cruises throughout Europe and North Af-
    rica including ports in the Mediterranean, Canary Islands, Norwe-
    gian fjords, British Isles, Ireland and Spitzbergen. The Belorussiya
    makes seven-to 11-day cruises of the South Pacific departing from
    Sydney

MV GRUZIYA

Built: 1975
Registry: Ukraine
Length: 512 ft.
Beam: 72 ft.
Speed: 18 knots
Officers: Ukrainian
Crew: 250, Ukrainian
Passengers: 420
Cabins: 200. All cabins have individually controlled heat and air-con-
    ditioning, telephone, private bath with shower or tub and radio
    (some with TV and tub). Most cabins have twin beds, some have
    berths for third or fourth person. Suites have tub and bidet; some

have refrigerator.

Dining: Two dining rooms, single seating. Cuisine is international with Ukrainian specials.

Facilities: Four lounges, five bars, library, swimming pool, sauna, massage, boutique, theater, salon for shows, disco, casino. Russian atmosphere. Medical facility with general practitioner, surgeon and dentist.

Activities: Russian tea ceremonies, language lessons, balalaika demonstrations, cooking seminars, Russian entertainment in the evening. Shore excursions to Mayan ruins, snorkeling and diving on barrier reef in Belize.

Youth Program: Children's program on holidays.

Access for Disabled: Not accessible to wheelchairs.

Rates: From $1,095 to $2,395 per person, including airfare form U.S. gateway cities.

Itinerary: Seven-day cruises from Tampa, Florida to Puerto Cervos; Honduras; Belize City, Belize and Cozumel, Mexico. Also seven-day cruises from Montreal along the St. Lawrence and Saguenay Rivers to Prince Edward Island and Quebec, along Canada and U.S. East Coast. Also in fall are 18- and 27-day transatlantic cruises with stops in the Azores, Spain, Italy, Turkey, Ukraine, Israel, Egypt, Morocco, Canary Islands, and St. Thomas.

MV KARELIYA

Built: 1976

Registry: Ukraine

Former Name: *Leonid Brezhnev*

Length: 515 ft.

Beam: 73 ft.

Speed: 20 knots

Officers: Ukrainian

Crew: 250, Ukrainian

Passengers: 550. Singles 5%, couples 85%, families 10%.

Cabins: 231. Some have two beds, some have two to four upper and lower berths. All have air-conditioning. Some inside cabins have bath shared between connecting cabins. Eight suites.

Dining: Two restaurants. Continental cuisine. Usually a single seating.

Facilities: Main lounge, four bars, cinema, nightclub, casino, swimming pool, sauna, hairdresser, laundry.

Activities: Sports deck, shuffleboard, ping pong. Ukrainian night by crew.

Youth Program: Playroom. Children's program during school holidays.

Access for Disabled: Not recommended.

Rates: Ten-night cruises from $1,495 to $1,655 double occupancy per

OdessaAmerica Lines

person; $2,638 to $5,773 for 22- to 37-night cruises.

Itinerary: Long cruises of 23- to 59-nights around the west, south, and east coasts of Africa through the Suez Canal back to the Mediterranean. Ten- to 17-day cruises of Scandinavia, Northern Europe, the Mediterranean, Canary Islands, Baltic capitals and St. Petersburg, and the Black Sea.

ODESSAMERICA/ CRUCEROS AUSTRALIS
MV TERRA AUSTRALIS
Built: 1984
Registry: Chile
Former Name: *Savannah*
Length: 213 ft.
Beam: 42 ft.
Speed: 11 knots
Officers: Chilean
Crew: 37, Chilean
Passengers: 100. About 40% singles, 60% couples.
Cabins: 62. All cabins are outside, have individually controlled air-conditioning, private bath with shower, radio, picture windows, phone. Two suites.
Dining: Regional specialties, seafood, Chilean wine.
Facilities: Lounge, bar, library, gift shop. Medical facilities, physician on board.
Activities: Lecture slide shows on local history. Viewing glaciers, penguin colonies.
Youth Program: None.
Access for Disabled: No provisions for disabled.
Rates: Per person double occupancy from $1,075 to $3,020.
Itinerary: Seven-day cruises from Punta Arenas through the Strait of Magellan and Chile's inland waterways to Beagle Channel glaciers,

Tierra de Fuego and Magdalena Island.

ORIENT LINES
1510 S.E. 17th St., Ft. Lauderdale, FL 33316
800-333-7300; 305-527-6660

MV MARCO POLO
Built: 1993
Registry: Bahamas
Length: 578 ft.
Beam: 77 ft.
Speed: 19 knots
Officers: Scandinavian
Crew: Filipino
Passengers: 800. (On Antarctic sailings, passengers limited to 400 to protect the environment.)
Cabins: 425. Private bath with shower and hairdryer, TV, music, telephone, individual thermostat control. Six suites have refrigerator.
Dining: Cafe for casual lunch by the pool; at dinner serving Oriental specialties at tables for two to six. Main bi-level dining room serves continental and American cuisine. Two sittings; smoking or non-smoking areas.
Facilities: The ship has an ice-strengthened hull, two tenders and a helicopter landing pad on the top deck. Main show room, nightclub, piano bar, saltwater swimming pool, three outdoor jacuzzis, small casino, library, gym, boutique, saunas, massage, hairdresser. Medical center with British or American physician and nurse.
Activities: Guest lecturers who are noted experts, discussing the culture, history, flora and fauna of the places visited, local cultural performances and folklore entertainment such as Maori dance performances, local wine tasting, zodiac landing craft and sightseeing. Dance classes.
Youth Program: Children's playroom.
Access for Disabled: Must be accompanied by passenger who will assist. Passengers confined to wheelchairs must provide their own collapsible chair (no wider than 22 1/2 inches), certain areas of the ship are inaccessible. Two wheelchair accessible cabins. Passengers confined to wheelchairs cannot participate in some shore excursions; some ports of call require tenders.
Rates: Seventeen- to 25-day cruises from $3,150 to $9,950 per person double occupancy (Antarctica higher). Rates include pre- or post-cruise hotel stays and air transportation.
Itinerary: Circumnavigates the world. Segments include from Africa to Antarctica, to New Zealand and Australia, to South Pacific; to Vi-

etnam, China, Japan and the Java Sea. Cruise program is designed so that you can take two or more cruises in a sequence without repeating parts of call.

OUT O' MYSTIC SCHOONER CRUISES

7 Holmes St., P.O. Box 487, Mystic, CT 06355
800-243-0416; 203-536-4218

MYSTIC CLIPPER and MYSTIC WHALER

Built: 1982, 1967
Registry: United States
Length: 125 ft., 100 ft.
Beam: 26 ft.
Speed: Sail plus diesel power
Crew: American
Cabins: 4. Two cabins have upper-lower bunks, hot and coldwater washbasin, shared heads and showers. Owner's cabin has private bath with shower and double bunk. Great room (co-ed) has upper and lower single bunks, shared bath and shower, curtains for privacy. No smoking below deck. Passengers tend their own cabins and bunks.
Dining: Meals served family style in dining salon or as buffet on deck.
Facilities: Both are two-masted gaff-rigged schooners, with centerboards, drawing 7 ft. with the board up and 13 ft. with the board down. Bring soft luggage only, casual clothes, foul-weather gear. Ice chest on deck for beverages.
Activities: The itinerary and the activities are decided by the weather. You may help crew or take the helm if you wish. Threeday cruises have pirate treasure hunting party on shore.
Access for Disabled: Not recommended.
Rates: Per person from $219 (coed room, three days) to $589 for owner's cabin for five days.
Itinerary: Two- to five-day sails from Mystic, Connecticut to various coastal islands and small towns of New England such as Sag Harbor, Greenport, Block Island, Newport, Cuttyhunk, Martha's Vineyard or Dering Harbor, depending on wind and tide.

P & O FAIRSTAR CRUISES

c/o International Cruise Connections
99 Long Ct., Thousand Oaks, CA 91360
800-433-8747; 805-496-0548

TSS FAIRSTAR

Built: 1957

Registry: Liberia
Former Name: *Oxfordshire*
Length: 613 ft.
Beam: 78 ft.
Speed: 16 knots
Officers: Italian
Crew: 460, Australian
Passengers: 976. Passengers over age 75 need certificate of fitness
from physician.
Cabins: 480. Two- to six-berth cabins; most have private bath with
shower; 68 have shared facilities. Five suites.
Dining: Two restaurants, pizzeria. Two seatings.
Facilities: Three lounges, disco, cinema, casino, five bars, shops, swim-
ming pool, laundry, hairdresser, gym. Medical facilities with physi-
cian and nurses on board.
Activities: Full PADI dive facility on board, instruction and certifica-
tion on most cruises, resort dives for novices. Diving top sites.
Stops in major ports, small villages, and on uninhabited private islands.
Youth Program: Playpen, nursery and activities year round on every
sailing.
Access for Disabled: Not wheelchair accessible.
Rates: Per person double occupancy, five- to seven-day cruises from
$1,190 to $2,310; nine- to 14-day cruises from $1,650 to $4,990.
Itinerary: Cruises to South Pacific, Melanesia and to Cairns, Whitsunday and other Austrian and New Zealand Coastal towns.

P & O LONDON
c/o Golden Bear Travel, 16 Digital Dr., Novato, CA 94948
800-551-1000; 415-382-8900

CANBERRA
Built: 1961
Registry: England
Length: 249 ft.
Beam: 103 ft.
Speed: 20 knots
Officers: British
Crew: 800, British
Passengers: 1,641. Singles 20%, couples 70%, families 10%. Mostly Brit-
ish.
Cabins: 780. All have air-conditioning, radio, some without private
bath. Premier cabins with sitting area. Variety of accommodations
from inside four-berth cabins with washbasins (passengers share

bathroom facilities) to large suites. Unique court cabins with windows that open onto a communal foyer.

Dining: Two restaurants serving mostly British fare. Passengers are assigned to a dining room based on the location of their cabin (i.e. passengers in higher-priced cabins eat in a restaurant with larger menu choice).

Facilities: Lounges for entertainment and dancing, wraparound observation bar, three pools, theater, disco, casino, library, hairdresser, shops, self-service laundries on every deck.

Activities: Lectures, deck tennis, deck games with matches between officers and passengers, singalong entertainment and classical music concerts.

Youth Program: Playroom, activities, pool, separate early suppers, babysitting, mainly in the summer.

Rates: Per person double occupancy for 10- to 26-day cruises from $3,031 to $16,387; for 30- to 90-day cruises from $4,780 to $65,802; includes airfare and two nights hotel in London.

Itinerary: In summer, 10- to 26-day cruises from Great Britain to Canary Islands, Mediterranean and Scandinavia. In winter, cruises to Caribbean and a 90-day world cruise (available in segments).

ORIANA
Built: 1995
Registry: England
Length: 852 ft.
Beam: 104 ft.
Speed: 24 knots
Officers: British
Crew: International
Passengers: 1,828
Cabins: 914. Cabins have air-conditioning, private bath with shower or tub, TV, radio, phone; some with picture window, some with balcony. Eight suites.
Dining: Two restaurants.
Facilities: Lounges, bars, duty free shop, three pools, sauna, massage, jacuzzi, gym, laundry, dry cleaning. Medical facilities.
Activities: Deck sports, jogging track, nightly entertainment. Shore visits.
Youth Program: Yes.
Access for Disabled: Wheelchair access.

SEA PRINCESS
Built: 1965
Registry: England
Former Name: *Kungsholm*

Length: 659 ft.
Beam: 87 ft.
Speed: 20 knots
Officers: British
Crew: 400, British
Passengers: 714. Singles 20%, couples 70%, families 10%.
Cabins: 368. All have air-conditioning, radio, some without private
   bath. Six suites. Premier cabins with sitting area, TV.
Dining: Continental and English cuisine; two sittings.
Facilities: Three lounges with live bands and dancing, piano bar, ca-
   sino, two outdoor pools, indoor pool, sauna, whirlpool, gym, hair-
   dresser, shop, laundry, library, theater, playroom for children.
   Medical facilities.
Activities: Aerobics and dance lessons.
Rates: Full 92-day cruise from $18,790 to $59,136 per person double oc-
   cupancy, includes airfare and two nights stay in a hotel. Segments
   of 18- to 55-nights range from $4,677 to $35,114.
Itinerary: A 92-day world cruise (available in segments); and 10- to 30-
   day cruises of the Canary Islands, Mediterranean, Suez Canal,
   Scandinavia, Canada and Caribbean.

P & O SPICE ISLAND CRUISES
c/o Esplanade Tours, 581 Boylston St., Boston, MA 02116
800-426-5492; 617-266-7465; 800-323-7308

MV ISLAND EXPLORER and MV SPICE ISLANDER
Built: 1985
Registry: Indonesia; Panama
Length: 134 ft.; 121 ft.
Beam: 40 ft.
Speed: 10 knots
Officers: Indonesian
Crew: 21, Indonesian
Passengers: 36-42. Singles 15%, couples 80%, families 5%.
Cabins: All cabins are outside, have air-conditioning, private bath
   with shower and hairdryer, phone, music. Some suites with picture
   window.
Dining: International, with local specialties. Single seating.
Facilities: Catamaran design with shallow draft allows access to re-
   mote islands. Lounge, library and laundry. Complete diving facil-
   ity. Zodiacs and skiffs. Nurse on board.
Activities: Scuba, snorkeling, water skiing, fishing and windsurfing.
   Some tanks, weight belts, snorkels and fins on board. Lecturer provides seminars and briefings. Shore excursions emphasize less-vis-

ited destinations such as game reserves with rare Javan rhinos as well as jungle cats, and villages isolated from outside influence until about 15 years ago, also events such as buffalo races, grass-fist boxing matches, traditional dance and music. Often makes spontaneous stops to join a wedding party or harvest festival.
Access for Disabled: Passage only for persons in good health without physical disabilities.
Rates: Double occupancy rates per person from $1,962 to $3,075.
Itinerary: Seven- and eight-day cruises of islands in Indonesia. From Bali to Kupang and from Jakarta to the Krakatau Volcano and Ujung Kulon rainforest.

PAN ORAMA CRUISES

800-881-8484

SC PANORMA

Built: 1993
Registry: Greece
Length: 174 ft.
Beam: 40 ft.
Speed: 13 knots
Officers: Greek
Crew: 16, European, American
Passengers: 48
Cabins: 24. All cabins have air-conditioning, private bath with shower, phone, radio, picture window, twin beds, some of which convert to double. Three cabins have pullman child berth
Dining: Local and international cuisine. Single seating.
Facilities: A three-masted sloop. Main salon.
Activities: Shore excursions, shore-based entertainment, exercise classes, watersports.
Rates: Per person double occupancy from $995 to $2,250
Itinerary: Seven-day cruises of the Caribbean and Mediterranean.

PAQUET FRENCH CRUISES

1510 S.E. 17th St., Ft. Lauderdale, FL 33316
800-556-8850; 305-772-8600

MS MERMOZ

Built: 1957
Registry: Bahamas
Length: 532 ft.
Beam: 65 ft.
Speed: 16 knots

Officers: French
Crew: European, Indonesian
Passengers: 530. Singles 10%, couples 85%, families 5%. Mostly French.
Cabins: 275. All cabins have individually controlled air-conditioning, radio, phone, private bath with shower, some with tub. Two suites. Most have twin beds.
Dining: Passengers are assigned to one of two restaurants, depending on their cabins category; dinner is single seating; French and some lighter nouvelle cuisine. Indoor/outdoor grill.
Facilities: Theater, showroom, piano bar, disco, casino, hydrotherapy, two outdoor pools, sauna, boutiques, hairdresser, laundry, library, dry cleaning. Medical facilities, doctor on board.
Activities: Lectures by guest experts on the history and culture of the ship's destination. Theme cruises such as Music Festival at Sea. Berlitz French immersion course during the 18-day transatlantic crossing. Parisian cabaret, local entertainers, French and English-language films, exercise equipment and classes, ping pong, shuffleboard, skeet shooting.
Youth Program: Counselors and activities during French school holidays.
Access for Disabled: Cabins and public rooms not wheelchair accessible.
Rates: Per person rate start at $1,795. Berlitz course is extra. During some cruises children under age 16 may travel free when sharing a cabin with two adults.
Itinerary: Sails the Caribbean in late winter and early spring, a seven-day loop from Guadaloupe to St. Barts, Antigua, Martinique, Barbados, St. Lucia, Bequia. Also visits the Galapagos Islands and transits the Panama Canal on a 15-day voyage from Ft. Lauderdale to Cozumel, Colombia, Costa Rica, San Blas Islands, Panama and Ecuador. Eight- to 15-day cruises of Baltic capitals, Norwegian fjords, Iberian shores, Greece, Turkey, Egypt and the Red Sea, Emirates and the Persian Gulf, India, Ceylon and the Arabian Sea.

PEARL CRUISES
1510 SE 17th St., Ft. Lauderdale, FL 33316
800-426-3588; 800-556-8850; 305-764-3500

MV PEARL
Built: 1967
Registry: Bahamas
Former Names: *Pearl of Scandinavia; Finnstar; Ocean Pearl*
Length: 517 ft.
Beam: 66 ft.

MV PEARL

Speed: 20 knots

Officers: European

Crew: 232, Filipino, European

Passengers: 480. Singles 15%, couples 85%.

Cabins: All cabins have individually controlled air-conditioning, private bath with shower, radio phone. Thirteen suites.

Dining: Dining room seats 260, two sittings. Cuisine is European, American and Asian. Cafe for casual breakfast and lunch.

Facilities: Nightclub, small casino, cabaret entertainment, piano bar, theater, indoor and outdoor pools, gym, two saunas, hairdresser, shops, laundry, library. Medical facilities.

Activities: Deck sports, ping pong. Port and special interest lectures.

Rates: Double occupancy rates per person from $2,750 to $8,995, including hotel stays before and after the cruise.

Itinerary: Ten- through 14-day cruises of Australia, the Indian Ocean, Africa, China, Spice Islands, Japan, Vietnam, Burma, Siam, Thailand, Indonesia and Malaysia.

PEN BAY PACKET COMPANY

70 Elm St., Camden, ME 04843

800-999-7352; 207-236-3520

MV PAULINE
Built: 1947
Registry: United States
Length: 83 ft.
Beam: 18 ft.
Speed: 8 knots
Officers: American
Crew: 5, American
Passengers: 12
Cabins: 6. Upper and lower berths, sink with hot and cold water,
    shared bath facilities. No smoking in cabins.
Dining: Family style.
Facilities: Main salon. Tender.
Activities: Shore excursions, snorkeling, lobster bakes.
Rates: Per person double occupancy $965.
Itinerary: Seven-day cruises of the coast of Maine.

STEPHEN TABER
Built: 1871
Registry: United States
Length: 68 ft.
Beam: 22 ft.
Officers: American
Crew: 5, American
Passengers: 22
Cabins: 12. Sink with hot and cold water, shared bath facilities. No
    smoking in cabins.
Dining: Family style.
Facilities: Main salon. Two tenders.
Activities: Shore excursions, snorkeling, lobster bakes.
Rates: Per person double occupancy $675.
Itinerary: Schooner makes seven-day cruises of the coast of Maine.

POLAR EXPEDITIONS See MARINE EXPEDITIONS

PREMIER CRUISE LINES

400 Challenger Rd., Cape Canaveral, FL 32920
407-783-5061; 800-327-7113

SS ATLANTIC
Built: 1982
Registry: Liberia

Premier Cruise Lines

Length: 671 ft.
Beam: 90 ft.
Speed: 21 knots
Officers: International
Crew: 535. International
Passengers: 1,090. Mostly families.
Cabins: 549. All cabins have air-conditioning, private bath with
    shower, radio, phone; some with tub, TV. All 52 suites with sitting
    area, TV, tub.
Dining: Galaxy Dining Room seats 735. Two seatings for dinner.
Facilities: Revues at club, piano bar, disco, cinema, casino, fitness
    equipment, outdoor and indoor pools, whirlpool, conference
    rooms, shops, laundry. Medical facilities, doctor on call.
Activities: Sunrise Terrace just for adults. Shuffleboard, skeet shoot-
    ing, golf driving range, ping pong. Snorkeling equipment and in-
    struction. At Sanctuary Bay in Port Lucaya guests encounter
    Underwater Explorers Society dolphins.
Youth Program: Activities program all year for children and teens.
    Cartoon characters on board. Teen nightclub.
Access for Disabled: Limited wheelchair accessibility; traveling com-
    panion required.
Rates: Double occupancy per person from $445 to $1,345, including
    airfare. Children under 12 receive special rates during promotions.

Cruise may be combined with stay at Orlando theme parks.
Itinerary: The "Big Red Boat" makes three- and four-day cruises of the
Bahamas, leaving from Port Canaveral, Florida. Three-night cruises
to Key West; four-night cruises to Cozumel from Tampa Bay West.

SS MAJESTIC

Built: 1972
Registry: Bahamas
Former Names: *Sun Princess; Spirit of London*
Length: 535 ft.
Beam: 74 ft.
Speed: 19 knots
Officers: International
Crew: 380, International
Passengers: 760.
Cabins: 380. All have private bath with shower, air-conditioning, ra-
dio, phone. Four suites have combination tub/shower.
Dining: Dining rooms seats 504. Two seatings for dinner.
Facilities: Revues in club, dancing at the cabaret, piano bar, disco, cin-
ema, casino, outdoor pool, children's pool, whirlpool, massage
shops, hairdresser, laundry. Medical facilities.
Activities: Aerobics classes, skeet shooting, shuffleboard, ping pong,
snorkeling instruction and equipment.
Youth Program: All year for children and teens. Cartoon characters on
board. Beach activities. Teen nightclub.
Access for Disabled: Wheelchair mobility limited. Travel companion
required.
Rates: Double occupancy per person from $445 to $1,739.
Itinerary: Four-day cruises from Port Everglades, Florida to the Bahamas and Key West.

SS OCEANIC

Built: 1965
Registry: Bahamas
Length: 782 ft.
Beam: 97 ft.
Speed: 22 knots
Officers: International
Crew: 535, International
Passengers: 1,180
Cabins: 590. All have private bath with shower, air-conditioning, ra-
dio, phone; some with TV, tub; several connecting cabins and five-
berth family staterooms available. Suites with sitting area, picture
window, veranda.
Dining: A different style of cuisine prepared each night (including Ital-

ian, French and Caribbean). Dining room seats 812 with two seatings for dinner.

Facilities: Showroom, dancing at the cabaret, piano bar, disco, two-level cinema, casino, two outdoor pools, whirlpool, massage, conference rooms, hairdresser, shops, laundry. Medical facilities, doctor on board.

Activities: Jogging track, exercise classes, skeet shooting, shuffleboard, golf driving range, ping pong, snorkeling instruction and equipment.

Youth Program: Children's recreation center. Teen program.

Access for Disabled: Wheelchair mobility limited.

Rates: Double occupancy rate per person from $445 to $1,739.

Itinerary: Three- and four-day cruises of the Bahamas.

PRINCESS CRUISES

10100 Santa Monica Blvd., Los Angeles, CA 90067
800-421-0522; 310-553-1770

CROWN PRINCESS and REGAL PRINCESS

Built: 1990, 1991

Registry: Liberia

Length: 811 ft.

Beam: 105 ft.

Speed: 19 knots

Officers: Italian

Crew: 696, primarily European

Passengers: 1,590. Singles 15%, couples 80%, families 5%.

Cabins: 795. All have individually controlled air-conditioning, phone, walk-in closets, refrigerator, TV, radio. All 14 suites, 36 mini-suites and 134 outside cabins have veranda and large windows.

Dining: Two-tiered main restaurant, several cafes, pizza parlor.

Facilities: A three-story atrium plaza with boutiques. Variety of restaurants, bars and lounges, nightclub, disco, three pools, library, youth center, sauna, massage, hairdresser, Broadway-style reviews, theater, casino, shops. Medical facilities.

Activities: Language lessons, lectures, dancing on the pool deck on Fiesta Night. Deck sports, fitness center, exercise classes, pool games,, ping pong, pool volleyball, trapshooting. Jogging track equals 1/5 mile. A private beach call at Princess Cay (Eleuthera) provides barbecue, shopping, dancing, sailing, banana boats, snorkeling, scuba diving.

Youth Program: Youth program is run when there are at least 15 children on board.

Access for Disabled: Ten cabins designed for wheelchair access.

REGAL PRINCESS

Rates: Double occupancy per person for seven-day cruise from $1,399
to $4,299.
Itinerary: Seven-day cruises of the Caribbean, Mexico, and Alaska,
and repositioning cruises through the Panama Canal.

FAIR PRINCESS

Built: 1957
Registry: Liberia
Former Names: *Fairsea; Carinthea*
Length: 608 ft.
Beam: 80 ft.
Speed: 19 knots
Officers: Italian
Crew: 430, primarily European
Passengers: 890
Cabins: 445. Air-conditioned with radio and phone, suites with TV.
Most have two extra upper berths.
Dining: Two dining rooms, each with two sittings.
Facilities: Showroom, piano bar, theater, casino, disco, library, meeting
rooms, hairdresser, shops, laundry, ironing room, fitness center,
sauna, massage, three swimming pools. Doctor on call.
Activities: Deck sports, exercise classes, ping pong.
Youth Program: Children's counselors, group activities year-round.
Shallow children's pool with pool games and snorkeling lessons.
Teen program includes Italian lessons and karaoke. PG movies in
youth center. No babysitting services; children must be at least 24

months old to travel with Princess.

Access for Disabled: Ten wheelchair cabins, but some public areas are not accessible.

Rates: Per person double occupancy from $1,130 to $6,138.

Itinerary: Seven- through 10-day cruises of Mexico, Alaska, the South Pacific and Hawaii.

GOLDEN PRINCESS

Built: 1973

Registry: Bahamas

Former Names: *Royal Viking Sky; Sunward; Birka Queen*

Length: 674 ft.

Width: 83 ft.

Speed: 19 knots

Officers: Finnish, British, and Italian.

Crew: 410.

Passengers: 830

Cabins: 415. Cabins have individually controlled air-conditioning, TV, radio, phone, bath with shower. Nine suites with verandas.

Dining: Dining room seats 452. Two sittings.

Facilities: Observation lounge, disco, theater, casino, shops, hairdresser, massage, sauna, two pools, whirlpool, gym, library. Medical facility.

Activities: Paddle tennis, golf driving.

Youth Program: Children's counselors. Teen center.

Access for Disabled: Staterooms and some public areas not accessible to wheelchairs.

Rates: Per person double occupancy rate for seven-day cruises from $1,399 to $4,299; for 10- to 16-day cruises from $1,665 to $11,987.

Itinerary: Seven-day cruises of Alaska; one- to 10-day cruises of Mexico; 10- to 16-day cruises of Hawaii and Tahiti; 14-day cruises of southeast Asia, Australia and New Zealand.

ISLAND PRINCESS and PACIFIC PRINCESS

Built: 1972

Registry: Britain

Former Names: *Island Venture; Sea Venture*

Length: 553 ft.

Beam: 80 ft.

Speed: 19 knots

Officers: British

Crew: 305, primarily European

Passengers: 640. Singles 5%, couples 90%, families 5%.

Cabins: 305. Air-conditioned cabins with radio, phone. Suites have sitting area, refrigerator, tub.

Dining: Split-level dining room, two sittings. Casual breakfast and lunch on deck.

Facilities: Various lounges, four with dance floors and shows, disco, casino, theater, two outdoor pools, gym, two saunas, massage, library, hairdresser, laundry, dry cleaning. Medical facilities, doctor on board.

Activities: Deck sports, golf driving, ping pong, skeet shooting, exercise classes, jogging track.

Youth Program: Only when more than 15 children are on board.

Access for Disabled: Several equipped cabins. All four elevators are accessible.

Rates: Per person double occupancy for 11- to 14-day cruises from $3,140 to $10,587; for 16- to 19-day cruises from $4,138 to $11,387.

Itinerary: Eleven- to 34-day cruises of South America, Africa, Mediterranean, Hawaii, Tahiti, Australia, New Zealand, India, Asia, Europe and Holy Land.

MV ROYAL PRINCESS

Built: 1984

Registry: Britain

Length: 757 ft.

Beam: 106 ft.

Speed: 20 knots

Officers: British

Crew: International

Passengers: 1,200

Cabins: 600. All are outside. Penthouse, suites, mini-suites and some cabins on the Aloha Deck have private verandas. All cabins have bathtubs, refrigerators, and large windows, air-conditioning, radio, TV, phone, dressing area.

Dining: A two-level restaurant with large outside windows. Two sittings. Cafe for casual breakfast and lunch.

Facilities: Observation lounge atop the ship, two main rooms for shows, whirlpool, two saunas, two massage rooms, gym, lap pool, seven bars, four entertainment lounges, casino, theater, disco, library, gift shop, hairdresser, full-service laundry, dry cleaning, self-service laundrette. Medical facilities with physicians.

Activities: Exercise classes, golf driving, ping pong, pool sports, shuffleboard, skeet shooting. An unobstructed circuit of the ship allows fitness walks and jogging, 3.5 laps equals 1 mile.

Youth Program: Youth program when more that 15 children are on board.

Access for Disabled: All cabins can accommodate a standard wheelchair, but the cruise line limits the number of cabins available to disabled passengers to 10 per cruise.

Rates: Double occupancy per person from $2,600 to $12,787.
Itinerary: Ten- to 14-day cruises include Panama Canal, Baltic, Canada and New England/Colonial America, Scandinavia and Russia.

TSS SKY PRINCESS
Built: 1984
Registry: Britain
Former Name: *Fairsky*
Length: 789 ft.
Width: 98 ft.
Speed: 19 knots
Officers: British
Crew: 535. Primarily European.
Passengers: 1,200. Singles 5%, couples to 35 4%, couples over 55 64%, families 5%.
Cabins: 600. Air-conditioned, radio, TV, phone. Suites have bathtubs and verandas. Many cabins have two upper berths to accommodate a third or fourth passenger.
Dining: Two dining rooms. Continental cuisine.
Facilities: Horizon lounge atop the ship, health club, sauna, massage room, 25-seat whirlpool, jogging track on top deck, three pools, gym, seven bars, five entertainment lounges with dancing, showroom, casino, cinema, theater, disco, library, piano bar, shops, hairdresser, meeting rooms, laundry and self-serve laundromat. Medical facilities, doctor on call.
Activities: Exercise classes, paddle tennis, ping pong, pool games, shuffleboard, skeet shooting, volleyball.
Youth Program: Children's program with counselors. Snorkeling lessons, pool. For teenagers, exercise classes, arts and crafts, Italian lessons, movies, teen room, disco open in early evening, karaoke lip sync talent contest. Children must be at least 24-months old, no babysitting services.
Access for Disabled: Ten cabins with wheelchair access, all six elevators accessible to wheelchairs.
Rates: From $1,299 to $9,292 per person double occupancy.
Itinerary: Seven- to 15-day cruise of Panama Canal and Alaska.

STAR PRINCESS
Built: 1989
Registry: Liberia
Former Name: *Fair Majesty*
Length: 805 ft.
Width: 105 ft.
Speed: 19 knots
Officers: Italian

Crew: 600. Primarily European.
Passengers: 1,470
Cabins: 735. Air-conditioned, radio, TV, phone, refrigerator, dressing area, twin beds that convert to queen size. Suites have separate sitting areas, king-size beds, and verandas. Outside cabins have picture window.
Dining: Dining room seats 800. Two sittings.
Facilities: Three-story atrium lobby, observation lounge, show lounge, casino, cinema, gym, three pools, four whirlpools, sauna, massage, steamroom, seven bars, casino, theater, disco, library, piano bar, shops, hairdresser,laundry, self-serve laundromat, dry cleaning, ironing room. Medical facilities, doctor on call.
Activities: Fitness program, massage, beauty treatments, exercise classes, shuffleboard, skeet shooting, volleyball. For jogging, five laps of Sun Deck equals 1 mile.
Youth Program: Children's program all year. Shallow depth pool for children with snorkeling lessons. For teenagers, exercise classes, arts and crafts, Italian lessons, movies, teen room, disco open in early evening, karaoke talent show. Children must be at least 24-months old, no babysitting services.
Access for Disabled: Ten cabins for disabled passengers, all elevators accessible to wheelchairs.
Rates: For seven-day cruises from $1,399 to $4,299 per person double occupancy.
Itinerary: Seven-day cruises of Caribbean, Alaska, Mexico, Panama Canal.

SUN PRINCESS

Delivery: 1995
Registry: Italy
Length: 856 ft.
Beam: 106 ft.
Speed: 21 knots
Passengers: 1,950
Cabins: 1,050. Suites and outside cabins have verandas.
Dining: Two dining rooms, pizzeria, international food court.
Facilities: Two atrium, lounges, shops, bars, disco, casino, two main showrooms, three pools, gym.
Itinerary: Caribbean and Alaska.

QUARK EXPEDITIONS

980 Post Rd., Darien, CT 06820
800-356-5699; 203-656-0499

AKADEMIK SERGEY VAVILOV
Built: 1988
Registry: Russian
Length: 386 ft.
Beam: 59 ft.
Officers: European
Crew: 35, European
Passengers: 75
Cabins: All are outside, with two lower beds, some have private bath with shower, some share bathroom between two cabins. Four suites.
Dining: International cuisine.
Facilities: Ice-rated polar research vessel. Conference room/library. Main lounge with bar, gym, two saunas, small heated pool. Three zodiacs. Medical facilities, physician on board.
Activities: Lecture programs, educational and entertainment videos. Shore excursions by zodiacs to study icebergs and wildlife.
Rates: For three-day cruise from $4,550 to $6,960 per person double occupancy, including one night hotel before the cruise in Santiago, Chile.
Itinerary: Twelve-night cruises from Falkland to the Antarctic, including King George Island, Deception Island, and Port Lockroy, subject to weather, sea and ice conditions.

KAPITAN DRANITSYN
Built: 1980
Registry: Russia
Length: 437 ft.
Beam: 87 ft.
Officers: Russian
Crew: 35, Russian, western
Passengers: 75
Cabins: All are outside, with windows, and have private bath with shower. Five suites.
Dining: European chefs, international menu, local seafood specialties.
Facilities: Ice-breaker polar research vessel. Gym, heated indoor pool, sauna, library, zodiacs, two helicopters. Medical facilities, physician on board.
Activities: Expert lecturers and expedition leaders, educational and entertainment videos. Shore excursions by zodiacs and helicopters to study icebergs and wildlife. Open bridge.
Rates: For 12-night cruise, from $5,580 to $8,980 per person double occupancy, including one night hotel before the cruise, shore and helicopter excursions; for 19-day cruise from $9,950 to $15,950.
Itinerary: Twelve-night cruises from Longyearbyen, Norway to the

fjords of Spitzbergen and the island archipelago of Franz Josef Land. A 19-day cruise continues on to New Siberian Islands, Wrangel Island and Provideniya.

KAPITAN KHLEBNIKOV
Built: 1981
Registry: Russia
Length: 437 ft.
Beam: 87 ft.
Speed: 15 knots
Officers: Russian
Crew: 60, Russian
Passengers: 106
Cabins: 56. All outside, have private bath with shower. Several suites.
Dining: International menu, European chefs, with local specialties such as Arctic char and Greenland shrimp.
Facilities: Ice-rated polar research vessel that works part of the year as an ice-breaker in the seas of northern Siberia. Two lounges with bar, gym, sauna, indoor heated pool, lecture theatre, library. Three zodiacs. Helideck and hanger for two helicopters. Medical facilities, physician on board.
Activities: Lecture programs, educational and entertainment videos. Shore excursions by zodiacs to study icebergs and wildlife. Reconnaissance and excursions by helicopters to otherwise inaccessible locations. Visit to Macquarie Island, breeding ground of elephant seals and most of the world's 3 million royal penguins. Arctic expedition usually encounters polar bears, enters the area of the north magnetic pole and visits native Inuit settlements and archeological sites.
Rates: For the Antarctic expedition, from $11,950 to $18,500 per person double occupancy, including shore excursions, helicopter time and one night hotel before the cruise in Santiago, Chile. For the Arctic expedition, $5,950 to $8,950.
Itinerary: A 27-day semi-circumnavigation of Antarctica including Peter Island and the Ross Ice Shelf and visits to sub-Antarctic islands of New Zealand and Australia. In late summer, an 11-day Canadiana Arctic expedition from Resolute to Greenland and Ellesmere and Baffin Islands.

YAMAL
Built:
Registry: Russia
Length: 500 ft.
Speed: 18 knots
Officers: Russian

Crew: 35. Russian
Passengers: 100
Cabins: 50. All are outside, with windows, and have private bath with
    shower. Twenty suites and mini-suites.
Dining: European chefs, international menu.
Facilities: Ice-breaker polar research vessel with 2-inch-thick rein-
    forced steel bow and 75,000 horsepower to drive through pack ice
    6 ft. thick at 10 knots. Lounge, gym, heated indoor pool, sauna, lec-
    ture theater, library, zodiacs, two helicopters. Medical facilities.
Activities: This will be a working expedition of scientists for an ice-
    breaking voyage across the Arctic Ocean in an attempt to reach the
    North Pole, accomplished only rarely by ship. Expert lecturers and
    expedition leaders on board. Open bridge. Shore excursions by zo-
    diacs and helicopters to study icebergs and wildlife, visit Siberian
    towns and native Chukchi and Eskimo villages. Barbecue and
    champagne on the ice at the North Pole.
Rates: From $5,590 to $8,980 per person double occupancy, including
    one night hotel before the cruise, shore and helicopter excursions.
Itinerary: One 14-day expedition from Murmansk to Franz Josef Land,
    and the geographic North Pole, then to islands of the Siberian
    Coast. Stops are subject to weather, sea and ice conditions.

REGAL CRUISES
4199 34th St., St. Petersburg, FL 33711
800-270-7245; 813-867-1300

MV REGAL EMPRESS
Built: 1953
Registry: Bahamas
Former Name: Caribe I
Length: 612 ft.
Beam: 80 ft.
Speed: 17 knots
Officers: European
Crew: 350, International
Passengers: 1,180
Cabins: 450. All have air-conditioning, phone. Suites have separate sit-
    ting room, picture window, TV, VCR, some have two baths. Some
    cabins accommodate five passengers.
Dining: Dining room seats 562 in two seatings; serves continental cui-
    sine.
Facilities: Six bars, four lounges, disco, casino, theater, piano bar, out-
    door pool, sauna, gym, jogging track, two whirlpools, massage, li-
    brary, gift shop, hairdresser.

Activities: Scuba-diving, snorkeling, shuffleboard, skeet shooting. The Promenade Deck is partially enclosed and air-conditioned; six laps equal 1 mile.

Youth Program: None.

Access for Disabled: Cabins with wheelchair access; travel companion required. Some public areas are inaccessible to wheelchairs. There is a 2- to 12-inch step to the bathroom in cabins. Must provide own wheelchair.

Rates: Double occupancy per person for four-night cruises from $299 to $529.

Itinerary: Four-night Mexican cruise from Tampa Bay to Playa del Carmen and Cozumel.

RECENCY CRUISES

260 Madison Ave., New York, NY 10016
800-388-5500; 800-388-6600; 212-972-4499

REGENT JEWEL and REGENT SPIRIT

Registry: Bahamas

Length: 425, 495 ft.

Beam: 59-63 ft.

Speed: 16-17 knots

Officers: Greek, European

Crew: International

Passengers: 400-500

Cabins: 211. All outside, have individual air-conditioning, private bath with shower, phone, radio, some cabins have large windows and bath with tub, two lower beds or one large double bed. Suites with large window. *Regent Jewel* has TV.

Dining: Dining room serves continental and French cuisine, regional specialties; two seatings. Two formal nights.

Facilities: Six lounges, four bars, outdoor pool, gym, sauna, massage room, theater, disco, library, casino, duty free boutiques, hairdresser. Medical facilities, physician and nurse.

Activities: Day shore excursions, dancing, exercise equipment, ping pong, cooking classes by French chef, golf driving range, exercise class, wrap-around promenade for jogging, lessons and video instruction of snorkeling, lectures on ports of call, performances by native folkloric dancers.

Youth Program: Children's activity programs are available only on designated cruises.

Access for Disabled: The structure of the vessel may prevent access to certain areas and facilities.

Rates: Seven-day cruises from $1,095 to $2,695 and 14-day cruises from $2,945 to $4,945 double occupancy per person.

Itinerary: *Regent Jewel* sails seven-day cruises from Turkey to Israel, Haifa, Rhodes, Santorini, Cyprus, Greece and Crete; and from Greece to Turkey, Crimea, Ukraine, Romania, Yalta, Odessa and Constanta on the Black Sea and return to Turkey. *Regent Spirit* sails seven-day cruise from Nice to the French and Italian Rivieras and to Tunisia, and in the Caribbean.

REGENT RAINBOW
Built: 1958
Registry: Bahamas
Former Name: *Santa Rosa*
Length: 599 ft.
Beam: 84 ft.
Speed: 19 knot
Officers: Greek, European
Crew: 420, European, International
Passengers: 960
Cabins: 484. All have individually controlled air-conditioning, phone, TV, radio, hairdryer; some cabins with picture window, bathtub, and sitting area; two suites.
Dining: Dining room with international and French cuisine. Two seatings per meal.
Facilities: Lounge with orchestra, showroom with nightly stage performances, disco, court and piano entertainment, casino, gym, outdoor pool, two saunas, three jacuzzis, massage, promenade deck for jogging, library, hairdresser, shops, meeting room, laundry. Medical facilities.
Activities: Exercise classes, skeet shooting, shuffleboard and ping pong. Gentlemen hosts on some cruises.
Youth Program: Playrooms and counselors.
Access for Disabled: Four cabins with wheelchair access.
Rates: Five-day cruise from $395 to $525 per person double occupancy.
Itinerary: Five-day Yucatan cruise from Tampa to Playa del Carmen, Cozumel, and Key West.

REGENT SEA
Built: 1957
Registry: Bahamas
Former Name: *Gripsholm*
Length: 631 ft.
Beam: 83 ft.
Speed: 18 knots
Officers: Greek
Crew: 365, European

Passengers: 729

Cabins: 361. Nearly all staterooms are outside. All have air-conditioning, radio, phone, some with double bed. Eleven suites with additional sitting area, refrigerator and hairdryer.

Dining: Continental and French cuisine, regional specialties. Two seatings for dinner.

Facilities: Lounge with orchestra and shows, piano lounge, disco, theater, casino, gym, aerobics, two outdoor pools, sauna, whirlpools and massage, hairdresser, shops, library, laundry. Medical facilities.

Activities: Skeet shooting, shuffleboard, ping pong, driving range, dance lessons, lectures on topics of local interest, snorkeling and scuba instruction. Sun Deck has unobstructed circuit for jogging. Jazz-theme cruises. Gentlemen hosts as dancing and bridge-partners. Excursions to Tikal, Quirigua, Copan, Altun Ha and Lamanai.

Youth Program: Children's services during holidays.

Access for Disabled: Two cabins with wheelchair access.

Rates: Seven-day cruises from $1,185 to $2,065 double occupancy per person, except in Alaska at $1,215 to $2,935.

Itinerary: Seven-day Mayan cruise from Montego Bay to Playa del Carmen, Cozumel, Belize, Guatemala and Honduras. In summer, seven- and 14-day cruises of Alaska between Vancouver and Seward.

REGENT STAR

Built: 1957

Registry: Bahamas

Former Names: *Statendam; Rhapsody*

Length: 642 ft.

Beam: 79 ft.

Speed: 19 knots

Officers: Greek

Crew: 450, European

Passengers: 950

Cabins: 485. Staterooms have air-conditioning, radio, phone; some cabins with double bed, sitting area and tub.

Dining: Continental and French cuisine. Two seatings for dinner.

Facilities: Lounge with orchestra and nightly shows, lounge and disco for dancing, theater, piano and trios, casino, gym, indoor/outdoor pool, spa, sauna, whirlpool, massage, shops, hairdresser, library, laundry. Medical facilities, doctor on staff.

Activities: Aerobics, shuffleboard, skeet shooting, ping pong, golf driving range, dance lessons, snorkeling and scuba diving instruction, lectures on topics of local interest. Gentlemen hosts as dancing and bridge partners. Jazz theme cruises.

Youth Program: During holidays.

Access for Disabled: Two cabins with wheelchair access.
Rates: Seven-day cruises from $1,095 to $1,855 double occupancy per
  person. Airfare free on 50-day cruise.
Itinerary: Seven-day cruises in Alaska and Caribbean from Montego
  Bay.

REGENT SUN
Built: 1964
Registry: Bahamas
Former Names: *Shalom; Doric; Royal Odyssey; Hanseatic*
Length: 627 ft.
Beam: 81 ft.
Speed: 19 knots
Officers: Greek
Crew: 390, International
Passengers: 836. Mostly over age 55.
Cabins: 418. All with air-conditioning, shower, radio, phone. Some
  suites have sitting area, tub and hairdryer. Double bed in 23 suites.
Dining: Continental and French cuisine. Two seatings for dinner. Cafe
  for casual breakfasts and lunch.
Facilities: Lounge seats 400 for shows and orchestras; piano lounge, li-
  brary, theater, disco, casino, indoor and outdoor pools, sauna, mas-
  sage, hairdresser, gym, meeting room, laundry. Medical facilities,
  physician on call.
Activities: Dance lessons, exercise classes, golf driving and putting,
  skeet shooting, deck tennis, shuffleboard, ping pong, snorkeling
  and scuba programs, lectures, jazz-theme cruises, gentlemen hosts
  as dancing and bridge partners.
Youth Program: During holidays and summer.
Access for Disabled: Two outside cabins with wheelchair access.
Rates: From $1,095 to $5,130 per person double occupancy.
Itinerary: Seven- to 14-day cruises of the Caribbean from San Juan;
  seven-day cruises in New England and eastern Canada.

RENAISSANCE CRUISES
1800 Eller Drive, Suite 300, Ft. Lauderdale, FL 33335
800-525-2450; 305-463-0982

RENAISSANCE I-VIII
Built: 1989 to 1992
Registry: Liberia
Length: 290-297 ft.
Beam: 50 ft.
Speed: 15 knots
Officers: Italian

RENAISSANCE I-VIII

Crew: 67-72, European

Passengers: 100-114

Cabins: 50-57. All are outside suites with large windows overlooking the sea, sitting area, phone, TV, VCR, and refrigerated bar, bathroom with shower, hairdryer; some with private balcony. Option of queen or twin beds.

Dining: Open seating. Buffet breakfast and lunch on deck.

Facilities: Three bars, one main lounge, library, pool, jacuzzi, casino, piano bar, gift shop, hairdresser, massage, full-service laundry. Doctor on board.

Activities: Zodiacs, sailfish, snorkeling equipment, scuba certification course. A water-sports platform that lowers from the stern allows access to the water when the ship is at anchor for water skiing, sailing and swimming. Three decks offer an unobstructed circuit for fitness walks. Open bridge policy. The ships sail primarily at night, and are in port during the day. Cruises feature lectures on history, architecture and culture of each port.

Youth Program: None

Access for Disabled: Cruises may be too strenuous for non-ambulatory passengers.

Rates: From $3,995 to $10,995 per person for cruise with airfare and two nights in hotels. Cruise-only rates from $1,995 for seven-day

Caribbean cruises, $2,995 for other seven-day cruises, $5,995 for 14-day cruises and $8,995 for 21- and 23-day cruises. Past guests save up to 40%.

Itinerary: To the Seychelles Islands and Africa; theCaribbean; the Baltic, including Northern Europe and Russia; the Mediterranean and Aegean Seas; and the Asian Islands and India. Cruises can be combined to create a two or three-week program aboard the same ship without repeating ports. Typical cruises: seven days from Athens to Rome; seven days between Barcelona, Rome, and Las Palmas; 14 days from London to Stockholm; seven days from Stockholm to Copenhagen; seven days from Istanbul to Athens; 23 days from Istanbul to Bombay; 14 days from Bombay to Singapore; 14 days from Singapore to Bali. Cruises in the Caribbean have ports of call in Antigua, St. Kitts, St. Croix, Virgin Gorda, St. Maarten, St. Barts, Dominica, St. Lucia, St. Vincent, Bequia, Martinique and Montserrat.

ROYAL CARIBBEAN CRUISE LINE
1050 Caribbean Way, Miami, FL 33132
800-327-6700; 305-539-6000

MAJESTY OF THE SEAS
Built: 1992
Registry: Norway
Length: 880 ft.
Beam:106 ft.
Speed: 21 knots
Officers: Norwegian
Crew: 822, Norwegian and International
Passengers: 2,354, mostly American
Cabins: 1,177. All have private bath with shower, phone, TV, radio, individually controlled air-conditioning; most have twin beds that convert to double bed. Suites have private veranda, refrigerator. One suite for up to six passengers is available, with two bedrooms, two baths, sitting room and balcony.
Dining: Caribbean and continental cuisine. Two dining rooms, two seatings for dinner. Cafe for indoor/outdoor breakfast and lunch.
Facilities: Viking Crown Lounge cantilevered from ship's funnels, the signature of every Royal Caribbean vessel. Five-deck atrium, 10 shops, four lounges, nightclub, 80-person conference center, cinema, 2,000 volume library, casino, two outdoor pools, hairdresser, shops, laundry, dry cleaning, fitness center, whirlpools, sauna, massage. Medical center, two doctors, three nurses.
Activities: Golf program with rounds in port. Exercise classes, dance classes, jogging track, snorkeling instruction.

Youth Program: Children's playroom and pool, teen nightclub. Children's menu. Year-round programs.
Access for Disabled: Two outside and two inside cabins with wheelchair access. Travel companion required.
Rates: Double occupancy per person from $1,180 to $3,595.
Itinerary: Year-round seven-night cruises from Miami to Playa del Carmen/ Cozumel, Mexico; Georgetown, Grand Caymen and Ocho Rios, Jamaica.

MONARCH OF THE SEAS
Built: 1991
Registry: Norway
Length: 880 ft,
Beam: 106 ft
Speed: 22 knots
Officers: International
Crew: 822. International
Passengers: 2,354.
Cabins: 1,177. All have private bath with shower, phone, TV, radio, individually controlled air-conditioning; 99% of staterooms convert to double bed configuration. A two - bedroom suite available with two baths, sitting room and balcony . Twelve suites feature sitting area, bar and private balcony, some have tub.
Dining: Two dining rooms. Casual meals in the cafe.
Facilities: Four lounges, nightclub, Viking Crown Lounge around funnel stack, 80-person conference center, cinema, 2,000 volume library, indoor/outdoor cafe, casino, two outdoor pools, two whirlpools, hairdresser, sauna, massage, jogging tracks, five-deck atrium, glass-enclosed elevators, Las Vegas-style revues and headline entertainment in 1,075-seat lounge, live music, dancing and entertainment in many spots, 10 shops, gym. Medical center.
Activities: Exercise classes, dance classes, jogging track, ping pong, skeet shooting and shuffleboard.
Youth Program: Year-round program. Children's playroom, teen nightclub. Children's menu.
Access for Disabled: Two outside and two inside cabins with wheelchair access. Travel companion required.
Rates: For seven-night cruises per person double occupancy from $1,399 to $3,799
Itinerary: From San Juan to Martinique, Barbados, Antigua, St. Maarten and St. Thomas, year-round.

NORDIC EMPRESS
Built: 1990
Registry: Liberia

Length: 692 ft.
Beam: 100 ft.
Speed: 19 knots
Officers: International
Crew: 671, International
Passengers: 1,600. Almost half are singles.
Cabins: 800. All have phone, TV, radio, individually controlled air-conditioning, private bath with shower, some with tub. Six suites have balcony.
Dining: Double-deck dining room seats 1,000. Italian, Caribbean or French cuisine. Two seatings for dinner. Indoor/outdoor cafe for breakfast, lunch and snacks.
Facilities: Nine-deck atrium with glass elevators and three-deck landscaped fountain. Las Vegas-style revues in 740-passenger showroom; entertainment and dancing in smaller lounge with floor-to-ceiling windows. Conference center, casino, pool, four whirlpools, hairdresser, boutique, sauna, massage. Viking Crown lounge becomes dance club after dark. Medical center.
Activities: Exercise and dance classes, gym, jogging track, putting green, ping pong, shuffleboard, skeet shooting, snorkeling instructions.
Youth Program: Year-round program. Children's space stationplayroom with bubbleball pool. Children's menu. Teen center.
Access for Disabled: Two outside and two inside cabins with wheelchair access. Travel companion required.
Rates: Double occupancy per person from $579 to $1,799.
Itinerary: Three- or four-nights from Miami to the Bahamas year round.

MS NORDIC PRINCE

Built: 1971
Registry: Norway
Length: 637 ft.
Beam: 80 ft.
Speed: 18 knots
Officers: Norwegian
Crew: 400, International
Passengers: 1,018
Cabins: 506. All have private bath with shower, phone, radio, individually controlled air-conditioning.
Dining: Dining room seats 580. Two seatings for dinner. Pool cafe for casual buffet breakfasts and lunches.
Facilities: Viking Crown Lounge around the funnel stack, casino, shops, hairdresser, sauna, pool, conference room for up to 580 people, dry cleaning, laundry, library, professional revues in the 580-

person show lounge; dancing, live music and other entertainment in the forward lounge. Medical center, doctor on call.

Activities: Fitness program, exercise equipment, jogging track, ping pong, basketball, shuffleboard, aerobics, golf driving and putting, skeet shooting. Golf privileges at ports of call.

Youth Program: During summer and major holidays. Children's menu.

Access for Disabled: Wheelchair access is limited. Doorways throughout the ship have lips, and public bathrooms have no facilities for the handicapped. Disabled passengers must bring their own traveling wheelchair. Must be escorted by a companion.

Rates: Double occupancy per person from $899 to $4,345.

Itinerary: Seven nights from Vancouver to Alaska during the summer. Six and seven nights from Los Angeles to the Mexican Riviera during the winter.

SONG OF AMERICA

Built: 1982

Registry: Norway

Length: 705 ft.

Beam: 93 ft.

Speed: 19 knots

Officers: Norwegian

Crew: 535, Norwegian and International

Passengers: 1,402

Cabins: 701. All have private bath with shower, phone, TV, radio, individually controlled air-conditioning; 50% of staterooms convert to double bed configuration. Some staterooms have sitting area, refrigerator, tub.

Dining: Theme dinners. Two seatings in dining room; floor-to-ceiling windows. Outdoor cafe. Several formal nights.

Facilities: Lounges including Viking Crown Lounge, casino, shopping center, twin pools, live music, dancing and entertainment, 70-person conference center, gym, hairdresser, sauna, massage. Medical center, doctor on board.

Activities: Golf putting, ping pong, dance lessons, snorkeling lessons, shuffleboard, skeet shooting. Both the Sun Deck and the Promenade Deck have unobstructed circuit of the ship. Golf priviledges at ports of call. Caribbean jazz cruise.

Youth Program: During summer and holidays.

Access for Disabled: Wheelchair access is limited. Public bathrooms have no facilities for the handicapped. Passengers must bring their own traveling wheelchair. Must be escorted by a companion.

Rates: Double occupancy per person from $1,222 to $4,349.

Itinerary: Seven nights from New York to Bermuda during the summer. Seven, 10 and 11 nights from San Juan and Miami during the winter to St. Croix, St. Kitts, Guadeloupe, St. Maarten, St. John, St. Thomas.

SONG OF NORWAY
Built: 1970
Registry: Norway
Length: 637 ft.
Beam: 80 ft.
Speed: 18 knots
Officers: Norwegian
Crew: 423, Norwegian, International
Passengers: 1,040
Cabins: 502. All have private bath and shower, air-conditioning; some have sitting area, tub, refrigerator.
Dining: Dining room seats 610, with two seatings. Casual pool cafe for buffet breakfasts and lunches. More extensive menu in the dining room.
Facilities: *Song of Norway* is the first cruise ship to have a cocktail and observation lounge cantilevered from its smokestack, now the hallmark of all Royal Caribbean vessels. Lounges, casino, hairdresser, pool, professional revues in the aft lounge, dancing and other entertainment in smaller lounge, shops, gym. Medical center.
Activities: The Promenade and Sun decks have unobstructed circuits of the ship. Exercise classes, golf driving and putting, ping pong, shuffleboard, skeet shooting, snorkeling lessons. Golf playing privileges at ports of call.
Youth Program: During the summer and major holidays.
Access for Disabled: Wheelchair access is limited, with lips in doorways throughout the ship. The Viking Crown lounge is inaccessible to wheelchairs. A travel-size wheelchair and a traveling companion are required.
Rates: For 10- to 12-night cruises per person double occupancy from $1,849 to $5,199.
Itinerary: Twelve-night Mediterranean cruises from Barcelona and Venice; 12-night cruises from Harwich to Scandinavia and Russia. Nine-, 10-, and 11-night cruises from Acapulco and San Juan through the Panama Canal during winter. Twelve-night transatlantic cruise.

SOVEREIGN OF THE SEAS
Built: 1988
Registry: Norway
Length: 874 ft.
Beam: 106 ft.
Speed: 18 knots

SOVEREIGN OF THE SEAS

Officers: Norwergian
Crew: 808, International
Passengers: 2,276
Cabins: 1,138. All have private bath with shower, phone, TV, radio, individually controlled air-conditioning. Some staterooms furnished
   with sitting area. Most have refrigerator and tub, twin beds that
   convert to doubles.
Dining: Two dining rooms, two seatings. Italian, French, Caribbean,
   and American theme dinners. Indoor/outdoor cafe for casual
   breakfasts and lunches.
Facilities: Five-deck atrium known as the Centrum, revues and headline entertainment in the two-deck lounge (seats 1,050); dancing
   and entertainment in lounge amidships, library, twin cinemas, casino, hairdresser, boutiques, two swimming pools, whirlpools, 100-
   person conference center, exercise equipment, jogging tracks,
   sauna, massage, Viking Crown Lounge seats 275. Medical center.
Activities: Exercise classes, ping pong, shuffleboard; golf program ar-

ranges playing priviledges at ports of call, video previews of ports of call and shore excursions. At Coco Cay (in the Berry Islands) passengers have beach games, sailboats, rocket rafts, and dancing to a steel drum band. Caribbean jazz cruise.

Youth Program: Year-round. Children's playroom and menu.

Access for Disabled: Ten inside cabins have wheelchair access, wide bath doors, grab bars. Travel companion required.

Rates: For seven-night cruise double occupancy per person from $1,329 to $3,845.

Itinerary: Sails from Miami year-round to San Juan, St. Thomas and Coco Cay in the Bahamas.

MS SUN VIKING

Built: 1972

Registry: Norway

Length: 563 ft.

Beam: 80 ft.

Speed: 20 knots

Officer: Norwegian

Crew: 341, Norwegian, International

Passengers: 714

Cabins: 357. All have private bath with shower, phone, radio, individually controlled air-conditioning. Some have sitting area, refrigerator, tub.

Dining: Dining room seats 610 with two seatings for dinner. Theme dinners. Informal cafe for lunch and breakfast.

Facilities: Revues in the aft lounge, dancing and other entertainment in the forward lounge, sauna, massage, swimming pool, laundry, hairdresser, Viking Crown lounge, shops, exercise equipment, Promenade and Compass deck have unobstructed circuits of the ship for fitness walks. Medical center.

Activities: Exercise classes, golf driving and putting, ping pong, shuffleboard, skeet shooting. Golf playing privileges at ports of call on golf cruises.

Youth Program: During the summer and major holidays.

Access for Disabled: Wheelchair access is limited, with lips in doorways throughout the ship. A portable wheelchair and a traveling companion are required.

Rates: Double occupancy per person from $999 to $5,895.

Itinerary: In summer, 10- to 11-nights from Vancouver to Alaska. In winter, seven- to 11-nights through the Caribbean from Miami and San Juan. A 14- to 15-night Panama Canal transit between San Juan and Los Angeles.

VIKING SERENADE
Built: 1982
Registry: Bahamas
Former Names: *Scandinavia; Stardancer*
Length: 623 ft.
Beam: 89 ft.
Speed: 18 knots
Officers: International
Crew: 612, International
Passengers: 1,512
Cabins: All have private bath with shower, phone, TV, radio, individually controlled air-conditioning. Suites have sitting area, picture window, balcony.
Dining: Two dining rooms. Two seatings for dinner. Breakfast and lunch buffet in cafe.
Facilities: Show lounge, 133-person conference center, exercise equipment, sauna, massage; observation lounge (nightclub when the sun goes down), casino, outdoor pool, shops, hairdresser. Medical center, doctor on board.
Activities: Exercise classes, ping pong, shuffleboard, parcourse stations along outdoor jogging track. Lectures on wildlife and ports of call.
Youth Program: Year-round. Teen nightclub. Children's playroom and menu.
Access for Disabled: Four inside cabins with wheelchair access. Travel companion required.
Rates: Double occupancy per person from $545 to $1,899.
Itinerary: Three-night cruises from Los Angeles to Ensenada year round; four-night cruises add a stop at Catalina Island.

ROYAL CRUISE LINE
1 Maritime Plaza, San Francisco, CA 94111
800-227-4534; 415-956-7200

MS CROWN ODYSSEY
Built: 1988
Registry: Bahamas
Length: 614 ft.
Beam: 92 ft.
Speed: 22 knots
Officers: Greek
Crew: 470, Greek
Passengers: 1,052. Singles 20%, couples 75%, families 5%.
Cabins: 526. Sixteen apartments with private verandas, 54 suites. Out-

side staterooms have bay windows, large windows, or portholes. All staterooms have music, individually controlled air-conditioning, phone for worldwide communication, twin or queen bed, private bath with shower or tub.

Dining: Restaurant is built on two levels. Two seatings. Continental cuisine with Greek specialties. Two formal evenings (men usually wear a tuxedo or a dark suit with bow tie); other evenings tend to be semiformal.

Facilities: Domed penthouse lounge with 360-degree views, six bars, five lounges, cinema/conference center, library, casino, boutiques, indoor and outdoor swimming pools, two indoor and two outdoor whirlpools, saunas, massage, gym, hairdresser, laundry and dry cleaning. Medical facility with doctor and two nurses.

Activities: Lecturers on fitness, nutrition, and self-improvement. Greek Night, passenger talent night, costume party. Gentlemen hosts for dancing and shore excursions. Big bands featured on transatlantic cruises. Classical music cruise to North Cape and Norwegian fjords. Culinary cruise from Lisbon to London.

Youth Program: Occasionally on Christmas holiday cruise.

Access for Disabled: Four cabins equipped with grip bars and wheelchair access.

Rates: Double occupancy per person range from $1,799 to $18,398.

Itinerary: Eight- through 24-night cruises of Hawaii, Mexico, Panama Canal, Caribbean, Mediterranean, British Isles, Scandinavia, and Canary Islands.

MS GOLDEN ODYSSEY

Built: 1974

Registry: Bahamas

Length: 427 ft.

Beam: 63 ft.

Speed: 22 knots

Officers: Greek

Crew: 200, Greek

Passengers: 450

Cabins: 237. All cabins have music, individually controlled air- conditioning, twin beds, phone, private bath with shower; many have tubs.

Dining: Restaurant serves 252. Two seatings. Continental cuisine. Luncheon buffet poolside.

Facilities: Three bars, three lounges, boutique, hairdresser, casino, library, theater/seminar meeting room, swimming pool, two saunas, massage. Medical facilities.

Activities: Open Promenade Deck has full circuit for fitness walks. Exercise classes, ping pong, shuffleboard. Two formal nights. Gentle-

MS STAR ODYSSEY

men hosts.
Access for Disabled: All cabins can accommodate 23" portable wheel-
    chairs. Bathroom sill is 2 1/2".
Rates: From $1,255 to $9,680 per person double occupancy.
Itinerary: Panama Canal cruises between Acapulco and Aruba or New
    Orleans; seven-day cruises from New Orleans to Caribbean; and 11-
    day Amazon cruises between Aruba and Manaus.

MS ROYAL ODYSSEY
Built: 1973
Registry: Bahamas
Former Name: *Royal Viking Sea*
Length: 676 ft.
Beam: 83 ft.
Speed: 21 knots
Officers: Greek
Crew: 410, Greek
Passengers: 750. Singles 20%, couples 75%, families 5%.

Cabins: 399. Nine penthouse apartments with private verandas, 52 suites, 267 outside staterooms, 49 single occupancy staterooms. Outside staterooms feature picture windows or portholes. All staterooms feature music, television, twin beds, individually controlled air-conditioning, private telephone for worldwide communication, shower. Some staterooms have hairdryers, tub and refrigerator.

Dining: Restaurant with single-seating dining. Outdoor cafe for casual breakfast and lunch.

Facilities: Six lounges and bars, cinema/conference room, library, casino, boutiques, outdoor swimming pool, three outdoor whirlpools, sauna, massage, hairdresser, laundry, dry cleaning. Medical facility with doctor and two nurses.

Activities: Paddle tennis, shuffleboard, ping pong, golf driving range, lectures, parcourse, walking track, gymnasium, exercise and dance classes. Gentlemen hosts for dancing and shore excursions.

Youth Program: None.

Access for Disabled: Anyone confined to a wheelchair must travel with a companion and provide 22" wheelchair. There is a step up to cabin bathrooms. No handicap-designed cabins.

Rates: Double occupancy rates per person for 12-day cruises from $4,058 to $9,688. Around-the-World cruise: $14,023 to $30,719.

Itinerary: 12- to 28-night cruises of Australia and New Zealand, Mediterranean, the Black Sea, and the Orient, including Vietnam. Around-the-World cruise (56 days) goes from Sydney to Asian ports, through the Suez Canal, to Greek ports, ending in Rome. The 1995 schedule includes Alaska, Canada and New England.

STAR ODYSSEY

Built: 1972

Registry: Bahamas

Former Names: *Royal Viking Star; Westward*

Length: 674 ft.

Beam: 83 ft.

Speed: 19 knots

Officers: Norwegian

Crew: 370, International

Passengers: 750

Cabins: 416. Each cabin has individually controlled air-conditioning, TV, radio. Seventeen suites, some of which have separate bedrooms, floor-to-ceiling windows, private balcony.

Dining: Dining room has single seating. Snack bar.

Facilities: Four lounges, show lounge, theater, casino, disco, variety of bars, shopping arcade, hairdresser, library, laundry, two heated pools, jogging tracks, fitness center with exercise equipment, two steam baths, two saunas, six massage rooms. Medical facilities, one

ROYAL VIKING QUEEN

doctor and two nurses.

Activities: Paddle tennis, golf driving, aerobics.

Youth Program: None.

Access for Disabled: All cabins have a step up into the bathroom and doors aren't wide enough for a wheelchair.

Rates: From $1,255 to $3,095 per person double occupancy.

Itinerary: Seven- to 15-nights to Alaska, New England, Canada, Caribbean and transcanal. In 1995 will cruise the Amazon, the Mediterranean, and Africa.

ROYAL VIKING LINE

95 Merrick Way, Coral Gables, FL 33134
800-422-8000; 305-447-9660

ROYAL VIKING QUEEN

Built: 1992
Registry: Bahamas

Length: 438 ft.

Beam: 62 ft.

Speed: 19 knots

Officers: Norwegian

Crew: 135, Scandinavian, International

Passengers: 212

Cabins: 106. All staterooms are outside suites and have private bath with shower and hairdryer, air-conditioning, TV, VCR, radio, phone, walk-in closet, refrigerator, twin beds that convert into a queen, large window, sitting area; some with veranda.

Dining: Restaurant seats 212. Single open seating. Cafe for casual breakfasts and luncheons.

Facilities: Lounge doubles as a theater or nightclub. Piano bar, casino, gym, whirlpools, saunas, steam rooms, massage, swimming pool, hairdresser, shops, library, TV satellite link-up and live teleconferencing, laundry. Medical facilities.

Activities: Exercise classes, dance lessons, lectures on ports by noted experts. Oceanographer Jean-Michel Cousteau, for example, is the guide for the 71-day trip circling South America.

Youth Program: None.

Access for Disabled: Cabins with wheelchair access. Travel companion required.

Rates: Double occupancy per person from $7,995 to $31,390.

Itinerary: Nine- through 20-day cruises to South Pacific, the Orient and Southeast Asia, Africa, Scandinavia, Mediterranean, South America and the Caribbean.

ROYAL VIKING SUN

Built: 1988

Registry: Bahamas

Length: 673 ft.

Beam: 95 ft.

Speed: 21 knots

Officers: Norwegian

Crew: 300, Scandinavian, International

Passengers: 740

Cabins: 370. Mostly outside. All have private bath with shower and hairdryer, TV, VCR, radio, phone, air-conditioning, some with refrigerator, bar, tub.

Dining: Dining room seats 760. Continental cuisine featuring traditional and nouvelle dishes. One seating. Alternative dining in grill. Cafe for casual dining.

Facilities: Show lounge, piano lounge, theater, casino, two outdoor pools, two saunas, whirlpool, massage, library, conference facilities, hairdresser, shops. Medical facilities.

Activities: Dance and golf lessons, aerobics, ping pong, wrap-around promenade deck, enrichment lectures given by authors, political leaders and journalists. Gentlemen hosts for dancing and bridge. World Affairs program offered in cooperation with Georgetown University.

Youth Program: None.

Access for Disabled: Ramp access, cabins with wheelchair access, wide bathroom doors, grab bars.

Rates: Double occupancy per person from $2,795 to $135,150.

Itinerary: World cruises of 102 days from San Francisco to London; and nine- to 16-day cruises of Scandinavia, Europe and the Mediterranean.

ST. LAWRENCE CRUISE LINES

253 Ontario St., Kingston, Ontario, Canada K7L 2Z4
800-267-7868; 613-549-8091

MV CANADIAN EMPRESS

Built: 1981

Registry: Canada

Length: 108 ft.

Beam: 30 ft.

Speed: 12 knots

Officers: Canadian

Crew: 14, Canadian

Passengers: 64. Singles 20%, couples 80%, mostly from U.S. and Canada.

Cabins: 32. All are outside with screened windows that open. Most are twin singles, some doubles; climate-controlled.

Dining: Grand Salon, open seating, two sittings. For dinner, men usually wear sport jacket.

Facilities: Dining room doubles as a lounge with entertainment, library, gift shop. Iron and ironing board available.

Activities: Entertainment nightly, skeet shooting, kite flying, shuffleboard, evening dance, historical commentary en route. Visits to castles, museums, forts, historic villages; tours of Ottawa, Montreal and Quebec City.

Youth Program: None. Minimum age for cruising is 12.

Access for Disabled: Limited.

Rates: Per person double occupancy from $768 to $1,188 including shore excursions.

Itinerary: This is a replica of a steamboat with four- and five-night cruises of St. Lawrence, Ottawa and Saguenay Rivers in Canada. Boarding ports include Kingston, Ottawa, Montreal and Quebec City.

SCHOONER J. & E. RIGGIN
Box 571, Rockland, ME 04841
800-869-0604

J. & E. RIGGIN
Built: 1927 for oyster dredging; rebuilt 1977
Registry: United States
Length: 90 ft.
Beam: 23 ft.
Speed: No inboard engine, 16-ft. diesel-powered yawl for maneuvering.
Crew: 5
Passengers: 26. Minimum age is 16.
Cabins: Ten two-berth and two triple cabins have sink with cold running water, window that can be opened. Toilets and hot showers above deck are shared.
Dining: Maine home-cooking on wood cook stove for family-style in the galley or on deck.
Facilities: This schooner is designated as a National Historic Landmark. Beer and liquor may be brought aboard.
Activities: Guests help crew or take a turn at the wheel. Yawlboat to explore, peapod for a row, shore for steamed lobster.
Rates: Three- to six-day cruises $320 to $615 per person.
Itinerary: Penobscot and Blue Hill Bay area of the Maine Coast.

SEABOURN CRUISE LINE
55 Francisco St., San Francisco, CA 94133
800-929-9595; 415-391-7444

SEABOURN PRIDE and SEABOURN SPIRIT
Built: 1988, 1989
Registry: Norway
Length: 439 ft.
Beam: 63 ft.
Speed: 18 knots
Officers: Norwegian
Crew: 140, European
Passengers: 204. Singles 10%, couples 90%.
Cabins: 100. All are outside suites with air-conditioning, sitting area, stocked bar/refrigerator, walk-in closets, picture window, large marble private bath and shower, hairdryer, TV, VCR, CD, radio, phone.

Dining: Restaurant seating is not assigned; passengers can dine at any time during meal hours. International cuisine. Two formal evenings each week. Gentlemen are expected to wear a jacket and tie on other nights. Cafe for informal breakfast and lunch.

Facilities: Three bars, two entertainment lounges, piano bar, small casino, conference facilities, outdoor pool, two saunas, three whirlpools, steamroom, massage, hairdresser, shops, full-service laundry and laundromat, library, and underwater viewing room has a window that looks through the bottom of the ship. Medical facilities with doctor on call.

Activities: On most evenings there is cabaret entertainment or local entertainment brought aboard at ports. American Contract Bridge instructor on board all cruises. Lectures on subjects ranging from Spanish treasure fleets to art appreciation. Deck sports, water sports, exercise equipment and classes, health and beauty treatments (herbal wraps, facials), dancing, ping pong, shuffleboard, skeet shooting. Platform in stern lowers for use of two tenders, a glass-bottom boat, a zodiac, sailboats, windsurfers and paddleboats. Snorkels and masks are provided. Port excursions include sightseeing in major cities, as well as a visit to the village of former head-hunters and a visit to an orangutan sanctuary on Borneo.

Youth Program: None.

Access for Disabled: Three suites have wheelchair access. All elevators and public areas are accessible. Travel companion required. Tenders used to ferry passengers ashore can pose difficulties.

Rates: Double occupancy per person from $3,965 to $18,525. No tipping. Rates include air from North America, one night in a hotel pre-cruise, some port excursions.

Itinerary: *Seabourn Pride*: Seven- through 14-day cruises of northeast Canada, the Caribbean, Mexico, the Panama Canal, South America, Europe and Scandinavia. *Seabourn Spirit*: Fourteen- to 21-day cruises of the Mediterranean, Black Sea, Red Sea, Southeast Asia and the Orient, including Vietnam. One 14-day Asian cruise goes to unusual ports in Sumatra, Java, Sulawesi and Borneo, while another goes from Bali to Komodo, Flores Islands, Malaysia and Singapore.

SEA CLOUD CRUISES See SPECIAL EXPEDITIONS

SEAWIND CRUISE LINE
1750 Coral Way, Miami, FL 33145
800-258-8006; 305-854-7800

TSS SEAWIND CROWN

Built: 1961
Registry: Panama
Former Name: *Vasco de Gama*
Length: 642 ft.
Beam: 81 ft.
Speed: 17 knots
Officers: Greek, Portuguese
Crew: 300, International
Passengers: 624
Cabins: 312. Air-conditioned, each has private bath with shower and
    hairdryer, TV, music, phone, mini-refrigerator; some have picture
    window and tub. Twenty suites have sitting room with sofa bed.
    Rooms for nonsmokers.
Dining: Restaurant seats 420. Two seatings for dinner. Cuisine incorpo-
    rates fresh Caribbean seafood and spices into continental meals.
    Themes each night includes French, Spanish, Mediterranean and
    Caribbean. Tavern for light meals.
Facilities: Five bars and lounges, show lounge, cinema, casino, two
    outdoor pools, whirlpool, sauna massage, meeting and conference
    rooms, library, hairdresser, shops, laundry. Medical facilities.
Activities: Aerobics, jogging track, volleyball, squash, ping pong, gym.
Youth Program: During major holidays and summer months. Chil-
    dren's playroom.
Access for Disabled: Two outside cabins with wheelchair access.
    Travel companion required. Guide dog allowed.
Rates: Double occupancy per person from $895 to $3,095, including
    airfare from gateway cities.
Itinerary: Seven-day cruises of the Caribbean, departing from Aruba
    to Curacao, Grenada, Barbados and St. Lucia.

SEVEN SEAS CRUISE LINE

333 Market St., Suite 2600, San Francisco, CA 94105
800-285-1835; 415-905-6000

MS HANSEATIC

Built: 1992
Registry: Bahamas
Length: 403 ft.
Beam: 59 ft.
Speed: 17 knots
Officers: German
Crew: 125, European
Passengers: 170, from Europe and North America.

Cabins: 90. Staterooms all with outside views. Each stateroom features a separate sitting area, bathroom with tub/shower, hairdryer, individual temperature control, TV, radio, refrigerator stocked with non-alcoholic beverages. There are four deluxe two-room suites that include a walk-in closet.

Dining: Continental cuisine. Single open seating dining allows you to be seated when, where and with whom you choose.

Facilities: Laundry, library, beauty services, fitness center, exercise equipment, sauna, whirlpool, massage, outdoor swimming pool and an observation room where you can follow the ship's course. There is an open bridge visitation policy. Medical facilities.

Activities: Cabaret-style entertainment, orchestra, documentary and feature films, lecture program, four tenders and 14 zodiacs enable landing on remote shores.

Access for Disabled: Yes.

Rates: Per diem including airfare range from $400 to $1,100. Special offers: Early booking discount of $500 per person. Most shore excursions are complimentary. No tipping.

Itinerary: Early summer, 13- 15-day cruises to North Polar regions, including Orkney Islands, Faeroe Islands, Vestmannaeyjar Islands, Iceland, Greenland, Norway, Finland, Sweden, Russia, Poland, Estonia, and Spitsbergen. (Ship has 1A1 Ice Safety Classification.) A 28-day cruise through the Northwest Passage goes from Greenland through the ice fields of Disko Bay to Baffin Bay, Resolute Bay, Barrow Strait, Beaufort Sea, Barrow, Point Hope, Nome and Anchorage, Alaska. An 11-day cruise goes from Anchorage to Vancouver, and a 13-day cruise from Vancouver to Acapulco. From October through December, 15- to 19-day cruises go through the Panama Canal to the San Blas Islands, Guatemala, Belize, Key West, Dominican Republic, British Virgin Islands, St. Barts, Barbados, Grenada, Trinidad, the Orinoco River and the Coast of Venezuela, Galapagos Island, Peru, the Chilean Fjords, the Strait of Magellan, Patagonia, Argentina, Falkland Islands to Antarctica. March cruises include South Africa, Madagascar and the Seychelles. In April, the ship cruises the Red Sea to Egypt, the Suez Canal and Greece.

MS SONG OF FLOWER

Built: 1974 as a container ship; rebuilt 1986 as cruise ship
Registry: Norway
Former Names: *Explorer; Begonia*
Length: 407 ft.
Beam: 52 ft.
Speed: 14 knots
Officers: Norwegian
Crew: 144, European

Passengers: 172

Cabins: 98. All have outside view, air-conditioning, private bath with shower and hairdryer, TV, VCR, radio, phone, refrigerator and complimentary mini-bar; many with picture window. Some cabins include convertible sofa bed in sitting area. Twenty suites, 10 with private veranda. Cabins for nonsmokers. Lower grade cabins are only half the size of top grades. The top suites are two cabins put together.

Dining: Continental cuisine, single seating. Passengers eat when they choose, and can sit where they like every night. All bar, cabin and restaurant drinks are free with exception of top-priced vintage wines.

Facilities: Nightclub with marble dance floor, show lounge, observation lounge, hairdresser, casino, health club, outdoor swimming pool, whirlpool, library with 2,000 books and 300 videos. Medical clinic with doctor and nurse.

Activties: Aerobics classes, deck sports including putting green and driving range, snorkeling equipment, dance lessons. A 120-passenger excursion vessel, the "Tiny Flower," with bow landing capabilities for direct access to remote shores. Open bridge policy.

Youth Program: None. Children under 12 not accepted.

Access for Disabled: Yes.

Rates: $2,995 to $8,775. No tipping.

Itinerary: Seven- through 14-day cruises off-the-beaten-path destinations of southeast Asia, the Red Sea, the Mediterranean, British Isles, Scandinavia and northern Europe.

SHERATON NILE CRUISES

Ahmed Packa St. 4, Garden City, Cairo EG

800-325-3535

HS ANNI; HS ATON; HS HOPT; HS TUT

Built: 1970

Length: 72 ft.

Beam: 36 ft.

Speed: 18 knots

Officers: Egyptian

Crew: 115, Egyptian

Passengers: 150.

Cabins: Air-conditioning, shower, radio, phone and picture window. Two to eight suites. Cabins for nonsmokers.

Dining: International and oriental cuisine.

Facilities: Lounge/bar doubles as disco, outdoor pool, ping pong, hairdresser, shops, library. Medical facilities.

Activities: Shore excursions.
Rates: For seven-day cruise $2,016 for cabin.
Itinerary: Three-, four- and seven between Luxor and Aswan on the
    Nile River.

SILVERSEA CRUISES
110 E. Broward Blvd., Ft. Lauderdale, FL 33301
800-722-6655; 305-522-4477
MV SILVER CLOUD and MV SILVER WIND
Built: 1994
Registry: Italy
Length: 514 ft.
Beam: 70 ft.
Speed: 19 knots
Officers: Italian
Crew: 185, European
Passengers: 296
Cabins: 148. All are outside suites and have air-conditioning, walk-in
    closet, sitting area, private bath with shower and hairdryer, refrig-
    erator, TV, VCR, direct dial phone; some with verandas. Five suites
    have two bedrooms.
Facilities: Observation lounge, show lounge, casino, two saunas with
    verandas, thalassotherapy and massage facilities, boutique, hair-
    dresser, fitness center, library, outdoor pool, two whirlpools, meet-
    ing room with computers, on-board film developing. Medical
    facility with doctor, nurse.
Activities: Guest lecturers, language courses, deck games, water-
    sports, aerobic classes, bridge instruction and tournaments, dance
    bands, cabaret shows, folkloric performances. Open bridge.
Youth Program: Yes.
Access for Disabled: Two suites. Guests requiring wheelchair must
    provide their own collapsible wheelchair.
Rates: For seven- to 14-day cruises from $4,195 to $16,195 per person
    double occupancy. Includes beverages throughout the ship, shore
    events, airfare from major U.S. and Canadian cities, pre-cruise ho-
    tels, all gratuities.
Itinerary: Mostly seven- to 14-day cruises of the Mediterranean, west-
    ern Europe, the Baltic, Canada, Colonial America, South America,
    Caribbean, transpanama, Africa, Seychelles. Several 20- to 44-day
    cruises.

SPECIAL EXPEDITIONS

720 5th Ave., New York, NY 10019
800-762-0003; 212-765-7740

CALEDONIAN STAR

Built: 1966
Registry: Bahamas
Former Name: *North Star*
Length: 293 ft.
Beam: 46 ft.
Speed: 12 knots
Officers: Scandinavian
Crew: 60, International
Passengers: 110. Almost all couples.
Cabins: 68. All are outside with air-conditioning, private bath with shower, TV, VCR, radio, refrigerator. Two suites. Cabins for non-smokers. Most cabins have twin beds, one of which folds into a sofa.
Dining: International cuisine.
Facilities: This expedition cruiser has a restaurant, two lounges, bar, lecture, theater, library, pool, hairdresser, shop, laundry. Medical facilities with physician.
Activities: Briefings about ports of call, water sports, snorkeling, diving. Zodiac shore excursions are limited to small groups, accompanied by guide.
Rates: Seychelles cruise from $4,800 to $7,300; Indonesian archipelagoes cruise from $6,780 to $9,100; Bali cruise from $5,100 to $7,600; 22-day Shanghai cruise from $7,620 to $11,620; 18-day Shanghai cruise from $6,360 to $9,610.
Itinerary: Fifteen-day cruises of the Seychelles and Comoros islands and Madagascar; 20-day cruises of Indonesian and Malaysian archipelagoes from Singapore to Bali; 16-day cruises from Bali to islands of Indonesia and Malaysia; 22-day cruises from Saigon to Shanghai exploring the coastline and islands of Vietnam, Hong Kong and China; 18-day cruises from Shanghai to the Russian Far East.

MS POLARIS

Built: 1960
Registry: Bahamas
Length: 238 ft.
Beam: 43 ft.
Officers: Swedish
Crew: 44, Filipino, Swedish
Passengers: 80
Cabins: 41. All outside cabins with twin beds, private bath with

shower, individual climate control, and music. The cabins are tiny, but have large picture windows for views of the sea.

Dining: Many meals are German and Scandinavian. Meals are served in single open seating.

Facilities: Small lounge/bar, library, sauna, gift shop, hairdresser, full-service laundry. Small hospital with doctor on board.

Activities: Schedules and excursions are subject to change. Sometimes passengers may be called on to decide whether the ship should follow a pod of whales or head for nearby fishing village. Lectures given by naturalists and historians on the wildlife and culture of the ports of call. No organized entertainment on board. Occasionally local performers play or sing in the lounge. Glass-bottom boat for underwater viewing. Zodiac landing craft, snorkeling. Natural history staff with guidance ashore and traditional recap at night of the day's events.

Children's Program: None.

Access for Disabled: Not recommended for the disabled or for those in poor health.

Rates: Amazon and Orinoco River cruise from $3,200 to $10,010; Costa Rica, Panama and Belize cruises from $3,990 to $7,800; Mayan coast cruise from $2,980 to $4,780; coastal Iberia cruise from $6,360 to $10,140; Isles of Britain cruise from $5,400 to $8,640; Estonia cruise from $6,330 to $9,570; Arctic Circle cruises from $4,380 to $9,570; Russia cruises from $9,600 to $14,800.

Itinerary: Sixteen-day cruise of the Amazon from Belem, Brazil to Iquitos, Peru; nine-day cruise of the Upper Amazon; nine-day cruise of the Orinoco River and Canaima; 12-day cruise of Costa Rica and Panama; 13-day cruise from Belize including a transit of the Panama Canal; nine-day cruise of the Mayan Coast; 16-day cruise of Coastal Iberia, France and Britain; 13-day cruise of the Isles of Britain and Ireland; 15-day cruise of Estonia, Latvia, Lithuania and St. Petersburg; 16-day cruise north of the Arctic Circle; 12-day cruise of Arctic Norway and Spitsbergen; 24-day cruise of Russia, Baltic and Scandinavia from St. Peterburg to Bergen, Norway, exploring 10 countries.

MV SEA BIRD and MV SEA LION

Built: 1981, 1982
Registry: United States
Length: 152 ft.
Beam: 31 ft.
Speed: 12 knots
Officers: American
Crew: 21, American
Passengers: 70

Cabins: 36. All are outside, have individually controlled air- conditioning, private bath with shower, hairdryer, radio, lower beds. The cabins are very small.

Dining: Single open seating.

Facilities: Open bridge policy, observation lounge, full-service laundry. A doctor is on board on the Baja cruise; otherwise, the ship is never far from land for any needed medical aid.

Activities: Lectures. Naturalist guides for ashore trips, snorkeling, barbecues, slide shows, search for finback and blue whales, dolphins, and birds, swim among sea lions. Zodiac craft for shore excursions. Bow ramp allows for direct access onto beaches.

Access for Disabled: Not recommended for the disabled or for those in poor health.

Rates: Alaskan cruise from $3,130 to $4,360; Columbia River cruise from $1,890 to $$2,820; San Juan Island cruise from $1,350 to $2,000; California cruise from $730 to $2,490; Sea of Cortez and Baja cruises from $2,170 to $4,800 (includes one night hotel in La Paz).

Itinerary: Ten-day cruise of Alaska's Inside Passage, including Glacier Bay, Tracy Arm; seven-day cruise along the Columbia and Snake rivers from Oregon to Hells Canyon, Idaho; six-day cruise of San Juan islands with stops in Vancouver, Victoria and Seattle; four and nine-day cruise of San Francisco Bay and Sacramento Delta; nine- to 12-day whale watch cruise in Baja, California and Sea of Cortez

SY SEA CLOUD

Built: 1931

Registry: Malta

Former Name: *Hussar*

Length: 316 ft.

Beam: 49 ft.

Speed: 12 knots

Officers: International

Crew: 65, International

Passengers: 60

Cabins: 47. All staterooms (including 11 fully-restored original cabins) are outside with private bath and shower. Two Owner's Suites with antiques, double bed, bathtub and shower. Cabins are for non-smokers.

Facilities: Originally the private yacht of Marjorie Merriweather Post and E.F. Hutton, the *Sea Cloud* has an old-fashioned elegance. Has 4 masts and 29 sails, marble fireplaces, two bars, antique furnishings. Medical facilities.

Activities: Water sports, lectures. Several guides so tour groups are divided according to interests.

Rates: Ten-day cruise from $5,370 to $9,350; 11-day cruise from $5,200 to $8,900.

Itinerary: Ten-day cruise of the Caribbean from St. Lucia to Grenada, Dominica, Tobago, Marie-Galante; 11-day cruise of the Mediterranean including Sicily and Malta. Six-day cruises of Pacific Northwest from Seattle to Vancouver.

STAR CLIPPER
4101 Salzedo Ave., Coral Gables, FL 33146
800-442-0551; 305-442-0550

STAR FLYER and STAR CLIPPER
Built: 1991
Registry: Luxembourg
Length: 360 ft.
Beam: 48 ft.
Speed: 17 knots
Officers: Scandinavian, European, American
Crew: 60, Scandinavian, European, American
Passengers: 180. Almost all couples.
Cabins: The top five catagories have twin beds which will convert into doubles. Cabins in the lowest category have upper and lower berths. All have ocean views, private bath with shower and hairdryer, air-conditioning, TV.
Dining: Open seating. International cuisine.
Facilities: A modern clipper sailing ship. Restaurant/conference room, two pools, library, piano bar, boutique, laundry. Medical facilities.
Activities: Passengers are encouraged to view themselves as shipmates. Each morning is "Cap'n's Storytime" when the ship's Master tells his company what's in store that day. Snorkeling gear is issued to all on the first day, and a fleet of zodiacs carry passengers and windsurfing boards to remote coves. Local bands provide music for dances. Passengers can help hoist the sails or sit and watch the experts.
Youth Program: None.
Access for Disabled: These ships are not for anybody who isn't reasonably fit and active.
Rates: From $745 to $2,095 for six- and seven-day cruises; $1,745 to $2,945 for 10 days. 50% off for second person.
Itinerary: *Star Flyer* cruises the Caribbean. The *Star Clipper* cruises the Mediterranean out of Cannes and Monte Carlo during the summer, reverting to seven-day Caribbean itineraries in the winter out of St. Maarten. Transatlantic repositioning cruises.

STARLAURO CRUISES

420 Fifth Ave., New York, NY 10018
800-666-9333; 212-764-4800

MV ACHILLE LAURO

Built: 1947
Registry: Italy
Length: 642 ft.
Width: 82 ft.
Officers: Italian
Passengers: 788.
Cabins: 387.
Facilities: Two pools, casino, gym, theatre.
Rates: For seven nights from $1,170 to $2,560.
Itinerary: Seven, 11, and 14-night cruises in the Mediterranean.

SUN LINE CRUISES

1 Rockefeller Plaza, New York, NY 10020
800-468-6400; 212-397-6400

MS STELLA MARIS

Built: 1960
Registry: Greece
Former Name: *Bremerhaven*
Length: 300 ft.
Beam: 45 ft.
Speed: 15 knots
Officers: Greek
Crew: 110, Greek
Passengers: 180. Mostly retired.
Cabins: 93. Mostly outside. All have private bath with shower, air-con-
    ditioning, radio. Deluxe cabins have sitting area, picture window
    and combination tub/shower.
Dining: Dining room seats 164. International cuisine with Greek spe-
    cialties.
Facilities: Lounge, cabaret, theater, boutique, outdoor pool, hair-
    dresser, laundry. Medical facilities.
Activities: Nightly dancing with live orchestra, feature films, jogging,
    shuffleboard, skeet shooting, paddle tennis, ping pong, exercise
    classes, dance lessons, lectures on ports of call.
Youth Program: None.
Access for Disabled: No elevators.
Rates: Double occupancy per person from $1,195 to $2,140.
Itinerary: Seven-day cruises in the Mediterranean during the spring,

summer and fall; seven- to 14-day cruises in the Caribbean in winter.

MS STELLA OCEANIS

Built: 1965
Registry: Greece
Former Name: *Aphrodite*
Length: 350 ft.
Beam: 53 ft.
Speed: 16 knots
Officers: Greek
Crew: 140, Greek
Passengers: 300
Cabins: 159. Most are outside. All have private bath with shower or combination tub/shower, air-conditioning, radio. Six suites have additional sitting area.
Dining: Dining room seats 200. Two seatings for dinner. International menu featuring Greek specialties.
Facilities: Lounge with entertainment and dancing, bars, outdoor pool, casino, duty free boutique, hairdresser, meeting room, library, laundry. Medical facilities with doctor and nurse.
Activities: Exercise classes, shuffleboard, paddle tennis, ping pong, skeet shooting, jogging, dance lessons. Greek crew performs native songs and dances on Greek Night.
Youth Program: None.
Access for Disabled: Not recommended for wheelchairs.
Rates: Double occupancy per person from $500 to $1,360.
Itinerary: Three- and four-day cruises around the Greek Isles during spring, summer and fall.

TSS STELLA SOLARIS

Built: 1973
Registry: Greece
Former Name: *Camboge*
Length: 544 ft.
Beam: 72 ft.
Speed: 22 knots
Officers: Greek
Crew: 320, Greek
Passengers: 620
Cabins: All have private bath with shower or combination tub/shower, air-conditioning, radio, phone; 66 suites have sitting area, picture window, TV.
Dining: Dining room seats 450; two seatings for dinner. Continental cuisine featuring Greek specialties. One formal evening is held on

the seven-day cruises, three cruises lasting longer than 12 days. Men are requested to wear a jacket and tie for all "informal" dinners.

Facilities: Bars, lounges featuring entertainment and dancing, piano, bar, disco, theater, casino, two outdoor pools, sauna, massage, hairdresser, shops, library, meeting room, laundry. Medical facilities with doctor and nurse.

Activities: Dance lessons, ping pong, skeet shooting, shuffleboard. There is an unobstructed circuit of the ship; 7 laps equal 1 mile. Spanish lessons. Lectures on topics related to ports of call. Local performers often brought on board to perform. Greek night includes dancing, ethnic food, bouzouki music, toasts with ouzo or wine. Caribbean cruises have excursions to Mayan ruins.

Youth Program: Children's services on some cruises.

Access for Disabled: Guide dogs allowed. Access for the disabled is limited. Entrances to cabins or cabin bathrooms have raised thresholds. The width of the door into the bathroom is 21 1/2". Any passenger confined to a wheelchair must be accompanied by an able-bodied passenger.

Rates: Double occupancy per person for seven- to 15-day cruises is from $1,155 to $8,310; for 28-day Amazon cruise is $3,435 to $5,350, including free air from gateway cities.

Itinerary: Seven-day to 15-day cruises of the Mediterranean, South America, the Caribbean, the Panama Canal and Amazon. The Christmas/New Year's cruise is a 14-day loop out of Fort Lauderdale to Caribbean. In February and March, a 12-day Panama Canal from Galveston to Ocho Rios, Cristobel, the San Blas Islands, Port Limon, Cozumel and Playa del Carmen. Repositioning cruises between Ft. Lauderdale and Greece in spring and autumn. A seven-day Black Sea cruise to Greece, Turkey, Bulgaria, Ukraine and Romania.

SVALBARD See EUROCRUISES

SWAN HELLENIC CRUISES

c/o Esplanade Tours, 581 Boylston St., Boston, MA 02116
800-426-5492; 617-266-7465

NILE MONARCH
Built: 1991
Registry: Egypt
Length: 235 ft.
Beam: 36 ft.

Speed: 20 knots
Officers: Egyptian
Crew: Egyptian
Passengers: 74
Cabins: 40. All are outside. Twin cabins all have individually control-
    led air-conditioning, TV, VCR, radio, phone, minifridge, private
    bath with shower and hairdryer. Four suites with combo
    tub/shower.
Dining: Main restaurant serves international cuisine and seats 80.
    Open seating.
Facilities: Lounge, swimming pool, library, hairdresser, laundry, shop.
    Clinic, British doctor on board.
Activities: Guest lecturers. Special ornithological cruises link Egyptian
    history with contemporary bird life. Ornithologists with experience
    of Middle Eastern birds work along with Egyptology lecturer.
Youth Program: None.
Rates: Twelve-day cruises from $3,625 to $4,375; 18- to 20-day cruises
    from $4,980 to $8,240 double occupancy per person. Cost includes
    round trip airfare from gateway cities, two nights at hotel in Lon-
    don, all excursions and gratuities.
Itinerary: Seventeen-day cruises between Cairo and Aswan with the
    exception of December and January, when low water levels make
    cruising along the lower Nile uncertain. At this time, ship takes 15-
    day cruises between Aswan and Luxor and as far as Nag Hamadi.
    Special excursion to Lake Qaran in the Fayoum for birding cruise.

MTS ORPHEUS

Built: 1969, rebuilt 1987
Registry: Greece
Length: 264 ft.
Beam: 50 ft.
Speed: 14 knots
Officers: Greek
Crew: 110, Greek
Passengers: 288
Cabins: 166. All have air-conditioning, radio, phone, private bath with
    shower or tub. Most have two lowers, some with upper and lower.
    Eight suites.
Dining: Greek and international cuisine. Open single seating. No
    smoking. Buffet-style meals are in the tavern, and more formal
    luncheon and dinner in the restaurant. Two dressy nights.
Facilities: Lounge with dancing, two bars, shops, casino, library, bou-
    tique, outdoor pool, hairdresser, laundry. Medical facility.
Activities: Very little traditional cruise entertainment. Lectures. Shore
    excursions to sites of early civilization. Greek night by crew. Spe-

cial interest cruises on ornithology, marine biology, volcanology and astronomy.

Access for Disabled: Not accessible.

Rates: Fourteen-day cruises from $3,590 to $7,935 per person double occupancy. Rates include airfare from gateway cities, two night hotel accommodation, most shore excursions and all gratuities.

Itinerary: Cruises in the West and East Mediterranean, Red Sea, Aegean through the Bosphorus into the Black Sea mostly of two week's duration. Two one-week cruises can also be linked with adjacent itineraries to form two, three, or four week holidays.

REMBRANDT VAN RIJN

Built: 1985

Registry: Netherlands

Length: 390 ft.

Beam: 34 ft.

Speed: 25 knots

Officers: European

Crew: European

Passengers: 90. For passengers over age 75, a medical certificate is required from doctor stating that you are fit enough to undertake the cruise.

Cabins: Staterooms have individually controlled air-conditioning, twin beds, TV, private bath with shower. Some cabins with VCR radio, phone, hairdryer. No smoking.

Dining: Main dining room seats 90. Single open seating.

Facilities: Bar and lounge, small shop and library.

Activities: Guest lecturers, including botanist on cruises through bulb fields. Excursions accompanied by guides.

Youth Program: None.

Access for Disabled: Not accessible.

Rates: Eight- to 10-day cruises from $2,065 to $2,685 and 13- to 18-day cruises from $3,795 to $5,945 per person double occupancy, including airfare, shore excursions, two nights hotel and gratuities.

Itinerary: Eight- and 10-day cruises of Holland from Amsterdam; 13-day Rhine-Mosel cruise between Arnhem and Basel; 13- to 18-day cruises of the Rhine, Mosel, Main and Danube Rivers; 16-day Danube cruise between Budapest and Nuremberg; 16- to- 18-day Main to Danube cruise including Rhine, Main and Danube Canal.

TALL SHIP ADVENTURES

1010 S. Joliet St., Aurora, CO 80012

800-662-0090; 303-341-0335

SV *SIR FRANCIS DRAKE*
Built: 1917
Registry: Honduras
Former Name: *Godewind*
Length: 165 ft.
Beam: 23 ft.
Speed: 9 knots; sails whenever possible
Officers: International
Crew: 14, International
Passengers: 28. Singles 5%, couples 90%, families 5%.
Cabins: 14. Small, air-conditioned, most with upper and lower berths, some with side-by-side or double bed. Sailboat-type shower.
Dining: Family-style in salon. No dressy clothes needed.
Facilities: Salon is only public room, used for dining, TV, VCR, bar, socializing. Most time is spent on deck or shore. Open bridge. Library.
Activities: This is an authentic tall sailing ship, a three-masted schooner, offering a non-structured cruising experience. Sunfish, snorkeling equipment, picnics, barbecue, water sports. Guests may participate in sailing the ship, but are not obligated.
Youth Program: None.
Access for Disabled: Not accessible.
Rates: Double occupancy rates per person from $420 to $1,395.
Itinerary: Three- to seven-day cruises leaving from St. Thomas to ports in the U.S. and British Virgin Islands.

TALL SHIP FRIENDS
Hammer Landstr. 220, D-20537, Hamburg 73, Germany
49 40 678-9000; 49 40 219-4619

SEDOV
Built: 1921; rebuilt 1979
Registry: Russia
Former Names: *Magdalene Vinnen, Kommodore Johnson*
Length: 386 ft.
Officers and Crew: 75, Russian
Trainees: 150
Passengers: Passengers can be men or women, must be at least 15 years old, in good health and capable of understanding simple commands in English. Some 3,000 people from ages 15 to 79 have sailed with Tall Ship Friends.
Cabins: Accommodations are with trainees in pullman berths. Shared facilities.
Dining: Dining room serves four meals per day.
Facilities: This is the world's largest old windjammer with more than

45,000 square feet of sail. She is a four-masted barque with 178 ft. high masts. The ship is a training vessel for the Russian merchant marine service, and all passengers sail as trainees. Medical facilities with doctor on board.

Activities: Passengers are joint-sailors, undergoing watches and other shipboard routines just as the trainees do; however, working aloft in the rigging is voluntary.

Rates: For six-day cruise from $776 to $1,136 per person.

Itinerary: Five- to seven-day cruises from wherever the ship is in port, sometimes in the Baltic Sea, sometimes in tall ship regattas, sometimes rounding Cape Horn.

Note: Other tall ships are also available for booking.

TRANSOCEAN See MARQUEST

TRAVERSE TALL SHIP COMPANY

13390 W. Bay Shore Dr., Traverse City, MI 49684
800-678-0383; 616-941-2000

SV MANITOU

Built: 1975
Registry: France
Length: 114 ft.
Beam: 22 ft.
Speed: Sail power
Crew: American
Passengers: 24.
Cabins: 12. The cabins have two bunks, washbasins. Common heads and showers on deck level. No maid service. No smoking below deck.

Dining: Meals served family-style in main cabin or as buffet on deck.

Facilities: This tall ship is a traditional two-masted gaff-rigged topsail schooner. Bring soft luggage only for easy storage, casual clothes and foul-weather gear.

Activities: The itinerary and the activities are decided by the weather. You may help crew if you wish. Sailboards, sea kayaks and dingy are on board. Hiking and beachcombing.

Youth Program: None. Minimum age for passengers is 16.

Rates: Per person double occupancy from $375 to $899.

Itinerary: Three- or six-day cruises from Northport, Michigan through the waters and islands of Lake Michigan and Lake Huron. No established route; depending on wind, ports may include Manitou Islands in the Sleeping Bear Dunes National Lakeshore, Harbor

Springs, Beaver Island, Mackinac.

WESTOVER BOAT COMPANY
c/o Fenwick's, 900 4th Ave., Seattle, WA 98164
800-243-6244; 206-382-1262

MV BARKIS and MV PEGGOTTY
Built: 1986
Registry: England
Length: 75 ft.
Beam: 11 ft.
Speed: 8 knots
Officers: English
Crew: 4, English
Passengers: 10. Singles, 5%, couples 80%,, families 15%.
Cabins: 5. All have twin beds, private bath with shower, window.
Dining: Family style. International cuisine with English specialties.
Facilities: The *Barkis* and the *Peggotty*, named after characters in Dickens' *David Copperfield*, travel in tandem, one ship containing staterooms, the other having the salon, galley and dining room.
Activities: Minibus for land excursions. Bicycles available.
Youth Program: None. Children under age 10 not allowed unless charter.
Access for Disabled: Not recommended because of stairs.
Rates: Double occupancy per person from $1,995 to $2,350.
Itinerary: Six-day cruises through the inland waterways of England, leaving from Brampton, England.

WINDJAMMER BAREFOOT CRUISES
P.O. Box 120, Miami Beach, FL 33119-0120
800-327-2600; 305-543-7447

MV AMAZING GRACE
Built: 1955
Registry: Honduras
Former Name: *Pharos*
Length: 234 ft.
Beam: 40 ft.
Officers: British
Crew: 40, West Indian
Passengers: 96
Cabins: All with air-conditioning, some have shared bathroom facilities. Suites have queen bed, private bath, stereo, TV, VCR, wet bar. Cabins for non-smokers.

SV FANTOME
S/V FANTOME
HOMEPORT-ANTIGUA(WINTERS)
FREEPORT/NASSAU(SUMMERS)
ACCOMMODATIONS-98
CREW-45
LENGTH-202 FT
BEAM-40 FT
DRAFT-15 FT

SV FANTOME

Dining: Two seatings for dinner.
Facilities: Formerly a British Navy vessel, now the *Amazing Grace* is a
    working cargo ship. It keeps Windjammer's sailing fleet supplied,
    while offering her passengers a cruise of the Caribbean. Whirl-
    pool, antique fireplace in the piano room, library. Medical facilities.
Activities: Beach excursions, snorkeling, exploring ports of call.
Youth Program: No special program. Children under 7 not accepted.
Access for Disabled: Not recommended.
Rates: Double occupancy per person $950 to $2,800.
Itinerary: Thirteen-day cruises between Freeport, Bahamas and Gre-
    nada, following the Tall Ships to supply them.

SV FANTOME
Built: 1927
Registry: Honduras
Former Name: *Flying Cloud*
Length: 282 ft.
Beam: 40 ft.
Speed: 10 knots
Officers: British
Crew: 45, West Indian
Passengers: 128
Cabins: Upper and lower berths, shower, air conditioning. Two cabins with double bed (or two twins that convert) and refrigerator. Two suites with jacuzzi, TV and VCR. No smoking in cabins.
Dining: Dining salon seats 100, with two seatings for dinner. Family-style meals.
Facilities: Originally owned by the Duke of Westminster, the *Fantome* is a four-masted schooner. Medical facilities.
Activities: Beach picnics and parties, snorkeling and scuba diving, fishing and knot tying and dance lessons. The crew offers informal sailing classes and encourages guests to assist in the operation of the ship.
Rates: From $950 to $1,125 per person for six-day cruise. Children age seven to 11 are half price.
Itinerary: From Antigua to islands such as St. Barts, St. Maarten, St. Kitts, Montserrat, Dominica, Guadeloupe, Isle des Saintes, depending on the wind. In summer and fall from Nassau or Freeport to islands such as Gun Cay, Bimini, Great Stirrup, Rose Island, Chub, Whale, Egg, Gorda or Sweeting's Cay.

SV FLYING CLOUD
Built: 1935
Registry: Honduras
Former Names: *Oisseau des Isle; Ave de Tahiti*
Length: 208 ft.
Beam: 32 ft.
Speed: 8 knots
Officers: British
Crew: 25, West Indian
Passengers: 78
Cabins: 18. All have private bath with shower, air-conditioning, tile floors. Cabins are non-smoking. One suite with TV, VCR, CD, waterbed. Stateroom to share for six.
Dining: Dining salon seats 74; two seatings for dinner.
Facilities: Three-masted barquentine travels to remote harbors and secluded beaches. Bar.

Activities: Beach parties, snorkeling and scuba, diving equipment available. The crew offers informal sailing lessons and encourages guests to participate in the daily operation of the ship.

Youth Program: None.

Access for Disabled: Not recommended.

Rates: Per person from $650 to $1,125. Children are half price.

Itinerary: Six-day cruises of the Caribbean, departing from Tortola of some of the following: Salt Island, Virgin Gorda, Beef Island, Green Cay, Sandy Cay, Norman Island, Deadman's Bay, Cooper Island, Jost Van Dyke, Peter Island, depending on the wind, weather and island events.

SV MANDALAY

Built: 1923

Registry: Honduras

Former Names: *Hussar; Vema*

Length: 236 ft.

Beam: 33 ft.

Speed: 9 knots

Officers: British

Crew: 28, West Indian

Passengers: 72

Cabins: All cabins have air-conditioning, most have private bath with shower. Suites have double bed, refrigerator. Some cabins share bathroom facilities. Cabins are non-smoking.

Dining: Dining salon seats 50; two seatings for dinner. Family-style dinners.

Facilities: Formerly the luxury yacht of E.F. Hutton and a research vessel for Columbia University.

Activities: Beach picnics, parties, fishing, knot-tying, snorkeling and scuba. The crew offers sailing lessons.

Youth Program: None.

Access for Disabled: Not recommended.

Rates: For 13-day cruises from $1,450 to $1,750 per person. Children to 11 are half price.

Itinerary: From Antigua or Grenada to a selection of Palm Island, Mayreau, Tobago, Bequia, St. Vincent, St. Lucia, Martinique, Dominica, Isle des Saintes, Nevis, Montserrat, Carriacou, depending on the wind.

SV POLYNESIA

Built: 1938

Registry: Honduras

Former Name: *Argus*

Length: 248 ft.

Beam: 36 ft.
Speed: 10 knots
Officers: British
Crew: 45, West Indian
Passengers: 126
Cabins: 52. All have private bath with shower, air-conditioning; two
suites have double bed, refrigerator. Bachelor and Bachelorette
Quarters sleep up to six people each. Cabins are non-smoking.
Dining: Dining salon seats 70; two seatings for dinner.
Facilities: A four-masted tall ship once part of the Portuguese Grand
Banks fleet.
Activities: Snorkeling, scuba, fising, exercise classes, dance lessons.
The crew members give informal sailing lessons and encourage
guests to assist in the operation of the ship. The ship's mascot par-
rot keeps watch. Theme cruises, singles cruises offered each month.
Youth Program: None.
Access for Disabled: Not recommended.
Rates: Per person from $650 to $1,025.
Itinerary: Six-day cruises of the Caribbean from St. Maarten to St.
Barts, St. Kitts, Saba, Nevis, Prickly Pear, Anguilla, Montserrat, de-
pending on the wind.

MV VAGABOND
Delivery: 1994
Registry: France
Former Name: *Polestar*
Length: 210 ft.
Crew: West Indian
Passengers: 78
Facilities: This is the baby sister to *Amazing Grace*, a second supply
ship of the Windjammer sailing ships, carrying passengers.
Access for Disabled: No recommended.
Rates: Per person double occupancy from $950 to $2,800.
Itinerary: Thirteen-day cruises that follow the routes of the sailing
ships in the Bahamas and the Caribbean. Windjammer's Tall Ships
are at the call of the winds and so itineraries often change from
week to week.

SV YANKEE CLIPPER
Built: 1927
Registry: Honduras
Former Names: *Cressida; Pioneer*
Length: 197 ft.
Beam: 30 ft.
Speed: 9 knots

WIND SPIRIT

Officers: British
Crew: 29, West Indian
Passengers: 65
Cabins: All have bath with shower and air-conditioning. Most with
    upper and lower berths, 10 with double or queen beds. Cabins are
    non-smoking.
Dining: Dining salon seats 36; two seatings for dinner. Family-style
    meals, island specialties.
Facilities: Once owned by the Vanderbilts, this three-masted sailing
    vessel has been restored.
Activities: Beach parties, snorkeling, scuba, fishing, knot-tying, exer-
    cise classes, dance lessons. The crew encourages guests to partici-
    pate in the operation of the ship and offers impromptu sailing
    lessons.
Youth Program: None.
Access for Disabled: Not recommended.
Rates: Per person from $775 to $850. Children ages 7 to 11 are half
    price.
Itinerary: Six-day cruises of the Caribbean, leaving from Grenada to
    Petit St. Vincent, Bequia, Mayreau, Palm Island, Union Island,
    Young Island or Carriacou.

WINDSTAR CRUISES
300 Elliott Ave. W., Seattle, WA 98119

800-626-9900; 800-258-7245; 206-281-3535

WIND STAR; WIND SONG; WIND SPIRIT

Built: 1986, 1987, 1988

Registry: Bahamas

Length: 440 ft. including bowsprit

Beam: 64 ft.

Power: Four masts with six triangular, self-furling, computer-operated sails. Ship uses sails whenever possible; also has three diesel engines.

Officers: Norwegian

Crew: 91, European, Indonesian, Filipino

Passengers: 148

Cabins: 74. All are outside with sitting area; queen-size beds convert to two twins; some cabins offer third berth. All have TV, VCR, radio, minibar, international direct-dial phone, private bath with shower and hairdryer, air-conditioning.

Dining: Restaurant accommodates all passengers at one sitting. Open seating. Open-air breakfast and lunch buffet on Veranda. Men wear sports coats for evenings. Ties are not required.

Facilities: Lounge featuring live entertainment nightly, disco, book and video libraries, watersport platform off stern of ship, piano bar, laundry, small casino, sauna, boutique, hairdresser, fitness center, masseuse. Doctor's office.

Activities: No structured daily regime. Shore excursions, cultural tours and watersports activities available at each destination. Typical activities are a rainforest tour, exploring lagoons in an outrigger canoe, feeding sharks off Bora Bora's coral reefs, horseback riding, helicopter sightseeing, jungle river cruise, glass-bottom boating, picnics, golf, deep sea fishing, and sailing a regatta on an America's Cup racer. Unobstructed circuit of ship for jogging (12.5 laps equals 1 mile). Exercise classes, snorkeling equipment and underwater cameras available.

Youth Program: Windstar Cruises discourages passengers from bringing their children. There are no facilities for childcare.

Access for Disabled: Almost impossible for disabled passengers to move through ship.

Rates: Per person from $1,995 to $5,995 depending on length of cruise and destination. Low-cost air add-ons.

Itineraries: *Wind Spirit* cruises from Singapore and Bangkok to Phuket (Thailand), Penang, Langkawi and Tioman Island, Terengganu, and Pulau Perhentian (Malaysia) and Ko Samui (Thailand). 10-day Christmas cruise departs Singapore, making port calls at Phuket, and Phi Phi Island (Thailand), Port Kelang, Langkawi, Penang and Malacca (Malaysia). An 11-day New Year's cruises departs Singapore to visit Port Kelang, Langkawi, Penang, Malacca (Malaysia), Phi Phi Island, the Similan Islands, and Phuket (Thailand). *Wind Star*: Seven- and 14-day cruises to the Windward and Leeward Islands, departing from Barbados to Bequia, Tobago Cays, Grenada, Carriacou, Martinique, St. Lucia, Iles de Saintes, St. Martin, St. Barthelemy and St. Kitts. In the spring it repositions with a transatlantic 13-day sailing from Barbados to Portugal with an uninterrupted 12 days on open seas. It has a 15-day cruise with port calls at Casablanca, Lisbon, Gibraltar, Porto Banus, Ibiza, Barcelona, Monte Carlo, and Rome; then an 11-day leg to ports in Italy, Sicily, Malta, Crete, Greece and Piraeus. Other cruises include seven-day cruises to ports in Greece and Turkey. Other cruises go to Patmos, Kas, Fethiye, Istanbul, Monemvasia, Capri, Portoferraio, Villefranche, Malaga, Gibraltar, and Casablanca.

Wind Song: All year, seven-day cruises of Society Islands, departing Papeete, Tahiti, to visit ports at Huahine, Raiatea, Bora Bora, and Moorea.

WING TOURS & NILE CRUISES

2065 York Rd., Timonium, MD 21093
800-869-4647; 410-560-7206

MS JASMIN and MS ORCHID

Built: 1988
Registry: United States
Length: 223 ft.
Beam: 42 ft.
Officers: Egyptian
Crew: 75, Egyptian
Passengers: 124
Cabins: 62. These sister ships have air-conditioned, outside cabins with picture window, phone, radio, private bath with shower.
Dining: Single seating. International and Egyptian cuisine.
Facilities: Nightclub, outdoor pool, jacuzzi, hairdresser, boutique, laundry.
Activities: Guided tours. Ping pong.
Youth Program: None.
Access for Disabled: Not accessible.
Rates: Double occupancy per person from $799 to $1,309.
Itinerary: Four- and six-day cruises of the Nile River between Luxor and Aswan.

WORLD EXPLORER CRUISES

555 Montgomery St., San Francisco, CA 94111-2544
800-854-3835; 415-391-9262

SS *UNIVERSE*

Built: 1954
Registry: Liberia
Former Name: *Atlantic*
Length: 564 ft.
Beam: 76 ft.
Speed: 15 knots
Officers: Chinese
Crew: 200, Filipino, Chinese, American
Passengers: 500. Singles 10%, couples 90%.
Cabins: 314. Cabins are tiny and plain, have private bath with showers; no TV or phone. Inside double cabins have upper and lower berths. Suites look out onto a promenade, not the sea; some have tubs.
Dining: Seafood is purchased fresh in Alaska. Two seatings for lunch and dinner, with passengers assigned to tables. A classical guitarist or string quartet often plays during dinner. Two semiformal evenings each cruise.
Facilities: The *Universe* began as a freighter and was transformed into a transatlantic liner. The lounge is the site of most lectures, evening shows, largest bar on the ship. There is also a nonsmokers' lounge, smokers' lounge, piano lounge, library with 12,000 volumes, theater, gift shop, hairdresser, children's playroom, laundry and self-serve laundromat. A doctor is on board.
Activities: Exercise equipment, bikes, rowing machines, massage. Enclosed Promenade Deck has an unobstructed circuit of the ship; 12 laps equal 1 mile. The *Universe* is really a floating campus that accepts members of the public during the summer. At-sea times are packed with classes, slide presentations and educational films. Experts lecture on subjects ranging from Alaskan anthropology to history, glaciers, whales and oceanography. College or tenure credit is offered at an extra fee to those who write a paper. During the rest of the year on the *Universe*, the University of Pittsburgh offers "Semester at Sea" while sailing around the world.*
Youth Program: None
Access for Disabled: Some doorways have raised thresholds. The elevator does not reach the Main Deck cabins. Handicapped passengers must be escorted by an able-bodied companion.
Rates: Double occupancy per person ranges from $2,995 to $4,095. A no-cost, two- to three-day stay in Vancouver or Seattle is an early-

booking incentive.

Itinerary: Sails from Vancouver on 14-day, round-trip Alaska cruises to Wrangell, Juneau, Skagway, Glacier Bay, Columbia Glacier, Valdez, Seward, Sitka, Ketchikan and Victoria.

* For further information: University of Pittsburgh, Semester at Sea Program and Caribbean Seminar at Sea, 800-854-0195.

YANKEE SCHOONER CRUISES

Box 696, Camden, ME 04843

800-255-4449; 207-236-4449

ROSEWAY

Built: 1925

Registry: United States

Length: 112 ft. on deck

Beam: 25 ft.

Speed: 10 knots, sail plus diesel engine, but sail alone when underway

Crew: 7

Passengers: 30. Passengers include individuals, couples, families and groups. Minimum age is 16. Passengers should bring casual clothes; radios and tape players with headphones are welcome.

Cabins: 14. Cabins have sink. Two heads, hot showers on deck are shared. No smoking below deck.

Dining: Downhome, downeast cuisine prepared on woodburning stove. Fresh native seafood, fresh baked breads and pastries.

Facilities: Schooner spent 32 years in the pilot service off Boston Harbor and was the last pilot schooner active in the U.S. Main salon for dining and socializing.

Activities: Lobster bake on shore. Hiking, windsurfing, scuba, snorkeling gear provided. Theme cruises: art, photo, video production, music cruises with experts on board. Passengers may participate in shipboard task including sailing, navigating, and galley help. Ship spends five to seven hours a day sailing.

Access for Disabled: Not accessible.

Rates: Three- to six-night cruises from $429 to $849.

Itinerary: Sails from St. Thomas during the winter to islands such as St. John, Virgin Gorda, George, Dog, Jost Van Dyke, Norman Island, Salt Island and Peter Island; in summer, three- to six-night cruises in Maine from Camden to island coves, coastal fishing harbors such as Eggemoggin Reach, Isle au Haut, Swans Island, Blue Hill Bay, Mount Desert, Snug Harbor.

TRAVELING BY FREIGHTER

Hopping a freighter evokes a romantic image of escape. What is it really like?

The old conventional cargo vessels are pretty much obsolete; today's freighters are mostly container vessels and spend less time in port, but they still offer unique opportunities to travel.

Passenger accommodations on cargo ships are quite comfortable and spacious, usually consisting of a cabin with twin beds and private bath, with occasional availability of a suite or an owner's cabin with a separate sitting room.

Food is plentiful and good, but not up to the gourmet feasts one expects on luxury cruise ships. Dining is informal, and many ships have a pantry where passengers may help themselves to snacks. There usually is a lounge where you can meet with other passengers and the officers.

There may or may not be a swimming pool and sauna, and there are only small areas of deck space for lounging or reading. Most freighters have cabins for only a few passengers, usually no more than 12, and even with only a few, they may not all be booked. Crews may speak little or no English. There is usually no entertainment. Young children are usually not accepted, nor are persons over 75 years of age; those over age 65 must provide a medical certificate signed by a physician stating that they are fit to travel, and all passengers must have insurance. No doctor is required on board unless there are more than 12 passengers.

The costs are less per day on a cargo vessel than on a cruise ship, but the voyages are often longer, so the overall cost is about the same.

Plan on a broad range of travel dates instead of specific times and dates. Dates of departure and arrival, and even ports of call, are often subject to last-minute changes. If you are flexible, then hopping a freighter can still be one of life's great adventures. But take some books.

SOME MAJOR FREIGHTER/ PASSENGER LINES

BANK LINE
Clydebank, Forthbank, Ivybank, Moraybank
Capacity 8 passengers each; outdoor pool.
Year round—Round-the-world cruises of 110 to 115 nights, departing from Antwerp, returning to Rotterdam, calling at Dunkirk, Le Havre, various islands in the South Pacific and Singapore. Transits Panama and Suez Canal. From $11,825 to $13,575.

BLUE STAR PACE LINE
Columbia Star, California Star
Capacity 12 passengers; outdoor pool.
Year round—Cruises of 41 to 44 nights from Los Angeles to Australia, calling at Noumea, Sydney, Melbourne, Brisbane, Wellington, Auckland, Suva, Honolulu, New Caledonia, Fiji, and Seattle. Fare: $4,400 to $4,550.
America Star, Melbourne Star, Queensland Star, Sydney Star
Capacity 11 passengers each; outdoor pool.
Year round—Cruises of 65 to 70 nights from Jacksonville to Australia and New Zealand, calling at Houston, Melbourne, Sydney, Brisbane, Port Chalmers, Wellington and Auckland. Transits Panama Canal. From $5,400 to $7,700.
Southland Star, Wellington Star
Capacity 2 passengers each.
Year round—Cruises of 35 to 40 nights from the West Coast of the United States to New Zealand, calling at Papeete, Tonga, Suva, Honolulu and ports in Australia. Fare: $5,100.

CAST FREIGHTER CRUISES
Cast Husky, Cast Muskox, Cast Otter
Capacity 12 passengers each; outdoor pool.
April to November—Transatlantic cruises of approximately 32 nights from Montreal, calling at ports in the St. Lawrence River and at Zeebrugge (Belgium) and occasionally London, Antwerp or Rotterdam. Fare: $3,890.

CHILEAN LINE
Laja, Lircay
Capacity 12 passengers each; outdoor pool.
Year round—South American cruises of approximately 45 nights from Los Angeles, calling at Arica, Iquique, Antofagasta, Valparaiso, San

Antonio, Callao, Guayaquil, Esmerales, and other ports. From $3,750 to $4,050.

Year round—Far East cruises of approximately 65 nights from Los Angeles, calling at Yokohama, Nagoya, Kobe, Kagoshima, Busan, Keelung, Hong Kong, and other ports. From $5,500 to $5,950.

COLUMBUS LINE

Columbus America, Columbus Australia, Columbus Queensland, Columbus New Zealand
Capacity 8 to 12 passengers each; outdoor pool.

Year round—Cruises of 65 to 70 nights from Jacksonville, Florida returning to Philadelphia, calling at New Orleans, Houston, Melbourne, Brisbane, Sydney, Auckland, Wellington and Port Chalmers. Transits Panama Canal. From $5,450 to $7,650.

Columbus Victoria, Columbus Virginia, Columbus Wellington
Capacity 8 passengers each; outdoor pool.

Year round—Cruises of 42 to 45 nights from Los Angeles returning to Seattle, calling at Melbourne, Sydney, Wellington, Auckland and occasionally Honolulu. Fare: $4,798 to $5,400.

Oregon Star
Capacity 8 passengers; outdoor pool.

Year round—Cruises of 42 to 45 nights from Los Angeles returning to Seattle, calling at Melbourne, Sydney, Auckland, Noumea, New Caledonia and Suva. Fare: $5,150 to $5,400.

COMPAGNIE POLYNESIENNE de TRANSPORT MARITIME

Aranui
Capacity 60 passengers; outdoor pool.

Year round—Cruises of 15 nights departing approximately once a month from Papeete, calling at Takapoto, Ua Pou, Nuku Hiva, Hiva Oa, Fatu Hiva, Ua Huka, Tahuata and Rangiroa. From $2,730 to $3,740.

CONTAINERSHIPS REEDERI

Lorraine, Pacific Span
Capacity 8 to 9 passengers, respectively; outdoor pool.

Year round—Cruises of 46 nights from Long Beach, calling at Le Havre, Thamesport, Rotterdam and Bremerhaven. Transits Panama Canal. Fare: $4,375 to $4,685.

Sea Breeze
Capacity 9 passengers; outdoor pool

Year round—Cruises of 55 nights from Charleston, calling at Norfolk, Spain, Bombay, Malta. Transits Suez Canal. Fare: $5,200 to $5,600.

EGON OLDENDORFF LINE

Columbus Olivos

Capacity 8 passengers; outdoor pool.

Year round—Cruises of about 42 nights from Philadelphia returning to New Jersey, calling at Baltimore, Martinique, Barbados, Trinidad, Santos, Buenos Aires, Montevideo, Rio Grande, Itajai, Rio de Janeiro, Salvador, and other ports. Fare: $4,570.

Explorer, Voyager

Capacity 8 passengers; pool.

Year round—Cruise of 60 days from New Zealand, calling at Suva, Manila, Hong Kong, Keelung, Buson, Hiroshima, Osaka, Yokohama, to Auckland. Fare: $5,250.

Magdalena Oldendorff

Capacity 7 passengers; outdoor pool.

Year round—Cruises of 89 to 114 nights from Savannah, calling at Philadelphia, Tampa, occasionally Los Angeles and ports throughout Japan. Transits Panama Canal; extensive port time in Japan. Fare: $8,750.

Neptune Lazuli

Capacity 9 passengers.

Year round—Cruise of 57 nights from New York to Halifax, Sri Lanka, Singapore, Taiwan, Hong Kong. Transits Suez Canal. Fare: $5,090 to $5,430.

Oakland, Yokohama

Capacity 6 passengers each; outdoor pool.

Year round—Round-the-world cruises of 84 nights from Long Beach, calling at Oakland, Japan, Korea, Taiwan, Hong Kong, Singapore, Belgium, the Netherlands, England, Germany, New York, Norfolk and Savannah. Transits Suez and Panama Canals. Fare: $6,190 to $7,960.

HANSEATIC MARINE

American Senator

Capacity 4 passengers; outdoor pool.

Year round—Round-the-world cruises of 84 nights from Long Beach, calling at Oakland, Japan, Korea, Taiwan, Hong Kong, Singapore, Belgium, Germany, the Netherlands, France, New York, Norfolk and Savannah. Transits Suez and Panama Canals. Fare: $7,960.

IVARAN LINES

Americana

Capacity 88 passengers; outdoor pool, gym, slot machines.

Year round—Cruises of 43-44 nights from New York and Miami, calling at Savannah, Rio de Janeiro, Santos, Buenos Aires, Montevideo, Rio

Grande, Itajai, Salvador, Fortaleza, San Juan, Norfolk and Baltimore. From $8,550 to $14,535.

Salvador, Santa Fe
Capacity 12 passengers each; outdoor pool.

Monthly—Cruises of 50 to 52 nights from Houston returning to New Orleans, calling at Rio de Janeiro, Santos, Buenos Aires, Montevideo, Rio Grande, Itajai, San Juan, Santo Domingo and Barbados. From $6,000 to $6,875.

LAEISZ LINE
Panama Senator, Paris Senator
Capacity 6 passengers each; outdoor pool.

Year round—Round-the-world cruises of about 84 nights from Long Beach, calling at Oakland, Japan, Korea, Taiwan, Hong Kong, Singapore, Belgium, the Netherlands, England, Germany, New York, Norfolk and Savannah. Transits Suez and Panama Canals. Fare: $8,400 to $8,850.

LEONHARDT & BLUMBERG
Provence
Capacity 5 passengers; indoor pool.

Year round—Cruises of 46 nights from Long Beach, calling at Le Havre, Thamesport, Rotterdam and Bremerhaven. Transits Panama Canal. Fare: $4,685 to $5,000.

LYKES LINE
Adabelle Lykes, and 16 other cargo vessels
Capacity 4 to 12 passengers.

Year round—Cruises of 32 to 50 nights from New Orleans or other Gulf ports or the Great Lakes, calling in the Mediterranean, northern Europe and Africa, and along the west coast of South America. From $2,800 to $5,000.

MARCON LINE
Nedlloyd Hong Kong
Capacity 10 passengers; outdoor pool.

Year round—Cruises of about 80 days from Costa Rica, calling at Yokohama, Kobe, Pusan, Hong Kong, Singapore, and ports in Ecuador, Chile, Peru and Columbia. Fare: $7,340 to $8,600.

MEDITERRANEAN SHIPPING COMPANY
Alexa, Barbara, Sandra
Capacity 8 to 12 passengers; outdoor pool on *Alexa*.

Every eight weeks—East Africa cruises of 35 nights from Antwerp, calling at Felixstowe, Mogadishu, Dar es Salaam, Tanga, Mombasa, Port Said, Leghorn and Valencia. Transits Suez Canal. Fare: $3,500.

Aniello, Regina D, Rosa M

Capacity 12 passengers each; all but the *Rosa M* with outdoor pool.

Every twenty days—Indian Ocean cruises of 59 nights from Antwerp, calling at Rouen, Dunkirk, Réunion, Mauritius, Tamatave, Felixstowe, Rotterdam, Bremen and Hamburg. Fare: $5,800.

Aurora, Michele, Mirella, Rosemary, Sextum

Capacity 12 passengers each; all but the *Sextum* with outdoor pool.

Weekly—South Africa cruises of 48 nights from Antwerp, calling at Felixstowe, Cape Town, Port Elizabeth and Durban. Fare: $4,500.

Chiara, Rafaela S, Sabrina, Watergina

Capacity 8 to 12 passengers; two with indoor pools.

Year round—Transatlantic cruises of 27 nights from Boston, calling at New York, Baltimore, Newport News, Le Havre, Antwerp, Bremen, Hamburg and Felixstowe. Fare: $3,200.

Diego, Giovanna

Capacity 12 passengers each; outdoor pool.

Every two weeks—Eastern Mediterranean cruises of 27 nights from Antwerp, calling at Felixstowe, Limassol, Ashdod, Haifa, Alexandria, Naples and Lisbon. Fare: $3,200.

Emilia, Francesca

Capacity 12 passengers each; outdoor pool.

Every two weeks—South Africa cruises of 55 nights from Leghorn, calling at Genoa, Marseilles, Barcelona, Cape Town, Port Elizabeth, Durban, Réunion, Mauritius, Madagascar and Valencia. Fare: $5,500.

Presidente Frei

Capacity 6 passengers.

Monthly—South American cruises of 40 nights from New York, calling at Baltimore, Charleston, Miami, Cristobal, Callao, Arica, Iquique, Valparaiso and Antofagosto. Transits Panama Canal. Fare: $4,000.

MINERAL SHIPPING LIMITED

Christiane, Patty

Capacity 7 passengers each; outdoor pool on *Christiane*.

Year round—Cruises of about 32 to 35 nights from Savannah returning to another East Coast port, calling at ports in the Gulf of Mexico, Rotterdam, Delfjizl and occasionally Germany. Fare: $2,725.

Clary, Julia

Capacity 12 passengers each; outdoor pool.

Year round—Cruises of about 70 nights from Savannah returning to another East Coast port, usually calling at Genoa, Civitavecchia, Ancona, Monfalcone and Yerakini and occasionally Rotterdam and Delfzijl. Fare: $5,775.

POLISH OCEAN LINES
Kosciuszko, Pulaski, Sikorski, Starzynski
Capacity 6 passengers each; outdoor pool.
Weekly—Transatlantic crossings of 8 to 10 nights, depending on port of disembarkation, departing on Monday from Port Newark for Le Havre, Rotterdam and Bremerhaven. From $950 to $1,045.

PROJEX LINE
Asian Senator
Capacity 5 passengers; outdoor pool.
Year round—Round-the-world cruises of 84 nights from Long Beach, calling at Oakland, Japan, Korea, Taiwan, Hong Kong, Singapore, Belgium, Germany, the Netherlands, France, New York, Norfolk and Savannah. Transits Suez and Panama canals. Fare: $7,960.

YUGOSLAV GREAT LAKES LINE
Biokovo
Capacity 4 passengers.
Year round—Cruises of 35 to 40 nights from Montreal, calling at Koper, Trieste, Naples/Salerno, Genoa and Leghorn. Fare: $2,880 to $3,400.

Split
Capacity 9 passengers; indoor pool.
Year round—Cruises of 35 to 40 nights from Montreal, calling at Koper, Trieste, Naples/Salerno, Genoa and Leghorn. Fare: $2,880 to $3,400.

Solin
Capacity 8 passengers; indoor pool.
Year round—Cruises of 35 to 40 nights from Montreal, calling at Koper, Trieste, Naples/Salerno, Genoa and Leghorn. From $2,880 to $3,500.

INSIDER TIP: WHAT'S BEING "WAIT-LISTED" MEAN?
- On a cruise ship, it usually means your name is on a list to be called in the event another passenger with confirmed reservations cancels. But when booking a freighter, the term is used differently, meaning roughly, "to have your name on the list as having requested a cabin for an approximate departure time."

ITINERARIES

The following are the major countries from which cargo vessels operate. The listings are made alphabetically by country, with the port of departure and the usual ports of call, followed by the name of the shipping line, and the vessel or vessels cruising that itinerary. If you decide to take a freighter, contact your travel agent for arrangements or contact the cruise line directly. Be sure to confirm dates of sailings, the restrictions on passengers, the length of any specific trip, whether one-way fares are available, whether layovers are possible, and what shore excursions are available.

From AUSTRALIA

Melbourne, Victoria - Sydney, New South Wales - Brisbane, Queensland - Osaka, Japan - Yokohama, Japan - Nagoya, Japan - Yokkaichi, Japan

Eastern and Australian Steamship Company Limited *Ariake*

Sydney - Melbourne - Brisbane - Pusan Korea - South - Osaka, Japan -Yokohama, Japan - Brisbane - Melbourne - Sydney, New South Wales

Egon Oldendorff *Pyrmont Bridge* **(9 passengers)**

From BELGIUM

Antwerp - Dunkerque, France - Le Havre, France - Panama Canal - Papeete, French Polynesia - Apia, Samoa - Suva, Fiji - Noumea, New Caledonia - Honiara, Solomon Islands - Lae Papua, New Guinea - Kieta Papua, New Guinea - Rabaul Papua, New Guinea - Kimbe Papua, New Guinea - Darwin, Australia - Singapore, Singapore - Suez Canal - Rotterdam, Netherlands

Bank Line *Forthbank* **(9 passengers);** *Moraybank* **(9 passengers);** *Ivybank* **(9 passengers);** *Clydebank* **(9 passengers)**

Antwerp/Hamburg, Germany - Port-Cartier Quebec, Canada - Baie-Comeau Quebec, Canada - Montreal Quebec, Canada - Quebec, Canada

Egon Oldendorff *Dora Oldendorf* **(10 passengers);** *United Venture* **(10 passengers)**

Antwerp/Rotterdam Netherlands/Hamburg, Germany - New Orleans, Louisiana, United States

Egon Oldendorff *Dora Oldendorf* **(10 passengers);** *United Venture* **(10 passengers)**

Antwerp/Rotterdam Netherlands/Hamburg Germany - Norfolk, Virginia, United States - Newport News, Virginia, United States

Egon Oldendorff *Dora Oldendorf* **(10 passengers);** *United Venture* **(10 passengers)**
Antwerp - Chester, Pennsylvania, United States - Philadelphia, Pennsylvania, United States - Richmond ,Virginia, United States - Antwerp
Transeste (ship to be advised)
Zeebrugge - Montreal, Quebec, Canada - Zeebrugge
Cast Line Ltd. *Cast Husky* **(70,912 tons, 12 passengers);** *Cast Muskox* **(70,837 tons, 12 passengers);** *Cast Offer* **(12 passengers)**
Lewisporte, Newfoundland - Nain, Newfoundland - Lewisporte, Newfoundland
Marine Atlantic *Northern Ranger* **(5 passengers)**

From FRANCE
Dunkerque/Le Havre - Fort-de-France, French, West Indies - Pointe-a-Pitre, French, West Indies - Fort-de-France, French, West Indies -Dunkerque/Le Havre
Compagnie Generale Maritime *Fort Royal* **(31,390 tons, 12 passengers);** *Fort Fleur D'Epee* **(32,184 tons, 12 passengers);** *Fort Desaix* **(12 passengers);** *Fort St. Charles* **(12 passengers)**

From GERMANY
Bremerhaven - Le Havre, France - Houston, Texas, United States - New Orleans, Louisiana, United States - Savannah, Georgia, United States - Rotterdam, Netherlands - Bremerhaven
Polish Ocean Lines *Prof Szafer* **(16,000 tons, 12 passengers);** *Prof Rylke* **(16,000 tons, 12 passengers);** *Prof Mierzejewski* **(12 passengers)**
Hamburg - Karachi, Pakistan - Bombay, India - Colombo, Sri Lanka - Madras, India - Calcutta, India - Antwerp, Belgium
Polish Ocean Lines *Grunwald* **(8 passengers);** *Major Sucharski* **(8 passengers)**
Hamburg - Valparaiso, Chile - Callao, Peru - Antofagasta, Chile - Arica, Chile - Guayaquil, Ecuador - Hamburg
Polish Ocean Lines *Polonia* **(12 passengers);** *Radom* **(12 passengers);** *Lublin* **(12 passengers);** *Lodz II*
Hamburg - Santo Domingo, Venezuela - Puerto Cabello, Venezuela - Cartagena, Colombia - Cristobal, Panama - Limon, Costa Rica - New Orleans, Louisiana, United States - Columbia, South Carolina, United States - Hamburg
Polish Ocean Lines *Kuznica* **(12 passengers);** *Jastarnia Bor* **(12 passengers);** *Wladyslawowo* **(12 passengers)**
Hamburg/Bremerhaven - Oslo, Norway - Fredrikstad, Norway - Gothen-

burg, Sweden - Malmo, Sweden - Copenhagen, Denmark - Hamburg/Bremerhaven

Beutelrock Lubeck *Carolin* **(4 passengers)**
Hamburg - Bremen - San Juan, Puerto Rico - Veracruz, Mexico - Tampico, Mexico - Rio Haina ,Dominican Republic - San Juan, Puerto Rico - Antwerp, Belgium - Hamburg

Deutsche Seereederei Rostock *Pasewalk* **(9,231 tons, 6 passengers);** *Pritzwalk* **(6 passengers);** *Glauchau* **(6 passengers)**
Hamburg/Antwerp, Belgium/Le Havre, France - Ponta Delgada, Azores, Portugal - Pointe-a-Pitre, French West Indies - Fort-de-France, French West Indies - Cayenne French Guiana - Santo Tomas de Castilla ,Guatemala - Le Havre, France/Antwerp, Belgium/Hamburg

Horn Line *Hornbay* **(12 passengers);** *Horncliff* **(12 passengers);** *Horncap* **(12 passengers);** *Hornstar; Horngulf; Hornwind*
Hamburg - Tenerife, Spain - Rio de Janeiro, Brazil - Montevideo, Uruguay - Buenos Aires, Argentina - Santos, Brazil - Ilheus, Brazil -Tenerife, Spain - Hamburg

Polish Ocean Lines *Warszawa* **(12 passengers);** *Krakow* **(12 passengers);** *Bydgoszcz* **(12 passengers)**
Hamburg/Kiel/Bremerhaven - Aarhus, Denmark - Gothenburg, Sweden - Copenhagen, Denmark - Hamburg/Kiel/Bremerhaven

Reederei Martin Spaleck *Atlantis; Gisela; Sabine; Pinguin* **(2 passengers)**

From ICELAND

Reykjavik - Immingham, United Kingdom - Hamburg, Germany - Antwerp, Belgium - Rotterdam, Netherlands - Immingham, United Kingdom - Reykjavik

Elmskip Iceland Steamship Company) *Bruarfoss* **(12 passengers);** *Laxfoss* **(12 passengers)**

From ITALY

Genoa - Paranagua, Brazil - Santos, Brazil - Rio de Janeiro, Brazil -Livorno - Genoa

Grimaldi Group *Repubblica di Pisa* **(70 passengers);** *Repubblica di Venezia* **(70 passengers)**
Genoa - Marseille, France - Barcelona, Spain - Fortaleza, Brazil - Salvador, Brazil - Santos, Brazil - Buenos Aires, Argentina - Montevideo, Uruguay - Livorno

Dollart Reederei/Bremen *Calapadria* **(10 passengers)**
Genoa - Valencia, Spain - Montreal, Quebec, Canada - Larnaca, Cyprus -Izmir, Turkey - Naples - Genoa

Deutsche Seereederei Rostock *Sachsen* **(2 passengers);** *Branden-burg* **(2 passengers)**
Livorno - Valencia, Spain - Fos-sur-Mer, France - Marseille, France -Ash-dod, Israel - Haifa, Israel
Grimaldi Medferry Lines *Valencia Bridge* **(12 passengers)**

From NETHERLANDS

Rotterdam - Le Havre, France - Piraeus, Greece - Jeddah, Saudi Arabia - Hodeidah, Yemen - Aqaba, Jordan - Yanbu, Saudi Arabia - Port Sudan - Salerno, Italy - Valencia, Spain - Thamesport, United Kingdom - Antwerp, Belgium - Rotterdam
Concordia Shipping Line *Concordia* **(7 passengers)**
Rotterdam - Lisbon, Portugal - Algeciras, Spain - Valletta, Malta -Piraeus, Greece - Naples, Italy - Palermo, Italy - Algeciras, Spain -Lisbon, Portugal - Leixoes, Portugal - Felixstowe, United Kingdom -Rotterdam
Transeste *Ritscher* **(6 passengers)**
Rotterdam - Algeciras, Spain - Piraeus, Greece - Izmir, Turkey - Thessaloniki, Greece - Piraeus, Greece - Algeciras, Spain - Felixstowe, United Kingdom - Rotterdam
Containerschiffs-Reederei/Elsfleth *Alum Bay* **(6 passengers)**
Rotterdam/Delfzijl - Savannah, Georgia, United States - Rotterdam
Mineral Shipping Company *Patty* **(7 passengers)**

From NEW ZEALAND

Auckland - Napier - Nelson - Timaru - Tauranga - Suva, Fiji - Noumea, New Caledonia - Manila, Philippines - Hong Kong, Hong Kong - Keelung, Taiwan - Pusan, Korea-South - Hiroshima, Japan - Osaka, Japan - Nagoya Japan - Yokohama, Japan - Suva, Fiji - Noumea ,New Caledonia -Auckland
Egon Oldendorff *T.A. Explorer* **(8 passengers);** *T.A. Navigator* **(8 passengers);** *T.A. Mariner* **(8 passengers);** *T.A. Adventurer* **(8 passengers);** *T.A. Discoverer* **(8 passengers)**

From POLAND

Gdynia - Aarhus, Denmark - Izmir, Turkey - Alexandria, Egypt - Casablanca, Morocco - Gdynia
Polish Ocean Lines *Radzionkow* **(8 passengers);** *Garwolin* **(8 passengers);** *Siemiatycze* **(8 passengers)**
Gdynia - Hamburg, Germany - Rotterdam, Netherlands - Antwerp, Belgium - Tunis, Tunisia - Valletta, Malta - Alexandria, Egypt - Latakia, Syria - Limassol, Cyprus - Mersin, Turkey - Larnaca, Cyprus - Gdynia
Polish Ocean Lines *Zeran* **(6 passengers);** *Wloclawek* **(6 passengers);** *Chodziez* **(6 passengers)**

Szczecin - Hamburg, Germany - Antwerp, Belgium - Dakar, Senegal - Freetown, Sierra Leone - Monrovia, Liberia - Abidjan Cote d'Ivoire - Lagos, Nigeria - Douala, Cameroon - Hamburg, Germany - Szczecin
Polish Ocean Lines *Zabrze* **(12 passengers);** *Zakopane* **(12 passengers);** *Zambrow* **(12 passengers);** *Zawichost* **(12 passengers);** *Zawiercie* **(12 passengers)**

From SPAIN
Valencia - Fos-sur-Mer, France - La Spezia, Italy - Larnaca, Cyprus -Jeddah, Saudi Arabia - Khor Fakkan, UAE - Singapore, Singapore - Kaohsiung, Taiwan - Hong Kong, Hong Kong - Singapore, Singapore - Khor Fakkan, UAE - Jeddah, Saudi Arabia - Larnaca, Cyprus - Valencia
Deutsche Seereederei Rostock *Mecklenburg* **(2 passengers);** *Thuringen* **(12 passengers)**
Valencia - Fos-sur-Mer, France - La Spezia, Italy - Larnaca, Cyprus -Port Said, Egypt - Jeddah, Saudi Arabia - Khor Fakkan, UAE - Singapore, Singapore - Kaohsiung, Taiwan - Hong Kong, Hong Kong - Singapore, Singapore - Khor Fakkan, UAE - Jeddah, Saudi Arabia - Suez, Egypt -Larnaca, Cyprus - Valencia
NSB Frachtschiff-Touristik *Choyang Star* **(11 passengers);** *Japan Senator* **(11 passengers)**
Cardiff - Santa Cruz de Tenerife, Tenerife, Spain - Jamestown, St. Helena - Georgetown, Ascension Island - Jamestown, St. Helena - Cape Town, South Africa - Edinburgh, Settlement Tristan da Cunha - Jamestown, St. Helena - Georgetown, Ascension Island - Jamestown, St. Helena - Santa Cruz de Tenerife, Tenerife, Spain - Cardiff
St. Helena Shipping Co. Ltd. *St. Helena* **(128 passengers)**

From UNITED KINGDOM
Felixstowe - Bremerhaven, Germany - Le Havre, France - Veracruz, Mexico - Altamira, Brazil - Galveston, Texas, United States - Antwerp, Belgium - Felixstowe
Egon Oldendorff *Tete Oldendorff* **(6 passengers);** *Birte Oldendorff* **(6 passengers)**
Felixstowe - Rotterdam, Netherlands - Lisbon, Portugal - Algeciras, Spain - Leixoes, Portugal - Bilbao, Spain - Felixstowe
Transeste *Widukind* **(6 passengers)**
Felixstowe - Algeciras, Spain - Piraeus, Greece - Izmir, Turkey - Thessaloniki, Greece - Piraeus, Greece - Algeciras, Spain - Rotterdam, Netherlands - Felixstowe
H.W. Janssen GmbH *Sea Progress* **(6 passengers)**
Felixstowe - Antwerp, Belgium - Rotterdam, Netherlands - Hamburg,

Germany - Bremen, Germany - Limassol, Cyprus - Ashdod, Israel - Haifa, Israel - Felixstowe

H.W. Janssen GmbH *City of London* **(8 passengers)**

Felixstowe - Livorno, Italy - Naples, Italy - Suez Canal - Djibouti - Dar-es-Salaam, Tanzania - Tanga, Tanzania - Mombasa, Kenya - Tanga Tanzania - Dar-es-Salaam, Tanzania - Djibouti, Djibouti - Suez Canal - Naples, Italy - Livorno, Italy - Felixstowe

Mediterranean Shipping Company S.A. *Sextum* **(12 passengers)**; *Michele* **(9 passengers)**; *Alexa* **(4 passengers)**; *Rosemary* **(6 passengers)**; *Mee May* **(10 passengers)**; *Mirella* **(12 passengers)**

Felixstowe - Hamburg, Germany - Rotterdam, Netherlands - Dunkerque, France - Barcelona, Spain - Fos-sur-Mer, France - La Spezia, Italy -Port Said, Egypt - Suez Canal - Melbourne, Australia - Sydney, Australia - Noumea, New Caledonia - Keelung, Taiwan - Hong Kong, Hong Kong - Singapore, Singapore - Suez Canal - Port Said, Egypt - Salerno, Italy - Felixstowe

NSB Frachtschiff-Touristik *Contship Australia* **(6 passengers)**; *Contship la Spezia* **(10 passengers)**; *Contship Barcelona* **(10 passengers)**; *Contship Jork* **(10 passengers)**; *Contship France* **(10 passengers)**; *Contship Germany* **(10 passengers)**; *Contship Ipswich* **(10 passengers)**; *Koala Success*

Felixstowe - Le Havre, France - New York, United States - Norfolk, Virginia, United States - Savannah, Georgia, United States - Panama, Panama - Papeete, French Polynesia - Auckland, New Zealand - Sydney, Australia - Melbourne, Australia - Singapore, Singapore - Port Kelang, Malaysia - Colombo, Sri Lanka - Suez Canal - Alexandria, Egypt - La Spezia, Italy - Rotterdam, Netherlands - Felixstowe

NSB Frachtschiff-Touristik *Contship Europe* **(4 passengers)**; *Contship England* **(4 passengers)**

Felixstowe - Cape Town, South Africa - Port Elizabeth, South Africa -Durban, South Africa - Fremantle, Western Australia, Australia - Sydney, New South Wales, Australia - Melbourne, Victoria, Australia -Fremantle, Western Australia, Australia - Antwerp, Belgium - Rotterdam, Netherlands - Felixstowe

Mediterranean Shipping Company S.A. *Sabrina* **(6 passengers)**; *Alexandra* **(4 passengers)**; *Maria Laura* **(5 passengers)**; *Luisa* **(3 passengers)**

Felixstowe - Haifa, Israel - Suez Canal - Singapore, Singapore - Fremantle, Western Australia, Australia - Melbourne, Victoria, Australia - Sydney, New South Wales, Australia - Auckland, New Zealand - Port Chalmers, New Zealand - Panama Canal - New Orleans, Louisiana, United States - Charleston, South Carolina, United States - Philadelphia, Pennsylvania,

United States - Halifax, Nova Scotia, Canada - Zeebrugge, Belgium - Felixstowe

ABC Containers *Ellen Hudig* **(9 passengers);** *Cornelis Verolme* **(4 passengers);** *Martha II* **(3 passengers)**

Felixstowe - Alexandria, Egypt - Ashdod, Israel - Haifa, Israel - Limassol, Cyprus - Naples, Italy - Lisbon, Portugal - Hamburg, Germany - Bremerhaven, Germany - Antwerp, Belgium - Rotterdam, Netherlands -Felixstowe

Mediterranean Shipping Company S.A. *Viviana* **(4 passengers);** *Aurora* **(8 passengers)**

Felixstowe - Cape Town, South Africa - Port Elizabeth, South Africa -Durban, South Africa - Port Elizabeth, South Africa - Cape Town, South Africa - Antwerp, Belgium - Rotterdam, Netherlands - Felixstowe

Mediterranean Shipping Company S.A. *Sextum* **(12 passengers);** *Michele* **(9 passengers);** *Alexa* **(4 passengers);** *Rosemary* **(6 passengers);** *Mee May* **(10 passengers);** *Mirella* **(12 passengers)**

Felixstowe - Durban, South Africa - Fremantle, Western Australia, Australia - Melbourne, Victoria, Australia - Sydney, New South Wales, Australia - Brisbane, Queensland, Australia - Adelaide, South Australia, Australia - Fremantle, Western Australia, Australia - Jeddah, Saudi Arabia - Suez Canal - Genoa, Italy - Felixstowe

Baltic Shipping Co. *Pyotr Masherov* **(6 passengers);** *Skulptor Zalkalns* **(6 passengers);** *Anatoliy Vasiljev* **(6 passengers);** *Akademik Gorbunov* **(12 passengers);** *Smolensk* **(8 passengers);** *Skulptor Konenkov* **(6 passengers);** *Magnitogorsk* **(8 passengers);** *Georgiy Pyasetskiy* **(6 passengers)**

Felixstowe - Vlissingen, Netherlands - Hamburg, Germany - St. Petersburg, Russia - Kotka, Finland - Hamburg, Germany - Rotterdam, Netherlands - Felixstowe

Baltic Shipping Co. *Pyotr Masherov* **(6 passengers);** *Skulptor Zalkalns* **(6 passengers);** *Anatoliy Vasiljev* **(6 passengers);** *Akademik Gorbunov* **(12 passengers);** *Smolensk* **(8 passengers);** *Skulptor Konenkov* **(6 passengers);** *Magnitogorsk* **(8 passengers);** *Georgiy Pyasetskiy* **(6 passengers)**

Felixstowe - Antwerp, Belgium - Le Havre, France - New York, United States - Norfolk, Virginia, United States - Savannah,Georgia, United States - Cristobal, Panama - Long Beach, California, United States -Oakland, California, United States - Yokohama, Japan - Osaka, Japan -Pusan, Korea-South - Kaohsiung, Taiwan - Hong Kong, Hong Kong - Singapore, Singapore - Suez Canal - Port Said, Egypt - Rotterdam, Netherlands - Bremerhaven, Germany

NSB Frachtschiff-Touristik *Singapore Senator* **(11 passengers);** *Arabian Senator* **(10 passengers);** *New York Senator*

Felixstowe - Le Havre, France - Boston, Massachusetts, United States -New York, United States - Baltimore, Maryland, United States - Norfolk, Virginia, United States - Wilmington, North Carolina, United States -Boston, Massachusetts, United States - New York, United States - Baltimore, Maryland, United States - Norfolk, Virginia, United States -Rotterdam, Netherlands - Antwerp, Belgium - Bremen, Germany - Hamburg, Germany - Felixstowe

Mediterranean Shipping Company S.A. *Raffaela* **(12 passengers);** *Water Gina* **(12 passengers)**

Felixstowe - Dunkerque, France - Rouen, France - Nantes, France - Pointe des Galets, Reunion - Port Louis, Mauritius - Tamatave, Madagascar - Antwerp, Belgium - Felixstowe

Mediterranean Shipping Company S.A. *Sextum* **(12 passengers);** *Michele* **(9 passengers);** *Alexa* **(4 passengers);** *Rosemary* **(6 passengers);** *Mee May* **(10 passengers);** *Mirella* **(12 passengers)**

Grimsby - Esbjerg, Denmark

DFDS Liner Agency *Dana Cimbria* **(12 passengers);** *Dana Maxima* **(12 passengers);** *Dana Corona* **(12 passengers)**

Immingham - Cuxhaven Germany

DFDS Liner Agency *Dana Cimbria* **(12 passengers);** *Dana Maxima* **(12 passengers);** *Dana Corona* **(12 passengers)**

Liverpool - Ponce, Puerto Rico - Puerto Cabello, Venezuela - La Guaira, Venezuela - Bridgetown, Barbados - Port of Spain, Trinidad & Tobago - Willemstad, Neth Antilles - Oranjestad, Aruba - Rio Haina, Dominican Republic - Port-au-Prince, Haiti - Kingston, Jamaica - Belize City, Belize - Santo Tomas de Castilla,Guatemala - Puerto Cortes, Honduras - Limon, Costa Rica - Kingston, Jamaica - Rio Haina, Dominican Republic - Ponce, Puerto Rico - Felixstowe

Harrison Line *Author* **(6 passengers)**

Newcastle-upon-Tyne - Esbjerg Denmark

DFDS Liner Agency *Dana Cimbria* **(12 passengers);** *Dana Maxima* **(12 passengers);** *Dona Corona* **(12 passengers)**

Southampton - St. Johns, Antigua & Barbuda - Bridgetown, Barbados -George's Grenada - Kingstown, St. Vincent - Castries, St. Lucia - Basseterre, St. Kitts & Nevis - Roseau, Dominica - Southampton

Geest Line *Geestbay* **(12 passengers);** *Geetsport 7,729 tons,* **(12 passengers)**

Tilbury - Hamburg, Germany - Rotterdam, Netherlands - Antwerp, Belgium - Dakar, Senegal - Conakry, Guinea - Monrovia, Liberia - Lagos, Nigeria - Douala, Cameroon - Tema, Ghana - Paranagua, Brazil - Santos, Brazil -Rio de Janeiro, Brazil - Le Havre, France - Tilbury

Grimaldi Group *Repubblica di Genova* **(65 passengers);** *Repubblica di Amalfi* **(65 passengers);** *Repubblica di Roma*

Tilbury - Middlesbrough - Gdynia, Poland - Tilbury
Polish Ocean Lines *Inowroclaw* **(12 passengers)**
Tilbury - Hamburg, Germany - Bremen, Germany - Antwerp, Belgium -
Santos, Brazil - Buenos Aires, Argentina - Rio Grande, Brazil - Itajai, Brazil
- Santos, Brazil - Rio de Janeiro, Brazil - Salvador, Brazil -Rotterdam,
Netherlands - Tilbury
Blue Star Line *Argentina Star* **(12 passengers)**
Tilbury - Cape Town, South Africa - Port Elizabeth, South Africa -Durban,
South Africa - Port Elizabeth, South Africa - Cape Town, South Africa -
Tilbury
P & O Containers *City of Durban* **(6 passengers)**
Tilbury - Cape Town, South Africa
Safmarine *Helderberg* **(10 passengers);** *Sederberg* **(10 passengers);**
Waterberg **(10 passengers);** *Winterberg* **(10 passengers)**

From UNITED STATES

Charleston, South Carolina - New Orleans, Louisiana - Houston, Texas
-Melbourne, Australia - Sydney, Australia - Brisbane, Australia - Auck-
land, New Zealand - Wellington, New Zealand - Port Chalmers, New
Zealand - Philadelphia, Pennsylvania
Columbus Line *Columbus Queensland* **(8 passengers);** *Columbus*
Australia **(12 passengers);** *Columbus New Zealand* **(12 passengers);**
Columbus America **(12 passengers)**
Galveston ,Texas - Livorno, Italy - Naples, Italy - Izmir, Turkey - Haifa,
Israel - Alexandria, Egypt - Piraeus, Greece - Livorno, Italy - Galveston,
Texas
Lykes Lines (ship to be advised)
Galveston, Texas - New Orleans, Louisiana - Rotterdam, Netherlands
-Bremerhaven, Germany - Felixstowe, United Kingdom - Le Havre,
France -Norfolk, Virginia - Charleston, South Carolina - Miami, Florida -
Galveston, Texas
Lykes Lines (ship to be advised)
Long Beach, California - Oakland, California - Yokohama, Japan - Osaka,
Japan - Pusan, Korea - South - Kaohsiung, Taiwan - Hong Kong, Hong
Kong - Singapore, Singapore - Antwerp, Belgium - Rotterdam, Nether-
lands - Felixstowe, Suffolk, United Kingdom - Bremerhaven, Germany -
New York - Norfolk, Virginia - Savannah, Georgia - Long Beach, Califor-
nia
Laeisz Line *Paris Senator* **(6 passengers)**
Long Beach California - Savannah Georgia
Laeisz Line *Paris Senator* **(6 passengers)**
Los Angeles, California - Sydney, New South Wales,Australia - Mel-
bourne, Victoria, Australia - Wellington, New Zealand - Auckland, New

Zealand - Noumea, New Caledonia - Suva, Fiji - Honolulu, Hawaii -Seattle, Washington

Columbus Line *Act 9* **(8 passengers)**
Los Angeles, California - Sydney, New South Wales, Australia - Melbourne, Victoria, Australia - Wellington, New Zealand - Auckland, New Zealand - Seattle, Washington

Columbus Line *Columbus Victoria* **(8 passengers);** *Columbus Virginia* **(8 passengers);** *Columbus Wellington* **(8 passengers)**
Los Angeles, California - Tokyo, Japan - Osaka, Japan - Los Angeles, California

Leonhardt & Blumburg *Hansa Bremen* **(8 passengers);** *Hansa Visby* **(8 passengers);** *Hansa Lubeck* **(8 passengers)**
Los Angeles, California - Guayaquil, Ecuador - Callao, Peru - Arica, Chile - Iquique, Chile - Antofagasta, Chile - Valparaiso, Chile - San Antonio, Chile - Los Angeles, California

Chilean Line (ship to be advised)
Los Angeles, California - Yokohama, Japan - Nagoya, Japan - Kobe, Japan - Pusan, Korea-South - Keelung, Taiwan - Taichung, Taiwan - Kaohsiung, Taiwan - Hong Kong, Hong Kong - Los Angeles, California

Chilean Line (ship to be advised)
New Orleans, Louisiana - Antwerp, Belgium - Bremerhaven, Germany - Felixstowe, United Kingdom - Le Havre, France - New Orleans, Louisiana

Lykes Lines (ship to be advised)
New Orleans, Louisiana - Cartagena, Columbia - Barranquilla, Columbia - Balboa, Panama - Guayaquil, Ecuador - San Antonio, Chile - Valparaiso, Chile - Matarani, Peru - Callao, Peru - Buenaventura, Colombia - New Orleans, Louisiana

Lykes Lines (ship to advised)
New Orleans, Louisiana - Callao, Peru - Arica, Chile - Buenaventura, Colombia - Guayaquil, Ecuador - New Orleans, Louisiana

Lykes Lines (ship to be advised)
New Orleans, Louisiana - Dakar, Senegal - Monrovia, Liberia - Abidjan, Cote d'lvoire - Tema,Ghana - Douala, Cameroon - Cabinda, Angola - Cape Town, South Africa - Port Elizabeth, South Africa - East London, South Africa - Durban, South Africa - Maputo, Mozambique - Beira, Mozambique - Dar-es-Salaam, Tanzania - Mombasa, Kenya - New Orleans, Louisiana

Lykes Lines (ship to be advised)
New Orleans, Louisiana - Casablanca, Morocco - Algiers, Algeria - Tunis, Tunisia - Naples, Italy - Alexandria, Egypt - Ashdod, Israel -New Orleans, Louisiana

Lykes Lines (ship to be advised)
Newark, New Jersey - Savannah, Georgia - Miami, Florida - Rio de Janeiro, Brazil - Santos, Brazil - Buenos Aires, Argentina - Montevideo, Uruguay - Rio Grande, Brazil - Itajai, Brazil - Santos, Brazil - Rio de Janeiro, Brazil - Salvador, Brazil - Fortaleza, Brazil - San Juan, Puerto Rico - Norfolk, Virginia - Baltimore, Maryland -Newark, New Jersey

Ivaran Lines *Americana* **(108 passengers)**
New York - Savannah, Georgia - Miami, Florida - Rio de Janeiro, Brazil - Santos, Brazil - Buenos Aires, Argentina - Montevideo, Uruguay - Rio Grande, Brazil - Paranagua,Brazil - Itajai, Brazil - Santos, Brazil -Salvador, Brazil - Ilheus, Brazil - Bahia, Brazil - Fortaleza, Brazil -Norfolk, Virginia - Baltimore, Maryland - New York

Ivaran Lines - *Americana* **(108 passengers)**
Philadelphia, Pennsylvania - Baltimore, Maryland - Norfolk, Virginia -Jacksonville, Florida - Fort-de-France, French West Indies - Bridgetown, Barbados - Port of Spain, Trinidad & Tobago - Santos, Brazil - Buenos Aires, Argentina - Montevideo, Uruguay - Rio Grande, Brazil - Paranagua, Brazil - Santos, Brazil - Rio de Janeiro, Brazil -Fortaleza, Brazil - Norfolk, Virginia

Egon Oldendorff *Columbus Olivos* **(8 passengers)**
Savannah, Georgia - Fernandina Beach, Florida - Santos, Brazil - Buenos Aires, Argentina - Montevideo, Uruguay - Rio Grande, Brazil -Santos, Brazil - Norfolk, Virginia

Hanseatic Shipping Co. Ltd. *Alabama* **(4 passengers)**
Seattle, Washington - Coos Bay, Oregon - San Francisco, California -Los Angeles, California - Pago Pago American, Samoa - Nuku'Alofa Tonga - Suva, Fiji - Papeete, French Polynesia - Honolulu, Hawaii -Auckland, New Zealand - Wellington, New Zealand - Lyttelton, New Zealand

Blue Star North America Ltd. *California Star* **(18,326 tons, 12 passengers);** *Southland Star* **(11,393 tons, 2 passengers);** *Wellington Star* **(2 passengers)**
Seattle, Washington - San Francisco, California - Los Angeles, California - Sydney, New South Wales, Australia - Melbourne, Victoria, Australia - Noumea, New Caledonia - Suva, Fiji - Auckland, New Zealand

Blue Star North America Ltd. *Columbia Star* **(12 passengers)**

- Note: For more information on freighter travel and up-to-date ship and schedule changes, you may wish to contact Travel Tips Cruise and Freighter Travel Association, P.O. Box 218, Flushing NY 11358; 800-872-8584. They publish a bi- monthly magazine on freighter travel and can make reservations.

YOU CAN ALSO TAKE A MAIL SHIP OR A FERRY

A cruise aboard an official mail carrier to outlying places or a ferry is another possibility. For example, the mail ship *St. Helena* stops at the islands of Tenerife, St. Helena and Ascension Island on a 26-day cruise along a 6,000 mile route from Wales to Cape Town, South Africa. Twice a year it also goes another 1,800 miles from Cape Town to Tristan Dan Cunha (population 300).

Cabins are air-conditioned, there are sport and entertainment programs, and a small swimming pool. One-way fare from Cardiff to Cape Town ranges from $1,096 to $3,050.

If you are traveling with a car, ferries are a fast and convenient way to combine a sea voyage and the excitement of driving off at your destination. Some ferries have quite deluxe accommodations, and the difference between cruise ships and ferries is blurring. Many once humble ferries now have casinos, swimming pools, good restaurants, activities, lounges, and entertainment.

You can find ferries carrying both passengers and cars plying the waters of the Greek Islands, the Turkish coast, the Gaspe Peninsula, along the Norwegian coast, between England and Spain across the Bay of Biscay, and Alaska. Some only go overnight, but others go for several days, and allow stops along the way. They are inexpensive, and usually have local persons as passengers.

Talk to your travel agent. They can book you on ferries and mail ships with hotel or bed and breakfast stops in between as appropriate.

CHARTERING YOUR OWN BOAT

Chartering a boat for your own personal cruise is not as complex as you might think. You can charter a small sailboat or motor yacht to cruise off on your own without a captain (called bareboat), or you can charter a boat with a captain and crew and provisions in place. You can go with one friend or get a group together. The most popular places to cruise are in the Bahamas, the Caribbean, and the Mediterranean, but you can find boats to charter with your family or friends just about anywhere in the world: windjammers on the Maine coast, barges on the Rhine or the Nile, houseboats on Florida rivers, dive boats to explore the barrier reefs of Australia or Belize, yachts to island-hop in the South Pacific.

You can charter the big boats too. Indeed, just about any ship that you read about in the *Ship Profiles* can be chartered for a private cruise. Companies and organizations frequently charter ships such as the *Radisson Diamond* or the *WindSong* for large group travel. In fact, we were told that the *Radisson Diamond* is booking some 20 full-ship charters per year, and the three WindStar sailing ships charter out about 35 weeks per year.

In this section we'll give you names and phone numbers of some of the private outfits that charter sailing yachts, motor yachts, river barges and houseboats.

If you decide to cruise on your own, do some research

before you go. Read cruising guides and buy videos about the areas you'll cruise; talk to experts to find out about boating conditions, good anchorages, and points of interest. Know what equipment and provisions will be on board, and what you have to furnish.

Even if you're not an old salt, cruising on your own yacht is a dream you can fulfill, since both sail and powered yachts can be chartered complete with captain and crew. On a charter you can also have provisions supplied — sports equipment, gourmet meals (usually more than you can eat), and even wine. But it's cheaper to supply things yourself.

Even with a hired captain and crew, if you are a landlubber, you'll increase your enjoyment if you go to a boating school first; or if you are a sailor you might need some brushing up on navigation or instrumentation. If you decide to go bareboat, expect to be checked out for your boating skills. Some charter companies combine charters with sailing school courses.

CHARTER COMPANIES AROUND THE WORLD

The following is a list of companies from whom you can charter a boat with or without a captain and crew. We list their home bases and telephone numbers so you may call for brochures on their sail or motor yachts available, and their current rates. Many travel agents also can handle charter arrangements.

AMAZON:

Amazon Tours and Cruises
800-423-2791; 305-227-2266

ASIA:

Club Mariner
800-334-2435
Sunsail
800-238-7388
Yacht Connections
800-238-6912

AUSTRALIA:

Elite Yacht Charters;
213-552-7968
Roylen Endeavour Cruises
800-811-8484; 305-463-1922
Worldwide Travel
800-881-8484

BAHAMAS, CARIBBEAN

Abaco Bahamas Charters
Hopetown, Abaco
800-626-5690; 502-245-9428
ATM Yacht Charters
Guadeloupe, Martinique, St. Martin, Union Island
800-634-8822
Avery's Marine
St. Thomas
809-776-0113
Barefoot Yacht Charters
St. Vincent
800-677-3195; 809-456-9334
Bitter End Yacht Club
Virgin Gorda
800-872-2393; 312-944-5855
Caribbean Adventures
St. Thomas
800-626-4517; 809-776-7245
Caribbean Sailing Charters
St. Thomas
800-824-1331; 404-641-9640
Caribbean Yacht Charters
St. Thomas
800-225-2520; 617-599-7990
Club Mariner
800-334-2435
Conch Charters
Tortola
514-630-4802
CYOA
St. Thomas
800-944-2962; 809-774-3677
Discovery Yacht Charters
Tortola
800-268-8222; 705-368-3744

Eleuthera-Bahamas-Charters

Hatchet Bay, Eleuthera
800-548-9684; 508-255-8930; 809-335-0186

Elite Yacht Charters

213-552-7968

First Class Yachting

St. Lucia
800-922-0291; 201-342-1838; 809-452-0367

Freedom Yacht Charters

Virgin Gorda
800-99902909; 401-848-2900

Galapagos Cruise

San Cristobal Island
800-527-2500; 214-907-0414

Huntly Yachting Vacations

St. Martin
800-322-9224; 215-678-2628

Ideal Yacht Charters

Ocho Rios, Jamaica
809-974-0575

Island Yachts

St. Thomas
800-524-2019

Jet Sea

Marsh Harbour, Abaco, Guadeloupe, Martinique, St. Martin
800-262-5382

Leeward Islands Yacht Cruises St. Maarten

201-444-5560

Misty Isle Yacht Charters

Virgin Gorda
809-495-5643

Moorings

Treasure Cay, Abaco, Grenade, Guadeloupe, Martinique, St. Lucia, St. Martin, Tortola
800-535-7289; 813-535-1446; 809-494-2332

Nautorts Swan Cruises

St. Martin
800-356-7926; 401-848-7181

North South Yacht Vacations

Tortola
800-387-4964; 416-242-7426; 809-494-0096

Ocean Incentives

St. Thomas
800-344-5762; 809-775-6406

Offshore Sail and Motor Yachts
Tortola
800-582-0175; 809-494-4726
Privilege Charters
Guadeloupe, Tortola
800-262-0308; 305-462-6706
Proper Yachts
St. John
809-776-6256
Russell Yacht Cruises
Martinique
800-635-8895
Seabreeze Yacht Charters
Tortola
800-388-6224; 416-499-3102
Sunsail
Marsh Harbour, Abaco, Martinique
800-327-2276
Sun Yacht Charters
Tortola
800-772-3500; 800-327-2276; 207-236-9611; 809-494-5538;
809-495-4740
Thomas Sailing
St. Martin, St. Thomas, Tortola
800-258-8753; 809-494-0333
Tortola Marine Management
Tortola
800-633-0155; 203-854-5131
Trade Wind Yachts
St. Lucia, St. Vincent, Tortola
800-825-7245; 804-694-0881; 809-494-5523
Tropic Island Yacht Charters
Tortola
800-356-8938; 809-494-2450
Valef Yachts S.A.
800-223-3845; 215-641-1264; 215-641-0423
Via Carib Yacht Cruises
St. Lucia
514-274-0011
Virgin Islands Charter Yacht League St. Thomas
800-524-2061; 809-774-3944
Worldwide Travel
800-881-8484

CANADA:

Blue Pacific Yacht Charters
Vancouver, B.C.
604-682-2161; 604-682-5312

Bosun's Charters
Sidney, B.C.
604-656-6644

Canadian Yacht Charters
Gore Bay, Ont.
705-721-4297

Charter Associates
Powell River, B.C.
604-872-7210

Desolation Sound Yacht Charters
604-339-4914; 604-339-7222

Discovery Yacht Charters
Little Current, Ont.
800-268-8222

Executive Sailing Charters
Toronto, Ont.
416-203-3000

Fundy Yachts
St. John River
506-659-2769; 506-634-1530

Hindeloopen Charters
Sidney, B.C.
604-656-1768

Island Cruising
Duncan, B.C.
604-748-6575

Lion's Head Yacht Charters
Lion's Head, Ont.
519-793-4232

Sail Cape Breton
Cape Breton Island
902-345-2694; 207-594-4506

Seahorse Sailing
Sidney or Egmont, B.C.
604-655-4979

Venture Yacht Charters
Kingston, Ont.
613-549-1007

EUROPE RIVER/CANAL BARGES:
Abercrombie & Kent
800-323-7308; 708-954-2944
Carlisle Cruises
800-221-4542; 800-426-9297
Continental Waterways Ltd.
800-227-1281
European Canal Cruises
800-367-0303
Frontiers International
800-245-1950
Julia Hoyt Canal Cruises
800-852-2625; 508-535-5738

GALAPAGOS ISLANDS:
Elite Yacht Charters
213-552-7968
Galapagos Cruises
800-359-0365

MEDITERRANEAN AND MIDDLE EAST:
Elite Travel International
212-752-5440
Elite Yacht Charters
213-552-7968
Hillem Nooh
Bahrain
463 138
Huntley Yacht Vacations
800-322-9224; 215-678-2628
International Charter Connection
800-366-6532; 303-426-0914
Ocean Charters
800-922-4833; 908-671-2207
Sunsail
800-524-7388
Tradewind Yachts
800-825-7245; 804-694-0881
Valef Yachts S.A.
800-223-3845; 215-641-1624; 215-641-0423
Worldwide Travel
800-881-8484

Yacht Connections
800-238-6912
Zeus Tours and Yacht Cruises
800-447-5667; 212-221-0006

SEYCHELLES:
Seychelles Underwater Centre
Mahe, Seychelles
213-392-8054
Yacht Connections
800-238-6912

SOUTH PACIFIC:
ATM Yachts
800-634-8822; 714-650-0889
Club Mariner
800-334-2435
Elite Yacht Charters
213-553-7968
Ocean Charters
800-922-4833; 908-671-2207
Sun Yacht Charters
800-772-3500

U.S.: EAST COAST
Annapolis Bay Charters
Annapolis, MD
410-269-1776; 301-261-1815
Associated Mystic Yacht Charters
Mystic, CT
203-536-1949
AYS Charters
Annapolis, MD
410-267-8181
Bay Island Yacht Charters
Camden, ME
800-421-2492; 207-236-2776
Bight Services Inc.
Annapolis, MD
410-263-2838
C&C Charters
Pt. Pleasant, NJ, Grasonville, MD
800-638-0426; 908-295-3450; 800-773-7245; 410-827-7888

CSA Charter and Sail

Norfolk, VA
800-296-7245; 804-588-2022

Cape Yacht Charters

Falmouth, MA
800-345-5395; 508-540-5395

Carolina Wind Yachting Center

Washington, NC
800-334-7671; 919-946-4653

Chesapeake Sailing School

Annapolis, MD
800-966-0032; 410-269-1594

Classic Charters

Wiscasset, ME
207-882-5448

Coastline Sailing School & Yacht Charters

Noank, CT
800-749-7245; 203-536-2689

Dodson Boat Sales

Stonington, CT
203-535-1507

East Passage Sailing

Portsmouth, RI
800-922-2930; 401-683-5930

Eastern Shore Yacht Charters

Oxford, MD
800-854-0061; 410-226-5000

Elite Yacht Charters

213-552-7968

Free State Yachts

Annapolis, MD
410-266-9060

Freedom Yachts

Middletown, RI
800-999-2909; 401-848-2900

Hartge Chesapeake Charters

Galesville, MD
410-867-7240; 301-261-9040

Haven Charters

Rock Hall, MD
410-639-7140

Havre de Grace Sailing Services

Havre de Grace, MD
800-526-1528

Hinckley Yacht Charters
Bass Harbor, ME
207-244-5008

Julyan Chesapeake Charters
Oxford, MD
410-226-5777; 410-226-5450

La Vida Yachts
Chestertown, MD
410-778-6330

Long Reach Charters
Orr's Island, ME
207-833-6659

Manset Yacht Service
Southwest Harbor, ME
207-244-4040

McKibben Sailing Vacations
Burlington, VT
800-845-0028; 802-864-7733

Morris Yachts, Inc.
Southwest Harbor, ME
207-244-5509

Oyster Bay Sailing School
Oyster Bay, NY
800-323-2207; 516-624-7900

Paradise Bay Charters
Annapolis, MD
410-268-9330; 301-261-1709

Pelorus Marina
Rock Hall, MD
410-639-2151

Pleiades Yacht Charters
Bethesda, MD
301-530-8075

Prevailing Winds
Newport, RI
401-846-6096

The Sailing Emporium
Rock Hall, MD
410-778-1342

The Sailing Place
Atlantic Beach, NC
919-726-5664

Sail Westbrook
Westbrook and Norwich, CT
203-399-5515

Sigsbee Sailing Center
Port Washington, NY
516-767-0971

Spindrift Cruises
Tenants Harbor, ME
207-372-6245

Sun Yacht Charters
Camden, ME
800-772-3500; 207-236-9611

U-Sail-It
Colchester, VT
802-878-8888

Whittaker Creek Yacht Charters
Oriental, NC
919-249-0666

Yacht Services International
Green Brook, NJ, City Island, NY
908-752-1463

Yachting Operation Services
Henderson Harbor, NY
315-938-5495

U.S.: GREAT LAKES

Adventure Plus Yacht Charters
Sandusky, OH
419-625-5000

Apostle Islands Yacht Charter Assn.
LaPointe, MI
800-821-3480

Bay Breeze Yacht Charters
Traverse City, MI
616-941-0535

Burr Yacht Charters
Mt. Clemens, MI
800-445-6592; 313-463-8627

Door County Sailing
Sister Bay, WI
414-854-2124

Harbor North Charters
Huron, OH
800-451-7245; 419-433-6010

Michigan City Sailboat Charters
Michigan City, IN, New Haven, MI
219-879-7608
Northwind Sailing
Grand Marais, MN
218-387-1265
Port Clinton Yacht Charters
Port Clinton, OH
419-734-6207
Sailboats Inc.
Bayfield, Manitowoc, Sturgeon Bay, Superior, WI; Chicago, IL;
Hammond, IN; Mt. Clemens, MI; Thunder Bay, Ont.
800-826-7010; 715-392-7131

U.S.: SOUTH

A-B-Sea Sailing
New Port Richey and Marathon, FL
800-227-5127; 813-845-1726
Blue Water Yacht Charter
Ft. Lauderdale, FL
800-522-2992; 305-768-0695
Cedar Mills Marina
Lake Texoma, TX
903-523-4222
Corpus Christi International School of Sailing
Corpus Christi, TX
512-881-8503
Cruzan Yacht Charters
Coconut Grove, FL
305-858-2822
Easy Sailing Yacht Charters
Coconut Grove, FL
305-858-4001
Florida Yacht Charters
Miami Beach and Key West, FL
800-537-0050; 305-532-8600
Fort Myers Yacht Charters
Fort Myers, FL
800-468-1807; 813-466-1800
Fun in the Sun Yacht Charters
Dania, FL
305-923-2808

Gypsy Star Charters

St. Petersburg, FL;
813-867-5718

Kentucky Lake Sails

Grand Rivers, KY
502-362-8201

La Gringa Sailing Services

St. Petersburg, FL
813-822-4323

Landfall Charter Services

Ft. Lauderdale, FL
800-255-1840; 305-763-8464

Nautica Boat Club

Denison, TX
800-969-9622; 903-463-7245

O'Leary's Sarasota Sailing School

Sarasota, FL
813-953-7507

Royalty Yacht Charters

St. Petersburg, FL
813-898-0100

Sailboats Inc.

Longboat Key, FL
800-826-7010

Sailing South

Destin, FL
904-837-7245

Southern Yacht Charters, Inc.

Fairhope, AL
800-458-7245; 205-928-1283

Southernmost Sailing

Key West, FL
305-745-2430

Southwest Florida Yachts

N. Fort Myers, FL
800-262-7939; 813-656-1339

St. Petersburg Yacht Charters

St. Petersburg, FL
813-823-2555

Texas Sailing Academy

Lake Travis, TX
512-261-6193

Treasure Harbor Marine
Islamorada, FL
800-352-2628; 305-852-2458

Yachting Vacations
Punto Gorda, FL
800-447-0080; 813-637-6634

U.S.: WEST COAST AND ALASKA

ABC Yacht Charters
Anacortes, WA
800-426-2313; 206-293-9533

A Day on the Bay
San Francisco, CA
415-922-0227

Alaskan Wilderness Sailing Safaris
Valdez, AK
907-835-5175

Anacortes Yacht Charters
Anacortes, WA
800-233-3004; 206-293-4555

Aventura Sailing Association
Dana Point, CA
714-493-9493

Bellhaven Charters
Bellingham, WA
800-542-8812; 206-733-6636

California Sailing Academy
Marina del Rey, CA
310-821-3433

Cass' Charters & Sailing School
Sausalito, CA
800-472-4595; 415-332-6789

Charter Associates
Pt. Roberts, WA
206-945-0232

Club Nautique
Alameda and Sausalito, CA
800-343-7245; 510-865-4700

D'Anna Yacht Center
Oakland, CA
800-262-5959; 510-451-7000

Dana Harbor Yacht Charters
Dana Point, CA
714-493-1206

Elite Yacht Charters
Beverly Hills, CA
213-552-7968

58 22' North Sailing Charters
Juneau, AK
907-789-7301

Harbor Sailboats
San Diego, CA
800-854-6625; 619-291-9568

Intrepid Yacht Sales and Charters
Bellingham, WA
800-826-1430; 206-676-1248

Inside Passage Charter Co.
Ketchikan, AK
907-225-8551

Marina Sailing
Marina del Rey, Long Beach, Newport Beach, Redondo Beach, Channel Islands, San Diego, CA
800-262-7245; 310-822-6617

Marine Adventure Sailing Tours
Juneau, AK
907-789-0919

Northwest Marine Centers
Seattle, WA
800-659-3048; 206-283-3040

Olympic Sailing Club
Berkeley, CA
800-223-2984; 510-843-4200

Pacific Yachting
Santa Cruz, CA
800-374-2626; 408-476-2370

Penmar Marine Charters
Anacortes, WA
800-828-7337; 206-293-4839

San Diego Yacht Charters
San Diego, CA
800-456-0222; 619-297-4555

San Juan Sailing
Bellingham, WA
800-677-7245; 206-671-4300

Santa Barbara Sailing Center
Santa Barbara, CA
800-350-9090; 805-962-2826

Set Sail Yacht Cruises
San Diego, CA
800-553-7245; 619-224-3791

Spinnaker Sailing
Redwood City, CA
415-363-1390

Waltzing Bear Charters
Sitka, AK
907-747-3608

Windln Sails Yacht Charters
Friday Harbor, WA
800-752-4121; 206-378-5343

U.S.: HOUSEBOATS

Dale Hollow Marina
Celina, TN
615-243-2211

Herman & Helen's Marina
Stockton, CA
209-951-4634

Hontoon Landing
Deland, FL
800-248-2474; 904-734-2474

Houseboat Vacations
Astor, FL
800-262-3454; 904-759-3252

Lake Powell Resorts & Marinas
Phoenix, AZ
800-528-6154; 602-278-8888

Miller's Houseboats
Suwanee, FL
800-458-2628; 904-542-7349

Playmate Resort Marinas
Colorado River, Mohave Lake, Lake Mead, Lake Shasta, California Delta
800-752-9669; 213-691-2235

Remar Rentals
Thousand Islands, St. Lawrence Seaway
315-686-3579

Sunshine Line
Deland, FL
904-736-9422

INSIDER
PERSONAL
REPORTS

Your ship pulls against the lines holding it to the pier and seems as eager to go as you are; the lines are cast loose, the ship points to the sea, and it's free; with wind in your face and motion under your feet, the world beckons.

The following 20 Insider Personal Reports give you that kind of thrill. They recount exciting cruise adventures taken by professional travel writers on oceans, seas, rivers, coastal waters, fjords; first-class or third-class; on megaships, chartered boats, barges, and every type of vessel in-between; to the Arctic Circle and Antarctic; jungles and metropolises; everywhere and nowhere. They evoke the fun of cruising and discovery, the joy of encountering new people, cultures, and unspoiled regions.

There's a danger though — you may have an immediate and unexpected longing for sea air and blue water, for expeditions beyond the horizon, for acting out dreams.

We hope that you read these first-hand reports at leisure, and that they help make your dreams become reality.

SWIMMING WITH WHALES AT SILVER SHOALS BANK

by Marty Snyderman

The shallow waters of the 50-mile long Silver Shoals Bank are approximately 85 miles northeast of Puerto Plata in the Dominican Republic. Most of the deeper portions of the bank are only 70 to 90 feet, and in many sectors, towering coral heads rise to the surface. On the whole, the banks are not known for good scuba diving. However, during the winter months of the northern hemisphere more than 1,000 humpback whales migrate to the Silver Shoals from their northern feeding grounds off New England, Canada and Western Europe. For a whale watcher, the Silver Shoals are heaven on earth.

I was aboard *Coral Star* which normally operates as a dive charter boat, but during the winter months she carries whale watchers to Silver Shoals, as well as supplies for scientists who spend their winters studying the whales.

Due to the arrangements made by the government of the Dominican Republic and the scientists, a special permit allows a limited number of snorkelers to join *Coral Star* to observe the whales. The snorkeling operation is tightly regulated. Fully prepared to enter the water, the snorkelers go out in skiffs, but most of the observation is topside. Occasionally a whale, or perhaps a cow/calf pair, will become curious about a skiff. Sometimes these humpbacks circle the boat or dive below the boat and just hang in the water. When the whales seem interested, the snorklers are allowed to slip over the side. The strictly enforced rule, however, is no chasing. Despite their size, humpback whales can be very wary animals. All it takes to scare them away is a single snorkeler swimming toward them. However, once in a while a whale or a group of whales become so comfortable around swimmers that they will swim up to the snorkelers to check out their human counterparts. This is what happened to us.

We were returning by skiff to the mother ship after a morning of whale watching, and as we neared *Coral Star*, we saw a pair of playful whales swimming next to the boat. Soon we realized that Howard Hall and Bob Cranston were in the water with the whales. Howard and Bob were working on a *National Geographic* special about Caribbean marine life.

Cathy Cranston was scuba diving under the boat looking at Christmas tree worms and angelfish when she looked up and saw a pair of full-grown humpback whales looking at her from only a few feet away. Humpbacks have a keen sense of hearing, and the noise from scuba bubbles will usually send them off into the distance as soon as you exhale. But there are times when divers encounter humpbacks that are curious about divers and bubbles. I happened to be on the surface looking down at the scene when Cathy first looked up and saw the whales. All I can say is that she swims a mean backstroke, but there was no getting away. These whales were intent on investigation. Steve Drogin, Mark Thomas and I slipped over the side of our skiff to watch the whales, and soon the whales became curious about us.

Time after time the female swam toward us and cruised to within a few feet of us without ever bumping anyone. Many times the distance separating me from the whale was only a few inches. I felt certain that I could have reached out and touched her, but something inside of me felt like that might be a violation of her trust, so I refrained.

As the day progressed the whales continually swam around us. The female would go from one snorkeler to the next, and come back again, constantly maneuvering within our group. We spent the day free diving down to get a look at the whales and waiting on the surface as the whales came by to give us the once over time after time. They seemed equally adept at swimming on their stomachs, backs, sides or while constantly rolling over. Occasionally the female stood on her head and on her tail; once she swam right up to me while I was on the surface, only to lift her head out of the water above me as she supported herself with her tail before sliding back into the water next to me. Once again, not even a nudge.

At the end of the encounter, our legs were cramping, and our booties had worn holes in our feet, but we just couldn't get enough. As the whales finally swam away, we slowly crawled back into the zodiac, too tired and too stunned to say very much. Back aboard *Coral Star* someone started to say something profound about our encounter, but the four of us just shook our heads and started to laugh. We weren't sure that we believed what had just happened to us.

LOG OF ANTARCTICA & THE FALKLAND ISLANDS
by Kim Robertson
December 10
Port Stanley, the Falklands
Clear blue skies are the exception at Stanley. This day happened to be exceptionally clear, sunny, almost warm, with hardly any wind. After the long ride in from the Mount Pleasant airport we had a lavish lunch laid out in the pub known as Deano's, or Monty's (and variously miscalled Beano's, Manny's, Dinky's, Doozy's, and Bunky's). With most of the afternoon free and with the weather so inviting, most of us chose to walk around the town.
December 11
Bleaker Island/Sea Lion Island
Shortly after breakfast we arrived at our first destination, Bleaker Island, home to Finn Ferguson, the island's sole resident and land keeper.

We began our hike across the grassy plains to the Rockhopper penguin colony, a mile-long walk through tussock-grass mounds and sheep pasture. Along the way a rather large colony of Magellanic penguins looked like prairie dogs as they popped up from their burrows to investigate the new activity above ground.

We arrived at Sea Lion Island after lunch. The island has a perfect habitat for the rare Southern sea lion which breeds on its boulder beaches.

Clusters of portly Southern Elephant seals, seemingly indifferent to our presence, snorted and belched as we unloaded ourselves onto their beach. The larger groups of seals were sub-adult males who had come ashore to begin their "catastrophic molting" whereby they lose both their fur and epidermis. We were amazed at their 10' long, 4,000-lb. bodies, but learned that the dominant males or "beachmasters" can reach lengths of up to 15' and weigh five tons! Perhaps most endearing of all were the numerous five to six week old elephant seal pups asleep on the beach.

Many commented on the strange sight of domestic animals (sheep, cows) sharing the same habitat with Magellanic and Gentoo penguins. The Gentoo colony supported some 100 birds, all well into breeding season. Most of the eggs had hatched, and we had the opportunity to see a few of them poking their heads out to beg their parents for a bite to eat. Many of us made our way up to the Sea Lion Lodge where hot coffee and tea were served. Back near the beach, a pod of five Orca, or Killer, whales was spotted.

When the last zodiac returned from shore, we pulled anchor and headed south into the Drake Passage to Antarctica.

December 12
Drake Passage

By lunchtime, it was evident that we had come close to the Antarctic Convergence due to the thick fog bank we encountered. The Convergence is the point where the warmer waters of the South Atlantic meet the colder waters of the Antarctic. Black-browed Albatrosses were seen off and on during the day. Cape Petrels (also known, more poetically, as Pintado Petrels) were the most consistently seen birds of the day, showing off their flashy checkerboard pattern as they wheeled and glided over the wake of the ship.

Several lectures were given: a basic introduction to Antarctica, animal and bird species we were likely to encounter, a slide-talk on the rocks and ice of the Antarctic.

The evening was dedicated to the Captain's Welcome

Cocktail and Dinner party. We donned our best attire and toasted to a fantastic and successful voyage to the ice.

December 13
Elephant Island
   The skies were overcast and gray, and the fog hung low over the cold seas. We arrived at our first Antarctic landfall, Elephant Island, shortly after lunch. The fog continued to mask this 28-mile long island, but as we drew closer to the shores, the rock cliffs of Point Wild emerged with an awesome presence. It was here, on April 17, 1916, that Shackleton's men landed in their three small lifeboats after their expedition ship was crushed in the ice of the Weddell Sea. All of us tried to imagine what it must have been like to spend almost an entire winter here in these dreadful conditions.

December 14
Penguin Island/Arctowski Base-King George Island
   The higher bluffs off to the right of our landing beach were occupied by a nesting colony of Southern Giant-Petrels. These big birds — with the wings of albatrosses, but with the faces of scavengers — were nesting on the ground in rough rocky places, but with open ground nearby to allow them room for running take-offs. We kept a respectful distance, not wanting to experience the legendary spitting of the Giant Petrels, which are known to be capable of projecting a stream of proventricular oil for a distance of some six feet.
   Scattered along the beach like driftwood from a shipwreck were the remains of fur seals, elephant seals, and Weddell seals. Their partially mummified carcasses stood in stark contrast to the living beauty of the sleeping Weddell and Elephant seals, which allowed us to readily approach to get a closer look. The Weddell seals were particularly endearing, with their large eyes, upturned whiskers, and graceful lines. Although their motion on land was labored, underwater they dive to depths of 1,800 feet for up to 45 minutes, searching for food.
   After lunch we found ourselves just offshore from the Polish Arctowski station. A wet snow began to fall as we

lowered the zodiacs in preparation of our landing. Arctowski Station was built in 1977 by an expedition headed by Professor Stanislaw Rakusa-Suszczewski. This year-round station carries out investigations involving hydrobiology, marine biology, geology, and meteorology. We landed on the long rocky beach of Thomas Point, among several curious Gentoo penguins who watched us from a discrete distance. Whalebones of all sizes and shapes littered the beach on the way to the station. The Poles greeted us with smiles and hot coffee in the common room of their station. Many of us took the opportunity to stretch our legs on an extended walk to the end of the beach. Afterwards, we brought most of the station's personnel back to the ship for a visit and provisioned them with a few fresh vegetables until their next supply boat arrived.

December 15
Antarctic Sound/Paulet Island

We awoke to the sound of pack ice grinding along the hull of the ship. We had come into the Antarctic Sound overnight, and the waters were filled with chunks of loose pack ice in every shape and size. The *Explorer* slowly made her way through the maze of ice, bumping the larger pieces off to one side or the other. Captain Demel gave us an extremely close look at one large berg in particular; enough so that a few of us could reach out and touch it.

It was slow going through the ice, but we eventually made our way to Paulet Island. We arrived shortly after lunch and prepared to go ashore to see the massive Adelie penguin colony. We landed on Paulet Island, an extinct volcano which was covered by an enormous number of nesting birds. About a hundred yards inland on the north coast were the remains of a hut built from the local stones. This was where the crew of the Swedish ship *Antarctica* had spent the winter of 1903. The *Antarctica* (before the days of radio) was on her way to collect Dr. Otto Nordenskjold's expedition which had wintered further south at Snow Hill Island, when it was beset and foundered in the pack-ice of the Weddell Sea in February

1903. The crew managed to get ashore, about 25 miles, to Paulet Island with some provisions and stores. They built a hut where 22 men slept in their reindeer sleeping bags, roofed over by sails and sealskins.

The Adelie Penguin colonies stretched acre after acre, making up a thriving penguin city. Everywhere we looked there was action. Along the gravelly beach, Adelies were arriving constantly in little groups. Ten or twenty penguins would suddenly appear in the surf, swimming about in milling circles just offshore.

An arriving Adelie would walk in among the closely spaced nest sites — dodging the attacks of its neighbors, who would jab at it half-heartedly without getting up from the rockpiles that passed for their nests - until it reached its own nest. Then the greeting ritual would begin, as the mate on the nest stood up to face the mate arriving from sea. With much braying and craning of necks and bowing of heads and rolling of eyes, the two members of the pair would loudly go through the ritualized display that reaffirmed their devotion to each other; and finally the arriving bird would take its place on the nest, while the other would go off to feed.

On our return ride back to the ship, we toured through towers of icebergs. Incredible blues and aquas. One berg looked like a wall of glass. The evening was perfectly calm, and the light in the sky during our northward course was so spectacular that many of us were torn between sleep and the perfect picture.

December 16
Deception Island
"Thar she blows!" An early morning call announcing two humpback whales were sighted off the port bow raised many of us from a deep slumber. Two animals were apparently feeding just below the surface, as we could see their mouths open and close on two occasions. Captain Demel did an excellent job of positioning the ship so that all could get exceptional looks at the two whales. One animal, obviously interested in the presence of the ship, frequently raised its

head above the surface (known as "spyhopping") in an attempt to get a better look at us. We all tried to get photographs of the undersides of their flukes, for the Antarctic Humpback Catalog. We stayed with the whales for a good hour.

Deception Island is a doughnut-shaped volcanic island with a thin slice removed, allowing ships access to the hole of the doughnut. Early sealers recognized the protection this island offered and began using it during the early 1820's.

Our first of three stops at Deception Island began at Whaler's Bay, site of the old Hector Whaling Company that operated here from 1910 to 1931. Many climbed to the highest point they could find, while others searched out the Pintado petrel colony in the cliffs. The colony was spread out in many cracks and crevices throughout the rock face, and their monkey-like chirping could be heard all the way to the top of the rise. Later we wandered through the old British Antarctic Survey station that had been destroyed by a volcanic ash eruption in 1969 and subsequent flooding. Along the beach we could find areas of steaming sand as the tide went out.

After lunch we moved up the caldera to Telefon Bay, the site of a deep crater that was recently active. A lone Chinstrap penguin came ashore to investigate the crowds of people on the beach, and just stood there, watching all of us, watching him. This little bird stood directly in one of the hot vents seeping through the sand, seemingly oblivious to the 98-degree water swirling around his feet.

It was decided that he had the right idea, and we moved the ship to an area where several hot thermal vents rise through the sand, and heat the frigid waters of the caldera. The brave and/or foolish among us stripped down to our bathing suits (or equivalent) to take a plunge. Surprising to all was how great it felt — if you could find the perfect spot where hot meets cold. Even those of us who only lasted a minute or two were initiated into the Pendulum Cove Swimming Club.

December 17
Paradise Bay/Neumayer Channel
 We arrived at Paradise Bay under gray and cloudy skies. The bright red buildings of the abandoned Chilean base, Gonzales Videla, stood out against the pure-white backdrop of the glaciers behind it. We split into groups for a zodiac tour at the abandoned station.
 The experience of setting foot on the Antarctic Continent had an olfactory element added. The depth of the penguin guano underfoot may have been related to the fact that Gentoos are present year-around in the vicinity of their nesting colonies (unlike many penguin species which spend the off season well out at sea). Gentoos were incubating eggs in their rockpile nest all around the foundations of the buildings and sheds in the station area.
 A female Crabeater seal was spotted resting atop a small iceberg. She allowed the zodiacs to approach the iceberg and only occasionally acknowledged our presence with a yawn or a lazy glance before closing her eyes again. From such a close vantage point we had a chance to observe her sleek, dark-blond body and numerous scars. The long scars on the flank indicated that she had successfully escaped a leopard seal attack at an early age. The scars along her head are typical in Crabeaters as they are quite aggressive during the mating season when the males compete for females.
 After leaving Gonzales Videla, we slowly made our way out of Paradise Bay. The wind gained considerable strength as we worked our way south. Low clouds hung close to the water, masking the massive mountain peaks. We passed across the Bismark Strait to the LeMaire Channel in gusty 40-knot winds. By the time we entered the Lemaire, the wind was clocked at 65 knots, and the ice had been blown into the channel, choking our passage. This would be our furthest south point on our voyage; we could go no further in such conditions. We made a hasty retreat.

December 18
Foyn Harbor/Alcock Island
We arrived at the entrance to Foyn Harbor just after breakfast. The air was still and we were surrounded by beautiful bergs of every shape. Foyn Harbor was named for the godfather of modern whaling, Svend Foyn, who in 1865 invented the exploding grenade harpoon. This invention would forever change the pace of modern whaling and eventually lead to the demise of all the great whale stocks. The harbor itself was used as an anchorage for factory ships during the 1920's.

A zodiac tour around the harbor brought us to a half-sunken whaling vessel of unknown origin. Its exposed rusty decks were covered in patches of snow, and we could see the remaining aft section resting below the clear waters. A quick peek into one of the portholes showed the collapsed planks and rotted hull. The ship was probably abandoned when the whaling company ran short of funds, and the pressure of the pack ice over the years slowly crushed and eventually sank the vessel at its mooring. We drove around the small island to view several lichen and moss-covered rocks, the only real vegetation of the Antarctic. Bright-green mosses and burnt-orange lichens filled every possible crevice. Many of us had the opportunity to see a Leopard seal in the water on our way back to the ship. Numerous Crabeater seals lounged motionless on the bits of pack ice, giving us excellent looks and great photo opportunities.

We soon headed to our final stop in Antarctica—Alcock Island in Hughs Bay. Much to our delight, humpback whales were seen along the way! The ship slowed down for each group of whales so we could get photographs of their tails and observe their feeding behaviors. The animals were most likely cooperatively feeding just below the surface based on their swimming and diving patterns. As we neared Alcock Island, a crew member took a scout boat to shore to investigate that landing situation. He soon radioed back with bad news: the snow was chest-deep and we couldn't have made a proper landing. This is how expedition cruising goes...you never know the conditions until you get there. It was decided that we would take the zodiacs around the island to view the Chinstrap colony and intricate rock formations. Huge icebergs bobbed up and down in slow-motion near the deep waters around the island. Chinstraps marched along crowded "highways" to reach the top of their colony. Deep caves and colorful lichens appeared around every corner.

Two humpback whales were seen feeding near the ship, and we were able to approach these whales in the zodiacs to get a real sense of their true size. They hardly took notice of our presence as we followed them from a respectful distance. A few times they were seen to "tail breach" throwing the lower half of their body into the air, and slamming it back onto the water.

By dinnertime the seas had gathered strength and the wind soon gusted up to 45 knots. The *Explorer* rolled and pitched in the windswept seas. We were experiencing true Drake Passage weather. It was a long and exciting night at sea, as the ship creaked and shuddered with every smashing wave.

December 19
Drake Passage

We were crossing the Antarctic Convergence as evidenced by the thick fog bank surrounding us. It was a day of reflecting and relaxing, and several lectures were given.

December 20
Cape Horn

The seas were calmer. The ship was decorated with Christmas decorations, obviously done by the staff elves during the middle of the night.

We had a following of birds for much of the day. Black-browed Albatrosses were the most numerous, but we also had a number of Wandering Albatrosses. These huge birds, with their 11-foot wingspans, towered above all the lesser gliders in the vicinity. Sometimes the Wanderers would come in very close to the stern, inspiring a frenzy of focussing among the photographers on the pool deck; then the big birds would move away, looking ponderous and deceptively slow in flight, to disappear in the distance for a while before approaching again.

Blue Petrels were numerous during the morning, sometimes gliding close to the ship. When we were on the final approach to Cape Horn, scores of slender black seabirds appeared; these were Sooty Shearwaters, which nest all around the Cape.

On shore at Cape Horn, some members of our party noticed little birds flitting about the scrub — the first songbirds we had seen since leaving the Falklands. These were Rufous-Collared Sparrows, found all the way from southern Mexico to this, the absolute southernmost tip of South America. This was the height of summer for the sparrows of Cape Horn, and they were singing their clear whistles on all sides as we hiked up toward the great albatross monument that dominated the island.

That evening, the Captain hosted his Farewell Party. Our voyage to the Southern Ocean had been a fantastic one, filled with vivid images and exceptional experiences we will long remember.

SAFARI AND THE SEYCHELLES
by Shirley Linde

At 5:00 a.m. we were awakened by a call at the tent door, and soon we were bouncing and lurching in a land rover through the blackness along a pot-holed, rutted dirt road. Hyenas called. Scared by the headlights, a zebra bolted across the road. A gazelle bounded away on the left, and an ugly wart hog glowered.

We were on our way to a pre-dawn launch of a hot air balloon as part of a Micato Safari/Renaissance Cruise trip. We got our safety instructions as the fires roared at dawn to fill the balloons. As we soared off, the balloons seemed huge, and the heat and noise more than we had expected, but white knuckles soon relaxed as we sailed over the grasslands and began spotting wildlife: a herd of 12 elephants, a pride of lions, three ostriches running ungainly over the plain; later a rare black rhinoceros and her baby, wart hogs, hyenas, giraffes, zebra, wildebeests and gazelles. And at the end, a champagne breakfast in the field where we landed.

We had come on the safari after a night in Nairobi, flying in a 1942 DC3 over the Great Rift Valley to the 700 square mile Maasai Mara Game Reserve, land of the Maasai tribes just north of the Serengeti Plains and reputed to offer some of the finest game viewing in the world. We landed on a grass airstrip in the middle of nowhere, and immediately embarked on the first game run in a six-passenger van with open roof for picture-taking. There are two game runs per day of two to three hours each. Just driving to the camp we saw hundreds of zebra, groups of giraffes munching from the tops of trees, some cape buffalo and dozens of families of baboons (we were told they frequently get tipsy on fermented fruits from the sausage tree, also used with honey and sugar for a local beer).

Maasai tribesmen and women were in traditional dress as they walked the roads or tended their herds. (But if you want to get to know the Maasai, try to do it on an individual basis around a campfire, and skip the programmed visit to the village where we were badgered and harassed.)

We learned our first Swahili word from our driver: "Jambo!" for hello, and it was given with smiles wherever we went.

The cruise/safari trips are a combination vacation that allow you to sample several experiences as part of one trip; a three-day photo safari in Kenya, then a 12-day cruise to some of the world's most exotic ports.

The Renaissance carries only about 100 passengers, small enough to get into out-of-the-way ports. We started the cruise segment of the trip in the town of Mombasa in Kenya, then headed to sea with port stops at the exotic ancient towns of Lamu in Kenya and Zanzibar in Tanzania, then Anjouan island in the Comores, Nosy Be and Nosy Komba of Madagascar, and four of the Seychelle Islands.

The mix of various races and cultures—African, Arab,

Indian, Chinese, Portuguese, Turkish, British, French—showed up in an exciting mixture of varied architecture, music, dress and customs. We also saw flora and fauna found nowhere else on earth.

First Port — Lamu

Going to this African port is like stepping back into the 18th and 19th centuries. Donkeys are the main mode of transportation on land, and old-style boats called *dhows* are used for transport from island to island. As part of their Arab-Muslim heritage, many men still wear traditional full-length clothing and most women dress in black. There are old cannons on the seawall, narrow winding streets, and buildings with heavy ornately-carved doors. There are 31 Muslim mosques, the oldest built in the late 1300's, and a two-century old fort.

Old 18th-century guest houses are being authentically restored. We saw donkeys haul sand and coral to rebuild thick lime-and-water walls. The architecture is fascinating: kitchens are upstairs because of heat and smoke, doors face only north or south to protect from the sun, large steps keep children from going upstairs to adult bedrooms, fish are kept in the bathing water to eat mosquito larva.

I got lost in Lamu, separated from my group in the crowded narrow alleys, but found wonderful fabrics to bring home. Predominant colors: red made from mangrove bark, black, from ebony roots, and white from shells.

Historic Zanzibar

Ancient Zanzibar was the commercial center of east Africa for centuries, indeed was the most important town on the east African coast. Ruled by Omani Arabs, it was a center for ivory trade, the world's largest producer of cloves and the largest slave port on the east coast.

Take a walking tour of the town to see the ornate old houses, and some beautiful grill work and oiled carved teak doors among what is mostly neglected and rundown. Special places: the sultan's palace (it is rumored he later killed the workmen or cut off their hands so that nothing like it could ever be built again), the chilling former slave market, the Livingstone House where the explorer lived before his last expedition, and the church with the crucifix made from the tree under which Livingstone died.

The Bon-jour Bus of Anjouan

Anjouan is one of the Comoros Islands, with palm trees, beaches, rivers, a mile-high mountain, lakes and waterfalls. But the island is on a self-destruct course with overpopulation and an out-of-control birthrate. In the year 2,000 the population is expected to be double 1980. Trees are being felled for fuel; soil is eroding to the sea, destroying coral as it settles; schools and hospitals are on strike. There is one physician for 14,000 people.

The best way to see the island is by the local wooden-bench minibus that careens around the hills and curves. Friendly children line the streets, waving and shouting "bon jour" as you whiz past.

Good buys: the local perfume, *ylang-ylang*, and vanilla, the two major exports. Walk around the town of Matsamudu, the capital, to see old 17th-century houses, the marketplace, Muslim women with yellow mud packs on their faces designed to keep the skin soft for their husbands. Remember, in Muslim areas ask permission before taking photos, or unobtrusively use a telephoto lens.

Madagascar — Biologists' Heaven

Madagascar, one of the largest islands in the world, broke away from the African continent some 15 million years ago and has plants and animals not found anywhere else. There are 1,000 species of orchids, 30 species of lemur, and half of the world's chameleons. For decades, bands of pirates had their main Indian Ocean bases here, mostly living in the town of Libertalia. Government, schools, and communications are almost nonexistent. There are still pagan rites, such as turning the dead and taking relatives from their graves during certain celebrations. As in Anjuoan, the birthrate is exploding, deforestation is rampant, and much of the island's topsoil has washed away.

Our first Madagascar port stop was Nosy Be. Again some wonderful old architecture, but run down and in disrepair. There were excellent carvings to buy, and hand-embroidered tablecloths and shirts, and a handcraft unique to this area of stitched and cut-out linen. *Don't buy tortoise or ivory — you can't bring it back.* The children of Nosy Be came shipboard that evening in costume to present local folk dance and song.

The second Madagascar stop was Nosy Komba, a quiet dignified village with many crafts and a not-so-dignified colony of black lemurs, protected by the villagers who hold them sacred. Lemurs eat early in the morning and sleep midday, so we had our own breakfasts early and arrived by tender on the island by 8 with bananas. "Wear old clothes," our cruise director said. He was right. The lemurs came hurtling out of the trees, thudding onto our backs and shoulders, sometimes our heads, jumping from person to person, tree to ground to tree, grabbing and gorging on our bananas. Playing with the lemurs, then walking through the village was like stepping live from the pages of the *National Geographic.* I mentally wrote the caption "Lemur on Your Shoulder." The cruise director also explained about the short digestive systems of the lemurs: "Don't walk under the trees after 20 or 30 minutes." He was right about that too.

Praslin — Finding the Garden of Eden

Many plants and animals here are endangered species and many are not found anywhere else. The epitome was in the Vallee de Mai, on our first Seychelle island, Praslin (the s is silent). The forest is hushed and majestic. Coco-de-mer palms, found in only two or three known places in the world, soar a hundred feet above, their giant fronds making a patterned roof to the forest. Some are 900 years old. Is this the way the Garden of Eden looked? Or did a brontosaurus once munch on leaves in a forest such as this? The huge palms produce the heaviest seed in the world, each about 55 pounds. The dangling pistil of the male tree is ponderously evident, and the heavy seed of the female tree unquestionably a giant version of human female parts. The screech of a rare black parrot interrupts our reverie, and we reluctantly leave.

La Digue — Boulders and Beaches

Could anything be better than the Vallee de Mai? Well, perhaps La Digue. It shows dramatically that the Seychelles are really the peaks of the submerged mountainous continent formerly joining Africa and India. The beaches of La Digue are like no other. Huge granite boulders — the tops of underwater mountains — stand out against white sand beaches, and palm trees growing from crevices and cliffs hang out over hidden coves. There are no taxis on the island; you get to the beaches by bicycle or oxcart. You can stop to see the giant tortoises (it's okay to climb the fence and get in and feed them), photograph the island houses with their pastel colors and ornate grillwork, visit the old cemetery, climb to the top of the island, or snorkel and swim at one of the secluded beaches. Wherever you go, it will be quiet — the islanders don't like noise so they decided not to have any generators. The silence is wonderful.

Aride — Bird Sanctuary

Only seven people live on Aride — it's run by the society for the Promotion of Nature Conservation. You can only get on the island from the ship by zodiac. We were lucky and had calm seas so that we could go ashore. We saw thousands of rare sea birds including fairy terns, frigates, and noddys, and the always-present iguana lizards. Sometimes you can see roseate terns.

Mahe — Last Port and Best Place to Segae and Zuke

There's more to the Seychelles than seashores, and Mahe proves it. We're now only four degrees off the equator; the cruise has been 1,900 miles. Many people stay for a day or two after the cruise to see Mahe's miles of camera-worthy coastline with the outcrops of granite dating back millions of years. You can see tea, vanilla and cinnamon plantations and shop along the streets in Victoria or at Craft Village where local craftsmen and women embroider, weave, and construct model boats. At the Seypot cooperative, potters make original designs from local clay. You can eat local food at places such as the Marie Antoinette restaurant (Creole) or at the Round Island Restaurant, which is part of the Marine Preserve. You can hear local music at several hotels and clubs, such music as *segae*, *moogae*, and *zuke* and derivations from 18th century French dances, passed down from the early settlers. You can hike one of the newly laid out Nature Trails (brochures prepared by the Ministry of Tourism give detailed descriptions of each trail with line drawings of birds and plants).

We hiked the Morne Blanc trail in the Morne Seychollois National Park, and were rewarded at the top with a view over the island, looking at terns and frigate birds that were soaring *below* us.

If you want more time on a boat, you can hire a dive boat for a day or week and see the other wonderful world of the Seychelles — under water. There are at least 200 species of fish and 150 species of coral.

And you might wish to sample the breadfruit while you are there; it is said that if you eat it, you will return.

ALONG THE BALTIC TO FORMERLY OFF-LIMIT STATES
by Anne Kalosh

At a time when the tourism infrastructure of the Baltic nations is still developing, a cruise may be the ideal way to explore exotic "new" locations without experiencing the risks of vanishing hotel reservations, inferior rooms and uncertain rail and bus connections.

What is remarkable about sailing — besides the opportunity to visit virtually every Baltic port making headlines — is the chance to sail on a family-owned ship that is at home in these waters year round.

The *Kristina Regina* is operated by Finland's Kristina Cruises, a two-ship company with a "small is beautiful" philosophy, according to Captain Mikko Partanen, whose brother is the ship's chief engineer and whose sister works in cruise sales. It was the dream of their father to launch a sailing for Americans.

The Baltic States voyage on this intimate Finnish vessel is one of the summer's most dramatic itineraries. The destination-intensive, 11-day cruise-tour features ports in the Baltic republics of Estonia, Latvia, and Lithuania, as well as Russia, Poland, Germany, Denmark and Finland. All shore excursions — except overland options to Berlin, Vilnius (the one place requiring a visa) and Kronstadt — are included in the fare.

During its regular year-round schedule to Helsinki and Tallinn, *Kristina Regina* carries up to 400 passengers, most of whom are Europeans. For its special summer Baltic States sailing, sold exclusively in the U.S. by Euro-Cruises, the passenger limit is 220. That enables clients to enjoy the comfort of two lower berths, as well as single-seating dining.

The *Kristina Regina* is a converted steam vessel, built in 1960 and fully refurbished in 1990. A few passengers initially complained that their cabins were cramped, but with a busy itinerary keeping everyone ashore from sunrise to sunset, I found the accommodations adequate. For clients requiring more space, connecting cabins with his and her bathrooms are recommended.

The continental Finnish-accented cuisine earned high marks from passengers. Two lounges — one with a dance floor and live music nightly — are the core of the ship's social life. In addition, on several evenings passengers were treated to entertainment from ashore — either a lecture on an upcoming port or singing and dancing by a costumed folkloric group.

The *Kristina Regina* has two saunas, but no pool. The real strength of the gleaming white ship is its size: small enough to dock in the heart of every port city, and enabling passengers to develop a bond, which is virtually impossible on today's mega-liners.

I had never before sailed with such an interesting group of

people. They included a Navy-man-turned theatrical producer, a romance novelist, authors, university professors, a globe-trotting collector of chess sets and a retired Greek shipping tycoon and his wife.

There also was an ethnic contingent, including a Milwaukee man whose father had grown up in Koningsberg, East Prussia — since World War II a part of Russia and called Kaliningrad, a port on the itinerary.

There was a couple whose Lithuanian fathers met on an ocean liner while emigrating to America and a woman taking her college-age grandson to meet his Old World relatives in Latvia.

Excursions, which are included in this cruise-tour, consumed most of the day in every port. Without fail, guides spoke fluent English, were well-versed in their city's history and able to answer a range of questions. The itinerary began at the Danish capital of Copenhagen. Passengers arriving on early flights were dropped off downtown to explore while their luggage was taken to the ship in preparation for the late-afternoon departure.

At the German city of Lubeck, an old Hanseatic port, the ship docked downtown, and passengers took a guided walking tour past Gothic churches and old patrician manors.

Those who chose the optional tour to Berlin departed from here, overnighting at the first class Penta Hotel and stopping in Potsdam before rejoining the ship the following day at Rostock, Germany's biggest and most important port until hit by heavy bombing during World War II.

The Polish city of Gdansk, the birthplace of the Solidarity movement, was a favorite of many passengers, who said they were charmed by its canals and historical buildings, lovingly restored after the war. The tour included a visit to Sopot, the old resort town between Gdansk and Gdynia, where passengers strolled on Europe's longest wooden pier.

Kaliningrad, formerly the East Prussian capital of Koningsberg, was isolated by the U.S.S.R. as a top-secret naval base. A tour visited the city's amber quarry and factory and stopped at the cathedral ruins, which hold the tomb of philosopher Immanuel Kant.

At Klaipeda, a Lithuanian port, passengers on the optional tour of the capital of Vilnius departed for their overnight at the Lifuiva Hotel and sightseeing, including Gedeminas Square and a stroll through the Old Town. They rejoined the ship the following day at Riga, Latvia.

Riga was a personal favorite, with its lavishly decorated buildings, one with an ornate art nouveau facade. At Tallinn, the Estonian capital, we wandered along the cobblestone lanes of the ancient Upper Town, where Lutheran and Russian Orthodox churches were being restored after 50 years of neglect.

Two days were spent in St. Petersburg. Highlights included the gold-domed St. Isaac's Cathedral, and The Hermitage with its rooms of art treasures. After dinner on board, passengers attended a ballet ashore, and, on returning to the ship, got a glimpse of the city's famous "white nights."

The next day, passengers visited Pushkin in the Russian countryside, touring Catherine's Palace, which is set in a stately park. Some passengers chose instead to spend the second day in Russia on the optional excursion to Kronstadt to see its renowned maritime museum. The cruise ended the following morning in Helsinki, the Finnish capital.

FALL FOLIAGE ON THE UPPER MISSISSIPPI
by Shirley Linde

Fall foliage cruises are scheduled on the *Mississippi Queen* in September and October. I went to St. Louis with my new camera, taxied past the famous Gateway Arch of St. Louis and was soon on the brick-paved boat landing ready to board.

The *Mississippi Queen* is the largest steamboat ever built. Commissioned in 1976, she was designed by James Gardner (who also designed the *QE 2*), as the fleet sister of the legendary *Delta Queen*, built 50 years earlier in 1926, and now listed on the National Register of Historic Places.

The Queens are driven by a huge red wooden paddlewheel

astern. Each has a raucous steam-driven calliope played at each arrival and departure. (The *Mississippi Queen's* is the largest calliope every built — 44 pipes and a sound range of five miles.) With only an eight-foot draft, the paddlewheeler can travel north to where the navigable Mississippi ends at St. Paul, MN, almost at the river's headwaters. With the filigree, wrought iron, and brass, and the grand staircase with a crystal chandelier hanging from a mirrored ceiling, the ambiance takes you back to the spirit and elegance of the Great Steamboat Era of the 1800s.

The *Queen* is no speedster. She meanders along at about eight miles per hour, giving you a chance to capture some good pictures of morning river scenes with the mist rising, red leaves and weeping willows in the hazy autumn light, river barges and fishermen silhouetted at sunset. In between, you can watch the 26 locks and dams you go through, or join others flying kites off the top deck, dance to the ship's band or listen to its late-in-the-night jazz, blues and ragtime. Or you can sit in the Paddlewheel Lounge watching the bright red paddlewheel go round and round. Entertainment, like traveling, is not fast-paced.

I did visit the statue of Samuel Clemens (Mark Twain) and his house and his cave and the place in Hannibal, MO, where he grew up; you can picture Tom Sawyer, and Huckleberry Finn and Becky Thatcher living there.

You steamboat past Keokuk, Iowa, named after Chief Keokuk of the Sac and Fox Indians, located where the Des Moines and Mississippi Rivers meet. You wander on by Burlington and Davenport and Galena and then stop at Dubuque, a typical early river town based on lead mining and steamboat commerce, with the Woodward Riverboat Museum and a cable car taking you up a bluff for a magnificent view. The next day, you pass Prairie du Chien, the meeting place for fur traders many decades ago, and arrive at Lacrosse, Wisconsin, where the Mississippi, Black and La Crosse Rivers meet. (For bargains in down comforters and jackets, go to the factory outlet of The Company Store; for tasting, to Christina Wine Cellars in the 100-year-old Milwaukee Freight House or the Heileman Brewery; and for a good view go up to Grandad Bluff.) The next port is Wabasha, another former logging and fur-trading center with towering bluffs.

By now you have visited the pilot house and learned that the Mississippi is the crookedest river in the world and drains 41 percent of the United States, and that sandbars occur on the inner curves of the river bends, and that you call a vessel a "boat" on the river, not a ship, and that the speed on the river is in miles per hour, not knots as it is on the sea. And you have gorged on soul-satisfying food traditional to the river country — shrimp remoulade, crabmeat Louisianne, fried catfish, jambalaya, creole gumbo and pecan pie.

On the last day, many bends in the river later, you arrive in Saint Paul, the uppermost point of commercial navigation on the Mississippi. You may want to take some time there to take a tour of the twin cities, or head further north.

OFF-THE-BEATEN PATH IN PAPUA NEW GUINEA
by Gena Reisner

We arrived at Boagis Village on the remote Melanesian island of Woodlark unannounced, the first passenger ship ever to call there. Ashore, we found a beautiful little village; a few dozen stilt houses on a white-sand beach, coconut palms, and screeching red parrots. All along the beach, women and children were busily scrubbing sea cucumbers.

For our small group of expedition members, hungry for close encounters with exotic, untouched cultures, it was an ecstatic afternoon. And it got better.

As the late afternoon sun cast a golden glow over the scene, the men of the island returned home in lavishly carved and decorated outrigger canoes. They waded ashore, hauling sacks of sea cucumbers and loads of firewood. Suddenly, a little boy who had been fishing quietly all afternoon began running through the water, yelling "Catch! Catch!" He was so excited that his sarong slipped off, but he landed a foot-long fish, enough for his family's dinner.

My husband, Paul, and I lingered as long as we could, caught the last zodiac launch back to the ship, and climbed up on deck for a final look at Woodlark as we pulled out to sea. The evening would now unfold in the shipboard routine we had grown to love: first, a recap and briefing, where our lectures and naturalists would talk about the day's experiences and prepare us for the adventures to come; then an excellent meal with good conversation; and before going to bed early, a quick gaze at the Southern Cross.

Paul and I had joined 40 other passengers aboard *Explorer*, an expedition ship that offers a unique combination of adventure and creature comfort. Expeditions visit remote islands where even the mail boat doesn't call, seek out unusual flora and fauna, and stop at uninhabited paradisiacal islands where passengers can scuba dive, snorkel, or go beachcombing.

The 96-passenger *Explorer*, first launched in 1969, is no ordinary ship. Designed by Lars-Eric Linblad to be an expedition vessel, it soon pioneered leisure travel in Antarctica and successfully navigated the treacherous Northwest Passage. Run first by Linblad and then by Society Expeditions, it now belongs to Explorer Shipping Corporation (a joint venture of Abercrombie & Kent and a European shipping company), which has staffed it with the peerless Society Expeditions team.

The ship's small size, shallow draft, and robust construction give it far greater flexibility and maneuverability than most ships, allowing it to visit places inaccessible to other ships. The ship has an ice-strengthened hull for Antarctica cruising, and its rubber zodiac rafts allow passengers to land where the *Explorer* can't go.

Our quest was to follow the *kula* ring, a secret society of hereditary trading partners, through the remote islands of Milne Bay, then to visit the nearly inaccessible Asmat, famed in the art world for their wood-carving and believed to be the cannibal tribe that killed Michael Rockefeller. It was a journey that would take us from the idyllic South Sea Islands of everyone's dreams to a muddy world of whooping, feathered warriors, and finally to Indonesian islands famed for birds of paradise, pearls, and black magic. Along the way, we'd have a chance to snorkel and dive in some of the richest waters in the world.

We landed in Rabaul on the island of New Britain, part of Papua New Guinea (PNG) and about as far away as one can travel from the United States. Except for a whirlwind stop in PNG's capital, Port Moresby, Rabaul was the most accessible place we'd see for the rest of the cruise.

This landing was an expedition stop, where we were the first passenger ship ever to visit a village. First contact: It's the sort of thing that makes a would-be explorer's heart beat faster.

When we landed, everyone in the village rushed onto the beach to greet us and show us around. The ship's doctor made our visit especially welcome by setting up a clinic, something he did at several remote stops during the cruise.

The next day, we sailed to Milne Bay, and the world of the *kula* ring. Manoa, a member of a *kula* family and a PNG government employee who never had seen a cruise ship before, came along to help us plumb the ring's mysteries. In one rich conversation after another, Manoa told us folk tales from his childhood and fascinating details about the *kula* rituals.

Members of the *kula* ring trade shell necklaces and armbands around a ring of islands. Each trade object is ornately, bizarrely decorated and has its own name, pedigree, and set of trading partners. *Kula* people set off on trading expeditions in special trading canoes, which are beautifully carved and hung with gleaming cowrie shells. "It can take ten years for one armband to go around the circle," Manoa said.

For us, the fun was to seek out elaborate trade canoes pulled up on shore and to peek into all the houses until we found a trove of armbands and necklaces hung on a wall.

There's a practical side to all of this: The islands in the ring also trade essentials for their simple way of life. Woodlark supplies all the stone tools, for example, while Manoa's home island, Panaete, supplies red shells, pigs and canoes.

Our first glimpse of a *kula* object was on the back of a young woman on Kiriwina in the Trobriand Islands. We spotted it in the huge dance spectacle that the islanders put on for us. Other than her outlandish necklace, she looked like all the other women dancers: bare-breasted, garlanded with fragrant flowers, decorated with sprays of leaves, crowned with a mass of sulfur-crested cockatoo feathers, and sporting a red grass skirt and a face painted with asymmetrical black-and-white designs.

The men looked much the same, but they wore loincloths of pandanas leaf, and their dances were filled with boisterously erotic motions. "They call these the islands of love," a lecturer said.

We next followed the *kula* ring to Alcester Island, important to the ring as a go-between. Again, we arrived unexpected. "There's no way to inform them that we're coming — no telephone," Manoa said. "We did put out the word on the radio; there's one program a week in their language."

On Alcester, Manoa gently persuaded a man to show us his secret collection of *kula* armbands. Then we wandered along the sunny beach, with its lush palm trees and turquoise waters, until we found two trade canoes carefully sheltered under woven grass mats. That afternoon we visited Woodlard, the sea-cucumber island, where we peeked into each grass hut until we discovered a bunch of *kula* necklaces hung on a wall.

The climax of our *kula* circuit was a visit to Manoa's home island of Panaete. Here we were greeted by another vision out of Gauguin: an island beauty clad only in a profusion of perfumed white flowers and a plain grass skirt. The villagers put on a dance show that they seemed to enjoy immensely, shouting out comments followed by gales of laughter.

As our morning ashore drew to a close, people shyly began

to offer some items for sale. Everything, from a child-size red shell necklace to a carved ceremonial ax handle, seemed to have the same price of $10.

We returned to the ship and put aside thoughts of South Sea Islands. It was time to move on. We were sailing away from paradise and on to the most eagerly anticipated stop of our trip: the Asmat.

The itinerary called for a day at sea, a brief morning in Port Moresby, then three more days at sea. In that time we would cross the tricky border that bisects the island of New Guinea into the independent nation of Papua New Guinea and the Indonesian province of Irian. In fact, it is the rare and patient traveler who manages to see both sides of New Guinea in one trip.

During our days at sea, Tobias Schneebaum, who might know the Asmat better than anyone else, took center stage. Schneebaum lived among the Asmat for several years and wrote about his experiences in the fascinating book *Where the Spirits Dwell*. He ultimately became an expert on Asmat culture and art who collected, curated, and wrote the catalog for the important collection in the Asmat Museum in Agats, the Asmat capital.

Schneebaum regaled us with tales of his life among the Asmat. He taught us a scatological Asmat song that crystallized the tribe's raw, humorous, and graphic view of life. And he began preparing us for the traditional Asmat greeting: a guttural whoop that he rendered as "Whuh! Whuh! Whuh! Whuh!"

And the Asmat were ready for us. As we approached their first village in our fleet of zodiacs, they swooped out to meet us. Standing in dugout canoes, they were painted from head to toe, curved shells were threaded through their noses, and their heads and bodies were draped with feathers and fur. They beat their drums wildly, banged their paddles against the sides of their canoes, and shouted "Whuh! Whuh! Whuh! Whuh!" We were mesmerized.

They took control of the zodiacs and pulled us effortlessly

back to the village. There they lined us up in the shade and began to dance in the shimmering heat. The frenzy mounted as they dashed to and fro, tossing white lime at us in greeting, their feathers waving inches from our faces.

After the dance, they invited us into the men's house. We climbed a ladder made of logs and entered a long, stifling grass hut with a low thatched ceiling. Men were seated silently in front of the artifacts they had to sell: daggers made of cassowary bone, shell nosepieces, woven armbands with feather fobs, a few wood carvings. We all bought.

Amazingly, there were still more worlds for us to explore on this two-week cruise. Leaving Asmat, we sailed up the Indonesian archipelago toward the two intriguing islands that remained on our itinerary.

We stopped first at Dobu in the Aru Islands, the only source of the golden-plumed greater Bird of Paradise. Dobu also is a thriving Oriental emporium, where Chinese traders buy shark fins, bird nests, pearls, and spices.

We wandered the town on foot, visiting a market, a schoolyard, and a Chinese warehouse, while dodging frequent thunderstorms.

We had one last stop: the Gorong Islands, famed throughout Indonesia for black magic. The performance there was terrifying. First, a troupe of boys and men danced hypnotically to drums, as they slowly went into trances. Then the leader proved that they were in trances by sewing the little boys' cheeks and lips together and making them chew broken glass.

Happily, the afternoon's activity washed away the brutal magic. We snorkeled through a grotto, getting our last glimpse of clown fish and anemones, graceful butterfly fish, and banded sea snakes.

Finally, it was time to leave *Explorer*: Disembarking at Ambon, we were entertained and fed until flight time, then flown to heavenly Bali for dinner and the famous monkey dance. Not a bad ending.

But we couldn't help envying the dozen or more passengers who had stayed on board. They would sail up the Indonesian archipelago, snorkeling and diving in Indonesia's brilliant waters and visiting more remote, untouched, endlessly fascinating islands, living again an explorer's dream come true.

JOURNEY THROUGH THE GALAPAGOS
by Emily Rosen

It is the beginning of the world; it is the end of the world — six-hundred miles off the coast of Ecuador in South America, right there on the equator. It is 12 hours of sunlight and 12 hours of darkness in a place often referred to as the Isles of Enchantment.

It is the archipelago known as the Galapagos Islands, where Charles Darwin landed in the *HMS Beagle* in 1835, and launched his studies of the origin of the species.

Today, we take our voyage aboard the *Nortada*, for a nine-day (more or less) cruise around this group of 15 remote islands, discovered in 1535, with a swashbuckling history of renegades, buccaneers, and early exploitation by fur sealers and whalers.

"All travel in South America benefits from a sense of humor." — so sayeth the introductory words to our itinerary from Inca Floats, a Galapagos Tour Agency.

But, if you like boats, and water and hiking and wildlife, *and*, if adjusting to new people and sharing a bathroom with strangers, and eating whatever you are served with no recourse to "substitutions," *and* if you can survive living in quarters so close that two people must stand vertically belly to belly (sucked in) in order to occupy the same room at the same time, then hang in for the wondrous rewards of a visit to these magical islands.

We land on the island of Baltra, to the full confusion of guides meeting tourists. Finally sorted out, we bus and barge and bus once again to Santa Cruz Island, passing arid lands, verdant fields and unusual cacti, with a rewarding view of the hand-painted look of a deep-turquoise sea, calm as an unoccupied bath.

The dirt-road village of Porta Ayora, which boasts a hospital and a post office, is our destination. Once there, it is determined that the Hotel Galapagos — the intended place of rest for our travel-weary bodies — is overbooked. So, with no panic, we merely boat again, cross the bay, to land on the dock at the Hotel Delfine.

Here we are met by German-born Erna, our *hotelier*, and one of the first of the island's inhabitants, arriving here some 50 years ago. After a late lunch, while listening to wonderful stories about the islands, we deposit our belongings in our rooms, perform a quick clean up, and it's off again. Rodrigo, our land guide, escorts us to the Darwin Station and Museum, for a quick look at the famed land tortoises in captivity while being studied at the Darwin Research Center.

No wonder Darwin was intrigued and inspired! These tortoises are big ones! Some as old as 600 years — but no one knows for sure. They move slowly, but respond to touch. After a gentle caress by Rodrigo, they extended their necks fully from under their shells.

But, more than 24 hours of travel is exhausting, and after the turtles, it is an effort to keep our heads up for dinner at the Hotel Galapagos (another dinghy ride back across the water), where, despite some wariness of the raw fish, we down the rest of the meal with ease.

Now "re-fueled," a midnight swim in the Pacific from the beach at the Delfine sets a mood of infinite joy and contentment. We splash like children under the moon and the stars.

A series of false starts, diverted plans, and unexpected inconveniences are nothing more than what one must factor into the price to be paid for a trip to this heaven on earth. The next few days are a haze of mechanical failures, pursed lips, and remarkable displays of equanimity. Generator and water problems on board the *Nortada* puts the cruise on hold for a day or so. When we finally get underway, thanks to what may generously be called "a patch job," the worst consequences of significance are a few occasions when the air-conditioning konks out.

The days that follow are punctuated by morning and afternoon hikes, each day on a different island, sometimes two in one day. Each time we dinghy to our destination from the ship, landing on rock or on beach and prepared with the proper footwear. (The degree of "wetness" of a landing is always predicated on the tides at the precise moment of arrival.)

The Galapagos Islands were formed by volcanic eruptions and uplifts — they were never a part of the mainland, so the plants and animals native to the islands arrived by flying or floating on air currents, or by sea journeys.

The islands reach 16,000 feet above the ocean floor, and 5,600 feet above sea level. Their total land area is 3,043 square miles; the aggregate length of the coastline is less than 100 miles. The terrain ranges from lava rock to scrubby cactus growth to lush fields of agriculture and flowering plants. Some of the wildlife is different from island to island. There are always cool currents and comfortable breezes — although sunscreen and wide-brimmed hats are recommended as protection against the tropical sun.

Only five of the islands are inhabited, with a total resident population of 4,260, all making a living from a combination of tourism, cattle ranching, fishing and farming.

Organized tours began in 1969. Today, after Ecuador declared the islands a national park, there is a limit of 20,000 visitors a year. Forty-five sites were chosen by the park as biologically and scenically the richest for tourists, with a maximum permitted usage at any one time of between 12 and 90 people, depending on the island. This makes for an intensely personal, almost other-worldly, experience for our tour group, which consists of 12, plus our very necessary guide. In fact, no one may set foot on an island *without* a certified guide, whose responsibility, among others, is to enforce the strict park rules regarding respect for the surroundings: We do not litter; we do not pet the wildlife; we do not "lift" any of the flotsam, jetsam or assorted animals, vegetables or minerals. We leave only footprints.

We swim and snorkel almost every day, each time from a different beach and from a different coastline. Remarkably, each island holds a different fascination. Santa Cruz, with its main town of Porta Ayora, its hotels, its bustling village commerce and its well-built houses tucked into the roadsides, is a picture of Old World activity. The people are smiling and friendly.

On Santa Cruz, we visit the rain forests where tortoises roam freely and where visitors are allowed to get close enough to touch them. Those of us who prefer not to walk in the muddy light mist can go on horseback for the trek through the highlands. On this island, we also see our first pit craters.

From there, it's onto the uninhabited (by humans) islands, to catch glimpses of the true natives of this land: sea lions and iguanas, flamingos and pelicans, boobies (red foots, blue foots and masked) and herons, Darwin finches, albatrosses, sharks, penguins and frigate birds. In this atmosphere, one begins to care about the wildlife; while at home I screech at the sight of a lizard, here I long to pet an iguana, possibly the ugliest of all God's creatures. Etienne, our naturalist guide, born in Antwerp, regales us with information born from his love of the land and its inhabitants, of his acquired knowledge of biology and geology, to say nothing of his expertise in boating.

Dinghy rides take us through mangrove swamps at sunset, when sea turtles mate in evening silence unbroken except for the lapping of the water. We observe a male albatross perform his mating dance, complete with whistle, bill pecking and intricate choreography. We see a mother sea lion, lying exhausted, after just giving birth. We go close to white, fuzzy baby boobies and adult females atop their nests filled with eggs.

We watch as a female sea turtle shapes a tractor-like trail from the water onto the beach, to dig a sand hole to lay her eggs.

This is a multi-level, multi-dimensional experience. Each island is a landscape distinct from the others. Each day we see natural sights that we think cannot be equaled — until the ones we see the next day. The blow-holes on Hood Island, created when pressure of the waves made cracks in the lava rock, spray misty sea water in our faces. On Prince Philip's Steps on Tower Island, we inch into a 20 (or so) foot-high crevice, just wide enough for one body to fit, stepping gingerly — rock upon rock — until single file we reach the top, where, once again, we view the mating antics of the different bird species.

James Bay is the nearest thing to a sculpture garden I have ever seen. The lava rocks here are shaped in an artist's fantasy — tall, short, curved, straight, rough, edged, smooth, massive, minuscule. On Bartholome, we walk up 360 feet to its summit, pitted by what looks like moon craters. Out in the water rises the enormous Pinacle Peak lava rock, which broke off from the mainland and looks like a broad-based obelisk stretching hundreds of feet high, a beacon against the setting sun.

On Floreana, we stop at Post Office Bay, and follow a tradition of old-time mariners; checking the mailbox to see if anything is posted to an area near our homes. I "win" a postcard addressed to a town about 10 miles from where I live, and accept the responsibility of contacting the recipient and seeing to it that the message is personally received.

It's now New Year's Eve and our hotel chef bakes chocolate cake, and our tour group puts on our own show, and watch as the boat crew burns the old year in effigy, taking a five-foot-tall "doll," dressed in pants, jacket, shoes, socks, out in the dinghy, performing some voodoo-like chants, pouring gasoline, igniting all and sending the fiery pyre out into the water. Back on ship, ready to sail on again, we all fade shortly after the witching hour has struck.

Too soon, it is time to go home. We have forgotten the occasional clogged toilets, the sputtering generator, the empty water pipes, the Dramamine and Lomotil we consumed. We remember only the white sands and the black sands, the lava rocks and the turquoise water, the beaches, the tortoises, the diving boobies, the unity of the wildlife, Pinacle Peak in the sunset, the sounds of silence — nine days at the edge of the world.

CINDERELLA CRUISE TO NOWHERE
by Lea Lane

As a fortunate traveler who voyages to exotic places for a living, I have cruised through the Panama Canal, along the Yucatan Peninsula of Mexico, from Israel to Cyprus, and along Turkey's Turquoise Coast to Istanbul, and the Island of Rhodes. I have sailed to offshore islands of the Philippines, and to Brazil, rocked in hurricane-force winds in the Bay of Biscay overnight from England to Spain, and in the breezy southern Caribbean, and have crossed the seemingly endless archipelago of islands stretching from piney Finland to Sweden.

But one of the most memorable cruises I ever took went nowhere.

It wasn't remarkable for its itinerary (there was none), or its luxury, although it was Cunard's *Queen Elizabeth 2*, a grande dame of the sea, and I was splurging on first-class accommodations. No, it was because of a small incident that happened early in the voyage.

My tale starts when I was packing for the two-night party cruise, which was leaving from New York Harbor on the Hudson River — just like the grand old pre-jet days when people wore hats and threw streamers, and when a dozen ships were parked in the harbor, stocking up for their trips across the Atlantic. (Today, New York's harbor lies mostly empty except for day cruises up the river, the former air carrier *Intrepid*, now a museum, and occasional cruises such as the one I was booked on.)

As I packed, I carefully placed my clothing on my bed to make up outfits to wear on board. I was being very organized, as I had invited my mother, who wasn't used to the idea of luxury, and seemed a bit uncomfortable by the whole idea of sharing a first-class stateroom as a guest of her daughter.

Anyway, with all the things that came up, I closed my suitcase at the last minute and raced out the door to catch a cab to take us to the harbor.

On board, the old-style elegance of this great ship was thrilling. It was built for transatlantic and around-the-world voyages, and was like a floating city. The spa looked inviting. The high ceilings and fine furnishings reflected the stature of a ship that was built in 1969 as the last of the true ocean liners.

I walked around, and found a place that seemed cozy in a corner of the library. A huge puzzle of a still life — a vase of flowers — lay unfinished, with hundreds of pieces locked together by passengers before me. I would add my few pieces, perhaps a petal or two, on my tiny journey.

Our cabin, although not particularly large, was wood paneled, and had an old-fashioned porthole. We freshened up and then went on deck to watch the skyline of Manhattan recede into the distance as the ship pulled slowly out to wherever we weren't going.

At an informal get together, dressed in the slacks we came on board in, we met the captain — an extremely tall fellow with bootblack hair and a white outfit who, when asked said, "I have no idea where we're going. Maybe Block Island." We assumed somebody knew, but rationalized that it didn't matter much as there would be no stops. After all, it was the voyage that counted: dinner in the Grille, elegant parties. The works.

We went back to the cabin to unpack, shower, and dress up for dinner. I put my fancy clothes in the closet and my toiletries in the bathroom. But something seemed wrong. Something was missing. My jewelry? No. My scarves. No. My nightgowns. No. My shoes. *My shoes!*

I looked again in my suitcase, but it was empty, as was the bottom of my closet. In my super organization, I had packed my shoes in a bag — and left them on my bed at home.

I looked down at my feet. Sneakers. Not the thing to wear

to a formal dinner. I looked at my mother. She had her shoes in a neat row in her closet. Could I possibly...? But she was a size five and I was a size eight.

I rang in a panic for the room attendant, and she came in a minute.

"I need to buy some shoes," I said sheepishly.

"Well," she said in a tone somewhere between polite and bemused, "I'm so very sorry madame but there isn't a shoe store on the ship."

There was probably a store for everything else. Just my luck. Hadn't anyone else on board ever wanted to buy shoes? Here I was, going nowhere, and condemned to my room. What were my options? Wearing my grungy sneakers with my short silk dress? Going barefoot?

"Just a minute," said the attendant. "I'll see what I can do." And she left me feeling stupid and mad at myself, as my mother used all her restraint not to laugh at my plight.

Ten minutes later the attendant appeared. "Will these do?" she asked, placing before me an array of size-eight shoes, far nicer than the ones sitting on my bed back home. There were sandals, and pumps, and flats and deck shoes. They were black and white and cordovan and bone and taupe, and they were clean.

"How did you find these?" I asked incredulously, and gratefully.

"Oh we have our ways madame," she said. "I'm afraid you'll have to borrow them, but you can use them all if you'd like."

I picked a few pair, never happier. I wore them, they fit and nobody had a clue. I finally understood the meaning of luxury and service, and left a big tip.

I never forgot to pack my shoes again. And I'll never forget that little voyage to nowhere.

THE WEST INDIES — BY SCHOONER
by D. Rushforth Schild

In Idaho, sailing usually describes a mode of getting down

a ski slope, so a cruise on a West Indies schooner is about as familiar as piloting a rocket to the moon. The laid-back atmosphere of Windjammer Barefoot Cruises, however, makes riding the waves to exotic islands seem as comfortable as sipping snow-snake medicine around the living room hearth. Captain Mike Burke, a retired sea captain, began buying and restoring old sailing ships in 1947. He loved the beauty and simplicity of the islands and wanted to offer everyday folks the opportunity to sail through the scented salt air to dream destinations.

My West Indies adventure was on the *Polynesia*, one of his six ships in the Caribbean. Polished hardwood rails and gleaming brass adorn the smooth, gray wood decks. Shumba, the bright blue parrot, squawks "hello," while Klaus, the ship's portly cat, stares at the new batch of interlopers on her vessel. She gets more friendly at mealtime.

The top deck looks like a pirate vessel in the movies, with coiled ropes, towering masts and webbed rigging. There is an abundance of soft blue mats for daytime sunning or sleeping under the stars. Wooden-walled cabins are cozy and clean, with cool tile floors and roomy bunks. *Poly's* center has a shiny hardwood bar adorned with bunches of bananas and hand-painted batiks from St. Kitts. The glassed-in dining room has huge family-style tables and semi-circular benches anchored to the floor so dinner doesn't roll away at sea.

Before the flaming red sunset, *Poly's* approximately 125 passengers and 40 crew members were laughing together in homey comfort. (That's comfort, not luxury.) Family-style meals offer island fare, from fried plantains to sliced mango to shishkabobbed tuna, garlic-dipped shrimp and grilled swordfish. Cooks turn out gold-crusted breads and feather-fine pastries in a galley the size of a broom closet.

Poly's captain, Marcel Dekker, wears tee shirts, shorts and no shoes. Black ties on his ship are worn only for the toga party — to complement the wearer's sheet and whatever else is scrounged for the occasion.

Dekker, a muscular blonde with eyes the color of the changing sea, brings his Zimbabwean accent and a salty sense of humor to the trip. "The Caribbean is noted for its pirates and buccaneers," he said as *Poly* anchored off St. Barts. "They used to sail ships. Now they drive cabs."

He also offers a rundown on cuisine, recommending Le Select, the tiny French bar that reportedly inspired Jimmy Buffet's famous "Cheeseburger in Paradise." He mentioned a neighboring French restaurant, too. "Go there if you want to pay $4 for a cup of coffee and be insulted at the same time."

A day on St. Barts could be spent snorkeling at one of the several beaches (some nude, some not), devouring great French cuisine ranging from bread, wine and cheese beach picnics to elegant restaurant fare — or browsing through duty-free shops or dodging aggressive French drivers in the narrow cobbled streets.

St. Kitts the following day was the exact opposite. The proper British islanders are delighted to conduct tours of their homes. Our driver, Carlton, treated us to fresh-picked mangos as we drove through the steaming green rain forest to the Romney Batik Factory. There, island women hand paint bright patterns on cotton fabrics. The showroom is a primary color rainbow of skirts, shirts and scarves. This island also boasts wild green-backed monkeys, renovated sugar cane plantations and a walled fort with dozens of huge black cannons. One side of Carlton's island has black volcanic sand beaches; the other looks like the palms are standing in mounds of white sugar. *Poly* docked at St. Kitts overnight and a steel drum band came on board for a dance. Willowy women with sing-song accents sold batik and jewelry and braided our hair into unique Caribbean styles.

Some days were spent lazing on deserted island beaches and snorkeling coral reefs. At lunch-time, *Poly's* crew would wade ashore carrying picnic fare. On board, Dekker also organized hermit crab races (his first mate acted as bookie) and non-nautical boat races. Nearly every night ended in a dance as shipmates, single and paired, started moving to the always present tropical music.

The sea was wonderful and the islands exciting, but it was the warm friendships forged on the voyage that were the most valuable part of the trip. Passengers ranged in age from Howard, 70-something, who won the costume contest in a slip and headband, to a few kids celebrating the end of high school. Couples and singles forged friendships from the first swizzles and no one was ever alone unless they wanted to be. Shipmates unashamedly shared tears as they hoisted *Poly's* sails for the last time to the bagpipe strains of "Amazing Grace."

LEARNING ADVENTURE TO ALASKA
by Shirley Linde
The *SS Universe* gets its culture and academic background naturally — it sails for World Explorer Cruises during the summer, but during the rest of the year the ship is operated by the University of Pittsburgh and the Institute of Shipboard Education as a floating university on Semester at Sea round-the-world voyages.

No minks, tuxedos, gambling and glitz on this two-week cruise. Passengers dress in parkas and wool sweaters, explore spectacular glaciers, visit old gold-mining towns and Indian villages, and go to on-board lectures on Alaskan life and culture, Alaskan history, bird and animal life, marine biology, geology and art, (college credit available). Entertainment includes a jazz pianist, a string quartet at dinner, a flautist and classical guitarist, and well-known stars. There is an 11,000 volume library with information on where to shop, eat, visit and walk in each port.

Fitness programs, bingo, bridge games, ship horseracing, a costume parade, talent night, first run and classic films, films on Alaska, and other special events are available. And of course, there are the ports:
Wrangell. One of the oldest towns in Alaska, it was built along the Stikine River, used for hundreds of years by the Tlingit Indians as a fur-trading route. Unlike most of Alaska, temperatures seldom go below freezing, even in

the winter. (But it rains, so bring some hooded raingear to wear over a sweater or parka.) The highlight of Wrangell is the petroglyphs on the beach, primitive carvings in stone, estimated to be more than 8,000 years old. Take along papers and you can make rubbings using ferns growing nearby. You can buy garnets from children at the dock for as little as a quarter.

Juneau. You have a choice of going for two hours rafting on a river at the foot of a glacier, visiting an old gold mine and panning for gold, or flying over the Juneau Ice Fields — 1500 square miles of solid ice — to a lodge in the wilderness where you are served a fresh salmon dinner baked over an alder-wood fire, with wine chilled in glacier ice. You can also walk around town and visit the Alaska State Museum, the antique-filled Alaskan Hotel and the original golddiggers' hangout, the Red Dog Saloon.

Skagway. You can visit Burro Creek by boat to see a private salmon hatchery built trying to help preserve one of Alaska's treasures, or you can take a ride over the mountains and through the valleys of the historic Klondike Highway, imagining the thousands who walked these rugged paths during the gold rushes (where many died and few got rich).

The Inland Waterway. On about the third day of the trip you begin to see wildlife — a whale sighted off the side, an eagle soaring overhead. All along the waterway are deep uninhabited forests and snow-capped mountains, their peaks towering on both sides, dwarfing the ship.

Glacier Bay. Early in the morning the ship slows to a crawl in the ice-filled waters of Glacier Bay. You rush on deck to see the mist rising from the slushy undulating water. Icebergs and ice chunks float as far as you can see, some with seals lounging on them. Seagulls and puffins fly about. The ship inches forward to within 1,000 feet of the glacier. Bundled in a parka against the cold and drizzle, you stare in awe at the wall of ice hundreds of feet high, jagged, crevassed. This is ice layed down thousands of years ago —

some of it by snow falling at the time of Christ. As you watch, huge sheets of ice explode away with a thunderous roar: the rifle crack echoes through the vastness, and the wall falls slow-motion into the sea with awesome splashes and rolling waves.

Many passengers take a flight by helicopter or float plane over the glacier's ice fields. It is breathtaking as you hover over cliffs of ice and look down on pools of blue and jagged, yawning, mile-deep crevasses — hundreds of miles of ice as far as the eye can see, centuries old, still grinding mountains and carving valleys, as it did in the Ice Ages. The glaciers have been periodically advancing and retreating in this area for some 12 million years.

Anchorage. Its seafront is too shallow to be a seaport, so you board a bus, which drives onto a train, which goes through a mountain pass to a road on the other side. Here are excellent museums and art galleries, and a chance to shop for mukluks, local jade, old scrimshaw ivory and authentic prehistoric artifacts.

Sitka. This formerly Russian town is the ancestral home of the Tlingit tribes, and you will see many totems and magnificent basketwork in the Sheldon Jackson Museum. Be sure to take time for the peaceful walking trail through towering forests.

Ketchikan. Three hundred original handcarved totems are in the Totem Heritage Center. You can also help paddle a 37-foot canoe across a float plane to Metlakatla, the only Indian reservation in Alaska. Native arts and crafts are available for viewing and purchase.

AN UNCHARTED GREEK ODYSSEY
by Bea Tusiani

On the appointed Friday at the end of August, 29 of us from London, Paris, the U.S. and Zurich, descended in Athens for a five-day chartered cruise to the Greek Islands. The trip was to be a payback of sorts for the wives and children of eight families whose husbands traveled for business during most of the year.

Our intentions were to sail into the Aegean and visit the major islands in the Cyclades chain: Serifos, Mykonos, Paros and Santorini. What we hadn't planned on during this sybaritic island-hopping venture were the gale force winds that would ultimately turn our trip in another direction entirely.

We were in high spirits the morning of departure as 16 of us adults, six teenagers and seven children left for the dock in Piraeus to board the *Victoria*. The 108-foot vessel was tied up next to the infamous *City of Poros*, another boat which it was whispered had been repaired and renamed since it was attacked by a band of hooded terrorists two years before.

Climbing on board it hardly went unnoticed that the Europeans traveled light, flinging half-filled duffle bags onto the craft, while we Americans were bogged down with matching sets of luggage, armloads of video equipment and diving gear.

As the boat prepared for departure, all of us quickly set out to find our room assignments and checked out each others' accommodations. The ship itself was divided into four decks, the lowest housing the engine room and galley. Sixteen 8 x 6 foot cabins were distributed on the second deck — mercifully, with windows instead of portholes. The third contained the dining area, bar and wheelhouse; an open sundeck was at the top.

It wasn't until we'd gathered on this upper deck for a bon-voyage "ouzo party" that we learned the winds were going to be a problem. "Unusually strong for this time of year," I overheard the captain say to Dimitri, the only Greek among us. The term "Beaufort 8" was mentioned a number of times, and the faces of the men looked grim. Being in the shipping business, they were familiar with the Beaufort Scale of Wind Velocities.

A Beaufort 8, they said, signified gale-force winds of up to 46 miles per hour — on the sea that translates into 16 foot waves. Beaufort 12 indicated hurricane force winds.

And here we were about to shove off with a Beaufort 8! The Europeans shrugged it off and continued to drink their ouzo, but the Americans scrambled to follow the captain back down to the bridge.

Suddenly, all the initial fears I'd had about taking this trip came back to me. The nagging image of 13 nauseated children heaving their dinners overboard remained with me ever since the day I tried to convince my husband, without success, that five-year olds were too young for this sort of trip.

I was afraid that someone would fall overboard or the boat would capsize. When told that we would be traveling by night, I took comfort in knowing that at the very least, I could spend my nights in a life preserver atop the upper deck, so if the boat went down I could just swim away from it.

I distributed behind-the-ear anti-seasick patches to the American half of our group, and bore the brunt of ribbing directed at "patch people" from the heartier Euro-crowd.

When the captain made an on-the-spot decision to cruise close to the mainland rather than risk sailing out to the Cyclades under the wind conditions at sea, I was enormously relieved. All the others were clearly disappointed.

We stayed that night in Epidavros, and by 5 a.m. the next day the captain assured us we would receive further updates on the Beaufort status and, as the winds permitted, proceed to Serifos, the first of our island destinations.

With a reading of Beaufort 9 the following morning, we were once again advised to stick close to shore. Dropping anchor at a secluded spot in the Saronic Gulf, all 29 of us jumped into the salty sea; the Europeans from the bow of the boat (uncharacteristically wearing swimsuits out of respect for their puritan shipmates), the Americans more cautiously from a ladder that was lowered into the water (trying to be inconspicuous in our lifejackets).

It wasn't until the third night that there was a glimmer of hope that we might after all see one or two of the 39 Cyclades. We were docked at the island of Spetses when the captain passed the word along that the Beaufort has dropped down to 6 and if it remained under that level by five o'clock the next morning, we would be well on our way to Serifos. Raising our glasses of ouzo we toasted the captain in honor of the promising news.

At 3 a.m. the engines roared. I lay quietly in my bunk listening to the boat shift gears, assuming that the Beaufort had finally turned in our favor and we were on our way to Serifos. An hour later the boat was pitching roughly back and forth and I suddenly was struck with fear that the captain had made the wrong decision. Getting up enough courage to look out my window at the gale force wind that was heaving the boat wildly under my feet, I was amazed to discover that we hadn't yet moved from the dock.

Rousing my husband was useless, he mumbled something and turned toward the wall. As I ran out of my cabin the Frenchwoman next door quickly joined me, both of us heading for the deck. Relieved as we were that we hadn't yet left for Serifos in the middle of an ominous Beaufort, we were frightened to see the captain and crew running back and forth across the boat looking over the sides. Had someone fallen overboard?

Understanding nothing of what the Greek crew members were shouting, we clung to the side railings and groped our way below to wake Dimitri. As I banged frantically on his cabin door, the Frenchwoman quietly retreated to her room, leaving me the lone, crazed American on a boatful of 28 others, sputtering wildly that something was terribly amiss.

As it turned out, the chains from the boat's two anchors became entangled and the crew had been trying for the last hour to untwist them by spinning the boat around in circles.

By daybreak things had calmed down, but a reading of Beaufort 7 permanently scrubbed any hopes we had of seeing the Cyclades. Instead, Dimitri informed us that we would be taking an unexpected journey north into the Gulf of Corinth where we would view the ruins of the famed city of Delphi.

The mood seemed to change however when we entered the Canal of Corinth, a man-made waterway sliced into the middle of a mountain, measuring 27 yards from side to side. As our boat gently glided through the narrow canal, we watched from the upper deck in awe of the majestic stillness.

That eerie silence was broken when, as we came into the open gulf, some two dozen dolphins surfaced alongside our boat. Leaping by pairs into the air, they led us fairy-tale like to the entrance of their homeland, Delphi, which in Greek means dolphin.

Arriving at Mt. Parnassos just after dawn we seemed to be the sole travelers along the ancient path that led to what in the 5th Century B.C., was considered the center of the world. Dimitri's wife, Eleni, explained how the priestess Pythia was the oracle who dispensed wisdom to those who sought her advice, about the Temple of Apollo and of the original stadium where the very first Olympic games were held (even the 5-year old could relate to that).

Walking back down the Sacred Path, it soon became apparent that this stop along an unchartered course revealing the vastness of history and the minuteness of time had created a new inexplicable bond between us, European and American, adult and child.

Though the powers of the mighty oracle may have had something to do with drawing us to this magical spot, surely it was Sir Francis Beaufort who pointed us in the right direction.

A MIDSUMMER NIGHT'S DREAM, ON NORWAY'S FJORDS
by Vivian Kramer Fancher

The whole town turned out to greet Reidulf Maalen, commander of the *Crystal Harmony*, as he guided his cruise ship into Vagen Harbor. The welcoming populace assembled on Storkaia pier and cheered the waving passengers, who crowded the decks to watch the hero's homecoming. For the residents of Kristiansund it was a singular event. After three years at the helm it was the first time the captain had parked the boat in his own backyard, the city in which he grew up, attended maritime school and still has his home.

The stop was an agreeable surprise to most of the 600 passengers. When we signed on many months earlier for the two week North Cape cruise, an odyssey at a time of year, early summer, when the midnight sun is in action, Kristiansund wasn't in the line-up. The harbor was added to the itinerary as a thank you after Captain Maalen's skillful piloting five days earlier.

While cruising the coast to get the best possible view of Norway's incomparable Svartisen Glacier, Maalen had entered the narrowest of inlets, the largest ship of its size ever to do so, and had executed a daring turnaround, so close to the water's edge that we felt we could almost touch the shores.

That event marked the beginning of the ascent to the top of the world along the area called Nordland above the Arctic Circle. For five days the *Crystal Harmony* sailed in complete daylight. There was no sunrise or sunset, as the sun was continuously above the horizon line. And if the effect of living in 24 hours of daylight was stunning, so was all the scenery.

The excursions into the fjords—Sognefjord and Geirangerfjord—and the lands surrounding them, provided a panorama of everchanging, breathtaking vistas: rugged snowy peaks reflected in clear, deep, jade waters, the greenest of meadows, narrow gorges, tumbling feathery waterfalls, rushing rivers and Christmas-card hamlets.

The ship anchored in Flaam at the base of Aurlandsfjord, a web of Songnefjord, the country's longest and deepest fjord. Passengers traveled up the mountainside on the famous Flaam Railway that zigzags through tunnels and makes hairpin turns to Myrdal, 3,000 feet above sea level. The local train continues on to Voss, where following lunch, a bus carried us to the Stalheim Hotel with its celebrated view, and back to the boat that had moved to Gudvangen.

The excursion on the following day which began in

Hellesylt was just as dramatic. From the Dalsnibba Observation Point, reached by a road as twisted as a roller coaster, the drop is 5,000 feet down to the splendid and sprawling Geirangerfjord into which flows the very publicized waterfalls, the Seven Sisters. Cascades drop millions of misty gallons hundreds of feet. The most photographed sights in Norway are at Flydal Gorge, a rocky precipice located near the same byway. From here you can look upon sheer cliffs alternating with green patches of land in a pattern so artistic it belongs on a canvas, and we could see where the ship was anchored in the protective harbor.

The stops in port were like a series of enchanting short films, each port chosen for its unique charm and character.

Bergen, Norway's second largest city, is a metropolis that seems to have made the passage between centuries without architectural compromise. The colorful waterfront, home to the commercial center and fish market, is lined with wooden buildings dating from the 15th century Hanseatic period. A few squares away are modern structures of Scandinavian design.

Trondheim is a town of contrasts, too. Founded more than 1,000 years ago, it has the cluttered dignity of former times and a lively center where an open air market is filled with bright flowers, fresh fish and produce. The must-see sights are the Gothic-style Niadaros Cathedral dating from the Middle Ages, the Ringve Museum, a repository of 2,000 musical instruments, and the turf-roofed Trondelag Folk Museum.

Tromso, has been called "The Paris of the North" for its many cafes and restaurants. Located above the Circle, it is also tagged "Gateway to the Arctic," and is the largest city where the sun shines at midnight. The Northern Lights Planetarium and the Arctic Cathedral that houses Europe's biggest stained-glass painting are its major attractions.

Kristiansund is built on three tiny islands— · · · ·--dot is the busiest—so close to each other that they form one community. Although connected by bridges and accessible by bus, the best way to negotiate inter-island visits is by a ferry that regularly encircles the harbor.

The ship also put down in Honnigsvag, starting point for the trek to the North Cape, Europe's northernmost promontory which overlooks the vast expanse of the Arctic Ocean. Oslo, the last stop and the country's capital, was teaming with excitement, its tempo as upbeat as any great city on the Continent. By the time the ship reached Copenhagen, the point of disembarkation, it had been on a voyage not only of "northernmosts," but other "mosts" — the most impressive and the most memorable of journeys.

ADVENTURE ON THE ORINOCO
by Ed Kirk

Pairs of orange-winged parrots and blue-yellow macaws flew overhead, adding specks of color to the gray sky. Dozens of large-billed terns followed us upriver, their brilliant yellow mandibles flashing as they feasted on tiny crustaceans stirred to the surface by our wake. The silt-laden water was broken periodically by playful river dolphin. Dozens of cattle egret, snowy egret and great heron dotted the shore line, while red-haired howler monkeys sat sedentary in trees. Hoots of greeting from curious Warao Indians punctuated the peaceful scene as they paddled their dugouts as near as they could while we cruised by.

This was an afternoon cruising Venezeula's Orinoco, eighth largest river in the world. We were aboard the 138-passenger *Yorktown Clipper*, of Clipper Cruise Line's fleet of yacht-like ships. A well-rounded, personable naturalist staff had been added to Clipper's traditional all-American crew to transform our journey into a true destination-oriented voyage.

The *Yorktown Clipper* is a nimble vessel, but her yacht-like size and shallow draft result in accentuated motion in open sea, so stretches encompassing ocean waters were traveled at night after passengers had retired. Comments the morning after our departure from Tobago indicated that many had been taken by surprise by the rough passage. Waves crashing against the ship during the day attracted little attention as the naturalist staff presented an overview of the adventures that lay ahead. By evening, those affected were regaining their enthusiasm, recovery sparked by the calmer water of the approaching river and curiosity about the diverse area we had entered.

A full day and night cruising upriver brought us to the Indian village of Curiapo, built directly on the northern bank of the Orinoco. Houses are on stilts; streets are wooden boardwalks. The entire village seemed to be on hand to observe the visitors from our little white ship. The children were particularly anxious to greet us and shyly posed for pictures. Before returning to the *Yorktown*, we cruised up a nearby tributary in native boats observing the lush jungle terrain while passing fishermen in small dugouts proudly displayed their catch. Residents of scattered Indian homes observed us from the banks.

The new city of Ciudad Guayana, built at the western terminus for navigable shipping on the river was our next stop. Some passengers opted for a city tour, but most boarded buses for a short ride to the airport and flight to Canaima Jungle Camp, combined with an Angel Falls fly-by in venerable DC-3 aircraft.

Radio reports indicated that the falls were enshrouded with a cloak of clouds — a frequent occurrence — so the pilot headed directly for the camp, where passengers had a choice of activities and a Venezuelan barbecue lunch. Nestled deeply in the jungle of Canaima National Park, the camp is a peaceful retreat surrounded by natural beauty. Eerie rock *tepuys* rise majestically in the distance while tranquil, tannin-tinted lagoons invite swimmers, with a backdrop of canyons and waterfalls. Soon after lunch, we were urged to re-board the planes as word spread that the weather at Angel Falls had cleared.

Sandstone mesas abruptly broke the jungle savannah as we neared Devil's Canyon. An enigmatic feeling overcame us as we entered this "lost world" (featured in Speilberg movies), surrounded by jagged, pointed peaks rising through the clouds. Water cascaded above and below us as we flew by a series of small waterfalls streaking the sheer canyon walls. The clouds guarding Angel Falls had parted, and passengers could see the entire length of the world's tallest waterfall, an unbroken silver line plummeting over 3,200 feet from the flat mountaintop to the jungle below.

After a restful night, most were ready for more adventure on the river. At 7 a.m., the zodiacs were lowered and boarded by passengers and naturalists for an excursion up the Araguaito Tributary. The true value of the zodiacs now came into play. We were able to coast within feet of the shore line to observe a pygmy kingfisher perched atop a stake and a silver-beaked tanager nestled in the branches. Orinoco geese were spotted on a small bluff, and a cluster of small bats clung under a nearby log. A howler monkey carrying her baby traversed the branches directly above us. A young Indian woman stopped her furious beating of clothes against the rocks, the sight of our orange rubber boats giving her cause for respite from her wash-day chores. As the steamy heat of the day began to descend on the river, we reboarded the *Yorktown* for our voyage to Trinidad.

Our afternoon arrival at Port of Spain was timed to allow for a late excusion to Caroni Swamp. Here, we boarded wooden boats for a sunset cruise to a protected lagoon to await the arrival of hundreds of scarlet ibis. As we slowly made our way through the mangrove, we observed four-eyed fish swimming alongside. The ibis arrived in groups, first two at a time, then dozens, the dying sunlight reflecting on their brilliant plumage as they prepared to roost. Soon a favored mangrove resembled a tropical Christmas tree, as the red birds decorated its branches. The next morning featured a scenic drive through mountainous terrain to the Asa Wright Nature Center, deep in the forest of Trinidad's North Range. Tiny hummingbirds buzzed overhead as we strolled the paths lined with vegetation. Our guides pointed out dozens of birds, all easily visible, even to our untrained eyes.

My week aboard the *Yorktown* now came to a close, but the other passengers would continue on through the lower Caribbean. First, Cumana, the oldest settlement on the Spanish Main, where Dutch and English fought the Spaniards for the valuable salt flats throughout the Colonial period. Here passengers would be taken on a lantern-lit tour of the caves which serve as the daytime home of the nocturnal quacharo — the oil bird — valued for its oil-laden body fat used for lamps. Water and sea life would dominate the next several days in the beautiful Los Roques Archipelago, and Bonaire, with its exceptional snorkeling and diving. The Dutch architecture of Curacao would be explored via a walking tour, and many would enjoy the outstanding shops of Willemstad. The voyage would end in Aruba as the little ship headed for the next leg of her trek, through the Panama Canal and along the shores of Costa Rica.

TRADING AND TREKKING ON THE UPPER AMAZON
by Mark Glass

Although most of us with a marginal memory of grade-school geography think of the Amazon as being in Brazil, its first 700 kilometers, and many of its 1,100 major tributaries, are in Peru. Iquitos (e kee' tos) is the major city and starting point for expeditions. Because of its deep jungle location, Iquitos is only reachable by air and water; no roads exist to connect it with the rest of the country. There are direct flights to Miami via Faucett, a privately owned Peruvian airline with DC-8 fleet service.

Iquitos, with its population of approximately 500,000 lets you know quickly you are experiencing the third world. In brighter days, when the rubber industry was strong, this was a thriving and picturesque metropolis. Formerly elegant hotels, stores and homes are now past their prime, heaps of banana skins rot in the sun, and vultures fly overhead.

The people of the region live in close harmony with the rivers. All along the banks women do their laundry by hand. Dozens of native tribes still live beside the rivers, growing and hunting most of their food, making canoes and paddles from local trees, maintaining tribal languages and rituals. Our trip in September was at the lowest river-stage. Outside Iquitos is a village that consists entirely of houses on rafts, surrounded by lush greenery in September, but which would rise to float with the river and become islands within a few months.

Taxis within the cities are rickshaw-like vehicles propelled by motorcycles. Even more common are river taxis, which are long, thatched-roofed motor boats. On the Sunday of our arrival, the taxis were filled with locals travelling a few miles down river to the white sand beaches dotting the shoreline.

The Amazon Tours and Cruises Company has several boats available for excursions from one to seven days. The largest is the *M/V Amazonas* which can accommodate 42 passengers three to six nights (with flexibility to make special arrangements). Although accommodations are spartan, the rooms are air-conditioned, include private baths, and have filtered and bottled water, safe for American digestive systems.

Three lower-priced smaller boats also have private cabins, but shared bathroom facilities.

While the *Amazonas* covers the distance up and down river, the truly fascinating adventures are the side trips. In a two-day excursion we had seven such forays. We were able to take two treks through different parts of the jungle, visit two native villages, and fish for piranha. We also enjoyed an early-morning bird watch and a late-night trip up a small tributary to listen to the nocturnal sounds of the jungle.

The guides are fluent in English and conversant in every aspect of the region. For example, Beder Chavez not only knows all about the local wildlife, but is an accomplished artist, capturing it on canvas with the same mastery as when he pointed out and described its place in the ecosystem.

During the jungle walks, we learned how the natives live

with their environment. Many plants with medicinal value are still used by not only the jungle inhabitants, but much of the urban populace. While most of us would fear anacondas, boas, and other large snakes, numerous tribes consider them signs of good fortune. If nothing else, they eat insects and other small animals that would otherwise be a nuisance. Fortunately, some of the profuse bushes are effective snake-bite remedies.

We found varying blends of modern and primitive lifestyles. Huts on stilts (due to fluctuations in river level) are built from local wood with thatched roofs, with no windows or electricity. One hut which lacked walls had an old foot-powered sewing machine. Most natives primarily travel in hand-carved boats.

A highlight of the trip was our visit to a Bora village. The natives greeted us with tribal dances in their native apparel — the men in loincloths, the women wearing only short skirts and necklaces. We joined in one of the dances, and then bought native handicrafts, including jewelry made from local animals and plants, bark-cloth paintings, hand-made dolls, baskets and pottery.

Bargaining and bartering were customary, even though prices were amazingly low. My St. Louis Cardinal baseball caps were a valued trading commodity. In fact, when you go, take several expendable items with college, sport, rock, or other designs. You will go far with such bounty.

Once the Bora were finished performing the dances, trading with the tourists, and posing for photos, the women immediately changed to dresses, UCLA tee-shirts, and other western apparel. I guess there is a little showbiz in commerce wherever you go.

Among the sea life, pink and gray freshwater dolphins and manatees are protected species. Piranha may not be as bad as we think. When we fished for them at a bank where children were wading freely, they were too small to be a threat even to tots' toes.

For variety, the company also offers land accommodations

in the jungle overlooking the river and a short walk from the Yagua Village. The Amazon Tourist Camp is ideal for those who love to rough it. One can stay in bamboo huts, covered with thatched roofs, lit by kerosene lanterns. The rooms have private facilities, but showers are in a separate building. Buffet-style meals are in the dining room, and you know it is time to eat when you hear the beat of the log drums.

CRUISING FROM TAHITI
by Shirley Linde

The *Wind Song*, sailing on its seven-day cruise through French Polynesia in the South Pacific, isn't a typical cruise ship. There are few organized programs, and no assigned dining room seatings. Time is unstructured, announcements are few, you sit with whom you wish. There are only 148 passengers. You don't need a tux or an evening gown, or even a tie. The bridge is open to passengers at any time.

Typical of the informality, two passengers wanted to fish off the stern, so the captain went at trolling speed. Both got a hit at the same time — two big mahi mahis — and the captain slowed the boat to a crawl while they fought their fish and hauled them in. The chef served the fish for them at dinner.

One of the features of the *Wind Song* (and her sister ships *Wind Spirit* and *Wind Star*) is the diving platform/sports deck at the stern of the ship. The platform is lowered to water level when at anchor, permitting easy access to the sea. The ship provides equipment and instruction for snorkling, scuba, water skiing, or windsurfing, which you can do right from the platform; or you can swim or use a raft or kayak or sail a sunfish.

The *Wind Song* combines the mystique of the old tall ships that once sailed the tropics, but with sleek looks, luxury accommodations and modern technology. There are 21,000 square feet of sail, but no one needs to climb any yardarms — there are computer controls at the bridge that furl or unfurl the sails in two minutes.

The ship island-hops through five islands. It departs Sat-

urday evening under full sail at sunset from downtown Papeete, Tahiti, arriving the next morning in Huahine, departing that afternoon for Bora Bora. The next days and nights are
spent in Raiatea and Moorea, then back to Tahiti.

You can take a guided tour, or rent a bicycle, motorbike or
car and see the islands on your own, or you can sign up for
horseback riding or deep sea fishing or for a scuba or snorkeling trip to see the underwater fish and corals of the reefs
or lagoons, or you can get a view from above by helicopter.
Or you can just head for one of the beaches or hotels and
beachcomb, swim and bask in the sun.

On Huahine we visited a restored old Polynesian temple
site — called a *marae* — used for centuries as a meeting place,
a place of worship and sometimes as a place for human
sacrifice. Archeological studies are being done of these ancient temple sites, and you can see them on several of the
islands. On Raiatea, we took a short outrigger ride up the
Faaroa River and learned much about the uses of tropical
trees for medicines, mats, rope, food, utensils, clothing. Polynesians have for centuries been self-sufficient in living off the
land and the sea, and are doing much to retain their heritage
and culture. (They have also resisted investors who wish to
build condos and major hotels on the outer islands.)

On Bora Bora the ship held a beach barbecue on a little
island — called a *motu* — with tropical drinks served from a
floating rubber boat. In Moorea, we saw the legendary Mt.
Mouaroa, used as the basis for the song "Bali Hai." Snorkeling was magnificent just inside the reefs of several of the
islands.

At night there may be a Tahitian show — our favorite was
the children of Raiatea doing Polynesian dancing — or you
can play blackjack or the slots in the tiny casino, or sip a rum
drink and watch the moon rise, or dance, or if you are exhausted, you can borrow one of the many videocassettes and
collapse — each cabin has a VCR.

In Tahiti, check out Point Venus where the first known
Europeans set foot on the island, the waterfalls, the Paul

Gauguin Museum, Harrison Smith Botanical Garden, the fern grottos at Maraa Point. You can still see the breadfruit tree claimed to have been planted by Captain Bligh.

In downtown Papeete (the ship docks there), you'll not find a sleepy island village, but a din of taxis, buses, cars and bikes. Shops are expensive, but the International Market sells a reasonably priced sarong (called a *pareo*). We found fabric one of the less expensive ways to bring memories home. Most shops close for the lunch hour and at noon on Saturday. Nothing is open on Sunday except the native market (from 5 to 8a.m.).

In the evening you can visit the bars and clubs on the waterfront or see a sunset from the Maeva Beach or Beach-comber Hotels. If you want to use one of the local buses to get to town or your hotel, wave it down, or like the natives, put a rock on a breadfruit leaf.

BARGE TRIP INTO THE HEART OF AFRICA
by Catherine M. Senecal

Slightly south of the Sudan and west of the Ugandan border, in the middle of pygmy territory, I spent three hot, grueling days in the back of a beer truck as it lurched down a severely pot-holed track through the jungle to Kisangani.

Kisangani, formerly Stanleyville, was not a haphazard destination for those of us on the truck. The driver, for one, was delivering two goats to his uncle and taking 150 empty cases of beer bottles for refilling. I, on the other hand, was going to meet the Zaire River barge and repeat the last half of Henry Morton Stanley's journey of more than a hundred years ago, when he became the first known person to travel the river from its source to the Atlantic Ocean — some 1,400 miles downstream.

After three days on the road, however, my goal became less lofty, and I wanted only to wash up, eat and sleep, not necessarily in that order. When we finally arrived, the driver dropped me and my traveling companion, Joyce, in front of the slightly decrepit-looking Olympia Hotel. After sleeping in the back of a truck with goats, the place was no less than a vision before us. We washed up, wolfed down a plate of *spanakopita* (green spinach pastry), and went to bed.

Two days later, we were on the barge along with 1,000 or so other passengers as it pulled away from the bank and blew its final toot.

A main engine stern-wheeler with a flattened prow pushed two end-to-end barges of cabins and cargo down the river. Two carriers were lashed alongside one of these barges for a total of five barges longer than half a city block and wider than 50 feet. For ten days, this floating oddity hauled us from Kisangani — past masses of tangled equatorial forest, next to limestone cliffs, rolling plains — and out to Kinshasa, Zaire's capital, and the river mouth leading to the Atlantic Ocean.

I awoke early the first morning to explore. Narrow hallways outside second-class cabins and on lower decks became flourishing markets. Entrepreneurs set up miniature stalls and sold black-market penicillin, malaria pills, peanuts or jewelry. This constant buying and selling of goods proved to be the prime entertainment over the next 10 days.

The barge slowed if dozens of pirogues (canoes made from hollowed trees) were approaching it. I often heard the beat of distant drums as villages relayed the news of the barge's arrival. When we approached a settlement, villagers paddled up to the barge, their canoes piled high with bananas, avocados, freshly shot antelope or homemade bamboo chairs. They stood to paddle, enhancing the speed of their already swift, angled approaches to the fast-moving barge. With babies on their backs and hair a mass of wired pigtails, merchant women paddled in, grabbed railings and began to barter even before stepping on board. At times, up to a hundred pirogues were lashed to the boat.

Bartering reached chaotic proportions. Most Zairians spoke French, the official language, and one or two of the other major languages: Tshiluba, Kikongo or Kiswahili. For barge transactions, people spoke Lingala, language of the river. Sellers yelled out offers. Buyers responded with disbelieving guffaws. Women rolled their eyes and threw their hands in the air at especially ludicrous prices. Fishermen raced up stairs at breakneck speed dragging yard-long capitaine fish behind them for the cook's perusal.

More than once, I stepped outside my cabin door in the middle of the night to see what the racket was about. Nothing — this was normal life on the barge.

Once a villager sold all the bananas, palm wine or whatever filled the canoe, he or she stepped on board. Men bought cigarettes or razor blades and maybe sat for a haircut from the resident barber. Women bought cloth, soap and rice, then might treat themselves to a bottle of hand lotion. Afterward, they paddled back to their villages, by then miles upstream.

We went first-class, mainly because we wanted more than the one meal a day offered in second- or third-class. Also, sleeping in a cabin seemed like a reasonable idea. Third-class passengers established territory wherever they found two square yards of space on board. Our room was roughly 12 by 9 feet with two narrow cots, a small shower and a toilet. It was air-conditioned, though erratically, throughout the afternoon and night. Even at six in the morning, the temperature hovered at a humid 90 degrees.

Zaire is one massive river basin filled with forest. Larger than Alaska and Texas combined, this central African country is home to more than 35 million people from more than 200 different tribes. The river arches its way almost 2,900 miles from the south up and across the equator and back down. Shortly after Stanley's journey, the Belgians opened a trade route up the Zaire River into Kisangani to take out rubber and ivory. Later, Zaire became a major slave market for Belgium's King Leopold. In the 1960's, Kisangani was the scene of mass killings during Zaire's fight for independence. An uneasy calm has only recently settled over Kinshasa after civil unrest erupted in violence in 1993.

For many people aboard, this trip was no journey, but a job. Raja and Antoine, for example, two men who rode back and forth between Kisangani and Kinshasa, sold combs and other toiletry items. Other sellers collected goods in rural areas and hauled them to Kinshasa. In the capital, onions fetched 10 times what they cost in rural areas. Goats and chickens were transported alive. Chicks and baby crocodiles were cooked and eaten as a snack. Ten-foot crocodiles — too large for the refrigerator — were kept alive, jaws and tails bound to strong bamboo poles. For preservation, monkey was dried over a charcoal stove. Eels were sun-baked, then stacked in baskets.

In the first-class dining lounge, I was served fresh fish or roast beef with potatoes and gravy — a rare treat in Zaire. Meanwhile, the bazaar-bedecked third-class area dealt out its own fast-food fare: grubs, live or barbecued, sardines cooked in a hot pepper sauce, and deep-fried doughnuts. One evening, I tried fresh monkey meat — a common Zairian meal. It tasted like tender stew meat; better than grubs, which I tried after first imagining them as shrimps of the earth.

Every night, Zairian music floated from the dance hall. When we didn't go dancing, we climbed a ladder to the rooftop, settled in our portable bamboo stools (bought for $2 from a handy villager), and waited for the evening show — the setting sun. Near the equator, it appeared large and glowed pink, then orange, before dipping down into a yolky haze. We welcomed the cooling blackness as much as the captain disliked it.

Navigating at night was tricky. Sand shifted constantly with the flow of tributaries coming into the river. All night, the captain swept a searchlight from bank to bank looking for river buoys or markers showing these changes. If he couldn't spot one, he dropped anchor and moored for the night.

Just north of the equator on the sixth night of our journey, we stopped at Mbandaka, a major commercial port. Raja, Antoine, Joyce and I decided to walk into the village. Sipping beer around a table outdoors, we talked late into the night about the differences between Zaire and North America, not knowing when the whistle would blow and signal us to make a dash for the departing barge.

It left only the next morning. I awoke with a headache, surely from an excess of speaking French. From my deck, I watched morning fog rise to expose packets of bamboo stalks along the riverbank. I realized I was eager to arrive in Kinshasa. Although I was traveling in relative luxury compared with most people, the drain of being on a floating hotel with 998 other "guests" started to take effect.

Late on the ninth day, the captain anchored in Stanley's pool — a 15- by 20-mile lakelike bulge in the river. Night came as we waited, revealing the lights of Kinshasa and, to the north, Brazzaville, capital of the Congo. The widening of the river suggested we were near the Atlantic Ocean, yet we were still 300 miles inland. The next morning, we headed into the port of Kinshasa. We took a taxi to a cheap hotel in the "African quarters," close to night foodstalls and dancing establishments — focal points for an exciting time in a city that smacks of French atmosphere and African exuberance.

In the lobby, we met travelers who asked us about our journey. They listened intently as Joyce recounted sights that now seemed commonplace to me. I stared off into one of the far corners or the lobby and thought of the people who spend their lives making that river journey — back and forth, back and forth.

GOLFING THE INTRACOASTAL WATERWAY
by Shirley Linde

Imagine being on a small cruise ship, more like a private yacht, gliding along calm waters, then getting off every day or so with your own golf clubs to play some of the most well-known courses in the country.

That's the way it is on the Clipper Cruise Line golf cruises. The excursions travel the Intracoastal Waterway from Ft. Lauderdale, Florida, to Savannah, Georgia. (You go northbound or southbound according to the week you book.) After the cruise there is an optional post-cruise golf holiday at either Hilton Head Island in South Carolina or Sawgrass in

Florida. There are also shore tours in various ports, and time for personal sightseeing and shopping. On a typical cruise, guests board the ship at Pompano Beach near Ft. Lauderdale and pass waterfront homes, yachts, shrimp boats and fishermen. The scenery constantly changes as the ship zigzags through salt marshes and canals, past villages and cities, drawbridges opening as you go. Much of the cruise skirts along still-preserved wilderness areas. There are pelicans and herons, and manatees.

Golfers first get into the swing of things at PGA National at West Palm Beach, site of the PGA Championship and other professional tournaments. The next day in Cocoa Beach they are bused to Walt Disney World Golf Resort, and have a choice of playing on the Palm Course or the Magnolia Course, the site of the Disney World-Oldsmobile PGA Tournament. Or sometimes they play at the beautiful Grand Cypress Resort course in Orlando. At either course, your bag is ready on the cart when you arrive at tee-off time, all arranged by your port-to-port supercaddy who has driven by van to get them there while you lounged on the ship, enjoying the view.

In the next port — St. Augustine — golfers play the Ponte Vedra Ocean Course, about 30 minutes away, and non-golfers take a tour by tram of old St. Augustine, the oldest city in the United States, with its streets of ballast rock, restored buildings, old houses and museums. *The Clipper* docks at the city yacht pier, at the same inlet where Ponce de Leon landed in his search for the Fountain of Youth and Don Pedro Menendez de Aviles landed his mission for King Phillip I of Spain to start the settlement in 1565.

At St. Simons Island, Georgia, golfers play any two of three nine-hole courses at Sea Palms — Sea Palms West, Sea Tall Pines and Great Oaks. (On some cruises they play at St. Simons Island Club owned by The Cloister.) For non-golfers there is a bus tour of St. Simons with its historic lighthouse and museum, a fort and beautiful homes on nearby Sea Island. Slave cabins still stand, as well as massive live oaks and foot-thick grapevines growing on land that once was cotton plantations.

At Savannah the ship docks at the waterfront, where streets are paved with ballast stones and bricks from Savannah River mud. A bus tour of the city features some of the more than 1,000 homes being restored or renovated in one of the largest historical restoration projects in the nation.

The next day passengers disembark and, if they choose, are bused to Hilton Head for a three-day post-cruise extension. They stay at the Hyatt Regency Hotel and play at Palmetto and Harbour Town Links at Sea Pines Plantation where the Heritage Golf Classic is held, or they may play at the Arthur Hills course.

The golf cruise may be on either of two sister ships — the *Nantucket Clipper* or the *Newport Clipper*. Each is about 200 feet long with 51 cabins, with only an eight-foot draft so that it can dock at the town piers, easy for passengers to come and go to visit seaport museums and shops and wander about historic places. For the veteran traveler, besides the golf theme, the appeal is the casual atmosphere and the small size of the ship. It goes places the big ships can't. There is no gambling, no swimming pool, no beauty or gift shop. And no need for them.

UP THE SUWANNEE RIVER
by Adele Woodyard

Heavy mist hung thick above the still black water, hiding parts of trees in the early morning light. As it slowly burned off with the rising sun, I wondered if this is how the Suwanee River looks at its source — welling up, dark and mysterious, from the steaming ground of Georgia's Okefenokee Swamp, from where the river's 260 or so miles twist and turn through northern Florida on its way to the Gulf of Mexico. Along with three friends, I was cruising on a 44-foot chartered houseboat from Miller's Marina near where the Suwannee meets the Gulf. The water ranges from indigo to navy to black, so dark we can't see the bass, bluegills, perch, catfish, that lurk beneath the surface. Fed by 50 springs and three major rivers, the Suwannee here is opaque, a mirror reflecting sweetgum, maples, and loblolly pines in an unbroken line. The river was once a boundary dividing the Timucua and Apalachee Indians, and Suwannee Sound served as a rendezvous point for pirates in the 1780s. As our houseboat glided along, I could hear the waters whisper of long lost tribes, buried treasure, and a land untouched by civilization.

There is little to dispel the illusion. Settlements with names like Vista, Fowler's Bluff, and Clay's Landing barely intrude on mile after mile of wilderness. Mud turtles and large leatherbacks sun themselves on fallen logs. A blue heron waits in the shallows; another erupts in flight, its feet trailing splashes that gleam silver in the sun. Iridescent dragonflies dart above water that swirls in enigmatic circles. We watch an alligator slide into the wetness while, overhead, a large flock of ibises roost in a tree.

It was the bridge that spans the Suwannee between Fanning Springs and Old Town that brought me back to the present. Cars rumbled over concrete, and air that had resounded with bird songs was tainted by exhaust. Then we chugged around a long horseshoe bend to return once more to the serenity of the past.

Within our floating bungalow, Shirley practiced newly-learned dance steps to country-western music. White-haired Walt read a book and munched on boiled peanuts. Bobby, our unofficial captain, relaxed on the foredeck to listen to the sounds of silence, while I tried to steer the boat in a reasonably straight line. All of us are sailors with varying years of experience, but none of us had ever handled a houseboat before.

At first the size and shape of this waterborne vacation home was intimidating. "Nothing to it," Bill Miller, Jr. said. By the time he finished giving detailed instructions as he piloted us into the river, we believed him. It also helped to know there was an operations manual on board, and a VHF radio to call for help.

With three double-size beds and a hideabed (all linens supplied), a fully equipped galley, and head with shower and electric flush toilet, the houseboats can accommodate up to eight persons. Sliding glass doors open onto a foredeck that holds four patio chairs, a gas grill and ice chest, and two ladders, one for swimming, the other leading up to the sunroof, at the stern. There is an inboard/outboard engine, a generator, and batteries to furnish electricity for lights, heat and air-conditioning.

Fuel consumed is paid for at the end of the trip. The passengers supply food, paper towels, and personal items. I learned, too late, that groceries should include such items as spices and salt and pepper. Miller's campstore runs more to soft drinks, potato chips, lifevests and fishing tackle, than to food and condiments.

Reached by a narrow road from Old Town, Miller's Marina and Campground sprawls along a channel in an area renowned for salt and freshwater fishing.

"It's at its best during the winter months," Bill Miller, Sr. said, "and that's when most campers come."

To fish in the Gulf, it is necessary to either rent a john boat or bring your own, for houseboats are not allowed out on the "flats" at the river's mouth. However, East Pass along Hog Island is navigable and a good place to find drum, redfish, sea trout and flounder. Since any fishing we planned to do would be from the houseboat, we only had one of Miller's aluminum canoes strapped to the port rail.

A map of the Suwannee came complete with illustrations and tidbits of information neatly encased in a pink looseleaf binder. According to the map, along the 70 or so miles from the marina to the turnaround at Branford are several springs, one reputed to have spectacular rock faults that make it good for diving. Branford itself is a historic city where sternwheelers used to unload passengers. At nearby Roy Springs there is the wreck of the *Madison* to dive, a steamboat scuttled in 1863. An interesting side trip — you can float down the Ichetucknee on an oversize inner tube.

We dropped anchor off the entrance to Manatee Springs State Park. Unstrapping the canoe, three of us paddled in to tie up at the dock. Wooden walkways lead through towering cypress to a spring that boils up, a startling blue in the middle of water the color of tea. Unlike the river, it is crystal clear. Fish, from bait stealers to keepers, swam along the rocky bottom, and several spectators saw some snakes. "Cottonmouths," one gray-haired man insisted. It was an identification that did not seem to phase two scuba divers exploring the boil, or keep a family from splashing in the water off a sandy beach across the way. We saw several manatees for which the park was named. We watched three of the gentle creatures glide back and forth, feeding like the sea cows that some people call them. Later, we were able to record the sighting of other manatees in the river. Considered an endangered species after years of being on the losing side of run-ins with powerboats, the Florida Wildlife Service tries to keep track of their movements.

A pole near the park's concession stand and canoe rentals marks the years when the Suwannee overflowed its banks. In 1948 it actually flooded to a height of 16 feet. At the other extreme are shoals where water level can drop as low as two feet. Jack's Sandbar, says the river map, must be passed by hugging the far shore at low speed. A depth-finder on board loudly warns any skipper who comes too close.

Although an unseasonal cold snap called for heat at night, and kept us out of our bathing suits, we enjoyed a most relaxing cruise. Much too brief for those of us who revel in solitude after the din, dirt, and density of city life.

FINE WINE ON THE RHINE LINE
by Shirley Linde and Robert Linde

The KD German Rhine Line, the oldest and largest ship line on the Rhine, began carrying passengers in 1844. Today it also cruises the Main, Danube, Elbe, Seine, Rhone, Saone, and Moselle Rivers.

If you would enjoy sitting on the top deck of a cruise ship, watching castles appear out of the morning mist, seeing ruins and cathedrals loom from the cliffs, then stopping to visit vineyards and drink famous wines, the Floating Wine Seminar of the KD German Rhine Line is for you.

KD has several different cruises on the Rhine and the Moselle Rivers, but the special cruise for wine-appreciators is the Floating Wine Seminar. It is scheduled by KD in October, the height of the autumn grape harvest, so that you can see the grapes being harvested, in some places even taking a cable car over the heads of pickers in the huge vineyards. And, of course, you sample the wines.

The eight-day wine cruise is on the 192-passenger *Austria*, leaving from the old Dutch port of Nijmegen, continuing through Germany and France, and ending at Basel, Switzerland.

Lectures and wine-tasting on board and on shore focus on the wines of the Moselle, Ahr, Rheingau, Rheinhessen, Rheinpfallz, Alsace and Baden.

During shore excursions, wines are tested at Schloss Vollrads, an ancient castle; Kloster Eberbach, a medieval monastery that is one of the world's oldest wineries; Schloss Johannisberg, which produces Johannisberger Riesling; Schlagkamp-Desoye estate in Senheim; Cochem with its hilltop castle; Guntrum vineyards in Nierstein; the Burklin-Wolf estate in Wachenheim; the Schaetzel estate, and the Central Wine Cellars at Breisach in Germany's Black Forest. In Linz, the Ahrwein Society hosts a tasting of red wines.

The Rhine line also has a five-day Castles and Wine Cruise on the liner *Deutschland* that goes from Rotterdam to Basel. Wines are available on board from each of the major wine-growing areas along the cruise path. The ship stops for sightseeing tours to see castles, cathedrals and old villages at Linz, Mainz, Heidelberg, and Strasbourg.

The ships all go through the river valley, past vineyards and villages famous in the wine trade: Brauback, Boppard, St. Goar, Bacharach, Rudesheim, Bingen, Eltville, Nierstein, Oppenheim.

At Gernsheim you leave the ship for an excursion to Heidelberg, where in the cellar of the famous castle is the world's wine cask, holding nearly 50,000 gallons. Vintage views and vintage wines!

FIRST CRUISE BY A RELUCTANT CRUISER
by Ed Shriver
I managed to spend the first 50 plus years of my life without cruising anywhere, so taking the plunge, so to speak, was a matter of indifference to me. I wasn't particularly looking forward to being confined on a boat bobbing at sea for a week. I'd rather go to Paris.

Our cruise ship was the Royal Caribbean *Monarch of the Seas*. From perusing the brochures, it looked big and bright and busy, like a resort hotel that just happened to be spending a week moving from Puerto Rico to Martinique, Barbados, Antigua, Saint Maarten and St. Thomas — and back again to where we started.

We flew to San Juan, and managed to spend two nights enjoying the area before our ship sailed. Puerto Rico is a major cruise port and has always been my favorite Caribbean Island. It not only has beaches, rain forests, and mountains, but a thriving cultural life. The Old City has been painstakingly restored since the last time I was here, and now the Spanish-style buildings are pastel beauties, with balconies overlooking winding, narrow streets filled with shops and boutiques and galleries.

Since the big 500-year Columbus celebration the area has added parks streaming with hibiscus and bougainvillea, and esplanades and fountains. We stopped into some galleries, old churches and a museum or two with artworks from many countries. We had outstanding meals at restaurants featuring the best of the island, (I liked the chicken with mango salsa on painted plates) and went to a concert at the arts center. I felt I was in some European country, and definitely didn't want to get on the ship.

But we followed the signs to a modern port crowded with

brightly painted (large!) ships, and soon after clambered on board our grandly named vessel, which was indeed the biggest one around. The smiling staff whisked us from the gangplank to our quarters. OK, no standing around. That was a good act.

Small cabin but I liked how it made the most of the space available. Nice cabin actually; clean, enough drawers, fluffy towels, a good feeling.

A knock on the door and our baggage appeared. Now how could they do that so fast? We hung up our clothes, cleaned up and took a stroll down the carpeted, polished, well-marked passageway. Part of an old seagoing tradition that gives us the term "shipshape"?

We took a glass-paneled elevator that looked down on a plant-filled atrium, then strolled into the Monarch Viking Crown Lounge, 14 stories above sea level.

Huge windows (I had assumed a little round porthole would be the only way to look out) offered a panoramic view of the ocean and port. The ship had cast off while we were busying ourselves in our cabin. Now it was time for a glass of champagne, and a toast to possibilities. At dinner, a staff member escorted us to our table and introduced us to two other guests, total strangers who quickly talked about other trips and other times. I was embarrassed to admit this was my virgin voyage, but it came out anyway, and I was assured I would not suffer too much.

The food was good enough to entice me into ordering an unforgiving triple chocolate cake to go with my coffee. The wine served was acceptable, but I found a wine list, which I planned to use the next evening. There's something to be said for "learning the ropes" on a ship, even though we "sail" without canvas, rope or wind.

A trip back to our cabin revealed an envelope with an invitation to dine at the Captain's Table the next evening. Had someone tipped off the captain about my skepticism?

Sleeping at sea wasn't as hard as I thought it would be: after all, we were on a huge ship with stabilizers. It's pleasant, I had to admit, as had been everything so far; much better than I had anticipated. Maybe tomorrow there will be a storm and I'll get seasick. Would I hide in my room or watch from 14 stories up? Morning revealed calm water, strong sun and only more pleasures: breakfast by the pool, exploring the ship's themes and looks and available options. What I began to realize was that there was always something to do but no pressure to do anything. The isolation of being unhooked from mainland concerns was relaxing and restoring. The joy of "double hooky," from the social director's schedule as well, was deeply satisfying.

The captain and his navigator were interesting at dinner, and I got to talk a little philosophy, a little technology, a little cruise talk. An excellent 1982 Bordeaux wine was served.

Then we were off to the dance floor, and perhaps it was the lesson my friend insisted on, but we danced like Fred and Ginger (well, we danced better than we ever had). Later, we had a drink in a cozy bar near the dance floor, and listened to some soft music.

As the days passed, and we stopped at ports throughout the Caribbean, I enjoyed the subtle and not so subtle differences on each island. Mountains on some, flatlands on others; some with more smiling faces and others with better shopping. A gingerbread church here, a colorful marketplace there. The stops at each port were short, but my ambition was limited to enjoying myself.

On board I found myself playing in a bridge tournament, working out on a treadmill (so I could have more of that chocolate cake and maybe some ice cream on the side), losing at blackjack, reading a couple of long-put-off mysteries, window-shopping at a dozen stores, watching some old movies in a big theatre, sleeping a lot. And smiling more than I have in years. I figured out why cruises are so popular. They are easy on you. You can relax, and learn, and most of all, have fun. What's not to like?

DESTINATION PLANNER

Nouadhibou. Phi Phi Island. Naberevnye. These and other exotic world cruise ship ports—along with more familiar ones—are listed in this section. If you know (or even if you're wondering) where in the world you might want to cruise, but don't know which ships can get you there, when they leave, where they leave from, and which ports they go to, read on.

Using this specially created Destination Planner, similar to what a travel agent would use, you'll learn about oceans and rivers, names of towns you've never read about before, and the fabulous itineraries and ports of call throughout our planet.

The various maps included in this section will help you locate most ports, and a good atlas will pin even the smallest of them down.

Reading the Destination Planner

Major world cruising areas, for example ANTARCTICA, are to the left in bold letters, and in alphabetical order.

The embarkation port where you first board the ship is in italics; for example *Puerto Montt*

The ship name is in capital letters, the cruise line follows in parentheses; then, the month(s) the ship sails from that port, the number of days in the cruise(s), and the names of the ports of call.

Here is a typical Destination Planner entry:

ANTARCTICA
Puerto Montt
WORLD DISCOVERER
(Clipper) Nov. (17 days): Isla Chiloe, through Beagle Channel, Cape Horn, through Drake Passage, Elephant Is., Port Stanley (terminates).
If the word (terminates) follows the last port of call, the ship does not return to the embarkation port.

If a ship shuttles between two embarkation ports on alternate cruises, the names of the embarkation ports and ports of call are given only once:

Moscow-St. Petersburg
DOSTOYEVSKY
(Bolshoi) Jul.-Oct. (13 days): Uglich, Irma, Goritzky, Kizy, Valaam.

If a ship cruises to different ports of call from the same embarkation point, each itinerary is separated by "or":
SEABOURN SPIRIT
(Seabourn) Nov.-Mar. (14 days): Port Kelang, through Strait of Malacca, Semerang, Bali, Lombok Is., Kuching; or Penang, Port Kelang, Koh Samui, Bangkok, Kuching, Tioman.

If a ship always sails from embarkation ports on the same day of the week, the day is given:

Aswan-Luxor
SUN BOAT II
(Abercrombie & Kent) Tuesdays Dec.-Mar. (7 days): Kom Ombo, Idfu, Isna, Nag Hammadi, Abydos, Dandara.

In some cases, the names of embarkation ports and ports of call are listed serially, but sailing dates for each city are omitted to save space. For example:
DELTA QUEEN/MISSISSIPPI QUEEN
(Delta Queen Steamboat) Year round (3-12 days): Chattanooga, Huntsville, Decatur, Florence, Shiloh, Paducah, St. Louis, St. Genevieve, Cape Girardeau, New Madrid, Cave-in Rock, Henderson, Louisville, Madison, {etc.}

The previous example also illustrates how ships owned by the same cruise line, and going to the same ports, are listed with a slash (/) between their names.

If you don't find information about a particular ship in this section, you'll find general information about ports of call for additional vessels—including smaller ones—in the *Ship Profiles* section.

Our *Destination Planner* omits exact dates of departure because cruise calendar dates change from year to year. Cruise ships also make other changes, so when you've narrowed your choices, check for the ship's exact schedule with the cruise line or your travel agent.

ALASKA & BRITISH COLUMBIA

Anchorage

HANSEATIC

(Seven Seas) Sep. (11 days): Cook Inlet, Prince William Sound, Yakutat Bay, Glacier Bay Nat. Park, Skagway, Juneau, Le Conte Bay, Ketchikan, through Inside Passage, Vancouver (terminates).

SAGAFJORD

(Cunard/NAC) Jul.-Sep. (10 days): Cook Inlet, Homer, Kenai Fjord, Seward, Prince William Sound, College Fjord, Columbia Glacier, Valdez, Yakutat Bay/Hubbard Glacier, Juneau, Endicott Arm, Skagway, Sitka, Ketchikan, Vancouver (terminates).

Anchorage-Vancouver

FAIR/SKY/STAR PRINCESS

(Princess) Thur & Sat Jul.- Sep. (7 days): Seward, College Fjord, Columbia Glacier, Sitka, Skagway, Juneau, Ketchikan, through Inside Passage.

Juneau

SPIRIT OF ALASKA/DISCOVERY/ GLACIER BAY/'98

(Alaska Sightseeing) Alt. Thurs. & Sat. Jul.-Sep. (7 days): Tracy Arm, Sitka, Le Conte Glacier, Petersburg, Misty Fjord, Ketchikan, through Inside Passage, Seattle (terminates).

SPIRIT OF GLACIER BAY

(Alaska Sightseeing) Sep. (8 days): Glacier Bay, Sitka, Le Conte Glacier, Petersburg, Misty Fjord, Ketchikan, through Inside Passage, Seattle (terminates).

YORKTOWN CLIPPER

(Clipper) Jul.-Aug. (7 days): Tracy Arm Sitka, Glacier Bay Nat. Park, Haines, Skagway; or Sep. (14 days): Tracy Arm, Skagway, Haines, Glacier

WORLD DISCOVERER

Bay Nat. Park, Sitka, Misty Fjord, Ketchikan, Prince Rupert, Victoria, Friday Harbor, San Juan Is., Seattle (terminates).

Ketchikan-Sitka
SEA BIRD/SEA LION
(Special Expeditions) Jul.-Aug. (8 days): Misty Fjord, Le Conte Glacier, Tracy Arm, Haines, Point Adolphus, Glacier Bay Nat. Park.

Ketchikan
WORLD DISCOVERER
(Clipper) Sep. (10 days): Tracy Arm, Sitka, Wrangel, Misty Fjord, Queen Charlotte Is., Saltspring Is., through Strait of Belle Isle, Victoria, Vancouver (terminates).

Kodiak
WORLD DISCOVERER
(Clipper) Sep. (10 days): Kenai Fjord, Seward, College Fjord, Columbia Glacier, Prince William Sound, Tracy Arm, Wrangel, Misty Fjord, Prince Rupert (terminates).

Los Angeles
CUNARD CROWN DYNASTY
(Cunard Crown) May (9 days): San Francisco, Victoria, through Inside Passage, Misty Fjord, Ketchikan, Vancouver (terminates).

Nome
WORLD DISCOVERER
(Clipper) Jul.-Aug. (10 days): Little Diomede Is., King Is., St. Lawrence Is., Provideniya, crossing Intl. Date Line, Bering Strait, crossing Arctic Circle, Uelen; or Aug,-Sep (12 days): Provideniya Is., St. Lawerence, St. Matthew Is., Pribilof Is., Dutch Harbor, Semidi Is., Kodiak (terminates).

San Francisco
GOLDEN ODYSSEY
(Royal) May-Jun. (10 days): Victoria, through Inside Passage, Juneau, Sitka, Ketchikan.

GOLDEN PRINCESS
(Princess) Jul.-Sep. (10 days): Victoria, Vancouver, through Inside Passage, Juneau, Sitka, Ketchikan.

STAR ODYSSEY
(Royal) May-Jun. (10 days): Victoria, Sitka, Skagway, Juneau, Glacier Bay, Misty Fjord, Ketchikan, through Inside Passage, Vancouver (terminates).

Seattle
SPIRIT OF AMERICA
(Alaska Sightseeing) Sep. (10 days): Misty Fjord, Ketchikan, Wrangell, Petersburg, Tracy Arm, Sitka, Glacier Bay, Skagway, Haines, Juneau (terminates).

SPIRIT OF ALASKA/DISCOVERY
(Alaska Sightseeing) Sat Jul.-Sep. (7 days): through Inside Passage, Misty Fjord, Ketchikan, Petersburg, Le Conte Glacier, Sitka, Glacier Bay, Juneau (terminates); or Sep.-Oct.: Campbell River, Princess Louisa Inlet, Chemainus, Victoria, Vancouver, San Juan Islands, Friday Harbor, Orcas, Port Townsend

SPIRIT OF GLACIER BAY
(Alaska Sightseeing) May (10 days): Misty Fjord, Ketchikan, Wrangell, Petersburg, Tracy Arm, Sitka, Glacier Bay, Skagway, Haines, Juneau (terminates).

SPIRIT OF '98

(Alaska Sightseeing) Alt Thur Jul-Sep. (7 days): through Inside Passage, Misty Fjord, Ketchikan, Petersburg, Le Conte Glacier, Sitka, through Peril Strait, Tracy Arm, Juneau (terminates).

YORKTOWN CLIPPER

(Clipper) May-Jun. (7 days): San Juan, Friday Harbor, Victoria, Prince Rupert, Ketchikan, Misty Fjord, Glacier Bay Nat Park, Haines, Tracy Arm, Juneau (terminates).

Seward

CUNARD CROWN DYNASTY

(Cunard Crown) Alt Mondays May-Sep. (7 days): Hubbard Glacier, Skagway, Juneau, Petersburg, Ketchikan, Misty Fjord, through Inside Passage, Vancouver (terminates).

GOLDEN ODYSSEY

(Royal) Alt Mondays Jun.-Aug. (7 days): Yakutat Bay/Hubbard Glacier, Skagway, Glacier Bay, Juneau, Tracy Arm, Ketchikan, through Inside Passage, Vancouver (terminates).

ROTTERDAM

(Holland America) Alt Sun Jul.-Sep. (7 days): Valdez, Columbia Glacier, College Fjord, Hubbard Glacier, Sitka, Juneau, Ketchikan, through Inside Passage, Vancouver (terminates).

STAR ODYSSEY

(Royal) Alt Wed Jun.-Aug (7 days): Yakutat Bay, Hubbard Glacier, Skagway, Juneau, Glacier Bay, Ketchikan, through Inside Passage, Vancouver (terminates).

Sitka

SEA BIRD/SEA LION

(Special Expeditions) Jul.-Aug. (8 days): Point Adolphus, Glacier Bay Nat. Park, Haines, Tracy Arm, Le Conte Glacier, Misty Fjord, Ketchikan (terminates); or Sea Lion Aug.-Sep. (12 days) Glacier Nat. Park, Point Adolphus, Tracy Arm, Petersburg, Misty Fjord, Anthony Is., Skidegate, Queen Charlotte Is., through Inside Passage, Johnstone Strait, Vancouver (terminates).

Vancouver

AMERICAN PIONEER

(American Family) Fri May-Sep. (7 days): through inside passage, Ketchikan, Endicott Arm, Juneau, Skagway, Davidson Glacier, Sitka.

CUNARD CROWN DYNASTY

(Cunard Crown) Alt. Mon May-Aug. (7 days): through Inside Passage, Ketchikan, Tracy Arm, Juneau, Sitka, Hubbard Glacier, Seward (terminates)

COSTA RIVIERA
(Costa) Fridays Jul.- Sep. (7 days): through Inside Passage, Ketchikan, Endicott Arm, Juneau, Skagway, Davidson and Rainbow Glacier, Sitka.

CUNARD CROWN DYNASTY
(Cunard Crown) Sep. (12 days): through Inside Passage, Ketchikan, Tracy Arm, Skagway, Juneau, Misty Fjord, Victoria, San Francisco, Los Angeles (terminates).

FAIR PRINCESS
(Princess) Thur Jul-Sep,(7 days): through Inside Passage, Ketchikan, Juneau, Skagway, Sitka, Columbia Glacier, College Fjord, Seward, Anchorage (terminates),

GOLDEN ODYSSEY
(Royal) Alt. Mon & Wed Jun.-Aug. (7 days): through Inside Passage, Ketchikan, College Fjord, Tracy Arm, Juneau, Skagway, Yakutat Bay, Prince William Sound, Seward (terminates); or Aug.-Sep. (10 days): through Inside Passage, Ketchikan, Tracy Arm, Juneau, Glacier Bay, Victoria, Los Angeles (terminates); or through Inside Passage, Ketchikan, Tracy Arm, Juneau, Glacier Bay, Skagway, Sitka, Victoria, San Francisco (terminates).

NIEUW AMSTERDAM
(Holland America) Tues Jul.-Sep. (7 days): through Inside Passage, Ketchikan, Juneau, Glacier Bay, Sitka.

NORDIC PRINCE
(Royal) Sundays May-Sep. (7 days): through Inside Passage, Tracy Arm, Skagway, Haines, Juneau, Ketchikan, Misty Fjord, through Inside Passage.

NOORDAM
(Holland America) Thur Jul.-Sep. (7 days): through Inside Passage, Ketchikan, Juneau, Glacier Bay, Sitka.

REGAL/CROWN PRINCESS
(Princess) Sat/Sun Jul- Sep. (7 days): through Inside Passage, Juneau, Skagway, Glacier Bay, Ketchikan.

ROTTERDAM
(Holland America) Alternate Sundays Jul.-Sep. (7 days): through Inside Passage, Ketchikan, Juneau, Sitka, Glacier Bay, Columbia Glacier, College Fjord, Seward, Anchorage (terminates); or Sep. (7 days): through Inside Passage, Ketchikan, Juneau, Glacier Bay, Sitka.

SAGAFJORD
(Cunard/NAC) Jul.-Sep. (11 days): through Inside Passage, Ketchikan, Endicott Arm, Juneau, Skagway, Glacier Bay, Sitka, Yakutat Bay/Hubbard Glacier, College Fjord, Valdez, Seward, Kennai Fjord, Homer, Anchorage (terminates).

STAR ODYSSEY
(Royal) Alt. Wed Jun.-Aug. (7 days): through Inside Passage, Ketchikan, Tracy Arm, Juneau, Skagway, Yakutat Bay, Hubbard Glacier, Prince William Sound, Columbia Glacier, College Fjord, Seward (terminates).

SUN VIKING
(Royal) May-Sep. (10-11 days): Victoria, through Inside Passage, Sitka, Hubbard Glacier, Skagway, Haines, Juneau, Tracy Arm, Ketchikan, Wrangell

UNIVERSE
(World Explorer) May-Jun. (8 days): Wrangell,Juneau, Skagway, Glacier Bay, Yakutat Bay, Hubbard Glacier, Valdez, Seward, Ketchikan, Sitka, Victoria,

WESTERDAM
(Holland America) Sat Jul.- Sep. (7 days): through Inside Passage, Ketchikan, Juneau, Glacier Bay, Sitka.

WORLD DISCOVERER
(Clipper) May-Jun. (12 days): Belle Is., Saltspring Is., Queen Charlotte Is., Misty Fjord, Wrangell, Sitka, Tracy Arm, Misty Fjord, Ketchikan (terminates).

Vancouver-Whittier

REGENT SEA/STAR
(Regency) Alt. Fri Jul.-Sep. (7 days): through Inside Passage, Ketchikan, Endicott Arm, Juneau, Skagway, Lynn Canal, Sitka, Columbia Glacier, College Fjord.

AROUND AFRICA
Iberia, Canary Isles., North Africa

Agadir-Dakar

AURORA I
(Classical) Nov. (8 days): Lanzarote, Nouadhibou, Nouakchott, Banjul, Ziguinchor.

Barcelona-Southampton

PACIFIC PRINCESS
(Princess) Jul.-Sep. (12 days): Livorno, Civitavecchia, Cannes, Gibraltar, Tangier, Lisbon, Le Havre.

Barcelona

RADISSON DIAMOND
(Diamond) Oct.-Nov. (10 days): Malaga, Cadiz, Lisbon, Casablanca, Agadir, Lanzarote, Las Palmas (terminates).

RADISSON DIAMOND

SEABOURN PRIDE
(Seabourn) May (11 days): Palma, Malaga, Seville, Lisbon, Oporto, Bordeaux (terminates).

Bremerhaven
EUROPA
(Hapag-Lloyd Kreutzfahrten) Sep. (15 days): Bremerhaven, Dover, Le Havre, St. Peter Port, Villagarcia, Lisbon, Cadiz, Tangier, Malaga, Palma, Genoa (terminates).

Buenos Aires
ISLAND PRINCESS
(Princess) Apr.-May (19 days): Montevideo, Rio de Janeiro, Recife, Dakar, Las Palmas, Gibraltar, Barcelona (terminates).

Civitaveccia
STATENDAM
(Holland America) Oct. (15 days): Livorno, Genoa, Villefranche, Sete, Malaga, Las Palmas, Funchal, Lisbon (terminates).

Dover
VISTAFJORD
(Cunard/NAC) Sep. (15 days): Pauillac (Bordeaux), Oporto, Lisbon, Funchal, Barcelona (terminates).

Edinburgh
BERLIN
(Peter Dielmann Reederei) Sep. (13 days): Invergordon, Stornoway, Dublin, Waterford, Porto de Lexoes, Lisbon, Alicante, Barcelona, Marseille, Genoa (terminates).

Ft Lauderdale
VISTAFJORD
(Cunard/NAC) Apr. (13 days): Funchal, Casablanca, Malaga, Barcelona (terminates).

Genoa
COSTA CLASSICA
(Costa) Oct. (7 days): Gibraltar, Casablanca, Cadiz, Barcelona.

DAPHNE (Costa) Oct. -Nov. (14 days): Barcelona, Palma, Gibraltar, Tangier, Casablanca, Funchal, Santa Cruz Tenerife, Arrecife, Malaga, Alicante.
MONTEREY
(Starlauro) Jul.-Oct. (11 days): Barcelona, Malaga, Palermo, Ibiza, Casablanca, Palma.
SHOTA RUSTAVELLI
(Grandi Viaggi) Aug.-Sep. (14 days): through Strait of Gibraltar, Cadiz, Lisbon, Funchal, Santa Cruz Tenerife, Arrecife, Casablanca.

Hamburg
VISTAFJORD
(Cunard/NAC) Sep. (11 days): Dover, Pauillac (Bordeaux), Oporto, Lisbon, Funchal, Barcelona (terminates).

Harwich
SONG OF NORWAY
(Royal Caribbean) Sep. (12 days): Amsterdam, Le havre, Plymouth, La Rochelle, Vigo, Lisbon, Gibraltar, Barcelona (terminates).
SUN VIKING
(Royal Caribbean) Sep. (12 days): Amsterdam, Le havre, La Rochelle, Lisbon, Gibraltar, Barcelona, Genoa (terminates).

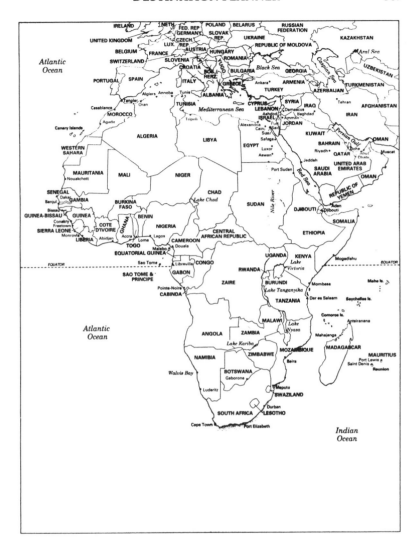

Le Havre
MERMOZ
  (Paquet French) Aug. (10 days): Guernsey, Vigo, Lisbon, Cadiz, Ibiza,
Barcelona, Toulon (terminates).

Lisbon
CLUB MED 1
(Club Med) Nov. (16 days): Cadiz, Casablanca, Lanzarote, Las Palmas, Fort de France (terminates).

Liverpool
AZERBAYDZHAN
(CTC) Sep.-Oct. (14 days): Lisbon, Funchal, Las Palmas, Santa Cruz Tenerife, Casablanca, Dublin.

London
AZERBAYDZHAN
(CTC) Aug.-Sep. (14 days): Porto Santo, Funchal, Las Palmas, Lanzarote, Casablanca, Gibraltar, Lisbon.

SONG OF FLOWER
(Seven Seas) Aug. (11 days): Zeebrugge, St. Helier, St. Malo, Concarneau, Oporto, Lisbon, Gibraltar, Puerto Banus, Barcelona (terminates).

Malaga
CUNARD PRINCESS
(Princess) Nov.-Apr. (10-15 days): Tangier, Lanzarote, Las Palmas, Santa Cruz de la Palmas, Funchal, Gibraltar, Santa Cruz de la Palma, Santa Cruz de la Tenerife,

Naples
VISTAFJORD
(NAC) Nov. (12 days): Ibiza, Malaga, Gibraltar, Casablanca, Agadir, Lanzarote, Las Palmas, Santa Cruz Tenerife, Funchal, Lisbon (terminates).

Nice
AURORA II
(Classical) Oct.-Nov. (11 days): Barcelona, Palma, Motril, Tangier, Seville, Agadir (terminates).

Piraeus
CROWN ODYSSEY
(Royal) Nov.-Dec. (21 days): Civitavecchia, Villefranche, Barcelona, Palma, Gibraltar, Casablanca, Funchal, Santa Cruz Tenerife, Barbados, Fort de France, St. Thomas, San Juan (terminates).

San Juan
CROWN ODYSSEY
(Royal): Apr. (12 days): St. Thomas, Funchal, Cadiz, Malaga (terminates).

Southampton
BLACK PRINCE
(Fred Olsen) Aug. - Sep. (14-18 days): Tangier, Mahon, Cannes, Alghero (Sardinia), Civitavecchia, Portofino (Elba Is.), Malaga, Ibiza, Lisbon; or Sep.-Nov.: Cadiz, Mahon, Cagliari, Civitavecchia, Valleta, Almeria, Tangier, Lisbon; or Nov-Jan.: Lisbon, Cadiz, Santa Cruz de la Palma, Santa Cruz de la Tenerife, Sebastian de la Gomera, Puerto del Rosario, Las Palmas, Arrecife, Agadir, Funchal.

CANBERRA
(P & O) Aug. - Jan. (10-13 days): Le Havre, Funchal, Gibraltar, Santa Cruz Tenerife, Lanzarote, Agadir, Puerto Vanus, La Pallice, Lisbon; or, Cadiz, Santa Cruz de la Palma, Santa Cruz de la Tenerife, San Sebastian de la Gomera, Puerto del Rosario, Las Palmas, Arrecife, Agadir, Funchal.

QUEEN ELIZABETH 2
(Cunard) Nov. (7 days): Lisbon, Funchal, Santa Cruz Tenerife.

PACIFIC PRINCESS
(Princess) Jul. -Aug. (12 days): Le Havre, Lisbon, Tangier, Gibraltar, Cannes, Civitavecchia, Livorno, Barcelona (terminates).

SEA PRINCESS
(P&O) Aug.- Sep. (12 days): Puerto Banus, Priaia da Rocha, Santa Cruz Tenerife, Las Palmas, Porto Santo, Funchal.

Indian Ocean

Ashdod
SEABOURN SPIRIT
(Seabourn) Nov. (23 days): through Suez Canal, Safaga, Aden, Bombay, Colombo, Phuket, Penang, Port Kelank, Singapore (terminates).

Bankok
PACIFIC PRINCESS
(Princess) Apr.-May (14 days): Kuantan, Singapore, Port Kelang, Phuket, Madras, Columbo, Goa, Bombay (terminates)

Bombay
PACIFIC PRINCESS
(Princess) Apr.-May (14 days): Safaga, through Suez Canal, Port Said, Alexandria, Haifa, Piraeus (terminates).

SEABOURN SPIRIT
(Seabourn) Mar.-Apr. (12 days): Aden, Safaga, through Suez Canal, Ashdod (terminates), or Nov. (11 days): Columbo, Phuket, Penang, Port Kelang, Singapore (terminates).

SEA GODDESS II
(Cunard Sea Goddess) Nov. (13 days): Goa, Mali, Phuket, Pulau Pangkor,

Kuala Lumpur, Singapore (terminates), or Mar.-Apr. (14 days) Hodeidah, Acaba, Sharm el Shiek, Hurgada, through Suez Canal, Alexandria (terminates).

SONG OF FLOWER
(Seven Seas) Oct.-Nov (14 days): Goa, Mangalore, Cochin, Male, Miladummadulu Atol, Penang, Kuala Lumpur, Mallaca, Singapore (terminates), or Mar.-Apr. (14 Days): Salalah, Aden, Hodeidah, Safaga, Sharm el Shiek, Suez (terminates)

Durban
LEV TOLSTOY
(Transocean/MarQuest) Feb. (19 days): Mossel Bay, Walvis Bay, Cape Town, Poet Elizabeth, Mutsamudu (Comoro Is.), Mombasa, (terminates).

Haifa
SEA GODDESS II
(Cunard Sea Goddess) Oct,-Nov.(14 days): Port Said, through Suez Canal, Hurgada, Aqaba, Djibouti, Bombay (terminates).

SEABOURN SPIRIT
(Seabourn) Nov. (23 days): Through Suez Canal, Safaga, Aden, Bombay, Goa, Columbo, Phuket, Panang, Port Kelang, Singapore (terminates).

Hurgada
LEV TOLSTOY
(Transocean/ Marquest) Jan. (17 days): Hodeidah, Victoria (Mahe Is.), Praslin Is., Dzaoudzi, Zanzibar, Mombasa (terminates).

Mahe Is. (Seychelles)
MERMOZ
(Paquet French) Dec. (9 days): Praslin Is., Diego Suarez, Nossi-Be, Ile de Mayotte, Anjouan (Comoro Is.), Mombasa (terminates).

RENAISSANCE VIII
(Renaissance) Nov.- Mar. (10-11 days): La Digue, Desproches (Seychelles), Poivre Is., Praslin Is., Aride Is., Cousin Is.

Mombasa
ISLAND PRINCESS
(Princess) Nov.-Dec. (16 days): Zanzibar, Nossi-Be, Mahe Is., Colombo, Panang, Kuala Lumpur, Singapore (terminates).

LEV TOLSTOY
(Transocean/Marquest) Jan.-Feb. (15 days): Moroni, Nossi-Be, Toamasina, Port Louis, Ft. Dauphin, Richards Bay, Durban (terminates), or Feb,-Mar. (16 days): Zanzibar, Nossi-Be, Diego Suarez, Victoria, La Digue, Male, Madras, Trincomalee, Colombo (terminates).

MARCO POLO
(Orient) Nov.-Dec. (18 days): Zanzibar, Ile de Mayotte, Nossi-Be, St. Denis de la Reunion, Port Louis (Mauritius), Durban, Port Elizabeth, Cape Town (terminates).

MERMOZ
(Paquet French) Dec (9 days): Anjouan (Comorp Is., Ile de Mayotte, Nossi-be, Diego Suarez, Praslin Is., Mahe Is. (Seychelles).

Nairobi
ROYAL VIKING QUEEN
(Royal Viking) Nov. (11 days):Nairobi, Zanzibar, Nossi-Be, Durban, Mossel Bay, Cape Town.

Piraeus
ISLAND PRINCESS
(Princess) Nov. (14 days): Alexandria, Tel Aviv-Yafo, through Suez Canal, Safaga, Mombasa (terminates).

MARCO POLO
(Orient) Oct.-Nov (20 days); Port Said, through Suez Canal, Suez, Aqaba, Safaga, Djibouti, Mahe Is., Praslin Is., Mombasa (terminates).

ORPHEUS
(Swan Hellanic) Nov. (17 days): Patmos, Rhodes, Latikia, Tartus, Limasol, Alexandria, Port Said, through Suez Canal, Sharm el Shiek, Safaga, Aqaba (terminates).

ROYAL ODYSSEY
(Royal) Nov.-Dec. (27-28 days): Ashdod, Port Said, through Suez Canal, Safaga, Bombay, Goa, Cochin, Colombo, Madras, Port Blair, Phukat, Penang, Singapore (terminates).

Singapore
QUEEN ELIZABETH 2
(Cunard) Mar. (11 days): Port Kelang, Madras, Mahe Is., Mombasa (terminates).

ROYAL ODYSSEY
(Royal) Mar.-Apr. (28 days): Ashdod, Port Said, through Suez Canal, Safaga, Bombay, Goa, Cochin, Colombo, Madras, Port Blair, Phuket, Penang, Singapore (terminates).

SEABOURN SPIRIT
(Seabourn) Mar.-Apr. (23 days): Port Kelang, Penang, Phuket, Colombo, Bombay, Aden, Safaga, through Suez Canal, Ashdod (terminates).

SEA GODDESS II
(Sea Goddess) Mar (13 days): Kuala Lumpur, Pulau Pangkor, Phuket, Male, Goa, Bombay (terminates).

SONG OF FLOWER

(Seven Seas) Mar. (14 days): Malacca, Kuala Lumpur, Penang, Male, Miladummadulu Atol, Cochin, Mangalore, Goa, Bombay (terminates).

Suez

SONG OF FLOWER

(Seven Seas) Oct. (14 days): Sharm el Shiek, Safaga, Hodeida, Aden, Salalah, Bombay (terminates).

Red Sea

Aqaba

ORPHEUS

(Swan Hellenic) Nov.-Dec. (15 days): Safaga, Suez, through Suez Canal, Port Said, Haifa, Ashdod, Limassol, Kos, Piraeus (terminates).

SEA PRINCESS

(P & O) Dec. (14 days): Suez, Port Said, Ashdod, Bodrum, Volos, Piraeus, Heraklion, Palma (terminates).

Bombay

PACIFIC PRINCESS

(Princess) Apr.-May (14 days): Safaga, through Suez Canal, Port Said, Haifa, Piraeus (terminates).

SEA GODDESS II

(Cunard Sea Goddess) Mar.-Apr. (13 days): Hodeidah, Aquaba, Sharm el Sheikh, Hurgada, through Suez Canal, Alexandria (terminates).

Colombo

LEV TOLSTOY

(Transocean/MarQuest) Mar. (16 days): Bombay, Muscat, Djibouti, Port Sudan, Hurgada (terminates).

Haifa

SEA GODDESS II

(Cunard Sea Goddess) Oct.-Nov. (14 days): Port Said, through Suez Canal, Hurgada, Aquaba, Djibouti, Bombay (terminates).

Piraeus

ISLAND PRINCESS

(Princess) Nov. (14 days): Alexandria, Tel-Aviv, Yafo.

MARCO POLO

(Orient) Oct. -Nov. (20 days): Port Said, through Suez Canal, Suez, Aquaba, Safaga, Djibouti, Mahe Is. (Seychelles), Praslin Is., Mombasa (terminates).

ORPHEUS

(Swan Hellenic) Nov. (17 days): Patmos, Rhodes, Latikia, Tartus, Limassol, Alexandria, Port Said, through Suez Canal, Sharm el Sheikh, Safaga, Aqaba (terminates).

ROYAL ODYSSEY

(Royal) Nov- Dec. (28 days): Ashdod, Port Said, through Suez Canal, Safaga, Bombay, Goa, Cochin, Colombo, Madras, Port Blair, Phuket, Penang, Singapore (terminates).

Southampton

SEA PRINCESS

(P & O) Nov.-Dec. (30 days): Gibraltar, Navplion, Kusadasi, Rhodes, Limassol, Port Said, through Suez Canal, Safaga, Aquaba, Suez, Port Sais, Ashdod, Bodrum, Volos, Piraeus, Heraklion, Palma.

Venice

LEV TOLSTOY

(Transocean/MarQuest) Dec.-Jan, (15 days): Valletta, Oiraeus, Heaklion, Antalya, Mersin, Haifa, Ashdod, Port said, through Suez Canal, Sharm el Sheikh, Hurgada (terminates).

ASIAN, INDIAN & FAR EASTERN WATERS

Ashdod

SEABOURN SPIRIT

(Seabourn) Nov. (23 days): Through Suez Canal, Safaga, Aden, Bombay, Colombo, Phuket, Penang, Port Kelang, Singapore (terminates).

Bali

AURORA II

(Classical) Oct. (11 days): Parepare, Pulau, Sipadan, Sandakan, Koto, Kinabalu, Miri, Kuching, Singapore (terminates).

FRONTIER SPIRIT

(Seaquest) Aug.- Sep. (14 days): Lembar, Palopo, Kabaena, Larantuka (Flores), Komodo Is., Santonda Is., Semerang, Jakarta, Tanjung Pinang, Singapore (terminates).

ISLAND EXPLORER

(Abercrombie & Kent) Apr.-Nov. (13 days): Sumbawa Is., Bima, Komodo Is., Flores Is., Solor Is., Kupang, Sawa Is., Komodo Is., Sumbawa Is. Lombok Is.

RENAISSANCE VI

(Renaissance) Jan.-Mar. (14 days): Komodo Is., Larantuka (Flores), Kalabahi, Ujung Pandang, Palopo, Lombok Is., Surabaya, Semerang, Jakarta, Krakatau (Rakata Is.), Singapore (terminates).

SEA GODDESS II

(Cunard Sea Goddess) Feb. (11 days): Palopo, Ujung Pandang, Semerang,

Palau Pelang, Singapore, Kuala Lumpur, Pulau Pangkor, Phuket (terminates).

SPICE ISLANDER
(Abercrombie & Kent) Mar.-Jan. (13 days): Sumbawa Is., Bimba, Komodo Is., Flores Is., Solor Is., Kupang, Sawu Is. Sumba Is., Komodo Is., Sumbawa Is., Lombok Is.; also available as 7-day trip to Kupang.

Bangkok
OCEAN PEARL
(Pearl) Mar. (13 days): through Strait of Malacca, Port Kelang, Jakarta, Bali, Semerang, Pulau, Sepa, Singapore (terminates).

PACIFIC PRINCESS
(Princess) Jan.-Feb. (14 days): Kuantan, Singapore, Bali, Sandkan, Koto Kimbalu, Canton, Hong Kong (terminates); or Apr. (14 days): Kuantan, Singapore, Port Kelang, Phuket, Madras, Colombo, Goa, Bombay (terminates).

SEABOURN SPIRIT
(Seabourn) Feb.-Mar; Dec. (7 days): Kuching, Toman, Singapore (terminates).

SEA GODDESS
(Cunard Sea Goddess) Mar. (11 days): Koh Samu, Kuantan, Troman, Penang, Phuket, Pulau, Pangkor, Kuala Lumpur, Singapore (terminates).

Bombay
RENAISSANCE VI
(Renaissance) Dec. (14 days): Dec. (14 days): Goa, Mangalore, Cochin, Port Blair, Phuket, Penang, Kula Lumpur, Singapore (terminates).

SEABOURN SPIRIT
(Seabourn) Mar.-Apr. (12 days): Aden, Safaga, through Suez Canal, Ashdod (terminates) Nov. (11 days): Colombo, Phuket, Penang, Port Kelang, Singapore (terminates).

SEA GODDESS II
(Cunard Sea Goddess) Nov. (13 days): Goa, Male (Maldives), Phuket, Pulau, Pangkor, Kuala Lumpur, Singapore (terminates).

Darwin
CUNARD CROWN MONARCH
(Cunard Crown) Jan.-Feb. (14 days): Komodo Is., Ujung Pandang, Lombok Is., Bali, Surabaya, Semerang, Jakarta, Singapore (terminates.

OCEAN PEARL
(Pearl) Jul. (13 days): Guangzhou, Nha Trang, Ho Chi Minh, Kota Kimbalu, Bandar Seri Begawan, Kuching, Port Kelang, Singapore (terminates), or Sep.-Oct. (10 days): Ningbo, Yangtze River Gorges, Nanjing, Shanghai, Dalian, Tianjin (terminates).

Ho Chi Minh
OCEAN
(American Pacific) Oct.-Nov. (7 days): Nha Trang, Da Nang, Haphong, Hong Kong (terminates).

Hong Kong
AURORA I
(Classical) Jan.- Feb. (11 days): Hanoi, Malong Bay, Da Nang, Ho Chi Minh, Rach Gia, Bankok (terminates).

CUNARD STAR MONARCH
(Cunard Star Monarch) Mar.-Apr. (14 days): Haiphong, Da Nang, Ho Chi Minh, Koh Samui, Bankok, Singapore (terminates).

MARCO POLO
(Orient) May-Oct. (10 days): Yangtze River, Zhenjiang, Nanjing, Shanghai, Quigdao, Salian, Tianjin (terminates),or; (12 days): Manila, through Makassar Strait, Bali, Semerang, Singapore (terminates).

OCEAN PEARL
(Pearl) Jul-Oct. (13 days): Guangzhou, Nha Trang, Ho Chi Minh, Kota, Kinabalu, Bandar Seri Begawan, Kuching, Port Kelang, Singapore (terminates); or, Sep.-Oct (10 days): Ningbo, Yangtze River Gorges, Nanjing, Shanghai, Dalian, Tianjin (terminates).

OCEAN STAR
(American Pacific) Oct.- Nov. (7 days): Haiphong, Da Nang, Nha Trang, Ho Chi Minh (terminates).

PACIFIC PRINCESS
(Princess) Feb.-Apr. (14 days): Canton, Kota Kinabalu, Sandakan, Bali, Singapore, Kuantan, Bangkok (terminates); or Shanghai, Dalian, Tianjin, Pusan, Nagasaki, Kobe (terminates).

ROYAL ODYSSEY
(Royal) Jan. (12 days): Canton, Da Nang, Kota Kinabalu, Brunei, Kuantan, Singapore (terminates).

Hurgada
LEV TOLSTOY
(Transocean/Marquest) Jan. (17 days): Hodeidah, Victoria (Mahe Is.), Praslin Is., Siego Suarez Is., Dzaqudz, Zanzibar, Mombasa (terminates).

Inchon
MARCO POLO
(Orient) Jun.-Sep. (14 days): Vladivostok, Hakodate, Tokyo, Kobe, Inland Sea, Shanghai, Tianjin (terminates).

Kobe
OCEANIC GRACE
(Oceanic) Sep. (10 days): Hakata, Quinhaungdao, Tianjin, or Nov. (4 days): Yaku Shima, Kochi (Shikoku), Tokyo (terminates).
PACIFIC PRINCESS
(Princess) Mar, (14 days): Nagasaki, Pusan, Tianjin, Dalian, Shanghai, Hong Kong (terminates).

Kupang
ISLAND EXPLORER/SPICE ISLANDER
(Abercrombie & Kent) Apr.; Jul.-Nov. (6 days): Sawu Is., Sumba Is., Komodo Is., Sumbawa Is., Lombok Is., Bali (terminates).

Mahe Is. (Seychelles)
MERMOZ
(Paquet French) Dec. (9 days): Praslin Is., Diego Suarez, Nossi-Be, Ile de Mayotte, Anjouam (Comoro Is.), Mombasa (terminates).
RENAISSANCE VIII
(Renaissance) Jul.-Jan. (10-11 days): La Digue, Desroches (Seychelles), Poivre Is., Praslin Is., Aride Is., Cousin Is.

Mombasa
ISLAND PRINCESS
(Princess) Nov.-Dec. (16 days): Zanzibar, Nossi-Be, Mahe Is. (Seychelles), Colombo, Penang, Kuala Lumpur, Singapore (terminates).
MERMOZ
(Paquet French) Dec. (9 days): Anjouan (Comoro Is.), Ile de Mayotte, Nossi-Be, Diego Suarez, Praslin Is.,(Seychelles) (terminates).
LEV TOLSTOY
(Transocean/MarQuest) Jan.- Feb. (15 days): Moroni, Nossi-Be, Diega Suarez, Victoria (Mahe Is.), La Digue, Male (Maldives), Madras, Trincomalee, Colombo (terminates).

Nigata
OCEANIC GRACE
(Oceanic) Sep. (7 days): Sakata, Akita, Aomori (Honshu), Sendai, Tokyo (terminates).

Osaka
OCEANIC GRACE
(Oceanic) Aug. (2 days): Toba, Toyko (terminates); or, Nov. (6 days): Shodoshima, Miyajima, Kobe, Shingo, Shimizu, Yokohama (terminates).

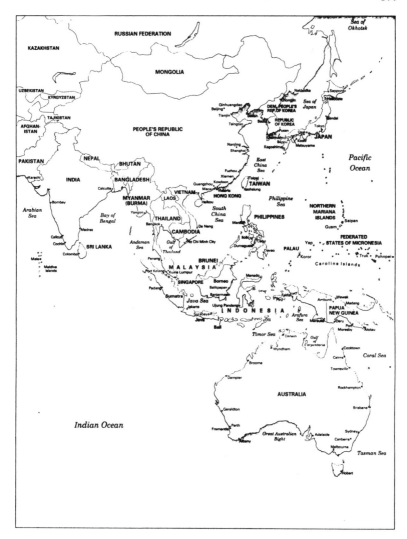

Otaru (Hokkaido)
EXPLORER
(Abercrombie & Kent) Jul. (9-10 days): Rishiri Is., Korsakov, Kuril Is., Petropavlovsk- Kamchatka (terminates).
OCEANIC GRACE
(Oceanic) Jul. (5 days): Rebun Is., Abashiri Is.; or (3 days): Hakodato, Tokyo (terminates).

Padang Bay (Bali)
OCEAN PEARL
(Pearl) Nov. (8 days): Komodo Is., Ujung Padang, Parepare, Semerang, Singapore (terminates).

Petropavlovsk-Kamkchatka
CALDONIAN STAR
(Seaquest) Jul.-Aug. (19 days): Aleksandrovsk, Kholmsk, Nevelsk, Vladivostok, Kanazawa, Matsue, Pusan, Inchon, Dalian, Tianjin (terminates).
EXPLORER
(Abercrombie & Kent) Jul. (12 days): Komandor Is., Kuril Is., Korsakov, Otaru (Hokkaido) (terminates).
OCEAN STAR
(American Pacific) Aug. (7 days): Paramushir Is., Kurilsk, Sakalin Is., Vladivostok, Kanazawa, Matsue, Pusan, Inchon, Dalin, Tianjin (terminates).

Phuket
SEA GODDESS II
(Cunard Sea Goddess) Feb.-Mar. (11 days): Langkawi Is., Penang, Pulau, Pangkor, Kuala Lumpur, Singapore, Tioman, Kuantan, Koh Samui, Bangkok (terminates).

Piraeus
ROYAL ODYSSEY
(Royal) Nov.- Dec. (28 days): Ashdod, Port Said, through Suez Canal, Safaga, Bombay, Goa, Cochin Columbo, Madras, Port Blair, Phuket, Penang, Singapore (terminates).

Singapore
AURORA
(Classical) Sep.- Oct. (11): Semerang, Madura Is., Benteng, Palopo, Watampone, Komodo Is., Lombok Is., Bali (terminates)..
CUNARD CROWN MONARCH
(Cunard Crown) Feb.-Mar. (14 days): Penang, Belawan, Sibolga, Padang, Jakarta, Semerang, Surabaya, Bali, Lombok Is.; or Mar. (14 days) Kuching, Bandar Seri, Begawan, Kota Kinabalu. Ho Chi Minh, Nha Trang, Canton, Hong Kong (terminates).
MARCO POLO
(Orient) May (10 days): Port Kelang, Ho Chi Minh, Da Nang, Canton, Hong Kong (terminates); or Jul.-Aug. (14 days): Semerang, Bali, through Makassar Strait, Manila, Hong Kong (terminates); or Aug. (12 days): Semerang, Bali, through Makassar Strait, Manila, Hong Kong (terminates).

OCEAN PEARL

(Pearl) Feb. (14 days): Through Strait of Malacca, Phuket, Nias Is., Padang, Krakatau (Rakata Is.), Jakarta, Semerang, Surabaya, Bali; or Krakatau, Jarkata, Semerang, Surabaya, Lombok Is., Palopo, Ujung Pandang, Kalabahi, Larantuka (Flores), Komodo Is., Bali (terminates); or Jul.-Aug. (13 days): Jakarta, Semerang, Parepare, Ujung Pandang, Komodo Is., Bali, Larantuka, Arafura Sea, Darwin (terminates); or Aug.-Sep. (12 days): Ho Chi Minh, Nha Trang, Da Nang, Haiphong, Hong Kong (terminates).

RENAISSANCE VI

(Renaissance) Nov.-Feb.(14 days): Krakatau (Rakata Is.), Jakarta, Semerang, Surabaya, Lombok Is., Palopo, Ujung Pandang, Kalabahi, Larantuka (Flores), Komodo Is., Bali (terminates); or Mar. (14 days): Kuala Lumpur, Penang, Phuket, Port Blair, Cochin, Mangalore, Goa, Bombay (terminates).

ROYAL ODYSSEY

(Royal) Dec.-Feb. (12 days): Semerang, Bali, Kota Kinabalu, Hong Kong (terminates).

ROYAL VIKING QUEEN

(Royal) Dec.-Jan. (18 days): Semerang, Bali, Lombok Is., Kuching, Koh Samui, Bankok, Ho Chi Minh, Hong Kong (terminates).

SEABOURN SPIRIT

(Seabourn) Nov.- Mar. (14 days): Port Kelang, through Strait of Malacca, Semerang, Bali, Lombok Is., Kuching: or Penang, Port Kelang, Koh Samui, Bangkok, Kuching, Tioman.

SEA GODDESS II

(Cunard Sea Goddess) Nov.-Feb. (10-11 days): Port Kelang, through Strait of Malacca, Semerang, Bali, Lombok Is., Kuching; or Mar. (13 days): Kuala Lumpur, Pulau Pangkor, Phuket, Male (Maldives), Goa, Bombay (terminates).

SEABOURN SPIRIT

(Seabourn) Mar.-Apr. (23 days): Port Kelang, Penang, Phuket, Colombo, Bombay, Aden, Safaga, through Suez Canal, Ashdod (terminates).

Sydney

BELORUSSIA

(CTC) Sep.-Oct. (28 days): Cairns, Rabaul, Guam, Yokohama, Kobe, Pusan, Shanghai, Hong Kong, Kuantan, Singapore (terminates).

PACIFIC PRINCESS

(Princess) Dec.-Jan. (16 days): Brisbane, Great Barrier Reef, Port Moresby, Bali, Singapore, Bankok (terminates).

Tanjung Priok
ISLAND EXPLORER
(Abercrombie & Kent) Mon. Nov.-Mar. (6 days): Peucang Is., Handeuleum, Labuhan, Meringg (Rakata Is.), Banten.

SPICE ISLANDER
(Abercrombie & Kent) Jan.- Feb. (6 days): Same ports as ISLAND EXPLORER.

Tianjin
CALDONIAN STAR
(Seaquest) Jul. (18 days): Dalian, Inchon, Pusan, Matsue, Kanazawa, Vladivostok, Nevelsk, Kholmsk, Aleksandrovsk, Petropavlosk-Kamchatka (terminates).

MARCO POLO
(Orient) Jul; Sep.-Oct. (10 days): Dalian, Quingdao, Yangtze River, Zhenjiang, Nanjing, Shanghai, Hong Kong (terminates).

OCEAN PEARL
(Pearl) Sep.-Oct. (10 days): Dalian, Yangtze River Gorges, Nanjing, Shanghai, Ningbo, Hong Kong (terminates).

Tokyo
OCEANIC GRACE
(Oceanic) Jul.-Nov. (2-6 Days): Ogasawara (Bonin Is.), Uwajima, Oki Is., Miyazu, Nigata (terminates), Kochi, Takamatsu, Tokushima, Osaka (terminates), Toba, Kobe, Shingu, Ohfunato, Sendai, Miyako, Imbari, Miyako, Sendai, Hiroshima, Kobe (terminates).

Vancouver
ROTTERDAM
(Holland America) Sep.-Oct. (30 days): Seattle, through inside passage, Glacier Bay Nat. Park, crossing Int'l Date Line, Hakodate, Vladivostok, Pusan, Tianjin, Naha (Okinawa), Hong Kong, Singapore (terminates).

Vladivostok
OCEAN STAR
(American Pacific) Jul.-Aug. (7 days): Sakhalin Is. Paramushir Is., Petropavlovsk- Kamchatka (terminates).

PANAMA CANAL
Acapulco
CROWN ODYSSEY
(Royal) Mar.-Apr. (11 days): Puerto Caldera, Aruba, Curacao, St. Thomas, San Juan (terminates).

CROWN PRINCESS
(Princess) Oct. (11 days): Cartegena, St. Thomas, private out is., Ft Lauderdale (terminates).

CRYSTAL HARMONY
(Crystal) Nov.-Dec. (14 days) Puerto Caldera, Curacao, St. Maarten, St. Thomas, San Juan, Nassau, Ft Lauderdale (terminates): or Dec. (17 days): Puerto Caldera, Aruba, St Maarten, St Thomas, Montego Bay, Grand Cayman, Playa del Carmen/Cozumel, Ft. Lauderdale (terminates); or Jan. (10 days): Aruba, St. Maarten, St. Thomas, San Juan (terminates).

GOLDEN ODYSSEY
(Royal) Nov. -Feb. (10 days): Isla San Jose, Ocho Rios, Grand Cayman, Tampa (terminates); or Nov.-Jan; Apr. (9 days): Puerto Caldera, San Blas Is., La Guaira., Curacao, Aruba (terminates); or Feb.-Mar. (12 days): Puerto Calderas, Ocho Rios, Grand Cayman, New Orleans (terminates).

NIEUW AMSTERDAM
(Holland America)
Oct. (12 days): Puerto Caldera, Balboa, Cristobal, San Blas Is., Grand Cayman, Tampa (terminates).

NOORDAM
(Holland America) Oct. (12 days): Balboa, Cristobal, Cartegena, Curacao, Montego Bay, New Orleans (terminates).

ROTTERDAM
(Holland America) Nov.-Dec. (12 days): Balboa, Cristobal, San Blas Is., Cartegena, Ocho Rios, Ft Lauderdale, Newport News (terminates).

ROYAL PRINCESS
(Princess) Nov.-Apr. (10 days) Puerto Caldera, Cartegena, St. Maarten, St. Thomas, San Juan (terminates).

STAR PRINCESS
(Princess) Oct. (10 days): Puerto Caldera, Cartegena, St. Thomas, San Juan (terminates).

SUN VIKING
(Royal) Oct. (14 days): Puerto Caldera, San Blas Is., Montego Bay, Grand Cayman, Cozumel, Key West, Miami (terminates).

WESTERDAM
(Holland America) Oct. (11 days): Puerto Caldera, Balboa, Cristobal, San Blas Is. Cartegena, Ocho Rios, Ft. Lauderdale (terminates).

Acapulco-San Juan
SONG OF NORWAY
(Royal Caribbean)Nov.-Apr.(10-11 days): Puerto Caldera, Curacao, St. Thomas

ROYAL PRINCESS
(Princess) Nov.-Mar. (10-11): Puerto Caldera. Cartegena, St. Maarten, St.

Thomas, Fort de France, Grenada, Caracas, Curacao; or Apr (14 days): add Bermuda, New York (terminates).

Acapulco-Ft. Lauderdale

CUNARD CROWN DYNASTY

(Cunard Crown) Oct.-May. (10-11 days): Puerto Caldera, Ocho Rios, Key West, Cozumel, Grand Cayman, Montego Bay.

SEABOURN PRIDE

(Seabourn) Nov.-Jan. (16 Days): Hautulco, Puerto Caldera, Fort de France, Aruba, Martinique, St. Barts, St. Maarten, Virgin Gorda, La Romana, Islas los Roques.

SKY PRINCESS

(Princess) Oct.-Dec.; Mar.-Apr. (11 days): Puerto Caldera, Cartegena, Ocho Rios, private out island.

Aruba

GOLDEN ODYSSEY

(Royal) Nov.-May (9 days): Curacao, San Blas Is., Puerto Caldera, Acapulco (terminates).

SEABOURN PRIDE

(Seabourne) Nov.-Dec. (8 days): Puerto Caldera, Acapulco (terminates).

Balboa-Colon

MAYAN PRINCE

(American Canadian Caribbean) Feb.-Mar (10-11 days): Punta Alegre, Contadora, Tobago Is., Porto Bello, San Blas Is., el Porvenir.

Barbados

CRYSTAL HARMONY

(Crystal) Nov. (10 days): Grenada, Aruba, Puerto Caldera, Acapulco (terminates).

Colon

YORKTOWN CLIPPER

(Clipper) Dec. (10 days): Portobelo, San Blas Is., Darien, Las Perlas Is., Cebaco Is., Manuel Antonio Nat. Park, Puerto Caldera (terminates).

Curacao

COLUMBUS CARAVELLE

(Transocean/MarQuest) Oct. (6 days): Oranjestad, San Blas Is., Darien, Las Perlas Is., Cebaco Is., Manuel Antonio Nat. Park, Puerto Caldera, Balboa (terminates).

EUROPA

(Hapag-Lloyd Kreutzfahrten) Dec.-Jan. (16 days): Ocho Rios, San Andres Is., Panama City, Puerto Quetzal, Acapulco, Puerto Caldera (terminates).

Cape Town
SAGAFJORD
(Cunard/NAC) Feb.-Apr. (69 Days): Durban, Mombassa, Mahe Is. Seychelles, Madras, Port Kelang, Singapore, Laem Chabang, Ho Chi Minh, Hong Kong, Shanghai, Pusan, Tokyo, Honolulu, Kahului, Maui, Los Angeles, Cabo San Lucas, Acapulco, Caldera, Oranjestad, Ft Lauderdale (terminates).

Ensenada
ODESSA
(Transocean/MarQuest) Mar (15 days): Cabo San Lucas, Mazatlan, Puerto Vallarta, Acapulco, Salina Cruz, Puntarenas, Balboa, Cristobal, San Blas Is., San Andres Is. (terminates).

Ft. Lauderdale-Acapulco
SKY PRINCESS
(Princess) Oct.; Dec.; Mar.-Apr (11 days): Princess Cays, Ocho Rios, Cartegena, Puerto Caldera.

Ft. Lauderdale
CRYSTAL HARMONY
(Crystal) Nov. (11 days): Key West, Playa del Carmen/Cozumel, Grand Cayman, Montego Bay, Puerto Caldera, Acapulco (terminates).

CUNARD CROWN DYNASTY
(Cunard Crown) Apr.-May (14 days): Grand Cayman, Cartegena, Puerto Caldera, Acapulco, Los Angeles (terminates).

CUNARD CROWN MONARCH
(Cunard Crown) Sep.-Oct. (14 days): Port Antonio, Cartegena, Puerto Caldera, Acapulco, Los Angeles (terminates).

RADISSON DIAMOND
(Diamond) Jan.(11 days): Key West,.Playa del Carmen/Cozumel, Grand Cayman, San Andres Is., Puerto Caldera (terminates).

ROYAL VIKING QUEEN
(Royal Viking) Dec, (16 days): Playa del Carmen/Cozumel, San Andres, Puerto Caldera, Acapulco, Cabo San Lucas, San Francisco (terminates).

SKY PRINCESS
(Princess) Jan.-Feb. (15 days): Princess Cays, Ocho Rios, Cartegena, Puerto Caldera, Acapulco, Cabo San Lucas, Los Angeles (terminates); or Apr.-May (18 days): add Vancouver (terminates).

VISTAFJORD
(Cunard) Dec-Jan, (14 days): Grand Cayman, Cartegena, Puerto Caldera, Acapulco. Cabo San Lucas, Los Angeles (terminates).

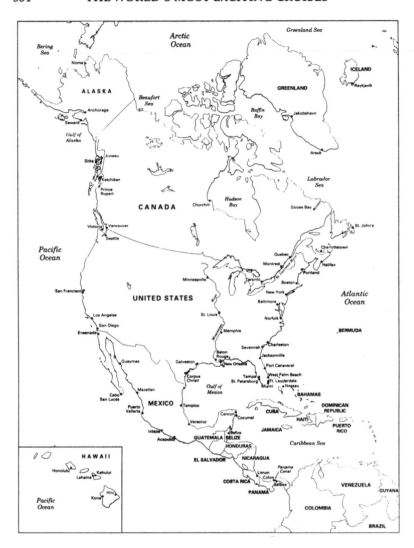

Ft. Lauderdale-San Francisco
ROYAL VIKING SUN
(Royal Viking) Dec.-Apr. (16 days): Aruba,.Puerto Caldera, Acapulco, Zihuatanejo, Cabo San Lucas, Los Angeles, San Francisco (terminates).

Hong Kong
SAGAFJORD
(Holland America) Mar.-Apr. (37 days): Shanghai, Pusan, Tokyo, Hono-

lulu, Kahului, Los Angeles, Cabo San Lucas, Acapulco, Caldera, Oranjestad, Ft. Lauderdale (terminates).

Honolulu
ROTTERDAM
(Holland America) Nov. (22 days): Lahaina, Hilo, Los Angeles, Cabo San Lucas, Acapulco, Caldera, Balboa, Cristobal, Cartagena, Ocho Rios, Ft Lauderdale (terminates).

Los Angeles
COSTA RIVIERA
(Costa) Sep.-Oct. (18 days): Cabo San Lucas, Zihuatanejo, Acapulco, Balboa, Cristobal, Cartegena, Curacao, St. Croix, Nassau, Ft. Lauderdale (terminates).

CUNARD CROWN DYNASTY
(Cunard Crown) Sept-Oct. (14 Days): Acapulco, Puerto Caldera, Cartegena, Ocho Rios, Ft. Lauderdale (terminates).

CROWN ODYSSEY
(Royal) Jan.-Feb (14 days): Cabo San Lucas, Acapulco, Puerto Caldera, Aruba, San Juan (terminates),

GOLDEN ODYSSEY
(Royal) Sep. (14 days): Puerto Vallarta, Zihuatanejo, Acapulco, Puerto Caldera, Ocho Rios, Nassau (terminates).

ISLAND PRINCESS
(Princess) Mar.-Apr. (14 days): Acapulco, Puerto Caldera, St. Maarten, St. Thomas, San Juan (terminates)

MAASDAM
(Holland America) Nov.-Dec.(16 days): Cabo San Lucas, Acapulco, Caldera, Balboa, Cristobal, Cartegena, Grand Cayman, Ft Lauderdale, Baltimore (terminates).

NIEUW AMSTERDAM
(Holland America) Oct. (15 days) Puerto Vallerta, Zihautanajo, Acapulco, Balboa, Cristobal, San Blas Is., Cartegena, Grand Cayman, Tampa (terminates).

NOORDAM
(Holland America) Sept.-Oct. (15 days): Cabo San Lucas, Acapulco, Caldera, Balboa, Cristobal, Cartegena, Grand Cayman, Cozumel, New Orleans (terminates).

ROTTERDAM
(Holland America) Nov.-Dec. (16 days): Cabo San Lucas, Acapulco, Balboa, San Blas Is., Cartegena, Ocho Rios, Ft Lauderdale, Newport News (terminates).

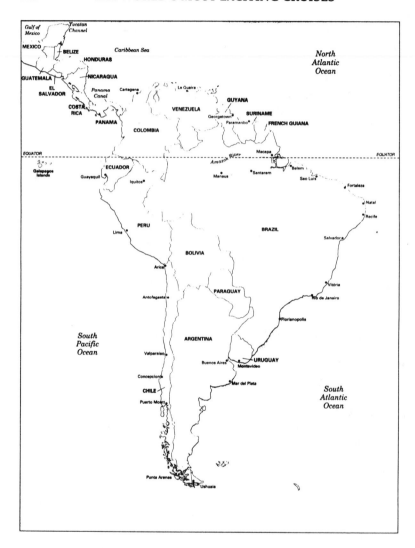

ROYAL PRINCESS
(Princess) Dec, (11 days): Cabo San Lucas, Acapulco, Puerto Caldera, Cartegena, St. Maarten, St. Thomas, San Juan (terminates).

SAGAFJORD
(Cunard/NAC) Sep. (14 days): Cabo San Lucas, Acapulco, Puerto Caldera, Oranjestad, Ft. Lauderdale (terminates).

SKY PRINCESS
(Princess) Oct.-Feb. (15 days): Cabo San Lucas, Acapulco, Puerto Caldera,

Cartegena, Ocho Rios, Nassau, private out island, Ft Lauderdale (terminates)

STARWARD
(Norwegian) Dec.-Jan.; Mar.(12 days): Acapulco, Puerto Caldera, Balboa, Cartegena, San Juan (terminates).

VISTAFJORD
(Cunard) Dec.-Jan.; Mar. (15-16 days): Cabo San Lucas, Acapulco, Puerto Caldera, Aruba, Ocho Rios, Grand Cayman, Ft Lauderdale (terminates).

WESTERDAM
(Holland America) Oct. (15 days) Puerto Vallarta, Ixtapa/Zihautanejo, Acapulco, Balboa, Cristobal, Cartegena, Curacao, St. Croix, Nassau, Ft. Lauderdale (terminates).

New Orleans
GOLDEN ODYSSEY
(Royal) Mar.-Apr. (12 days): Grand Cayman, Ocho Rios, Caldera, Acapulco (terminates).

NIEUW AMSTERDAM
(Holland America) Apr.-May (18 days): Ocho Rios, Cartegena, Cristobal, Balboa, Caldera, Acapulco, Cabo San Lucas, San Francisco, Vancouver (terminates).

NOORDAM
(Holland America) Apr.-May (18 days): Ocho Rios, Cartagena, Cristobal, Balboa, Caldera, Acapulco, Cabo San Lucas, San Francisco, Vancouver (terminates).

New York
ROYAL PRINCESS
(Princess) Oct.-Nov. (14 days): Bermuda, St Thomas, St. Croix, Curacao, Puerto Caldera, Acapulco (terminates).

QUEEN ELIZABETH 2
(Cunard) Jan. (13 days): Ft. Lauderdale, St Thomas, Cartegena, Acapulco, Los Angeles (terminates).

STATENDAM
(Holland America) Jan. (22 days): Ft Lauderdale, Cartagena, Cristobal, Balboa, Caldera, Acapulco, Cabo San Lucas, San Francisco, Honolulu (terminates).

Puerto Caldera (Costa Rica)
RADISSON DIAMOND
(Diamond) Jan (11 days): San Andres Is., Grand Cayman, Playa del Carmen, Cozumel, Key West, Ft. Lauderdale (terminates).

YORKTOWN CLIPPER

(Clipper) Dec. (10 days): Manuel Antonio Nat. Park, Cebaco Is., Las Perlas Is., Darien, San Blas Is., Portobelo, Colon (terminates).

San Diego

NOORDAM

(Holland America) Sep.-Oct. (16 days): San Diego, Cabo San Lucas, Acapulco, Balboa, Cristobal, Cartegena, Curacao, Montego Bay, New Orleans (terminates).

REGAL PRINCESS

(Princess) Oct. (15 days): Cabo San Lucas, Acapulco, Caldera, Cartegena, Grand Cayman, Playa del Carmen, Cozumel, Ft. Lauderdale.

REGENT SEA

(Regency) Oct, (15 days): Puerto Vallarta, Zihuatanejo, Acapulco, Costa Rica, Cartegena, Grand Cayman, Tampa (terminates).

San Francisco

GOLDEN ODYSSEY

(Royal) Sep. (15 days): Cabo San Lucas, Puerto Vallarta, Zihuatanejo, Acapulco, Puerto Caldera, Ocho Rios, Nassau (terminates).

NOORDAM

(Holland America) Sep.-Oct. (18 days): San Diego, Cabo San Lucas, Acapulco, Balboa, Cristobal, Cartegena, Curacao, Montego Bay, New Orleans (terminates).

REGENT STAR

(Regency) Oct. (15 days): Los Angeles, Puerto Vallarta, Zihuatanejo, Acapulco, Costa Rica, Cartegena, Montego Bay (terminates).

ROYAL VIKING SUN

(Royal Viking) Dec. (16 days): Santa Barbara, Puerto Vallarta, Zihuatanejo/Ixtapa, Acapulco, Puerto Caldera, Oranjestad, Aruba, Ft Lauderdale (terminates); or Apr.-May (16 days): Los Angeles, Acapulco, Puerto Caldera, San Andres, Playa del Carmen/Cozumel, New Orleans (terminates).

STAR ODYSSEY

(Royal) Sept. (15 days); Cabo San Lucas, Puerto Vallarta, Zihuatanejo, Acapulco, Puerto Caldera (Costa Rica), Ocho Rios, Nassau (terminates).

NIEUW AMSTERDAM

(Holland America) Sept.-Oct. (7 days): Cabo San Lucas, Acapulco, Puerto Caldera, Balboa, Cristobal, Aruba, Ocho Rios, Grand Cayman, Tampa (terminates).

San Juan

CROWN ODYSSEY

(Royal) Dec. (14 days): Aruba, Puerto Caldera, Acapulco, Zihuatanejo,

Puerto Vallarta, Los Angeles (terminates); or Feb.-Mar, (10 days): St. Thomas, Curacao, Puerto Caldera, Acapulco (terminates); or Mar. (11 days): St. Thomas, Curacao, Aruba, Puerto Caldera, Acapulco (terminates).

CRYSTAL HARMONY

(Crystal) Jan.-Feb. (14 days): St. Thomas, St. Maarten, Aruba, Acapulco, Zihuatanejo, Los Angeles (terminates).

PACIFIC PRINCESS

(Princess) Nov. (14 days): St. Thomas, St. Maarten, Caldera (Costa Rica), Acapulco, Los Angeles (terminates);

ROYAL PRINCESS

(Princess) Nov.-Mar. (11 days): St. Thomas, Fort de France, Grenada, La Guairi, Curacao, Acapulco (terminates); or Dec. (14 days): add Cabo San Lucas, Los Angeles (terminates),

STAR PRINCESS

(Princess) Apr.-May (17 days): St. Thomas, Curacao, Caldera, Acapulco, Cabo San Lucas, San Francisco, Vancouver (terminates).

SUN VIKING

(Royal Caribbean) Apr. (15 days): St. Thomas, Curacao, Puerto Caldera, Acapulco, Puerto Vallarta, Los Angeles (terminates).

Seattle

NIEUW AMSTERDAM

(Holland America) Sept. (19 days): San Francisco, Cabo San Lucas, Acapulco, Caldera, Balboa, Cristobal, Aruba, Ocho Rios, Grand Cayman, Tampa (terminates).

WESTERDAM

(Holland America) Sep.-Oct, (20 days): Los Angeles, Puerto Vallarta, Zihuatanejo, Acapulco, Balboa, Cristobal, Cartegena, Curacao, St. Croix, Nassau, Ft. Lauderdale (terminates).

Tampa

GOLDEN ODYSSEY

(Royal) Dec. (10 days): Grand Cayman, Ocho Rios, Isla San Jose, Acapulco (terminates).

NIEUW AMSTERDAM

(Holland America) Apr. (20 days); Grand Cayman, Ocho Rios, Aruba, Cristobal, Balboa, Puerto Caldera, Acapulco, Ixtapa/Zihuatanejo, Puerto Vallarta, Los Angeles, Vancouver (terminates).

Vancouver

NIEUW AMSTERDAM

(Holland America) Sept.-Oct. (18 Days): Los Angeles, Puerto Vallarta,

Zihuatanejo/Ixtapa, Acapulco, Balboa, Cristobal, San Blas Is., Cartegena, Grand Cayman, Tampa (terminates).

NOORDAM

(Holland America) Sept.- Oct. (20 days): San Francisco, San Diego, Cabo San Lucas, Acapulco, Cristobal, Cartegena, Curacao, Montego Bay, New Orleans (terminates).

REGAL PRINCESS

(Princess) Sep.-Oct. (20 days): San Diego, Cabo San Lucas, Acapulco, Puerto Caldera, Cartegena, Grand Cayman, Playa del Carmen, Cozumel, Ft Lauderdale (terminates).

SKY PRINCESS

(Princess) Sep.-Oct. (18 days): Los Angeles, Cabo San Lucas, Acapulco, Puerto Caldera, Cartegena, Ocho Rios, Nassau, Ft lauderdale (terminates).

WESTERDAM

(Holland America) Sept-Oct. (21 days): Seattle, Los Angeles, Puerto Vallarta, Zihuatanejo/Ixtapa, Acapulco, Balboa, Cristobal, Cartegena, Curacao, St. Croix, Nassau, Fort Lauderdale (terminates).

MEXICO, CENTRAL & SOUTH AMERICA & GALAPAGOS

Mexico

Acapulco

GOLDEN ODYSSEY

(Royal) May (8 days): Zihuatenejo, Puerta Vallarta, Mazatlan, Cabo San Lucas, Avalon, Catalina Is., Monterey, San Francisco (terminates).

REGAL PRINCESS

(Princess) Apr.-May (10 days): Zihuatanejo/Ixtapa, Puerto Vallarta, Mazatlan, Cabo San Lucas, Los Angeles, Vancouver (terminates).

STAR ODYSSEY

(Royal) May (8 days): Zihuatanejo, Puerto Vallarta, Mazatlan, Cabo San Lucas, Avalon, Catalina Is., Monterey, San Francisco (terminates).

Cabo San Lucas

SEA BIRD/SEA LION

(Special Expeditions) Dec.-Jan. (7 days): Isla Partida, Espiritu Santo, Isla Carmen, Bahia San Basilio, Isla Ildefonso, Isla Santa Catalina, La Paz (terminates).

WORLD DISCOVERER

(Clipper) Oct. (10 days): Isla Espiritu Santo, Isla San Jose, Isla San Francisco, Mazatlan, Manzillo, Zihuatanejo/Ixtapa, Puerto Escongido, Manuel Antonio Nat. Park, Puerto Caldera (Costa Rica) (terminates).

La Paz
SEA BIRD/SEA LION
(Special Expeditions) Dec.-Jan (7 days): Isla Partida, Espirito Santo, Isla Carmen, Bahia San Basilio, Isla Ildefonso, Isla Santa Catalina, Isla San Jose, La Paz (terminates).

AURORA II
(Classical) Mar. (6 days): Isla Santa Catalina, Isla Espirito Santo, Isla San Estaban, Angel de la Guarda, Sea of Cortez, Topolobampo (terminates).

Los Angeles
CROWN ODYSSEY
(Royal) Dec.-Jan. (12 days): Puerto Vallarta, Zihuatanejo, Acapulco, Manzanillo, Mazatlan, Cabo San Lucas.

FAIR PRINCESS
(Princess) Jan.-Apr. (10 days): Puerto Vallarta, Zihuatanejo, Acapulco, Mazatlan, Cabo San Lucas.

GOLDEN PRINCESS
(Princess) Jan.-Mar. (10 days): Cabo San Lucas, Mazatlan, Puerto Vallarta, Zihuatanejo.

JUBILEE
(Carnival) Sun year round (7 days): Puerto Vallarta, Mazatlan, Cabo San Lucas.

NORDIC PRINCE
(Royal Caribbean) Sun Oct.-Apr.(7 days): Cabo San Lucas, Mazatlan, Puerto Vallarta.

SEA BIRD and SEA LION
(Special Expeditions) Dec. Apr. (8-12 days): Los Cabos, Cabo San Lucas, Gorda Banks, Islas Partida, Espiritu Santo, Isla Carmen, Bahia San Basilio, Isla Ildefonso, Isla Santa Catalina, Isla San Jose, Isla Islotes, La Paz, San Carlos, Bahia Magdalena, Isla San Marcos, Isla San Pedro Matir, Isla San Estaban, Madriff Is. Guaymas, Isla Angel de la Guarda.

SOUTHWARD
(Norwegian) Fri year round (3 days): Catalina Is., Ensenada; or Mondays (4 days) adds San Diego.

VIKING SERENADE
(Royal Caribbean) Year round (3-4 days): Catalina Is., Ensenada.

San Diego
NOORDAM
(Holland America): Sep.-Oct. (4 days): Cabo San Lucas, Acapulco (terminates),

YORKTOWN CLIPPER

(Clipper) Nov. (15 days): Cabo San Lucas, Isla Espiritu Santo, Isla Santa Catalina, Isla San Jose, Isla San Francisco, Mazatlan, Isla Isobella, San Blas, Puerto Vallarta, Zihuatanejo/Ixtapa, Acalulpo (terminates).

San Francisco

NOORDAM

(Holland America): Sep.-Oct. (6 days): San Diego, Cabo San Lucas, Acapulco (terminates).

STAR PRINCESS

(Princess): Oct. (7 days) Cabo San Lucas, Mazatlan, Puerto Vallarta, Zihuatanejo/Ixtapa, Acapulco (terminates).

Topolobampo

AURODRA II

(Classical) Mar. (6 days): Sea of Cortez, Angel de la Guarda, Isla San Estaban, Isla Espiritu Santo, Isla Santa Catalina, La Paz (terminates).

Vancouver

CROWN PRINCESS

(Princess) Sep.-Oct. (10 days): San Francisco, San Diego, Cabo San Lucas, Acapulco (terminates).

NIEW AMSTERDAM

(Holland America): Sep.-Oct. (8 days): Los Angeles, Puerto Vallarta, Zihuatanejo/Ixtapa, Acapulco (terminates).

NOORDAM

(Holland America): Sep.-Oct. (8 days): San Francisco, San Diego, Cabo San Lucas, Acapulco (terminates).

STAR PRINCESS

(Princess) Oct. (10 days): San Francisco, Cabo San Lucas, Mazatlan, Puerto Vallarta, Zihuatanejo/ Ixtapa, Acapulco (terminates).

WESTERDAM

(Holland America): Sep.-Oct. (9 days): Seattle, Los Angeles, Puerto Vallarta, Zihuatanejo/Ixtapa, Acapulco (terminates).

Central America

Punta Renas

TEMPTRESS

(Temptress) Fri Jul.-Sep. (3 days):Manuel Antonio Nat, Park, Corcovado,, Nat. Park, Isla Del Cano (terminates); or Mondays (4 days): JunQuilla Bay, Santa Rosa Nat. Park, Isla Del Cano (terminates).

COLUMBUS CARAVELLE

South America

Balboa
COLUMBUS CARAVELLE
(Transocean/MarQuest) Oct. -Nov. (17 days): Salaverry, Callao, Pisco, Iquiqui, Antofagasta, Valparaiso (terminates).

La Libertad
WORLD DISCOVERER
(Clipper) Oct.-Nov. (16 days): Salaverry, Paracas, Arica, Iquiqu, Antofagasta, Isla Pan de Azucar, Isla Mocha, Ancud, Isla Chiloe, Puerto Montt (terminates).

Manaus
ISLAND PRINCESS
(Princess) Apr. (14 days): Amazon River, Recife, Rio de Janeiro, Sanyos, Montevideo. Buenos Aires (terminates).

Miami
AMERICANA
(Ivarian) Jan.- Nov. (44 days): Rio de Janeiro, Santos, Buenos Aires, Montivideo, Rio Grande, Itajia, Salvador, Forteleza, Norfolk, Baltimore, Port Elizabeth (NJ) (terminates).

Montevideo (Uruguay)
COLUMBUS CARAVELLE

(Transocean/MarQuest) Feb.-Mar. (15 days): Punte del Este, Rio Grande, Paranagua, Santos, Rio de Janeiro, Salvador, Recife, Natal, Fortaleza, Belem (terminates).

Ft.Lauderdale
SAGAFJORD

(Cunard/NAC) Oct.-Nov. (14 days): Barbados, Devil's Is., Fortaleza, Recife, Vitoria, Rio de Janeiro (terminates).

Rio de Janeiro
ODESSA

(Transocean/MarQuest) Jan. (18 days): Montevideo, Buenos Aires, Puerto Madryn, Port Stanley, Ushuaia, through Beagle Channel, through Strait of Magellan, Puerto Natales, Puerto Montt, Valparaiso (terminates).

Savona
ODESSA

(Transocean/MarQuest) Dec.- Jan, (18 days): Funchal, Santa Cruz de la Palma, Dakar, Natal, Recife, Salvador, Rio de Janeiro (terminates).

Tampa
REGENCY Cruises

(Regency) Oct.-Dec. (50 days): Grand Cayman, Puerto Moin (Costa Rica), through Panama Canal, crossing Equator, Guayaquil, Iquiqui, Valparaiso, Puerto Montt, through Strait of Magellan, Punta Arenas, Ushuaia, through Beagle Channel, Puerto Madryn, Buenos Aires, Montevideo, Rio de Janeiro, Salvador, Fortaleza, Belem, Amazon Delta, Devil's Is., Barbados, Antigua, St Thomas.

Valparaiso
COLUMBUS CARAVELLE

(Transocean/MarQuest) Nov. (11 days): Talcahuano, Isla Mocha, Valdivia, Puerto Montt, Puerto Eden, through Strait of Magellan, Puntarenas (terminates).

REGENT SEA

(Regency) Nov.-Dec. (35 days): Puerto Montt, through Strait of Magellan, Punta Arenas, Ushuaia, through Beagle Channel, Puerto Madryn, Buenos Aires, Montevideo, Rio de Janeiro, Salvador Fortaleza, Belem, Amazon Delta, Devil's Is., Barbados, Antigua, St. Thomas, Tampa (terminates).

Galapagos Islands

Baltra, Galapagos Is.

ISABELLA II

(Metropolitan) Tues Jul.-Dec. (7 days): Hood Is., Floreana Is., Puerto Ayora, Academy Bay, Santa Cruz Is., Tower Is., Isabela Is., Fernandina Is., James Bay, Bartolome Is.

SANTA CRUZ

(Metropolitan) Mon Jul.-Dec. (3 days): Batolome Is., Tower Is., Isabela Is., Fernandina Is.; or Thurs. (4 days): Hood Is., Floreana Is., Puerto Ayora, Academy Bay, Santa Cruz Is., Jervis Is., James Bay.

San Cristobal

GALAPAGOS EXPLORER

(Galapagos) Sat Jul.-Dec. (4 days): Bartolome Is., Tagus Cove, Punta Espinoza, Puerto Egas, Puerto Ayora; or Wed.(3 days): Punta Suarez, Gardiner Bay, Punta Cormorant, Floreana Is., Post Office Bay, Puerto Ayora, Santa Cruz Is., Darwin Research Station; or same ports Sat Oct.-Dec.(4 days) and Wed (3 days).

GALAPAGOS NETWORK

(Galapagos) Fri Jul.-Dec. (4 days): Tower Is., Bartolome Is., Puerto Egas, North Seymour Is., Puerto Ayora, Darwin Research Station.

RIVERS & CANALS

Amazon

Aruba

GOLDEN ODYSSEY

(Royal) Apr. (11 days): Grenada, Devil's Is., Macapa, Amazon River, crossing Equator, Alter do Chao, Santarem, Manuas (terminates).

Barbados

SEA GODDESS I

(Cunard Sea Goddess) Feb. (14 days): Tobago, Devil's Is., Porto Santana, Amazon River, Alter do Chao, Parinthos, Anavilhanas, Manaus (terminates).

Belem

COLUMBUS CARAVELLE

(Transocean/ MarQuest) Mar. (14 days): Breves Canas, Santarem, Manaus, Vendeval, Tabatinga, Letcia, Pevas, Iquitos (terminates).

Iquitos
ARCA
(Amazon River) Sun Jul.-Dec. (3 days): Pevas, Chimbote, Santa Rosa (terminates).
COLUMBUS CARAVELLE
(Transocean/MarQuest)
Mar. (7 days): Pevas, Leticia, Tabatinga, Anavilhanus, Manaus (terminates)
RIO AMAZONAS
(Amazon River) Sun Jul.-Dec. (3 days): Pevas, Cochaquinas River, Chinbote, Letcia, Tabatinga (terminates).

Manaus
COLUMBUS CARAVELLE
(Transocean/MarQuest) Mar. (7 days): Lago de Silves, Santarem, Pariso, Breves, Cayenne (terminates)
GOLDEN ODYSSEY
(Royal) Amazon River, Alter Do Chao, Santarem, Macapa, crossing Equator, Devil's Is., Grenada, Aruba (terminates).
SEABOURN PRIDE
(Seabourn) Feb.-Mar. (14 days): Anavilhanas, Parintins, Breves Canals, Devil's Is., Mayreau Is., St. Barthelemy, Tortola, Virgin Gorda, Ft Lauderdale (terminates).
SEA GODDESS I
(Cunard Sea Goddess) Feb. (10 days): Anavilhanas, Parintins, Alter Do Chao, Amazon River, Porto Santana, Devil's Is., Tobago, Barbados (terminates).

Ft. Lauderdale
SEABOURN PRIDE
(Seabourn) Feb. (16 days): La Romana, Virgin Gorda, Mayreau Is., Devil's Is., Breves Canals, Parintas, Anavilhanas, Manaus (terminates).

San Juan
ISLAND PRINCESS
(Princess) Apr. (11 days): St.Thomas, Fort de France, Barbados, Devil's Is., Santarem, Alter Do Chao, Boca Do Valetia, Manaus (terminates).

Santa Rosa
ARCA
(Amazon River) Wed Jul.-Dec. (3 days): Chimbote, San Pablo, Pevas, Iquitos (terminates).

Tatatinga
RIO AMAZONAS
(Amazon River) Wed Jul.-Dec. (3 days): sailing upriver, San Pablo, Iquitos (terminates).

Amstel (Holland, Belgium)

Amsterdam
LYS
(Waterways & Byways) Sun Jul.-Oct. (6 days): Amstel River, Leiden, Delft, Rotterdam, Ijssel River, Gouda, Oudewater, Utrecht, Amsterdam-Rhine Canal, Veecht River, Zaanse Schans, Haarlem (terminates)
MEANDER
(UK Waterways Holidays) Oct. (5 days): Amstel River, Drecht River, Alsmeer, Gouda, Delft, Haarlem, Zaandam, through Amsterdam Canals,

Amsterdam-Brugge
REMBRANDT
(Abercrombie & Kent) Alt. Sun Jul.-Oct. (6 days): Haarlem, Delft, Gouda, Gent, Gent-Ostend Canal.

Columbia

Portland
EXECUTIVE EXPLORER
(Alaskas Glacier Bay) Sep.-Jun. (5 days): Columbia River, Astoria, John Day Dam, McNary Dam, Snake river, Ice Harbor Dam, Sacajawea St. Park, Bonneville Dam, Columbia River Gorge.
SEA BIRD/SEA LION
(Special Expeditions) Sep. -Nov. (6 days): Columbia River, Snake River, Clarkston, Hell's Canyon, Columbia River Gorge, Hood River, Bonneville Dam, Astoria.

San Francisco
SPIRIT OF GLACIER BAY
(Alaska Sightseeing) Sat Sep.-Oct. (7 days): Columbia River, Columbia River Gorge, Bonneville Dam, Snake River, Hell's Canyon, Hood River, Astoria.
SPIRIT OF '98
(Alaska Sightseeing) Fri Oct. (7 days): Columbia River, Columbia River Gorge, Snake River, Hell's Canyon, Astoria.

Vancouver
SEA LION
(Special Expeditions) Sep, (9 days): Victoria, San Juan Is., Astoria, Port-

land, Columbia River Gorge, Bonneville Dam, Hood River, Snake River, Clarkston, Hell's Canyon, Pasco.

Danube

Budapest
MOZART
(DDSG-Donaureisen) Oct. (4-7 days): Esztergom, Vienna, Melk, Passau (terminates).

Constanza
DANUBE PRINCESS
(Peter Deilmann Reederei) Jun.-Aug. (10 days): Ruse, Turnu, Belgrade, Bezdan, Kalocsa, Budapest, Vienna, Melk, Grein, Passau (terminates).

Passau
DANUBE PRINCESS
(Peter Deilmann Reederei) Sat Mar.-Oct, (7 days): Duernstein, Budapest, Esztergom, Bratislava, Vienna, Melk, Grein; or Jun-Jul. (10 days): Duernstein, Vienna, Budapest, Kalocsa, Mohacs, Belgrade, Veliko, Gradiste, Turnu, Severin, Ruse, Constanza (terminates).
ROUSSE
(Luftner) Oct. (7 days): Vienna, Kalocsa, Budapest, Esztergom, Bratislava, Duernstein.

Vienna
MOZART
(DDSG-Donaureisen): Oct. (7 days): Melk, Passau, Duernstein, Vienna, Bratislava, Budapest, Esztergom.

Douro (Portugal)

Oporto
ALTODOURO
(Sea Air Holidays) Fri Oct. (7 days): Douro River, Entre-Os Rios, Aregos, Peso da Regua, Pocinho, Barca, D'Alva, Valera.

Gota Canal (Denmark)

Gothenburg-Stockholm
JUNO/WILHELM THAM
(Gota Canal Steamship) May-Sep. (4 days): Lilla Edet, Trollhatten, Vanersborg, Toreboda, Karlborg, Vadstena, Motala, Borensborg, Berg, Norsholm, Soderkoping, Sodertalje.

French Canals & Rivers

Agde-Trebes
ANJODI
(European) Sun Jul,-Nov, (6 days): Canal du Midi, Capestang, Homps, Marsiellette, Carcassone.

Auxerre
NYMPHEA
(European) Alt Sun Oct.- Nov. (6 days): Canal du Nivernais, Vermenton, Monte Carlo, Chatel Censoir, Clamecy, Chevroches.

Auxerre-Villiers
CRESTED GREBE
(European) Sun Jul.-Oct. (6 days): Canal du Nivernais, Clamecy, Mailly-le-Chateau, Chatel Censoir.

Auxerre-Melun
ESPRIT
(French Country) Sun Jul- Oct. (6 days): Seine River, Yonne River, Bassou, Sens.

Auxerre-Clamecy
LIBERTE
(French Country) Sun Jul,-Oct. (6 days): Canal du Nivernais, Yonne River, Joigny, Vincelles.

Auxonne
L'ESCARGOT
(Springer's) Sat Jul.-Oct. (6 days); St. Jean de Losne, Dijon, Fleurey-Sur-Ouche, Gissey-Sur Ouche, Pont D'Ouche (terminates)

Avignon-Macon
ARLENE
(French) Jul.-Oct. (7 days): Rhone Riner, Arles, Viviers, Tournon, Viviers, Tournon, Vienne, Lyon, Soane River.

Beaulieu-Montargis
LA JOIE DE VIVRE
(European) Fri Jul.-Oct. (6 days): Loire River, Briare, Rogny, Chatillon-Coligny, Montcresson.

Chateau Thierry-Compiegne
JULIANA
(Waterways & Byways) Sun Jul.-Oct. (6 days): Marne River, Damery, Canal Lateral, Canal de L'Ainse a la Marne, Reims, Soissons.

Chatel Censoir
VIOS/DE HOOP
(Carlisle) Sun Jul.-Oct. (6 days): Canal du Nivermais, Auxerre, Canal de Bourgogne, Tonnerre, Montbard (terminates).

Chatillon en Bazos-Villiers
CRESTED GREBE
(European) Jul; Aug-Sep. (6 days): Canal du Nivernais, Vezeley.

Dijon
LADY A
(European) Thur Jul.- Oct. (6 days): Canal de Bourgogne, Vandenesse-en-Auxos, Pont D'Ouche, La Bussiere-Sur-Ouche, Gissey-Sur-Ouche, Fleurey-Sur-Ouche, Vandenesse-en-auxois.

Dijon- St.Leger-Sur-Dheune
HORIZON II
(French Country) Alt Sun Jul.-Oct, (6 days): Canal du Centre, Yonne River, Seurre, Chalon-Sur-Saone, Chagny.

Dijon-Montchanin
L'ABERCROMBIE
(Abercrombie & Kent) Alt Wed Jul.-Nov. (6 days): Canal de Bourgnogne, St Jean de Losne, Dole, Saone River, Seurre, Chalone-Sur Saone, Canal du Centre, Rully.

Dijon-St. Leger-sur-Dheune
HORIZON II
(French Country) Sun Jul.-Oct. (6 days): Canal du Centre, Yonne River, Seurre, Chalon-sur-Saone, Chagny.

Dijon-Vandenesse-en-Auxos
NIAGARA
(Springer's) Oct (6 days): Canal de Bourgogne, Fleurey-Sur-Ouche, Pont de Pany, St. Marie-Sur-Ouche, Gissey-Sur-Ouche, La Bussiere-Sur-Ouche, Pont D'Ouche.

Fleurey-Sur-Ouche- Vandenesse-En-Auxos
LA REINE PEDALIQUE
(European) Alt Sat Aug.-Sep. (6 days): Canal de Bourgogne, Gissey-Sur-Ouche, Pont D'Ouche.

Honfleur- Paris
NORMANDIE
(French) Alt Sat Jul.-Oct. (6 days): Seine River, Caudebec, Rouen, Les Andelys, Vernon.

Lyon
PRINCESSE DE PROVENCE
(Peter Dielmann Reederei) Sat Mar.-Nov. (7 days): Tournus, Chalon-Sur-Soane, Trevoux, Tournon, Arles, Avignon, Veinne.

Lyon- Villeuve-Les-Avignon
NAPOLEON
(Abercrombie & Kent) Wed Jul.-Nov. (6 -7 days): Rhone River, Vienne, Tournon, Valence, Avignon, Arles.

Mittersheim-Strasburg
STELLA
(European) Alt Sun Jul.-Nov. (5 days): Canal de la Marne au Rhin, Xouxange, Lutzelbourge, Saverne, Waltenheim.

Mittersheim-Toul
LA VANCELLE
(European) Alt Sun Jul.-Nov. (6 days): Gondrexance, Lagarde, Maixe, Metz, Nancy, Liverdun.

Montbard-Tonnerre
LITOTE
(Abercrombie & Kent) Wed Sep.- Oct. (6 days): Canal de Bourgogne, Cry, Nuits-sur-Armancon, Ancy-le-Franc, Tanlay.

Nancy-Strasbourg
LINQUENDA
(Waterways & Byways) Sun Jul.- Oct. (6 days): Lagarde, Xouxange, Lutzelbourge, Saverne, Waltenheim, Erstein, Canal du Rhone, Au Rhin.

Nemours-Sancerre
LAFAYETTE
(Abercrombie & Kent) Wed Jul.- Nov. (6 days): Loire River, Montargis, Montbouy, Chatillon-Coligny, Rogny, Gien, Briare, Lere.

Tonnerre-Venarey-Les-Laumes
NENUPHAR
(French Country) Sun Jul.-Oct. (6 days): Canal de Bourgogne, Montbard, Ancy-le-Franc, Cry, Montbard, Vandenesse-en-Auxois, Dijon

Villiers-Joigny
LIBERTE
(French Country) Sun Jul.-Nov. (6 days): Canal du Nivernais, Yonne River, Clamecy, Vincelles, Auxerre.

German Canals & Rivers
Elbe River

Bad Schandau
CLARA SCHUMANN/THEODOR FONTANE
(KD German Rhine) Oct. (3 days): Dresden, Meissen, Torgau, Wittenburg
(terminates).

Dresden-Hamburg
PRUSSIAN PRINCESS
(Peter Dtelmann Reederei) Sat Apr.-Oct. (7 days): Bad Schandau, Decan, Pillnitz, Meissen, Wittenburg, Magdeburg, Tangermuende.

Lauenburg
CLARA SCHUMANN & THEODOR FONTANE
(KD German Rhine) Oct. (7 days): Wittenburg, Magdeburg, Wittenburg, Torgau, Meissen, Dresden, Bad Schandau (terminates).

Lovosice
CLARA SCHUMANN
(KD German Rhine) Oct. (6 days): Dresden, Meissen, Torgau, Wittenburg, Magdeburg, Wittenburg, Lauenburg (terminates).

Wittenburg
CLARA SCHUMANN & THEODOR FONTANE
(KD German Rhine) Oct. (5 days): Torgau, Meissen, Dresden, Decin, Lovosice (terminates).

Moselle River

Arnhem-Basel
REMBRANDT VAN RIJN
(Swan Hellenic) Aug.-Oct, (8 days): Cologne, Koenigswinter, Remagen, Moselle River, Cochem, Bernkastel, Treir, Koblenz, Oberwesel, Rudesheim, Mannheim, Karlesruhe, Strasbourg, Breisach.

Treir-Wuerzburg
SWITZERLAND II
(Sea Air Holidays) Aug,-Sep. (6 days): Trittenheim, Bernkastel, Cochem, Koblenz, Rudesheim, Miltenberg, Wertheim, Gemuenden am Main.

Treir
EUROPA/HELVETIA/ FRANCE
(KD German Rhine) Jul.-Oct. (2 days): Bernkastel-Kues, Cochem, Cologne (terminates).

Rhine River

Amsterdam-Basel
PRUSSIAN PRINCESS
(Cunard Europe American) Jul.- Oct. (6 days): Cologne, Duesseldorf, Mannheim.

URSULA III
(Sea Air Holidays) Jul.- Oct. (5 days): Cologne, Duesseldorf

Rudesheim, Mannheim, Strasbourg.

Amsterdam-Strasourg
DEUTSCHLAND/BRITANNIA
(KD German Rhine) Oct. (4 days): Duesseldorf, Cologne, Koblenz, Mannheim.

Arnhem-Basel
REMBRANDT VAN RIJN
(Swan Hellanic) Aug. -Sep. (9 days): Cologne, Koenigwinter, Remagen, Moselle River, Cochem, Bernkastel, Trier, Koblenz, Oberwesel, Rudesheim, Mannheim, Karlsruhe, Strasbourg, Breisach.

Bamberg
REMBRANDT VAN RIJN
(Swan Hellanic) Sep. (10 days): Schweinfurt, Ochenfurt, Wuerzburg, Karlstadt, Lohr am Main, Wertheim, Miltenberg, Aschaffenburg, Worms, Speyer, Karlsruhe, Strasbourg, Basel (terminates)..

Basel
AUSTRIA/HELVETIA
(KD GermanRhine) Thur Jul.-Oct. (3 days): Mannheim, Boppard, Cologne, Nijmegen (terminates); or Aug. (6 days): Antwerp, Middleburg, Rotterdam (terminates).
DEUTSCHLAND/BRITIANNIA
(KD German Rhine) Sat Jul.-Oct. (3 days): Strasbourg, Boppard, Koenigswinter, Cologne, Duesseldorf, Amsterdam (terminates).
REMBRANDT VAN RIJN
(Swan Hellenic) Sep.-Oct (9-10 days): Strasbourg, Worms, Aschaffenburg, Miltenberg, Wertheim, Lohr am Main, Karlstadt, Wuerzburg, Ochsenfurt, Volkach, Bamburg (terminates).
SWITZERLAND II
(Sea Air Holidays) Jul. (10 days): Strasbourg, Speyer, Ruedesheim, Koblenz, Andernach, Cologne, Duesseldorf, Rotterdam, Gouda, Utrecht, Amsterdam (terminates).

Cologne
BRITANNIA
(KD German Rhine) Dec. (6 days): Duesseldorf, Arnheim, Rotterdam, Willemstad, Nijmegan Duisburg; or Dec.-Jan. (6 days): Koblenz, Mainz, Mannheim, Strasbourg, Speyer, Boppard.
DEUTSCHLAND/BRITTAINIA
(KD German Rhine) Sat Jul.-Oct. (4 days): Linz, Rudesheim, Mainz, Speyer, Strasbourg, Basel (terminates).

EUROPA/FRANCE

(KD German Rhine) Fri Jul.-Oct. (2 days): Braubach, Rudesheim, Mainz, Frankfurt (terminates).

Frankfurt

EUROPA

(KD German Rhine) Fri Jul.-Oct. (3 days): Rudesheim, Koblenz, Alken, Cochem, Bernkastel-Kues, Treir (terminates).

EUROPA/FRANCE

(KD German Rhine) Sun Jul.-Oct.(3 days): Rudesheim, Koblenz, Alken, Cochem, Bernkastel-Kues, Treir (terminates).

Nijmegen

AUSTRIA

(KD German Rhine) Jul.- Oct. (4-7 days): Cologne, Linz, Cochem, Braubach, Oberwesel, Rudesheim, Eltville, Mainz, Speyer, Strasbourg, Breisach, Basel (terminates).

Rotterdam

REGINA RHENI

(Rederij Rijnvakantie) Jul.-Aug. (6-10 days): Duesseldorf, Cologne, Boppard, Andernach, Rudesheim, Cochem, Bernkastle, Zell, Koblenz, Emmerich

REX RHENI

(Rederij Rijnvakantie) Jul.-Aug. (13 days): Duesseldorf, Linz, Rudesheim, Speyer, Strasbourg, Basel, Breisach, Mannheim, Mainz, Boppard, Cologne, Emmerich

Strasbourg

DEUTSCHLAND/BRITANNIA

(KD German Rhine) Fri Jul.-Oct. (2 days): Speyer, Rudesheim, Cologne (terminates).

Treir

SWITZERLAND II

(Sea Air Holidays) Aug.-Sep. (6 days): Trittenheim, Bernkastel, Cochem, Koblenz, Rudesheim, Miltenberg, Wertheim, Gemuenden am Main, Wuerzburg (terminates).

Wuertzburg

SWITZERLAND II

(Sea Air Holidays) Aug, (6 days): Gemuenden am Main, Wertheim, Miltenburg, Aschaffenburg, Frankfurt, Mainz, Rudesheim, Koblenz, Cochem, Bernkastel, Trittenheim, Treier (terminates).

Mississippi & Tributaries
DELTA QUEEN/MISSISSIPPI QUEEN

(Delta Queen Steamboat) Year round (3-12 days): Chattanooga, Huntsville, Decatur, Florence, Shiloh, Nashville, Dover, Paduca, St. Louis, Chester, St. Genevieve, Cape Girardeau, New Madrid, Cave-in Rock, Henderson, Louisville, Madison, Cincinnati, Portsmouth, Maysville, Marietta, Wellsburg, Pittsburgh, Memphis, Helena, Pine Bluff, Little Rock, Petit Jean, St. Park, Ft. Smith, Vicksburg, Natchez, St. Francisville, Baton Rouge, Nottoway, New Orleans, Houmas House, Chalmette, Ft. Jackson, Lafitte, Morgan City, Oak Alley, Minneapolis/St. Paul, Wabasha, Winona, Prairie du Chien, Dubuque, Burlington, Hannibal.

New Orleans
NEW SHOREHAM II

(American Canadian Caribbean) Apr.-May (7 days): New Orleans, Houma, Morgan City, Atchafalaya River, Natchez, Baton Rouge.

Nile

Aswan-Luxor
HAPI

(Special Expeditions) Aug.-Sep. (7 days): Abydos, Dandera, Isna, Edfu, el Kab, Kom Ombo.

ISIS/OSIRIS

(Hilton) Jul. -Apr. (4 days): Isna, Idfu, Kom Ombo; or (6 days): add Dandara, Abydos. (Presidential Nile Cruises) Sat & Tues Jul, -Dec. (4 days): Isna, Idfu, Kom Ombo; or Wed (6 days): add Dandara, Abydos, Nag Hammadi; or Mondays (7 days): add Qena. (Nabila Nile Cruises) Jul.-Dec. (4 days): Isna, Idfu, Kom Ombo; or (6 days): add Dandara.

NEPHTIS

(Hilton) Jul. -Apr. (4 days): Isna, Idfu, Kom Ombo; or (6 days): add:Dandara, Abydos.

NILE MONARCH

(Swan Hellenic) Sep.-Mar. (6-11 days): Isna, Idfu, Kom Ombo, Dandara, Nag Hammadi.

SHEHRAYAR

(Oberoi) Jul.- Jan.(4 days): Isna, Idfu, Kom Ombo; or (6 days): add Dandara, Qena. (Sheraton Nile Cruises) Sat Jul.-Sep. (3 days): Isna, Idfu, Kom Ombo.

SHEHRAZAD

(Oberoi) Jul. - Jan. (4 days): Isna, Idfu, Kom Ombo, or (6 days): add: Qena, Dandara.

SUN BOAT I

(Abercrombie & Kent) Sep.-Apr. (4 days): Isna, Idfu, Kom Ombo.

SUN BOAT II

(Abercrombie & Kent) Alt. Tuesdays Dec.-Mar. (7 days): Isna, Idfu, Kom Ombo, Nag Hammadi, Agydos, Dandara.

Aswan-Cairo

NILE MONARCH

(Swan Hellenic) Sep.-Jun. (14 days): Isna, Idfu, Kom Ombo, Dandara, Nag Hammadi, el Kab, Abu Tig, el Til, Beni Hassan, Beni Suef. (Presidential Nile Cruises) Jul. - Oct. (10 days): Beni Suef, Beni Hassan, Assiut, Sohog, Nag Hammadi, Abydos, Dandara, Luxor, Isna, Idfu, Komombo.

SUN BOAT II

(Abercrombie & Kent) Sep.-Nov. (10 -11 days): Isna, Idfu, Kom Ombo, Luxor, Dandara, Nag Hammadi, El Balyana, Tell el Amarna, Beni Hassan, Beni Suef.

Russian Canals & Rivers

Khabarovsk

AMUR STAR

(American Pacific) Sun Jul.-Sep. (7 days): Komsomolsk Na Amure, Bogorodskoye, Nikolaevsk, Bulava, Ribalochny Is., Troitskoya.

Kiev

AKADEMIK GLUSHKOV

(Odessa America) Alte Mon Jul.-Oct. (7 days): Kaniv, Kremenchug, Dnepropetrovsk, Zaproshye, Novaya, Lakhovka, Kherson, Odessa (terminates); or Jul. (14 days): add Yevpatoriya.

Moscow

ANDROPOV

(Odessa America) Jul.-Sep. (14 days): Uglich, Kostroma, Yaroslava, Goritzky, Petrozavodsk. Kizhy, Valaam, St. Petersburg (terminates).

CHICHERIN

(Odessa America) Jul.-Sep. (21 days): Uglich, Kostroma, Nizhny, Novgorod, Kazan, Samara, Saratov, Volgograd, Astrakhan, Volgograd, Ulyanovsk, Cheboksary, Yaroslavl.

DIMITRI FURMANOV

(Czarina) Jul.-Sep. (8 days): Uglich, Yaroslavl, Gortzky, Petrozavodsk, Kizhv, Valaam, St. Petersburg (terminates).

DOSTOYEVSKY

(Bolshoi) Jul.-Oct. (13 days): Uglich, Irma, Goritzky, Kizhy, Valaam, St. Petersburg (terminates).

SERGEI KIROV

North-Western River Ship) Jul.-Oct. (7 days): Uglich, Yaroslavl. Goritzky, Kizhy, St. Petersburg (terminates).

Nikolaevsk
AMUR STAR
(American Pacific) Wed Jul.-Sep. (4 days): Bulava, Ribalochny Is., Troitskoya, Khabarovsk (terminates).

Odessa
AKADEMIK GLUSHKOV
(Odessa America) Alt Mon Jul.-Oct. (7 days): Kherson, Novaya, Kakhovka, Zaporosh'ye, Dnepropetrovsk, Kremenchug, Kaniv, Kiev (terminates).

St. Petersburg
ANDROPOV
(Odessa America) Jul.-Aug. (14 days): Valaam, Kizhy, Petrozavdsk, Goritzky, Yaroslavl, Uglich, Moscow (terminates).

DIMITRI FURMANOV
(Czarina) Aug.-Sep. (8 days): Valaam, Kizhy, Petrozavodsk, Goritzky, Yaroslavl, Uglich, Moscow (terminates).

DOSTOYEVSKY
(Bolshoi) Jul.-Aug. (13 days): Valaam, Kizhy, Goritzky, Irma, Uglich, Moscow (terminates).

SERGEI LIROV
(North-Western River Ship) Jul.-Sep. (6 days): Valaam, Kizhy, Goritzky, Uglich, Moscow (terminates).

Hudson River

New York
NANTUCKET CLIPPER
(Clipper) Oct.(7 days): Hudson River, Albany, Kingston, Poughkeepsie, West Point.

Sacramento & San Joaquin Rivers

San Francisco
SEA BIRD/SEA LION
(Special Expeditions) Nov. (3 days): Sacramento, San Joaquin River.

Thames & Rivers of England

Bath
HARLEQUIN
(UK Waterway) Apr.-Oct. (6 days): Bristol, Bradford-on Avon, Devizes, Avon River.

Brampton Old Mills
BARKIS/PEGGITY
(European) Sun Oct. (6 days): St. Ives, Earith, Huntingdon, Eaton Socon.

Henley
ACTIEF
(European) Oct. (3 days): Thames River, Sonning, Pangbourne, Oxford (Shillingford Bridge), (terminates).

Oxford (Shillingford Bridge)
ACITEF
(6 days): Thames River, Pangsbourne, Sonning, Henley, Hurley, Cliveden, Windsor (terminates).

Pyrford
VICTORIA
(UK Waterways) Fri Apr.-Sep. (3 days): Guildford, Weybridge (terminates).

Stratford-upon-Avon-Tewkesbury
BEVERLY/JEAN
(Waterways & Byways-Europe) Sun Jul.-Oct. (6 days): Avon River, Evesham, Pershore

Windsor
ACTIEF
(European) Oct. (6 days): Thames River, Cliveden, Hurley, Henley, Sonning, Pangbourne, Oxford (Shillingford Bridge) (terminates).

Yangtze

Chongquing-Yichang
BASHAN
(Abercrombie & Kent) Jul.-Nov. (3 days): Yangtze River.

Hong Kong
MARCO POLO
(Orient)) May-Sep. (10 days): Yangtze River, Zhenjiang, Nanking, Shanghai, Cingdoa, Dalian, Tianjin (terminates).

ANTARCTICA

Buenos Aires
HANSEATIC
(Seven Seas) Dec.-Jan. (19 days): New Is., Falkland Is., Carcass Is., Albatross Is., Grytviken, Scotia Sea, Coronation Is., South Orkney Is., Elephant

Is., Deception Is., King George Is., Port Lockroy, Paulet Is., Paradise Bay, Lemaire Channel, through Drake Passage, Cape Horn, Ushuaia (terminates).

MARCO POLO

(Orient) Jan. (15 days): Port Stanley, Hope Bay, King George Is., Paradise Bay, crossing Antarctic Circle, through Drake Passage, Ushuaia, through Beagle Channel, Punta Arenas (terminates).

Cape Town
MARCO POLO

(Orient) Dec. (21 days): Tristan de Cunha Is., South Georgia Is., Paulet Is., Paradise Bay, Cape Horn, Ushuaia, through Beagle Channel, Punta Arenas (terminates).

Port Stanley
WORLD DISCOVERER

(Clipper) Nov.-Dec. (11 days): Falkland Is., Elephant Is., through Drake Passage, Cape Horn, through Beagle Passage, Punta Arenas (terminates); or, Nov.-Dec. (15 days): South Georgia Is., South Orkney Is., Elephant Is., Falkland Is.; or, Feb.-Mar. (17 days): Falkland Is., Elephant Is., through Drake Passage, Cape Horn, through Beagle Channel, Isla Chiloe, Puerto Montt (terminates).

Puerto Montt-Port Stanley
EXPLORER

(Abercrombie & Kent) Nov.-Feb (9-20 days): Isla Chiloe, Puerto Eden, Laguna San Raphael, Puerto Natales, through Beagle Channel, Ushuaia, through Drake Passage, Anvers Is., Deception Is., King George Is., Elephant Is., Sea Is., Bleaker Is., South Georgia Is., South Orkney Is, Falkland Is.

Puerto Montt
COLUMBUS CARAVELLE

(Transocean/MarQuest) Nov.-Feb. (15-20 days): through Beagle Channel, Cape Horn, through Drake Passage, Carcass Is., King George Is., Laird Is., Danco Is., Galindez Is., Grytviken, Port Lockroy, Lemaire Channel, Paradise Bay, Deception Is., Hope Bay, Coronation Is., through Strait of Magellan, Port Stanley, Buenos Aires, Montevideo

HANSEATIC

(Seven Seas) Jan.-Mar. (12-14 days): through Beagle Channel, Cockburn Channel, Isla Riesco, New Is., West Falkland Is., Carcass Is., Elephant Is., South Shetland Is., Paulet Is., Deception Is., Baileys Head, through Drake Passage, Cape Horn, Tierra del Fuego, Isla Picton, Ushuaia (terminates).

WORLD DISCOVERER

(Clipper) Nov. (17 days): Isla Chiloe, through Beagle Channel, Cape

Horn, through Drake Passage, Elephant Is., Falkland Is., Port Stanley (terminates).

Puerto Williams
WORLD DISCOVERER
(Clipper) Dec.-Feb. (17 days): Cape Horn, through Drake Passage, Elephant Is., South Orkney Is., South Georgia Is., Port Stanley (terminates).

Punta Arenas
COLUMBUS CARAVELLE
(Transocean/MarQuest) Nov.-Jan. (11 days): through Beagle Channel, Cape Horn, through Drake Passage, King George Is., Paradise Bay, Deception Is., Hope Bay, through Strait of Magellan; or, Jan.-Feb. (16 days): through Strait of Magellan, Carcass Is., Port Stanley, through Drake Passage, Elephant Is., King George Is., Paradise Bay, Hope Bay, Deception Is., Cape Horn, through Beagle Channel; or, Feb. (14 days): through Strait of Magellan, through Beagle Channel, Cape Horn, through Drake Passage, Deception Is., Paradise Bay, King George Is., Port Stanley, Buenos Aires, Montevideo (terminates).

MARCO POLO
(Orient) Dec.-Jan. (15 days): through Beagle Passage, Ushuaia, through Drake Passage, crossing Antarctic Circle, Paradise Bay, King George Is., Hope Bay, Port Stanley, Buenos Aires (terminates), or Jan.-Feb. (23 days): through Beagle Channel, Ushuaia, through Drake Passage, Hope Bay, Paradise Bay, Bellinghausen Sea, Amundson Sea, Ross Sea, crossing Intl. Date Line, McMurdo station, Cape Royds, Cape Hallet, Cape Adare, crossing Antarctic Circle, Christchurch (terminates).

WORLD DISCOVERER
(Transocean/Marquest) Dec.-Jan. (11 days): through Beagle Channel, Cape Horn, through Drake Passage, Puerto Williams (terminates).

Ushuia
AKADEMIK IOFFE
(BCT/Overseas Adventure Travel) Dec.-Mar. (11-16 days): through Drake Passage, King George Is., Paulet Is., Deception Is., Paradise Bay, Elephant Is., Falkland Is., South Georgia Is., Cape Horn, Tierra del Fuego.

AROUND THE WORLD
Los Angeles
QUEEN ELIZABETH 2
(Cunard) Jan.-Apr. (87 days): Lahaina (Maui), Honolulu, Pago Pago, Lautoka, Auckland, Christchurch, Milford Sound, Melbourne, Sydney, Brisbane, Cairns, Lae, Manila, Kagoshima, Yokohama, Hong Kong, Ho Chi Minh, Bangkok, Singapore, Kuala Lumpur, Mahe Is. (Seychelles),

Mombasa, Durban, Cape Town, Walvis Bay, St. Helena Is., Dakkar, Agadir, Lisbon, Southhampton, Cherbourg (terminates).

STATENDAM

(Holland America) Jan.-Apr. (98 days): Kona, Honolulu, Kritimati (Christmas Is.), crossing Equator, Pago Pago, crossing Int'l Date Line, Suva, Port Vila, Cairns, Great Barrier Reef, Madang, Manila, Hong Kong, Laem Chabang, Bali, Semerang, Singapore, Port Kelang, Madras, Columbo, Seychelles, Zanzibar, Mombasa, Suez, through Suez Canal, Port Said, Haifa, through Dardenelles, Istanbul, Piraeus, Lipari, Civitavecchia, Malaga, Casablanca, Funchal, Ft. Lauderdale, New York (terminates).

New York
QUEEN ELIZABETH 2

(Cunard) Jan.-Apr. (100 days): Ft Lauderdale, St. Thomas, Cartegena, Acapulco, Los Angeles, continues with ports listed under Los Angeles.

Ft Lauderdale
QUEEN ELIZABETH 2

(Cunard) Jan.-Apr. (98 days): St. Thomas, Cartegena, Acapulco, Los Angeles, continues with ports listed under Los Angeles.

SAGAFJORD

(Cunard/NAC) Jan.-Apr. (108 days): St. Thomas, Barbados, Devil's Is., Recife, Salvador, Rio de Janeiro, Buenos Aires, through Strait of Magellan, through Beagle Channel, Ushuaia, through Beagle Channel, Cape Horn, Shetland Is., Admiralty Bay, Shetland Is., Port Stanley, Tristan de Cunha Is., Cape Town, Durban, Mombasa, Mahe Is. (Seychelles), Madras, Port Kelang, Singapore, Laem Chabang, Ho Chi Minh, Hong Kong, Shanghai, Pusan, Tokyo, Honolulu, Kuhului (Maui), Los Angeles, Cabo San Lucas, Acapulco, Caldera (Costa Rica), through Panama Canal, Oranjestad.

ATLANTIC COAST, NORTH AMERICA
Bahamas

Freeport
CORAL STAR

(Coral Bay) Jul. (7 days): Conception Is., San Salvador Is. Long Is., George Town (Great Exuma Is.) (terminates).

Georgetown (Great Exhuma Is.)
CORAL STAR

(Coral Bay) Sat (7 days): Long Is., San Salvador Is., Conception Is..

Miami
BRITANIS
(Fantasy) Fri (2 days): Nassau.
DOLPHIN IV
(Dolphin) Year round (3-4 days): Nassau, private out Is., Key West.
ECSTASY
(Carnival) Year round (3-4 days): Nassau, Freeport.
FANTASY
(Carnival) Year round (3-4 days): Freeport, Nassau.
NORDIC EMPRESS
(Royal Caribbean) Year round (3-4 days): Nassau, Coco Cay, Freeport.
ROYAL MAJESTY
(Majesty) Fri (3 days): Nassau, private out is.

New York
QUEEN ELIZABETH 2
(Cunard) Aug. (4 days): Nassau.
REGAL EMPRESS
(Regal), Sun Apr..- Oct., (7 days): Nassau, Freeport

Port Canaveral
ATLANTIC
(Premier) Year round (3-4 days): Nassau, Grand Bahama Is.
CARNIVALE
(Carnival) Year round (3-4 days): Nassau.
FANTASY
(Carnival) Year round, (3-4 days): Nassau, Freeport.
MARDI GRAS
(Carnival) Year round, (3-4 days): Nassau, Freeport.
OCEANIC
(Premier) Year round (3-4 days): Grand Bahama Is., Nassau.

Ft. Lauderdale
CUNARD CROWN JEWEL
(Cunard Crown) Year round (3-4 days): Nassau, Freeport.
MAJESTIC
(Premier) Year round (3-4 days): Grand Bahama Is., Nassau, Key West.
WESTWARD
(Norwegian) Year round (3-4 days): Key West, private out is., Nassau.

Nassau
FANTOME
(Windjammer Schooner) Jul.-Aug. (5 days): Chub Cay, Great Harbour Cay, Bimini, Freeport (terminates).
NEW SHORHAM II
(America Canadian Caribbean) Thur (12 days): Spanish Wells, Hatchet Bay, Governor's Is., South Palmetto Point, Sampson Cay, Pond Cay, Hawksbill Cay, Norman's Cay, Allan's Cay.

San Andres Is.
ODESSA
(Transocean/Marquest) Mar.-Apr. (12 days): Playa del Carmen, Cancun, New Orleans, Tampa, Key West, Havana, Miami, Nassau (terminates).

Bermuda

Alexandria
CROWN MONARCH
(Crown) Aug. (7 days): Bermuda

New York
DREAMWARD
(Norwegian) Sat Apr.-Oct. (7 days): St. Georges, Hamilton.
HORIZON
(Celebrity) Sun Oct. (7 days): Hamilton, St. Georges
MERIDIAN
(Celebrity) Sun July-Aug. (7 days): St. Georges, Hamilton.
SONG OF AMERICA
(Royal Caribbean) Sat May-Oct. (7 days): St. Georges, Hamilton.

San Juan
SONG OF AMERICA
(Royal Caribbean) Sun Apr.-May (7 days): St, George's, Hamilton, St. Maarten, St. Thomas, Antigua.

Continental Shelf

Baltimore
NANTUCKET CLIPPER
(Clipper) May-Jun. (8 days): Philadelphia, New York, Newport, Nantucket, Boston (terminates).

Boston
NANTUCKET CLIPPER
(Clipper) Sep. (11 days): Gloucester, Nantucket, Newport, New York,

Philadelphia, Baltimore, Annapolis, Washington, Alexandria (terminates).

SEABOURN PRIDE
(Seabourn) Sep.-Oct (14 days): Northeast Harbor, St. John, Lunenburg, St. Pierre-Miquelon, Quebec, Saguenay River, Baddeck, Halifax, Camden, Charlottetown, Montreal.

NANTUCKET CLIPPER
(Clipper) Aug.-Sep. (14 days):Halifax, Lunenburg, Digby, St. John, St. Andrews, Campobello Is., Bar Harbor, Camden, Gloucester.

Charleston-Jacksonville
NANTUCKET CLIPPER
(Clipper) Nov. (7 days): Beaufort, Hilton Head Is., Savannah, St. Simon's Is., Intracoastal Waterway.

Copenhagen
SEABOURN PRIDE
(Seabourn) Aug.-Sep. (16-17 days): Oslo, Bognes, Flam, Gudvangen, Lerwick, Shetland Is., Faroe Is., Reykjavik, L'Anse Aux Meadows, Baddeck, Halifax, Camden, Boston, or New York.

Ft. Lauderdale
SAGAFJORD
(Cunard/NAC) Sept.-Oct. (14 days): New York, Bermuda, Bar Harbor, St. John, Halifax, Saguenay River, Quebec, Montreal (terminates).

Gloucester
COLUMBUS CARAVELLE
(Transocean/MarQuest) Sep. (11 days): Newport News, Chesapeake & Delaware Canal, New York, Philadelphia, Baltimore, Charleston, Jacksonville, Fort Pierce, Miami, Freeport, Nassau (terminates).

Jacksonville
NANTUCKET CLIPPER
(Clipper) Oct.-Nov. (7 days): Intracoastal Waterway, St. Simons Is., Savannah, Hilton Head Is., Beaufort, Charleston (terminates).

Key West
CARIBBEAN PRINCE
(American Canadian Caribbean) Apr. (14 days): Marathon, Marco Is., Fort Myers, Sanibel Is., Sarasota, Carrabelle, Panama City, Ft. Walton Beach, Pensacola, Biloxi, Gulfport, New Orleans (terminates).

Kingston
CANADIAN EMPRESS
(St. Lawrence) Jul.-Oct. 4-5 days): Thousand Is., Ft. Wellington, Upper

Canada Village, Coteau Landing, Montreal, Carillon, Montebello, Ottawa.

Montreal
GRUZIYA
(Odessa America) Jul.-Sep. (7 days): Quebec, Saguenay Is., Gaspe, St. Pierre-Miquelon, Charlottetown, by Perce Rock, Halifax, Portland, Cape Cod, Newport, Philadelphia (terminates).
CANADIAN EMPRESS
(St. Lawrence) Jul.-Oct, (4 days): Cote Ste., Catherines, Upper Canada Village, Ft. Wellington, Rockport, Thousand Is., Kingston (terminates)

Nassau
GOLDEN ODYSSEY
(Royal) Sep, (7-8 days): Savannah, Charleston, Newport News, Baltimore, New York (terminates).
ODESSA
(Transocean/MarQuest) Apr. (20 days): Baltimore, Chesapeake & Delaware Canal, Philadelphia, New York, Horta, Ponta Delgada, La Coruna, Portsmouth, Bremerhaven (terminates).

Montreal-New York
CROWN DYNASTY
(Cunard Crown) July- Oct (7 days): Halifax, Bar Harbour, Portland, Provincetown, through Cape Cod Canal, Martha's Vineyard, Sydney, St Lawrence River, Saguenay Fjord, Quebec.
GOLDEN ODYSSEY
(Royal) Sept.- Oct. (7-14 days): Bar Harbor, Halifax, St. Lawrence River, Boston, through Cape Cod Canal, Saguenay, Sydney, Quebec.
REGENT SUN
(Regency) Sun, June-Sept. (7 days): Newport, Bar Harbor, Provincetown, Sydney, through Cape Cod Canal, Portland, Halifax, Saguenay Fjord, Quebec, passing Perce Rock.
ROYAL PRINCESS
(Princess) Sept.-Oct. (10 days): Quebec, Saguenay River, Charlottetown, Halifax, Bar Harbor, Boston, Newport.
SEABOURN PRIDE
(Seabourn) Sept. Oct. (7-14 days): Long Island Sound, through Cape Cod Canal, Northeast Harbor, Halifax, through Strait of Canso, Gaspe, St. Lawrence River, Quebec, Saguenay River, Baddeck, Lunenburg.

New Orleans
CARIBBEAN PRINCE
(American Canadian Caribbean) Apr. (14 days): Biloxi, Gulfport, Pensa-

cola, Sarasota, Sanibel Is., Fort Myers, Lake Okeechobee, West Palm Beach (terminates).

New York
CUNARD CROWN MONARCH
(Cunard Crown) July (5-7 days): Halifax, Bar Harbor, Portland, Provincetown, through Cape Cod Canal, Martha's Vineyard.

GOLDEN ODYSSEY
(Royal) Oct- Nov. (7-8 days): Baltimore, Newport News, Charleston, Savannah, Nassau (terminates).

NANTUCKET CLIPPER
(Clipper) Oct. (10 days): West Point, Kingston, Annapolis, St. Michaels, Yorktown, Norfolk, Washington, Alexandria (terminates).

QUEEN ELIZABETH 2
(Cunard) Jul. (4 days): Bar Harbor, Halifax, Martha's Vineyard; or Sept (6 days): Newport, Boston, St. John, Halifax, Martha's Vineyard.

REGAL EMPRESS
(Regal) Oct. (5 days): Martha's Vineyard, St. John, Bar Harbor, Newport.

STAR ODYSSEY
(Royal) Sept.-Oct.(7-14 days): Bar Harbor, Halifax, St. Lawrence River, Saguenay Fjord, Montreal, Quebec, Sidney, Boston, through Cape Cod Canal, Newport.

Ottawa
CANADIAN EMPRESS
(St. Lawrence) Jul.-Sep. (5 days): Montebello. Carillon, Sainte Anne de Bellevue, Montreal, Cote Ste. Catherines, Upper Canada Village, Brockville (terminates).

Ottawa-Kingston
CANADIAN EMPRESS
(St. Lawrence) Jun.-Oct. (5 days): Trois Riviers, Montreal, Coteau Landing, Upper Canada Village, Ft. Wellington, Thousand Islands.

Ottawa-Rochester
NANTUCKET CLIPPER
(Clipper) Jul.-Aug. (7 days): St. Lawrence River, Montreal, Prescott, Kingston, Thousand Islands.

Quebec-Warren
CANADIAN EMPRESS
(St. Lawrence) Oct. (5 days): Trois Rivieres, Montreal, Cote Ste. Catherines, Upper Canada Village, Ft. Wellington, Brockville, Thousand Is., Kingston (terminates).

THE WORLD'S MOST EXCITING CRUISES

CARIBBEAN PRINCE/MAYAN PRINCE/NEW SHORE-HAM II

(American Canadian Caribbean) Jun.-Oct. (12 days): Montreal, Bay of Eternity, Upper Canada Village, Clayton, Thousand Is., Oswego, Sylvan Beach, Eire Canal, Little Falls, Troy, Hudson River, West Point, New York, Long Is. Sound, Narraganset Bay,

Warren (R.I.)
CARIBBEAN PRINCE/MAYAN PRINCE

(American Canadian Caribbean) Oct.-Nov. (14 days): Long Island Sound, New York, Baltimore, Norfolk, Wrightsville Beach, Charleston, Beaufort, Savannah, Hilton Head Is., St. Simon's Is., St Augustine, Titusville, West Palm Beach (terminates).

Washington
NANTUCKET CLIPPER

(Clipper) Sep.-Oct. (8 days): Norfolk, Yorktown, St. Michaels, Annapolis, New York, Kingston, West Point, New York (terminates); or Oct. (11 days): Norfolk, Beaufort, Wilmington, Intracoastal Waterway, Charleston, Savannah, St. Simon's Is., Jacksonville (terminates).

West Palm Beach
NEW SHOREHAM II

(American Canadian Caribbean) Mar.-Apr. (14 days): Lake Okeechobee, Fort Myers, Sanibel Is., Sarasota, Carrabelle, Panama City, Ft. Walton Beach, Pensacola, Gulfport, Biloxi, New Orleans (terminates).

Antigua
EUROPA

(Hapag-Lloyd Kreutzfahrten) Dec. (9 days): St. Lucia, Pointe a Pitre, St. Kitts, Tortola, Santiago de Cuba, Curacao (terminates)

FANTOME (Windjammer Schooner)

Mon Nov.-Jun. (5 days): St. Barts, St. Maarten, St. Kitts, Nevis; or Montserrat, Pointe a Pitre, Iles des Saintes, Dominica.

MAYAN PRINCE

(American Canadian Caribbean) Dec. (11 days): Guadeloupe, Dominica, Martinique, St. Lucia, St. Vincent, Bequia, Canouan Is., Mayreau, Carriacou, Grenada.

RENAISSANCE III

(Renaissance) Sun Dec.-Apr. (7 days): St. Kitts, St. Croix, Virgin Gorda, St. Maarten, St. Barts; or alternate weeks Dominica, St. Lucia, St. Vincent, Bequia, Monserrat, Fort de France.

SEA CLOUD

(Special Expeditions) Feb.-Mar. (9 days): St. Lucia, Grenada, Tobaga, Carriacou, Dominica, Marie Galante.

STAR CLIPPER
(Star Clipper Schooner) Sat Nov.-Dec. (7 days): Iles des Saintes, Fort des France, St. Vincent, St. Lucia, Dominica, Montserrat, or St. Kitts, Anguila, St. Maartens, St. Barts, Saba, St. Eustatius, Nevis.

YORKTOWN CLIPPER
(Clipper) Jan. (10 days): Anguilla, Saba, St. Kitts, Iles des Saintes, Dominica, St. Lucia, Bequia, Union Island, Grenada (terminates).

Aruba
MAYAN PRINCE
(American Canadian Caribbean) Jan. (11 days): Bonaire, Curacao (terminates)

OCEAN BREEZE
(Dolphin) Sun Jul.-Dec. (7 days): Cartegena, Panama Canal (Gatun Lake only), San Blas Islands, Curacao (alt weeks) Grenada, Barbados, Fort de France, Curacao.

SEABOURN PRIDE
(Seabourn) Dec.-Jan. (8 days): Fort de France, St. Barts, St. Maarten, Virgin Gorda, Ft. Lauderdale (terminates).

SEAWIND CROWN
(Seawind) Sun Jul.-Dec. (7 days): Curacao, Grenada, Barbados, St. Lucia.

Baltimore
QUEEN ELIZABETH II
(Cunard) Oct.-Nov. (9 days): St. Maarten, Barbados, St. Lucia, St. Thomas.

Barbados
RADISSON DIAMOND
(Diamond) Dec.-Jan. (7 days): Pointe a Pitre, St. Kitts, St. Barts, St. John, St. Thomas, Virgin Gorda, San Juan (terminates).

SEA GODDESS I
(Cunard Sea Goddess) Feb. (7 days): Bequia, St Lucia, Fort de France, Nevis, St. Maarten, Jost van Dyke, St. Thomas (terminates).

Barcelona
PACIFIC PRINCESS
(Princess) Oct.-Nov. (12 days): Gibralter, Casablanca, Las Palmas, San Juan (terminates).

Buenos Aires
REGENT SEA
(Regency) Nov.-Dec. (23 days): Montevideo, Rio de Janeiro, Salvador, Fortaleza, Belem, Amazon Delta, Devil's Is., Barbados, Antigua, St Thomas, Tampa (terminates).

Cadiz
EUROPA
(Hapag-Lloyd Kreutzfahrten) Nov. (18 days): Arrecife, Santa Cruz de la Palma, Fort de France, Antigua, St. Thomas, Miami, Grand Cayman, Montego Bay (terminates)

Fort de France
CLUB MED I
(Club Med) Sun Nov.-Apr. (7 days): St. Lucia, Tobago Cays (Grenadines), Bequia, Mayreau Is., Barbados, Carriacou; or Marie Galante, St Kitts, Virgin Gorda, St. Maarten, Ile Tintamarre, Dominica; or Iles des Saintes, St. Barts, Jost van Dyke, St Thomas, Virgin Gorda, Nevis, or Isla las Roques, off Isla la Tortuga, Grenada, Barbados, Mayreau.

Ft. Lauderdale
CROWN PRINCESS
(Crown) Sat Jan.-Apr. (7 days):St. Maarten, St. Thomas, private out island; or alt weeks, private out island, Montego Bay, Grand Cayman, Playa del Carmen, Cozumel.

CUNARD CROWN JEWEL
(Cunard Crown) Sat year round (7 days): Ocho Rios, Grand Cayman, Cozumel Cancun; or alt weeks Puerto Plata, St. Thomas, St. John, Nassau.

DREAMWARD
(Norwegian) April (13 days): Aruba, St. John, St. Thomas, San Juan, St. Maarten, Tortola, Virgin Gorda, Bermuda, New York (terminates).

NOORDAM
(Holland America) Sat Jan.-Mar. (7 days): Nassau, San Juan, St. John, St Thomas; or alt weeks, Key West, Playa del Carmen, Cozumel, Ocho Rios, Grand Cayman; or Apr.(10 days): Aruba, Ocho Rios, Grand Cayman, Playa del Carmen, Cozumel, New Orleans (terminates).

MAASDAM
(Holland America) Dec.-Apr. (10 days): Aruba, Cartegena, San Blas Is., Limon, Grand Cayman; or Nassau, San Juan, St. Thomas.

MERIDIAN
(Celebrity) Nov. (10 days): Nassau, Tortola, St. Thomas, St. Maarten, Fort de France, Barbados, Grenada, San Juan (terminates)

REGAL PRINCESS
(Princess) Sat Oct.-Apr. (7 days): San Juan, St. Maarten, St Thomas, private out island; or alt weeks, private out island, Montego Bay, Grand Cayman, Playa del Carmen, Cozumel.

RADISSON DIAMOND
(Diamond) Jan.-Feb. (7 days): Nassau, private out island, St. Thomas, St. Maarten San Juan (terminates).

ROYAL VIKING SUN
(Royal Viking) Nov.-Jan. (11-17 days): Galveston, New Orleans, Playa del Carmen, Cozumel, Belize, Key West; or Tortola, San Lucia, Barbados, Scarborough, Grenada, Oranjestad, Aruba, Panama Canal (Gatun Lake only), Limon, Playa del Carmen, Cozumel.

SAGAFJORD
(Cunard/NAC) Dec. (16 days): Grand Cayman, Aruba, Grenada, Barbados, St. Lucia, Pointe a Pitre, St. Barts, St. Maarten, St. Thomas, Key West.

STATENDAM
(Holland America) Nov.-Dec. (10 days): St. Maarten, St. Lucia, Barbados, Dominica, Nassau; or Curacao, La Guaira, Grenada, Fort de France, St. Thomas, Nassau.

WESTERDAM
(Holland America) Sat Oct.- Jan (7 days): St.Maarten, St. Thomas, Nassau; or (8 days): add San Juan, Virgin Gorda, Tortola.

ZENITH
(Celebrity) Sat year round (7 days): San Juan, St. Thomas, St. Maarten, Nassau; or alternate weeks: Montego Bay, Grand Cayman, Cozumel, Playa del Carmen, Key West.

Freeport
AMAZING GRACE
(Windjammer) Jan.-Dec. (12 days): Nassau, Grand Turk Is., Tortola, St. Maarten, Antigua, Fort de France, St. Lucia, St. Vincent, Grenada (terminates).

FANTOME
(Windjammer) Oct. (5 days): Great Stirrup Cay, Gun Cay, Sandy Point (Abaco), Eleuthera, Nassau (terminates).

Funchal
STAR FLYER
(Star Clippers) Oct.-Nov. (19 days): Los Palmas, St Barts, St. Maarten (terminates).

Grenada-Antigua
MANDALAY
(Windjammer Schooner) Year round (12 days): Palm Is., Mayreau Is., Tobago Cays, Bequia, St. Vincent, St. Lucia, Fort de France, Dominica, Iles des Saintes, Carriacou, Montserrat, Nevis, Antigua (terminates)

Grenada
AMAZING GRACE
(Windjammer) Jan.-Dec. (12 days): Palm Is. (Grenadines), Bequia, Domin-

ica, St. Kitts, St. Barts, Conception Is. Gorda Cay, Jost van Dyke, Inagua Is., Freeport (terminates).

YANKEE CLIPPER

(Windjammer) Mondays Oct.-Dec. (5 days): Petit St. Vincent, Bequia, Mayreau Is., Palm Is., Union Is., Canquan Is., Carriacou.

YORKTOWN CLIPPER

(Clipper) Jan.-Mar. (12 days): Union Is., Bequia, St. Lucia, Dominica, Iles des Saintes, St. Kitts, Saba, Anguilla, Antigua (terminates).

Guaira

FIESTA MARINA

(Fiestamarina) Oct.-Dec. (7 days): Aruba, Santo Domingo, San Juan, St. Thomas.

Las Palmas

RENAISSANCE IV

(Renaissance) Nov. (14 days): Santa Cruz de la Palma, Santa Cruz Tenerife, Dakar, Cape Verde Is., St. Kitts, Antigua (terminates).

Lisbon

CRYSTAL HARMONY

(Crystal) Oct.-Nov. (12 days): Funchal, Agadir, Lanzarote, Las Palmas, Barbados (terminates).

VISTAFJORD

(Cunard/NAC) Nov.-Dec. (15 days): Funchal, Santa Cruz Tenerife, Barbados, Fort de France, Tortola, St. Thomas, Ft Lauderdale (terminates).

London

KARELIA

(CTC) Mar.-Apr. (33 days): Amsterdam, Punta Delgada, Barbados, St. Vincent, Bequia, Grenada, Ciudad Guayana, Tobago, St Lucia, Guadaloupe, Montserrat, St. Maarten, Antigua, Funchal

Miami

AMERICAN ADVENTURE

(American Family) Sat year round (7days): Nassau, Casa de Campo, Key West.

BRITANIS

(Fantasy) Sun year round (7 days): Key West, Playa del Carmen, Cozumel.

CELEBRATION

(Carnival) Sat year round (7 days): San Juan, St. Thomas, St. Maarten.

COSTA ALLEGRA

(Costa) Sun Dec.-May (7 days): San Juan, St. Thomas, Casa de Campo,

SS NORWAY

Nassau; or alt weeks Ocho Rios, Playa Del Carmen, Cozumel, Grand Cayman.

COSTA ROMANTICA

(Costa) Sun Nov.-May (7 days): San Juan, St. Thomas, Casa de Campo, Nassau; or alternate weeks, Ocho Rios, Playa del Carmen, Cozumel, Grand Cayman.

ECSTASY

(Carnival) July-Oct. (7 days): Nassau, San Juan, St. Thomas; or alternate weeks, Cozumel, Grand Cayman, Ocho Rios.

HOLIDAY

(Carnival) Sat year round (7 days): Cozumel, Grand Cayman, Ocho Rios.

MAJESTY OF THE SEAS

(Royal Caribbean) Sun year round (7 days): Playa del Carmen, Grand Cayman, Ocho Rios, Coco Cay; or alt weeks, Cozumel, Grand Cayman, Ocho Rios, Coco Cay.

NORWAY

(Norwegian) Sat Oct.-Dec (7 days): St. Maarten, St. John, St. Thomas, private out island.

ROYAL MAJESTY

(Majesty) Mon year round (7 days): Playa del Carmen, Cozumel, Key West.

SEABREEZE

(Dolphin) Sun year round (7 days): Playa del Carmen, Cozumel, Grand Cayman, Ocho Rios, Coco Cay; or alternate weeks, Nassau, private out island, San Juan, St. John, St. Thomas

SEAWARD

(Norwegian) Sun year round (7 days): Nassau, private out island, San Juan, St. John, St. Thomas; or alt weeks, Nassau, San Juan, St. John, St. Thomas.

SENSATION

(Carnival) Sun year round (7 days): Cozumel, Grand Cayman, Ocho Rios; or alt weeks, Nassau, San Juan, St. Thomas.

SONG OF AMERICA

(Royal) Dec.-Apr. (10 days): Coco Cay, St. Kitts, Dominica, Port of Spain, Fort de France, St. Maarten, St. Thomas, San Juan (terminates).

SOVEREIGN OF THE SEAS

(Royal) Sat year round (7 days): Coco Cay, San Juan, St Thomas.

SUN VIKING

(Royal) Oct.-Dec. (10 days): Coco Cay, St. Barts, Fort de France, Grenada, Dominica, St. Maarten, St. Thomas, San Juan (terminates).

Montego Bay

EUROPA

(Hapog-Lloyd Kreutzfahrten) Nov.-Dec. (24 days): Puerto Cortes, San Andres Is., San Blas Is., Cartegena, La Guaira, Grenada, Barbados, Bequia, Antigua, St. Lucia, Pointe a Pitre, St. Kitts, Tortola, Santiago de Cuba, Ocho Rios, Curacao (terminates).

REGENT SEA

(Regency) Sat Dec.-Apr. (7-13 days) Cozumel, Belize, St. Thomas, Puerto Cortes, Puerto Moin (Costa Rica), Panama Canal (Gatun Lake only), Cartegena, Aruba, Curacao.

REGENT SPIRIT

(Regency) Sun Nov.-Apr. (7 days): Port Antonio, Curacao, Bonaire, Aruba.

REGENT STAR

(Regency) Sun Oct.-Apr. (7 days): Puerto Moin (Costa Rica), Panama Canal (Gatun Lake only), Cartegena, Aruba.

Nassau

FANTOME

(Windjammer Schooner) Oct.-Nov. (5-12): Chub Cay, Harbour Cay, Bimini, Freeport, San Salvador Is., Grand Turk Is., Great Inagua Is., Tortola, Virgin Gorda, St. Maarten, St. Eustatius, St. Kitts, St. Barts, Antigua.

GOLDEN ODYSSEY
(Royal) Nov. (7 days): Key West, Grand Cayman, Ocho Rios, Curacao, Aruba (terminates).

STAR ODYSSEY
(Royal) Nov. (7 days) Key West, Grand Cayman, Ocho Rios, Curacao, Aruba (terminates).

New Orleans

ENCHANTED SEAS
(Commodore) Sat year round (7 days): Key West, Playa del Carmen, Cozumel, also Montego Bay some weeks.

GOLDEN ODYSSEY
(Royal) Mar, (7 days): Playa del Carmen, Cozumel, Grand Cayman, Ocho Rios.

NOORDAM
(Holland America) Oct.-Nov, Apr. (7 days): Ocho Rios, Grand Cayman, Playa del Carmen, Cozumel.

Newport News

ROTTERDAM
(Holland America) Dec.-Jan. (17 days): Ft Lauderdale, San Juan, St. Croix, Bonaire, Curacao, Puerto Cabello, St. Lucia, St. Kitts, St. John, St. Thomas, Ft Lauderdale (terminates).

New York

CROWN DYNASTY
(Cunard Crown) Oct. (14 days): Ft. Lauderdale, St. Thomas, St. John, San Juan, St. Maarten, Aruba, Port Antonio, Ft. Lauderdale (terminates).

DREAMWARD
(Norwegian) Oct. (15 days): St. Georges, Hamilton, San Juan, St. Thomas, Aruba, Panama Canal (Gatun Lake only), Limon, Grand Cayman, Ft. Lauderdale (terminates).

HORIZON
(Celebrity) Oct.-Nov. (7 days): Nassau, St. Thomas, St. Maarten, San Juan (terminates).

QUEEN ELIZABETH II
(Cunard) Oct.-Nov. (11 days): Baltimore, St. Maarten, Barbados, St. Lucia, St. Thomas, Baltimore.

REGENT SUN
(Regency) Oct.-Dec. (11 days): San Juan, St. Maarten, Antigua, St John, St. Thomas.

SEABOURN PRIDE
(Seabourn) Oct. (13 days): Philadelphia, Baltimore, Savannah, Port Ca-

naveral, Ft. Lauderdale, San Juan, Virgin Gorda, St. Maarten, St. Barts, St. Thomas (terminates).

SONG OF AMERICA

(Royal Caribbean) Oct.-Nov. (10 days): St. Georges, Hamilton, St. Maarten, St. Thomas, San Juan (terminates).

Piraeus

CROWN ODYSSEY

(Royal) Nov.-Dec. (21 days): Civitavecchia,Villefranche, Barcelona, Palma, Gibraltar, Casablanca, Funchal, Santa Cruz Tenerife, Barbados, Fort de France, St. Thomas, San Juan (terminates).

Port of Spain

YORKTOWN CLIPPER

(Clipper) Mar. (10 days): Cuidad Guayana, Orinoco River, Tobago, Bonaire, Curacao (terminates).

Rio de Janeiro

REGENT SEA

(Regency) Nov.-Dec. (18 days): Salvador, Forteleza, Belem, Amazon Delta, Devil's Island, Barbados, Antigua, St. Thomas, Tampa (terminates).

St. Maarten

POLYNESIA

(Windjammer Schooner) Oct.-Dec. (5 days): St Barts, Nevis, Montserrat, St. Kitts, Anguilla.

SIR FRANCIS DRAKE

(Tall Ship Adventures Schooner) Oct.-Nov. (7 days): Ile Tintamarre, St. Barts, Anguilla, Virgin Gorda, Norman Is., St. Thomas, St. John (terminates).

STAR FLYER

(Star Clippers Schooner) Nov.-Apr. (7 days): Anguilla, St. Thomas, St. Croix, Tortola, Norman Is., Virgin Gorda, St. Barts.

St. Petersburg

GRUZIA

(Odessa America) Dec. (7 days): Puerto Cortes, Belize, Cancun.

St. Thomas

MAYAN PRINCE

(American Canadian Caribbean) Dec. (11 days): St. John, Tortola, Virgin Gorda, Prickly Pear Cays, Anegada Is., Beef Is., Jost van Dyke, Sandy Cay, Norman Is.

NANTUCKET CLIPPER

(Clipper) Sat Jan.-Feb. (7 days): Francis Bay (St. John), Tortola, Norman

Island, Virgin Gorda, Jost van Dyke, Tortola (Soper's Hole), Norman Island, St. John.

SEA GODDESS I
(Cunard Sea Goddess) Sat Nov.-Jan., Mar. (7 days): St.John, St. Maarten, St Bart, Nevis, Virgin Gorda Jost van Dyke.

SAGAFJORD
(Cunard/NAC) Nov. (14 days): Salvador, Fortaleza, Belem, Tobago, St. Thomas, Ft. Lauderdale (terminates).

SEABOURN PRIDE
(Seabourn) Oct.-Nov., Jan.-Feb. (7 days): Mayreau Is., Antigua, Virgin Gorda, or Virgin Gorda, Jost van Dyke St. Maarten, Antigua, St. John, Ft. Lauderdale (terminates)

SIR FRANCIS DRAKE
(Tall Ship Adventures Schooner) Nov.-Jun. (7 days): St. John (Caneel Bay), Francis Bay (St. John). St. John (Cruz Bay), Jost Van Dyke, Norman Is., Tortola (West End); or as 3 day cruise to St. John.

San Juan
AMERIKANIS
(Fantasy) Mon year round (7 days): St. Thomas, Pointe a Pitre, Barbados, St. Lucia, Antigua, St. Maarten.

COSTA CLASSICA
(Costa) Sat Jan.-Apr (7 days): St. Maarten, Barbados, St. Thomas, Casa de Campo.

CUNARD COUNTESS
(Cunard Crown) Sat year round (7 days): Tortola, Antigua, Fort de France, Barbados, St Thomas; or alt weeks: St. Maarten, Pointe a Pitre, Grenada, St. Lucia, St. Kitts, St Thomas.

FESTIVALE
(Carnival) Sun year round (7 days): Aruba, Curaco, Tortola, Virgin Gorda, St. John, St. Thomas.

FIESTA MARINA
(Fiestamarina) Fri year round (7 days) St. Thomas, La Guaira, Aruba, Santo Domingo.

MERIDIAN
(Celebrity) Nov.-Mar. (10-11): Aruba, La Guaira, Grenada, St. Lucia St. Maarten, St. Thomas; also Panama Canal (Gatun Lakes only), San Blas Is., Fort de France, Curaco, St. John.

MONARCH OF THE SEAS
(Royal Caribbean) Sun year round (7 days): Fort de France, Barbados, Antigua, St. Maarten, St. Thomas.

RADISSON DIAMOND

(Diamond) Nov.-Dec., Feb.-May (3-7 days): Iles des Sainte, Barbados, Fort de France, Antigua, St. Thomas; or St. Thomas, St. Kitts, St, Maarten.

SONG OF AMERICA

(Royal Caribbean) Sat Nov.-Apr. (7-11 days): St. Thomas, St. Maarten, Fort de France, Port of Spain, Dominica, St. Kitts, St. Croix, Coco Cay, Miami (terminates)

REGENT SUN

(Regency) Dec.-Apr. (10-11): St. Thomas, Grenada, Port of Spain, Barbados, Fort de France, St Kitts, St. Maarten; or St. Lucia, Barbados, La Guaira, Curaco, Aruba, St. Barts, St. Thomas.

STAR PRINCESS

(Princess) Sat Oct.-Apr. (7 days): Barbados, Mayreau Is., Fort de France, St. Maarten, St. Thomas.

SUN VIKING

(Royal Caribbean) Sat Jan.-Apr.(7 days): St Croix, St. Barts, Pointe a Pitre, St. Maarten, St. John, St. Thomas; also Dominica, Tobago, Fort de France, Coco Cay, Miami (terminates).

TROPICALE

(Carnival) Sat year round with exceptions (7-11 days): St. Thomas, Pointe a Pitre, Grenada, La Guaira, Aruba; or Tortola, Curacao, Panama Canal (Gatun Lake only).

St. Vincent

AQUANAUT EXPLORER

(Aquanaut) Year round (7 days): Tobogo Cays, Chatham Bay, Carriacou, Union Is., Mayreau, Bequia.

Savona

ODESSA

(Transocean) Nov.-Dec. (29): Funchal, Barbados, Scarborough, St. Georges Cay, St. Vincent, St. Lucia, Fort de France, Pointe a Pitre, Antigua, Santa Cruz Tenerife.

Southampton

CANBERRA

(P & O) Nov.-Dec. (26 days): Funchal, St. Kitts, Montego Bay, New Orleans, Freeport, Ponta Delgado.

SEA PRINCESS

(P & O) Dec.- Jan. (23 days): Santa Cruz, Tenerife, Mayreau Is., Tobago, St. Lucia, Antigua, Tortola, Funchal.

Tampa
AMERICAN PIONEER
(American Family) Sun Jan.-Apr. (7-8 days): Cozumel, Jamaica, Playa del Carmen, Grand Cayman.
GRUZIYA
(Odessa America) Sat Oct.-May (7 days): Puerto Cortes, Belize, Cozumel, Playa del Carmen.
NIEUW AMSTERDAM
(Holland America) Sat Oct.- Apr. (7-11 days): Grand Cayman, Montego Bay, Playa del Carmen, Cozumel, Ocho Rios, Cartagena, Key West, San Blas Is.
REGENT RAINBOW
(Regency) Sun Oct.-Apr. (5 days): Playa del Carmen, Cozumel, Key West.

Tortola
FLYING CLOUD
(Windjammer Schooner) Nov.-Jun. (5 days): Salt Is. Virgin Gorda, Beef Is., Green Cay, Sandy Cay, Norman Is., Jost Van Dyke, Cane Garden Bay, Peter Is.

MEDITERRANEAN, ADRIATIC, IONIAN & BLACK SEAS
Ajaccio
ORPHEUS
(Swan Hellenic) Jul. (14 days): Naples, Salerno, Reggio Calabria, Naxos, Katakolon, Ithaca, Itea, through Corinth Canal, Piraeus, Delos, Mykonos, Kusadasi, Dikili, Mount Athos Pen., Thessaloniki (terminates).

Amsterdam
CRYSTAL HARMONY
(Crystal) Aug. (12 days): Guernsey, Puerto Banus, Palma, Barcelona, Cannes, Civitavecchia (terminates).
DAPHNE
(Costa) Sep. (10 days): Dover, Guernsey, La Caruna, Vigo, Porto de Leixoes, Malaga, Genoa (terminates).

Ashdod
RENAISSANCE VI
(Renaissance) Aug-Sep. (11 Days): Haifa, Antalya, Fethiye, Kos, Kusadasi, Chios, Istanbul (terminates).

SEABOURN SPIRIT
(Seabourn) Apr. (10 days): Port Said, Alexandria, Heraklion, Santorini, Bodrum, Kusadasi, through Dardanelles, Istanbul (terminates).

Barcelona
ACHILLE LAURO
(Starlauro) Jul-Oct. (14 days): Genoa, Naples, Alexandria, Port Said, Ashdod, Kusadasi, Istanbul, Piraeus, Messina.

AURORA I
(Classical) Jul.-Aug. (9 days): Camargue, Nice, Vaireggio, Bonifacio, Sorrento, Toarmino, Ravenna, Venice (terminates).

AUSONIA
(Grimaldi Siosa) Jul. (14 days) Messina, Yithion, Piraeus, Yalta, Odessa, Constanza, Istanbul, Taormina, Capri, Genoa

CUNARD PRINCESS
(Cunard Crown) Sep. (14 days): Mahon, Cagliari, Palermo, Valletta, Heraklion, Alexandria, Ashdod, Rhodes, Kusadasi, Piraeus (terminates).

RENAISSANCE II
(Renaissance) Aug. (7 days): Port Vendres, Port St. Louis, Monte Carlo, Portofino, Vaireggio, Civitavecchia (terminates).

RENAISSANCE IV
(Renaissance)
Oct. (14 days): Ibiza, Mahon, Port Vendres, Port St. Louis, Monte Carlo, Portofino, Porto Cervo, Vaireggio, Portoferraio (Elba Is.), Civitavecchia (terminates).

RENAISSANCE V
(Renaissance) Oct. (7 days): Port Vendres, Port St. Louis, Monte Carlo, Portofino, Vaireggio, Civitavecchia (terminates).

SEABOURN SPIRIT
(Seabourn) May-Jun; Aug. (14 days): St. Tropez, Monte Carlo, Portofino, Livorno, Porto Cervo, Civitavecchia, Sorrento, Taormina, Otronto, Venice (terminates),

SEA GODDESS II
(Cunard Sea Goddess) Jul.; Aug.-Sep. (7 days): Ibiza, Bonofacio, Porto Cervo, Portoferraio, Portofino, Monte Carlo (terminates) .

SONG OF FLOWER
(Seven Seas) Aug-Sep. (7 days) Ibiza, Palma, Collioure, Sete, Monte Carlo, Vaireggio, Civitavecchio (terminates).

VISTAFJORD
(Cunard/NAC) Sep. (14 days): Valletta, Skiathos, Yalta, Odessa, Istanbul, Mikonos, Kos, Kusadasi, Piraeus (terminates).

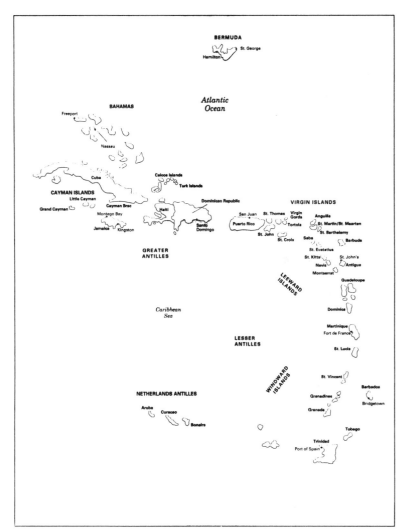

Barcelona-Venice
PACIFIC PRINCESS
(Princess) Aug.-Oct. (12 days): Cannes, Livorno, Civitavecchia, Messina, Piraeus, Mikonos, Selos, Katakolon.
SONG OF NORWAY
(Royal Caribbean) May; Sep.-Nov. (12 days): Palma, Villafranche, Livorno, Civitavecchia, Naples, Messina, Corfu.

Bremerhaven
EUROPA
(Hapag-Lloyd Kreutzfahrten) Sep. (13 days): Rouen, Plymouth, La Coruna, Lisbon. Tangier, Mahon, Villefranche, Genoa (terminates).

ODESSA
(Transocean/MarQuest) Sep. (12 days): London, St. Helier (Jersey), Brest, Lisbon, Tangier, Civitavecchia, Portoferraio (Elba), Savona (terminates).

LEV TOLSTOY
(Transocean/MarQuest) Sep.-Oct. (14 days): Southhampton, St/ Helier (Jersey), St. Nazaire, Porto de Leixoes, Lisbon, Portimao, Tangier, Malaga, Ibiza, Mahan, Ajaccio, Savona (terminates).

Capri
AUSONIA
(Grimalgi Siosa) Jul. (14 days): Genoa, Barcelona, Messina, Yithion, Piraeus, Yalta, Odessa, Constanza, Istanbul, Taormina.

Civitaveccia-Cannes
RADISSON DIAMOND
(Diamond) Jul,-Aug. (7 days): Monaco, Portofino, Livorno, Puerto Cervo, Sorrento.

Civitavecchia-Piraeus
RADISSON DIAMOND
(Diamond) Aug.-Oct. (7 days): Sorrento, Messina, Valleta, Heraklion, Santorini.

ROYAL ODYSSEY
(Royal) Apr.- May; Aug.; Nov. (12 days): Naples, Port Said, Alexandria, Ashdod, Limassol, Rhodes, Istanbul, Kusadasi, Mitiline, Volus.

Civitavecchia
CROWN ODYSSEY
(Royal) Nov. (12 days): Naples, Port Said, Ashdod, Limassol, Rhodes, Mytiline, Volus, Piraeus (terminates).

CRYSTAL HARMONY
(Crystal) Aug.- Oct (7 days): Naples, Venice, Mikonos, Istanbul, Yalta, Haifa, Ashdod, Piraeus (terminates); or (13 days): Naples, Valletta, Heraklion, Rhodes, Piraeus, Kusadasi, through Bosphorus, Yalta, Odessa, Istanbul (terminates).

RADISSON DIAMOND
(Diamond) Oct. (7 days): Porto Cervo, Ajaccio, Livorno, Portofino, St. Tropez, Marseille, Barcelona (terminates).

RENAISSANCE II
(Renaissance) Apr.-Oct. (7 days): Varreggio, Portofino, Monte Carlo, Port St. Louis, Port Vendres, Barcelona (terminates).

RENAISSANCE II/VI
(Renaissance) Jul.-Aug. (14 days): Sorrento, Lipari, Zakinthos Is.(Zante), Pylos, Kithira, Paros, Kos, Bodrum, Shios, Lesvos Is. Canakkale, Istanbul (terminates).

ROYAL VIKING SUN
(Royal Viking) Sep.-Oct. (12 days): Porto Empedocle, Kusadasi, Istanbul, Costanta, Odessa, Yalta, Mikonos, Piraeus; or Villefranche, Livorno, Porto, Ajaccio, Palma, Malaga, Gibralter, Casablanca, Lisbon (terminates).

SEABOURN SPIRIT
(Seabourn) Jun.; Aug, (7 days): Sorrento, Taormina, Otranto, Venice (terminates); Jul. (7 days): Livorno, Portfino, St. Tropez, Newcastle, Nice (terminates); Jul.-Aug. (7 days): Portoferrio (Elba Is,), Portofino, Monte Carlo, Cannes, Collioure, Barcelona (terminates); or Oct. (7 days): Aleghero, Valletta, Taormina, Sorrento, Portoferrio, Monte Carlo, Nice (terminates).

SEA GODDESS II
(Cunard Sea Goddess) Oct. (7 days): Sorrento, Capri, Taormina, Monemvasia, Mikonos, Piraeus (terminates).

SILVER CLOUD
(Silversea) Apr, (7 days): Taormina, Corfu, Katakolon, Itea, Navplion, Piraeus (terminates); or May, Porto Cervo, Barcelona, Ibiza, Malaga, Seville. Gibralter, Lisbon (terminates).

SONG OF FLOWER
(Seven Seas) May (7 days): Calvi, Portovenere, Portofino, Ile D'Hyeres, Colliqure, Barcelona (terminates); or Aug. (10 days): Sorrento, Taormina, Manfredonia, Venice, Corfu, Galaxidion, through Corinth Canal, Piraeus (terminates); or Sep, (9 days): Corfu, Galaxidion, through Corinth Canal, Skiathos, Volus, Piraeus (terminates); or Sep. (7 days): Sorrento, Toarmina, Corfu, Manfredonia, Ancona, Venice (terminates).

STATENDAM
(Holland America) Apr-May, (17 days): Malaga, Casablanca, Funchal, Ft, Lauderdale, New York (terminates).

SUN VIKING
(Royal Caribbean) Nov. (12 days): Civitavecchia, Naples, Messina, Villefranche, Barcelona, Tangier, Lisbon (terminates).

Corfu
ORPHEUS
(Swan Hellanic) Oct. (14 days): Heraklion, Limassol, Tasucu, Anamur,

434   THE WORLD'S MOST EXCITING CRUISES

Antalya, Finiki, Kas, Gulluk, Canakkale, Gemlik, Istanbul, Mt. Athos Pen., Thessaloniki (terminates) .

ZEUS

(Tours and Yacht) Sat Jul.- Aug. (7 days): Paxoi, Lefkas, Kefalonia, Zakinthos Is. (Zante), Ithaca, Venice (terminates).

Genoa

AUSONIA

(Grimaldi Siosa); Mar-Apr. (11 days): Naples, Istanbul, Dikili, Piraeus, Pylos, Siracusa, Barcelona; or (6 days): Naples, Lipari, Messina, Valetta, Tunis, Palermo, Naples (terminates); or (8 days) ; Barcelona, Palma Tunis, Palermo, Naples; or May-Jun. (11 days): Naples, Alexandria, Port Said, Ashdod, Limasol, Fethiye, Siracusa, Salerno; or May-Jun. (7 days): Naples, Porto Empedocle, Valleta, Gabes, Tunis, Ajaccio; or Jun. (14 days): Naples, Ibiza, Motril, Malaga, Cadiz, Lisbon, Funchal, Casablanca, Tangier, Marseille; or Jun. (10 days): Naples, Heraklion, Rhodes, Antalya, Mikonos, Santorini, Massina, Capri; or Jun.-Jul. (11 days): Naples, Heraklion, Tartus, Limasol, Rhodes, Santorini, Messina, Capri; or Jul. (14 days): Barcelona, Messina, Yithion, Piraeus, Yalta, Odessa, Constanza, Istanbul, Taormina, Capri; or Sat Jul.-Oct. (7 days): Barcelona, Ibiza, Palma, Tunis, Palermo, Capri.

BERLIN

(Peter Dielmann Reederei) Oct. (7 days): Olbia, LaGoullete, Valeta, Messina, Brindisi, Venice (terminates).

COSTA CLASSICA

(Costa) Sun Aug.-Oct. (7 days): Naples, Palermo, Tunis, Ibiza, Palma, Barcelona.

EUROPA

(Hapag-Lloyd Kreutzfahrten) Sep.- Oct. (14 days): Lipari, Syracuse, Corfu, Piraeus, Skiathos, Chios, Belos, Mikonos, Santorini, Valletta. Oct. (14 days): Toarmina, Kefalonia, Navplion, Piraeus, Istanbul, Mudanya, Kusadasi, Valletta; or Oct.-Nov. (15 days): Palermo, Heraklion, Rhodes, Antalya, Alexandria, Piraeus, Valleta, Cadiz (terminates).

MONTEREY

(Starlauro) Aug.-Oct. (11 days): Naples, Alexandria, Port Said, Ashdod, Kusidasi, Patmos, Piraeus, Capri; or Oct. (4 days): Barcelona, Palma, St. Tropez,.Valletta, Cadiz (terminates); or Apr.-May (16 days): Trapani, Valeta, Heraklion, Limassol, Istanbul, Canakkale, Katakolon, Catania; or May (13 days): Palermo, Katakolon, Hydra, Piraeus, Volos, Delos, Mikonos, Zakinthos Is., Valetta.

ROYAL ODYSSEY

(Royal) Jul.;Sep.-Oct (12 days): Villefranche, Portofino, Naples, Capri,

Navplion, Lipari, Civitavecchia, Malaga, Casablanca, Heraklion, Katakolon, Venice (terminates).

SHOTA RUSTAVELI

(Grandi Viaggi) Jul.(8 days): Palma, Malaga, Gibralter, Valencia, Barcelona, Ajaccio; or Jul-Aug. (13-18 days): Through Strait of Messina, Piraeus, through Dardenelles, Istanbul, Rhodes, Antalya, Alanya, Limassol, Latikia, Ashdod, Alexandria; or Messina, Katakolon, Piraeus, Mikonos, Istanbul, Nesebur, Odessa, Yalta, through Bosphorus, through Corinth Canal, Itea, Sarande, Corfu, Bari, Venice (terminates); Sep. (5 days): Valletta, Goulette, Capri.

SUN VIKING

(Royal Caribbean) Sep.-Oct. (12 days); Civitavecchia, Naples, Katakolon, Heraklion, Rhodes, Patmos, Mikonos, Kusadasi, Piraeus (terminates); or Nov. (12 days): Civitavecchia, Naples, Messina, Villefranche, Barcelona, Tangier, Lisbon (terminates).

TROPIC SUN

(Aquanaut) Apr.- May (6 days): San Remo, Nice, Cannes, St. Tropez, Monaco; or May- Jun.: Livorno, Elba, Rome, Naples, Catania, Malta.

VISTAFJORD

(Cunard/NAC) Oct. (15 days): Valletta, Skiathos, Yalta, Odessa, Istanbul, Mikonos, Marmaris, Patmos, Piraeus (terminates).

WORLD RENAISSANCE

(Renaissance) Aug. (14 days): Messina, Katakolon, Piraeus, Mikonos, Istanbul, Nesebur, Odessa, Yalta, through Bosphorous, through. Corinth Canal, Itea, Sarande, Corfu, Bari, Venice (terminates).

Haifa

STATENDAM

(Holland America) Apr. (25 days): through Dardenelles, Istanbul, Piraeus, Civitavecchia, Malaga, Casablanca, Funchal, Ft. Lauderdale, New York (terminates).

Heraklion

NEPTUNE

(Epirotiki) Thur and Sat Jul,-Oct. (3-4 days): Santorini, Palaion, Faliron, Mikonos, Kusadasi, Patmos, Rhodes.

Hurghada

LEV TOLSTOY

(Transocean/MarQuest) Mar.-Apr. (14 days): through Dardenelles, Istanbul, Piraeus, Lipari, Civitavecchia, Malaga, Casablanca, Funchal, Ft. Lauderdale, New York (terminates).

Istanbul-Piraeus

REGENT JEWEL

(Regency) Sat Apr.-Oct. (7 days): Dikili, Haifa, Limassol, Rhodes, Heraklion, Santorini.

RENAISSANCE VII

(Renaissance) Apr-May; Oct. (7 days): Canakkale, Kusadasi, Patmos, Rhodes, Mikonos, Santorini.

SEA GODDESS

(Cunard Sea Goddess) Oct. (7 days): Kusadasi, Bodrum, Lindos, Rhodes, Santorini, Mikonos, Santorini.

Istanbul

AURORA

(Classical) Sep.-Oct. (8 days): Thasos, Skopelos, Chios, Patmos, Leros Is., Naxos, Sifnos, Serifos, Piraeus (terminates).

CRYSTAL HARMONY

(Crystal) Aug.-Sep. (13 days): Odessa, Yalta, through Bosphorus, Kusadasi, Piraeus, Rhodes, Heraklion, Valletta, Naples, Civitaveccia (terminates).

ILLIRIA

(Classical) Oct. (9 days): Chios, Kusadasi, Lindos, Ayios, Nikolaos, Heraklion, Santorini, Yithion, Katakolon, Itea, Pireaus (terminates).

ORPHEUS

(Swan Hellanic)) Aug. (7 days): Cannakale, Kusadasi, Knidos, Kos, Mount Athos Pen., Volos, Thessaloniki (terminates).

RADISSON DIAMOND

(Diamond) Oct. (7 days): Canakkale, Kusadasi, Patmos, Rhodes, Delos, Mikonos, Santorini, Piraeus (terminates).

RENAISSANCE II

(Renaissance) Jul.- Oct. (7 days): Canakkale, Kusadasi, Patmos, Rhodes, Mikonos, Santorini, Piraeus (terminates); or Oct. (14 days): Canakkale, Lesvos Is., Chios, Bodrum, Kos, Paros, Kithira, Pylos, Zakinthos Is., Lipari, Sorrento, Civitavecchia (terminates).

RENAISSANCE V

(Renaissance) Sep. (7 days): Canakkale, Kusadasi, Patmos, Rhodes, Mikonos, Santorini, Piraeus (terminates).

RENAISSANCE VI

(Renaissance) Jul, (14 days): Canakkale, Lesvos Is., Chios, Bodrum, Kos, Paros, Kithira, Pylos, Zakinthos (Zante), Lipari, Sorrento, Civitavecchia (terminates); or Aug. (10 days): Canakkale, Kusadasi, Patmos, Rhodes, Mikonos, Santorini, Piraeus (terminates); or Aug. (10 days): Dikili, Samos Is., Bodrum, Kasterorizo, Haifa, Ashdod (terminates).

RENAISSANCE VII
(Renaissance) Oct. (7 days): Canakkale, Kusadasi, Patmos, Rhodes, Mikonos, Santorini, Piraeus (terminates).

ROYAL VIKING QUEEN
(Royal) Sep. (11 days): Trabzon, Sochi, Yalta, Odessa, Varina, through Dardenelles, Bodrum, Mikonos, Piraeus (terminates).

SEABOURN SPIRIT
(Seabourn) Apr. (11-14 days): through Dardenelles, Lesvos Is., Kusadasi, Rhodes, Santorini, through Corinth Canal, Katakalon, Otranto, Venice; or Jun-Sep. (14 days): through Dardanelles, Thessaloniki, Lesvos Is., Kusadasi, Rhodes, Piraeus, Mikonos, Poros, Navplion, Hydra, Piraeus, Santorini, through Corinth Canal, Katakolon, Corfu, Venice (terminates); or Oct.-Nov. (12 days): Kusadasi, Bodrum, Rhodes, Santorini, Alexandria, Port Said, Ashdod (terminates).

SEA GODDESS I/II
(Cunard Sea Goddess) Aug. (7 days): Kusadasi, Bodrum, Lindos, Rhodes, Santorini, Mikonos, Piraeus (terminates); or Oct. (10 days): Mytiline, Kusadasi, Bodrum, Marmaris, Lindos, Rhodes, Heraklion, Santorini, Delos, Mikonos, Patmos, Piraeus (terminates).

SILVER CLOUD
(Silverseas) Apr.-May (7 days): Canakkale, Kusadasi, Patmos, Volos, Mikonos, Santorini, Piraeus (terminates); or Volus, Delos, Mikonos, Piraeus, through Corinth Canal, Itea, Venice (terminates).

VOLGA/AJVASOVSKU
(DDSG Donaureissen) Sep. (9 days): Yalta, Izmail, Ruse, Nikopol, Baikal, Turnu Severin, Orsova, Budapest, Bratislava, Vienna (terminates).

SONG OF FLOWER
(Seven Seas) Sep. (9 days): Canakkale, Kusadasi, Bodrum, Rhodes, Hydra, through Corinth Canal, Katakolon, Zacinthos Is., Taorimuna, Sorrento, Civitavecchia (terminates).

Katakolon
LA PALMA
(Intercruise) Thur Jul.-Sep. (7 days):Venice, Corfu, through Corinth Canal, Piraeus, Kusadasi, Paymos, Rhodes.

Kusadasi
HALAS
(Abercrombie & Kent) Jul.- Sep. (3-6 days): Gocek, Yassicalar Is., Gemili Is., Domuz Is.

ISLAND PRINCESS
(Princess) Aug.-Sep. (12 days): Yalta, Odessa, Constanza, Istanbul, Izmir, Santorini, Katakolon, Venice (terminates).

KARELIA
(CTC) Mondays Aug.-Sep. (14 days): Piraeus, Yalta, Odessa, Istanbul, Kusadasi. Heraklion, Alexandria, Ashdod, Limassol, Rhodes.

LA PALMA
(Intercruise) Tuesdays Jul.-Sep. (7 days): Patmos, Rhodes, Katakolon, Venice, Corfu, through Corinth Canal, Piraeus.

SEA CLOUD
(Special Expeditions) Aug. (9 days): Antalya, Lindos, Rhodes, Bodrum, Santorini, Piraeus (terminates).

Lisbon

CROWN ODYSSEY
(Royal) Apr.-May (12 days): Tangier, Malaga, Villefranche, Civitaveccia, Messina, Katakolon, Venice (terminates); or Nov. (12 days): Tangier, Palma, Villefranche, Livorno, Ajaccio, Civitavecchia, Piraeus (terminates).

ILLIRIA
(Classical) Aug. (12 days): Cadiz, Motril, Barcelona, Port St. Louis, Bonifacio, Salerno, Taormina, Ravenna, Venice (terminates).

ROYAL ODYSSEY
(Royal) Oct.-Nov. (12 days): Tangier, Palma, Villefranche, Livorno, Ajaccio, Civitavecchia, Piraeus (terminates).

SEABOURN PRIDE
(Seabourn) Apr.-May (14 days): Seville, Tangier, Gibraltar, Vallencia, Ibza, Port Vendres, Monte Carlo, St. Tropez, Mahon, Barcelona (terminates).

London

AZERBAYDZHAN
(CTC) Aug. (14 days): Lisbon, Nice, Livorno, Alicante, Gibraltar, La Coruna

CROWN ODYSSEY
(Royal) Sep-Oct. (13 days): Zeebrugge, Le Havre, Oporto, Lisbon, Barcelona, Villafranche. Civitavecchia, Messina, Venice (terminates).

CRYSTAL HARMONY
(Crystal) Aug. (13 days): St. Helier, Le Havre, Lisbon, Livorno, Cannes, Barcelona, Civitavecchia (terminates).

KARELIA
(CTC) Aug. (14 days): Amsterdam, Lisbon, Tangier, Mahon, Nice, Civitavecchia, Naples, Messina, Kusadasi (terminates).

ROYAL VIKING SUN
(Royal) Aug.-Sep. (12 days): Amsterdam, Antwerp, Waterford, Oporto, Lisbon, Gibraltar, Malaga, Barcelona (terminates).

STATENDAM
(Holland America) Aug.-Sep. (12 days): Amsterdam, Zeebrugge, Le Havre, Lisbon, Cadiz, Malaga, Monte Carlo, Civitavecchia (terminates).

Malaga
CUNARD PRINCESS
(Cunard) Mar. (10 days): Alcante, Mahon, Cagliari, Palermo, Valletta, Messina, Corfu, Venice (terminates).

Malta
TROPIC SUN
(Aquanaut) Jun. (6 days): Syracuse, Crotone, Gallipoli, Korcula, Mali Losinj, Opatija, Rovinj; or Aug.: Catania, Naples, Rome, Livorno (pisa), Genoa (terminates).

Mombasa
STATENDAM
(Holland America) Mar.-Apr. (18 days): crossing Equator, Suez, through Suez Canal, Port Said, Haifa, through Dardenelles, Istanbul, Piraeus, Lipari, Civitavecchia (terminates).

Monte Carlo
ROYAL VIKING QUEEN
(Royal) Sep.-Oct. (10 days): Barcelona, Valencia, Palma, Porto Ajaccio, Civitavecchia, Livorno, Portofino; or St. Tropez, Valencia, Palma, Portoferraio, Livorono, Capri, Catania, Venice (terminates).

SEA GODDESS II
(Cunard) Jul.-Aug. (7 days): Portofino, St. Tropez, Calvi, Ibiza, Palma, Barcelona (terminates); or Jul.-Sep. (7 days): Portofino, Porto Cervo, Sorrento, Capri, Taormina, Zakinthos Is., Itea, through Corinth Canal, Navplion, Santorini, Mikonos, Piraeus (terminates); or Aug. (7 days): Portofino, Porto Cervo, Capri, Taormina, Corfu, Venice (terminates); or Aug. (11 days): Porto Cervo, Capri, Taormina, Monemvasia, Santorini, Mikonos, through Corinth Canal, Itea, Corfu, Venice; or Sep. (10 days): Portofino, Porto Cervo, Sorrento, Capri, Taormina, Monemvasia, Santorini, Mikonos, Piraeus (terminates).

SONG OF FLOWER
(Seven Seas) Sep. (7 days): Cannes, Portofino,Livorno, Bonifacio, Sorrento, Capri, Civitavecchia (terminates).

Naples
AUSONIA
(Grimaldi Siosa) Apr. (5 days): Porto Torres, Palma, Tunis, Palermo.

Nice-Venice
STELLIS MARIS
(Sun Line) Sat Jul.-Aug. (7 days): Portofino, Elba Is., Sorrento, Messina, Katakolon, Isola Tremiti.

Nice
ORPHEUS
(Swan Hellenic) Sep.-Oct. (14 days): Civitaveccia, Naples, Reggio, Calabria, Corinth, through Corinth Canal, Piraeus, Navplion, Yithion, Kalamata, Pylos, Navpactos, Katakolon, Corfu (terminates).

REGENT SPIRIT
(Regency) Alt Sun May-Oct. (7 days): Ajaccio, Civitavecchia, Capri, Palermo, Tunis; or Alt. Sun: Sete, Barcelona, Mahon, Alghero (Sardinia), Livorno, Portofino.

SEABOURN SPIRIT
(Seabourn) May; Jul-Aug. (14 days): Portovenere, Livorno, Sorrento, Civitaveccia, Portoferraio (Elba), Portofino, Monte Carlo, Cannes, Port Vendres, Barcelona,(terminates); or Aug. (14 days):Mahon, Port Vendres, Alghero (Sardinia), Livorno, Civitavecchia, Sorrento, Taormina, Otranto, Corfu, Venice (terminates).Sep.-Oct. (11 days): Portofino, Livorno, Monte Carlo, St. Tropez, Port Vendres, Barcelona, Mahon, Portovenere; or Oct. (14 days): Sorrento, Toarmina, Valleta, through Corinth Canal, Piraeus, Navplion, Bodrum, Lesbos, Istanbul (terminates)

WORLD RENAISSANCE
(Ipirotiki) Jul.-Sep. (14 days): Valencia, Motril, Malaga, Cadiz, Lisbon, Casablanca, Tangier, Gibraltar, Ibiza, Palma, Genoa (terminates).

Palaion Faliron
NEPTUNE
(Epirotiki) Fri Jul.- Oct, (3 days): Mikonos, Bodrum, Rhodes, Heraklion, Santorini; or Mondays (4 days): Mikonos, Kusadasi, Patmos, Rhodes, Heraklion, Santorini.

Patmos
LA PALMA
(Intercruise) Tuesdays Jul.-Sep. (7 days): Rhodes, Katakolon, Venice, Corfu, through Corinth Canal, Piraeus, Kusadasi.

Piraeus
AEGEAN DOLPHIN
(Dolphin Hellas) Mon and Fri Apr.-Oct. (3-7 days): Mikonos, Rhodes, Kusadasi, Patmos, Piraeus, Istanbul, Heraklion, Santorini.

AURORA I
(Classical) Sep. (8 days): Serfos, Sifnos, Naxos, Leros Is., Patmos, Chios, Skopelos, Thasos, Istanbul (terminates); or (8 days): Itea, Yithion, San-

torini, Herahlion, Ayios, Nikolaos, Lindos, Kusadsi, Chios, Istanbul (terminates); or Nov. (7 days): Santorini, Heraklion, Ayios, Nikolaos (Crete), Kas, Antalya, Lindos, Rhodes, Kusadasi (terminates).

BERLIN
(Peter Dolmann Reederei) Nov. (11 days): Limassol, Haifa, Ashdod, Port Said, Heraklion, Catania, Genoa (terminates).

CRYSTAL HARMONY
(Crystal) Oct.-Nov. (13 days): Mikonos, Venice, Catania, Valleta, Sicily, Cannes, Naples, Livorno, Barcelona (terminates).

CROWN ODYSSEY
(Royal) Oct.-Nov. (12 days): Volos, Mytiline, Rhodes, Limasol, Ashdod, Port Said, Naples, Civitavecchia (terminates).

CUNARD PRINCESS
(Cunard Crown) Oct. (14 days): Mikonos, Kusadasi, Rhodes, Limassol, Haifa, Alexandria, Heraklion, Corfu, Venice (terminates).

ISLAND PRINCESS
(Princess) Aug. (12 days): Yalta, Odessa, Constanza, Istanbul, Izmir, Santorini, Katakolon, Venice (terminates); or Oct. (12 days): Rhodes, Alexandria, Haifa, Limassol, Corfu, Venice (terminates); or (7 days): Santorini, through Corinth Canal, Itea, Corfu, Lipari, Sorrento, Civitaveccia (terminates).

ILLIRIA
(Classical) Oct,-Nov. (9 days): Mikonos, Santorini, Patmos, Kusadasi, Bodrum, Lindos, Rhodes, Alanya, Haifa (terminates).

LA PALMA
(Intercruise) Mondays Jul.-Sep. (7 days): Kusadasi, Patmos, Rhodes, Katakolon, Venice, Corfu, through Corinth Canal.

ORPHEUS
(Swan Hellanic) Aug. (14 days): Heraklion, Santorini, Rhodes, Symi Is., Fethye, Istanbul, Canakkale, Kusadasi, Kindos, Kos, Mount Athos Pen., Volos, Thessaloniki (terminates).

PALLAS ATHENA
(Epirotiki) Fri Oct. (7 days): Port Said, Ashdod, Limassol, Rhodes, Kusadasi, Patmos.

RADISSON DIAMOND
(Diamond) Jul. (7 days): Lesvos Is., Istanbul, Kusadasi, Patmos, Rhodes, Mikonos, Katakolon, Corfu, Venice (terminates); or Sep. (7 days): Delos, Mikonos, Santorini, Rhodes, Patmos, Kusadasi, Canakkale, Istanbul (terminates).

RENAISSANCE II
(Renaissance) Jul. (7 days): Santorini, through Corinth Canal, Itea, Corfu, Lipari, Sorrento, Civitavecciaa (terminates).

RENAISSANCE V

(Renaissance) Sep. (7 days): Santorini, through Corinth Canal, Itea, Corfu, Lipari, Sorrento, Civitaveccia (terminates).

RENAISSANCE VI &VII

(Renaissance) Jul- Aug; Oct. (7 days): Santorini, Mikonos, Rhodes, Patmos, Kusadasi, Canakkale, Istanbul (terminates)

ROYAL ODYSSEY

(Royal) Jun.-Oct. (12 days): through Dardenelles, through Bosphorus, Yalta, Odessa, Constanza, Istanbul, Kusadasi, Mikonos, Patras, Venice (Venice), or Oct: Civitaveccia, Elba Is., Livorno, Villefranche, Palma, Tangier, Lisbon (terminates).

ROYAL VIKING QUEEN

(Royal) Sep. (10 days): Kusadasi, Rhodes, Santorini, through Corinth Canal, Taormina, Capri, Portoferraio (Elba), St. Tropez, Monte Carlo (terminates).

ROYAL VIKING SUN

(Royal) Oct. (12 days): Haifa, Ashdod, Port Said, Alexandria, Rhodes, Heraklion, Catania, Civitavecchia (terminates).

SEABOURN SPIRIT

(Seabourn) Jul.- Oct. (7 days): Santorini, through Corinth Canal, Katakolon, Corfu, Venice (terminates); or Aug.-Sep. (7 days): Kusadasi, Thessaloniki, through Dardanelles, Yalta, Odessa, Constanza, Istanbul (terminates).Oct,-Nov. (12 days): Through Dardanelles, Istanbul, Lesvos Is., Kusadasi, Santorini, Rhodes, Antalya, Alexandria, Port Said, Ashdod (terminates).

SEA CLOUD

(Special Expeditions) Aug,-Sep. (9 days): Santorini, Lindos, Rhodes, Antalya, Bodrum, Kusadasi (terminates).

SEA GODDESS I

(Cunard Sea Goddess) Aug,- Sep, (7 days): Paatmos, Santorini, Mikonos, through Corinth Canal, Itea, Corfu, Venice (terminates); or Sep.-Oct (7 days): Mikonos, Symi Is., Lindos, Rhodes, Bodrum, Kusadasi, Istanbul (terminates); or, Oct. (11 days): Mikonos, Monemvasia, Taormina, Valletta, Ibiza, Puerto Banus, Malaga (terminates).

SEA GODDESS II

(Cunard Sea Goddess) Jul.-Aug. (7 days): Monemvasia, Taormina, Sorrento, Porto Cervo, Portofino, Monte Carlo (terminates); or Oct. (7 days): Mikonos, Karpathos, Lindos, Rhodes, Bodrum, Kysadasi, Istanbul (terminates).

SILVER CLOUD

(Silversea) Apr. (7 days): Limassol, Alanya, Antalya, Rhodes, Bodrum,

Chios, Istanbul (terminates); or Aug-Sep. (9 days): Santorini, Lindos, Rhodes, Antalya, Bodrum, Kusadasi (terminates).
SONG OF FLOWER
(Seven Seas) Apr. (11 days): Istanbul, Varna, Odessa, Constanta, through Dardenelles, Hydra, through Corinth Canal, Corfu, Pesaro, Venice (terminates);or Oct. (7 days): Kusadasi, Delos, Mikonos, Ayios, Nikolaos (Crete), Rhodes, Lindos, Antalya, through Suez Canal, Suez (terminates).
STELLA OCEANIS
(Sun Line) Fri Jul.-Oct. (3 days): Mikonos, Rhodes, Kusadasi, Patmos; or Mondays (4 days): Hydra, Heraklion, Santorini, Rhodes, Kusadasi, Mikonos.
STELLA MARIS
(Sun Line) Fri Sep.-Oct. (7 days): Istanbul, through Bosphorus, Kusadasi, Bodrum, Rhodes, Heraklion, Santorini, Delos, Mikonos.
STELLA SOLARIS
(Sun Line) Mondays Jul.-Oct. (7 days): Dikili, Istanbul, Kusadasi, Rhodes, Santorini, Heraklion, Delos, Mikonos.
SUN VIKING
(Royal Caribbean) Oct. (12 days): Kusadasi, Rhodes, Patmos, Mikonos, Heraklion, Katakolon, Naples, Civitavecchia, Genoa (terminates).
VISTAFJORD
(Cunard/NAD) Sep.-Oct. (14 days): Lesvos Is., Kusadasi, Mikonos, Rhodes, Santorini, Valleta, Messina, Sorrento, Civitavecchia, Elba Is., Villefranche, Genoa (terminates).
ZEUS
(Tours and Yacht) Fri Sep.-Oct. (7 days): Kea (Tzia), Paros, Santorini, Ios, Naxos, Mikonos, Tinos Is.

Rhodes
NEPTUNE
(Epirotiki) Jul.-Oct. (3-4 days): Heraklion, Santorini, Palaion, Faliron, Mikonos, Kusadasi, Bodrum, Patmos.
ZEUS
(Tours and Yachts) Thur Jul.-Sep. (7 days): Symi Is., Kos, Samos Is., Kusadasi, Patmos, Kalimnos.

Savona
ODESSA
(Transocean/MarQuest) Wed Jul.-Sep. (7 days): Katakolon, Venice, Corfu, through Corinth Canal, Piraeus, Kusadasi, Patmos; or Oct. (6 days): Ajaccio, Cagliari, Palermo, Civitavecchia, Portoferraio (Elba).

Singapore
ROYAL ODYSSEY
(Royal) Mar.-Apr. (28 days): Port Kelang, Penang, Phuket, Andaman Sea, Port Blair, Bay of Bengal, Madras, Colombo, Goa, Bombay, Luxor, Suez, through Suez Canal, Port Said, Ashdod, Piraeus (terminates).

Southhampton
BLACK PRINCE
(Fred Olsen) Oct. (22 days): Lisbon, Ibiza, Valleta, Corfu, through Corinth Canal, Piraeus, Santorini, Marmaris, Rhodes, Lindos, Heraklion, Taormina, Tangier.

CANBERRA
(P & O) Oct.-Nov. (16 days): Gibraltar, Port Said, Haifa, Piraeus, Lisbon.

QUEEN ELIZABETH 2
(Cunard) Oct. (10 days): Palma, Ajaccio, Naples, Gibraltar, Lisbon.

SEA PRINCESS
(P & O) Oct.-Nov. (14 days): Mahon, Toulon, Civitavecchia, Naples, Syracuse, Tunis, Gibraltar.

Suez
SONG OF FLOWER
(Seven Seas) Apr. (8 days): through Suez Canal, Antalya, Rhodes, Ayios Nikolaos (Crete), Delos, Mikonos, Kusadasi, Piraeus (terminates).

Sydney
ROYAL ODYSSEY
(Royal) Feb.-Apr. (58 days): Brisbane, Whitsunday Is., Great Barrier Reef, Darwin, Bali, crossing Equator, Singapore, Port Kelang, Penang, Phuket, Andaman Sea, Port Blair, Bay of Bengal, Madras, Colombo, Goa, Bombay, Luxor, through Suez Canal, Port Said, Ashdod, Piraeus, Volus, Mytiline, Chios, Rhodes, Limassol, Ashdod, Port Said, Naples, Civitavecchia (terminates).

Thessaloniki
ORPHEUS
(Swan Hellanic) Jul-Aug (14 days): Samothraki, Chios, Kusadasi, Gulluk, Kalkan, Rhodes, Rethimnon, Andros, Patmos, Samos Is., Skiathos, Skirob, Lemnos, Piraeus (terminates); or Aug.-Sep. (14 days): Canakkale, Istabul, through Bosphorus, Nesebur, Varna, Odessa, Yalta, Gemlik, Piraeus, through Corinth Canal, Corfu, Venice (terminates); or Oct,-Nov, (14 days): Kavala, Canakkale, Kusadasi, Antalya, Rhodes, Ayios, Nikolaos, Delos, Navplion, Katakolon, Itea, through Corinth Canal, Piraeus.

Toulon
MERMOZ
(Paquet French)) Aug.-Sep.(13 days): Civitavecchia, Gallipoli, Bodrum, Rhodes, Mikonos, Catania, Palermo.

Valencia
SEABOURN PRIDE
(Seabourn) May (7 days): Ibiza, Collioure, Monte Carlo, Mahon, Barcelona (terminates).

Venice
AURORA I
(Classical): Jul. (9 days): Ravenna, Taormina, Sorrento, Bonifacio, Viareggio, Nice, Camargue, Barcelona (terminates).

BERLIN
(Peter Deilmann Reedere) Sep.-Oct. (12 days): Corfu, Pylos, Salamis, Epidaurus, Rafina, Dikili, Kusadasi, Heraklion, Katakolon, Argostolion; or Oct.-Nov. (11 days): Levkas Is., Itea, Katakolon, Navplion, Heraklion, Santorini, Izmir, Canakkale, Delos, Mikonos, Piraeus (terminates).

COSTA ALLEGRA
(Costa) Jul.-Nov. (10-11 days): Bari, Corfu, Piraeus, Patmos, Kos, Antalya, Limassol, Alexandria, Isola Tremiti, or Alexandria, Port Said, Ashdod, Haifa, Rhodes, Kusadasi, Kithira; or, Aug.-Oct (11 days): Bari, Katakolon, Santorini, Istanbul, Yalta, Odessa, Varina, Mikonos, Piraeus.

CUNARD PRINCESS
(Cunard Crown) Mar-Apr. (14 days): Corfu, Heraklion, Alexandria, Haifa, Limassol, Rhodes, Kusadasi, Mikonos, Piraeus (terminates); or Jul.-Aug. (11 days): Bari, Katakolon, Santorini, Istanbul, Yalta, Odessa, Varina, Mikonos, Piraeus. Nov. (14 days): Corfu, Katakolon, Valleta, Messina, Sorrento, Cagliari, Mahon, Barcelona, Palma, Alicante, Gibralter, Malaga (terminates).

CROWN ODYSSEY
(Royal) May (12 days): Katakolon, Messina, Civitavecchia, Villefranche, Malaga, Tangier, Lisbon (terminates); or Oct. (12 days): Patras, Santorini, Mikonos, Kusadasi, Istanbul, Constanza, Odessa, Yalta, through Dardenelles, Piraeus (terminates).

CRYSTAL HARMONY
(Crystal): Sep.-Oct. (13 days): Piraeus, Istanbul, Kusadasi, Rhodes, Mikonos, Heraklion, Civitavecchia.

EUGENIO COSTA
(Costa): Jul.-Sep. (7 days): Bari, Katakolon, Santorini, Mikonos, Rhodes, Heraklion.

ISLAND PRINCESS

(Princess) Aug.-Oct. (14 days): Katakolon, Santorini, Izmir, Istanbul, Constanza, Odessa, Yalta, Piraeus (terminates); or Sep. (12 days): Katakolon, Piraeus, Mikonos, Delos, Messina, Civitavecchia, Livorno, Cannes, Barcelona (terminates); or Oct.-Nov (12 days): Corfu, Katakolon, Valleta, Messina, Sorrento, Cagliari, Mahon, Barcelona, Palma, Alicante, Gibraltar, Malaga (terminates).

LA PALMA

(Intercruise) Oct. (7 days): Corfu, through Corinth Canal, Piraeus, Kusadasi, Patmos, Rhodes, Katakolon.

ORPHEUS

(Swan Hellanic) Sep. (14 days): Trieste, Ravenna, Bari, Brindisi, Syracuse, Catania, Porto Empedocle, Trapani, Salerno, Civitavecchia, Livorno, Elba Is., Nice (terminates).

PACIFIC PRINCESS

(Princess) Oct. (12 days): Katakolon, Piraeus, Mikonos, Delos, Messina, Civitavecchia, Livorno, Cannes, Barcelona (terminates).'

ROYAL ODYSSEY

(Royal) May-Jul. (12 days): Katakolon, Herakalon, Santorini, Mikonos, Piraeus, Navplion, Naples, Capri, Portofino, Vallefranche, Genoa (terminates); or Jul.-Aug. (12 days): Patros, Santorini, Mikomos, Kusadasi, Istanbul, Constanza, Odessa, Yalta, Piraeus (terminates); or Sep. (12 days): Katakolon, Heraklion, Santorini, Mikonos, Piraeus, Navplion, Naples, Capri, Portofino, Villefranche, Genoa (terminates); or Oct. (12 days): Katakolon, Messina, Civitavecchia, Villefranchia, Malaga, Tangier, Lisbon (terminates).

ROYAL VIKING QUEEN

(Royal Viking) Oct. (10 days): Corfu, through Corinth Canal, Navplion, Santorini, Heraklion, Rhodes, Kos, Bodrum, Kusadasi, Piraeus (ter minates)

SEABOURN SPIRIT

(Seabourn) Apr.-May; Sep. (14 days): Taormina, Sorrento, Porto Cervo, Civitavecchia, Livorno, Portofino, St. Tropez, Monte Carlo, Nice (terminates); or Aug.-Sep. (14 days): Corfu, through Corinth Canal, Navplion, Santorini, Piraeus, Kusadasi, through Dardenelles, Yalta, Odessa, Constanza, Istanbul (terminates).

SEA GODDESS I

(Cunard Sea Goddess) Jul.;Sep (11 days): Zakinthos Is. (Zante), Itea, through Corinth Canal, Mikonos, Monemvasia, Taormina, Capri, Porto Cervo, Portofino, Monte Carlo (terminates); or Aug. (10 days): after Mikonos, Santorini, Lindos, Rhodes, Bodrum, Kusadasi, Istanbul (terminates); or (7 days): Corfu, Taormina, Sorrento, Portoferraio (Elba), Portofino, Monte Carlo (terminates),

SEA GODDESS II

(Cunard Sea Goddess) Jul.-Sep.(7 days); Zakinthos Is., Itea, through Corinth Canal, Mikonos, Karpathos, Kusadasi, Piraeus,

SILVER CLOUD

(Silverseas) May (7 days): Vieste, Zakinthos Is., Yithion, Heraklion, Rhodes, Santorini, Piraeus (terminates).

SONG OF FLOWER

(Seven Seas) May (7 days): Corfu, Galaxidion, through Corinth Canal, Delos, Mikonos, Kusadasi, Santorini, Piraeus (terminates); or Sep.-Oct. (11 days): Manfredonia, Corfu, through Corinth Canal, Hydra, through Dardenelles, through Bosporus, Varina, Odessa, Constanza, Istanbul, Piraeus (terminates).

SONG OF NORWAY

(Royal Caribbean) Oct.-Nov. (12 days): Corfu, Messina, Naples, Civitavecchia, Livorno, Villefranche, Palma, Barcelona (terminates).

STELLA MARIS

(Sun) Sat Jul-Aug. (7 days): Isola Tremiti, Corfu, Valletta, Messina, Capri, Elba Is., Portofino, Nice (terminates).

TROPIC SUN

(Aquanaut) Jun.- Aug. (6 days): Mali Losinj, Rab, Cres, Opatija, Pula, Rovinj.

Vienna

VOLGA / AJVASOVSKIJ

(DDSG- Donaureissen) Jul.-Sep. (16 days): Budapest, Belgrade, Turnu, Severin, Giurgiu, Olenita, Izmail, Istanbul, Yalta, Izmail, Ruse, Nikopol, Baikal Turnu Severin, Orsova, Budapest.

NORTHERN EUROPE

Baltic

Amsterdam

AURORA

(Classical) Aug,- Sep. (11 days): Ziebrugge, Rouen, St. Malo, St. Paul de Leon, Nantes, Pauillac, Muros, Aveiro, Lisbon (terminates).

STATENDAM

(Holland America) Jul.-Aug. (13 days): Oslo, Stockholm, Helsinki, St. Petersburg, Warnemuende, Copenhagen, London (terminates).

Bremerhaven

ODESSA

(Transocean/Marquest) Aug. (12 days): Kalmar, Stockholm, Tallinn, St.

Petersburg, Helsinki, Riga, Visby, Gdynia, Copenhagen, Kiel (terminates).

Copenhagen
AURORA II
(Classical) Jul. Aug. (8 days): Gdansk, Klaipeda, Riga, Stockholm, Tallinn, Helsinki, St. Petersburg, (terminates).

CROWN ODYSSEY
(Royal) Aug.-Sep. (12 days): Oslo, Stockholm, Helsinki, St. Petersburg, Warnemuende, through Kiel Canal, London (terminates).

CRYSTAL HARMONY
(Crystal) Jul.-Aug. (13 days): Stockholm, Tallinn, St. Petersburg, Warnemuende, Oslo, Amsterdam, London (terminates).

KRISTINA REGINA
(Kristina) Aug. (10 days): Luebeck, Rostock, Gdansk, Kaliningrad, Riga, Tallinn, St. Petersburg, Helsinki (terminates).

RENAISSANCE V
(Renaissance) Jul. (14 days): Luebeck, Ronne, Gdynia, Visby, Tallinn, St. Petersburg, Helsinki, Mariehamn, Stockholm (terminates).

ROYAL VIKING SUN
(Royal Viking) Aug. (12 days): Stockholm, St. Petersburg, Helsinki, Visby, Gdynia, Oslo, London (terminates).

SEABOURN PRIDE
(Seabourn) Jul. (14 days); Helsinki, St. Petersburg, Tallinn, Stockholm, Ronne, Luebeck, through Kiel Canal, Amsterdam, Zeebrugge, London (terminates),

Copenhagen-Stockholm
RENAISSANCE IV
(Renaissance) Sat Jul.-Sep. (7 days): Ronne, Visby, Tallinn, St. Petersburg, Helsinki.

Hamburg
ROYAL VIKING SUN
(Royal Viking) Jul. (12 days): Through Kiel Canal, Ronne, Bornholm, Gdynia, Riga, St. Petersburg, Helsinki, Stockholm, Copenhagen (terminates).

VISTAFJORD
(Cunard/NAC) Aug.-Sep. (13 days): Gdynia, Stockholm, Helsinki, St. Petersburg, Tallinn, Copenhagen, Oslo.

Harwich
SONG OF NORWAY
(Royal Caribbean) Jul. -Sep. (12 days): through Kiel Canal, Ronne, Born-

holm, Gdynia, Riga, St. Petersburg, Helsinki, Stockholm, Copenhagen (terminates).

Helsinki
KRISTINA REGINA
(Kristina) Jul. (3 days): Visby, Riga; or Aug. (10 days): St. Petersburg, Tallinn, Riga, Klaipeda, Kaliningrad, Gdansk, Sassnitz, Rostock, Copenhagen (terminates).

Kiel
EUROPA
(Hapag-Lloyd Kreutzfahrten) Aug. -Sep. (14 days): Riga, St Petersburg, Helsinki, Tallinn, Stockholm, Bremerhaven, Aarhus.

LEV TOLSTOY
(Transocean/MarQuest) Jul. (10): Klaipeda, Riga, Tallinn, St. Petersburg, Helsinki, Stockholm, Bremerhaven; or Aug. (12 days): Gdynia, Kaliningrad, Klaipeda, Riga, Tallinn, St. Petersburg, Helsinki, Stockholm; or Aug. -Sep. (3 days): Kalmar, Copenhagen.

VISTAFJORD
(Cunard/NAC) Jul. (13 days): Bornholm, Gdynia, Helsinki, St. Petersburg. Tallinn, Stockholm, Copenhagen, Kerteminde.

London
CROWN ODYSSEY
(Royal) Jun, Aug, (12 days): through Kiel Canal, Warnemuende, St. Petersburg, Helsinki, Stockholm, Copenhagen, Oslo.

KARELIA
(CTC) Jul. (14 days): Amsterdam, Oslo, Copenhagen, Copenhagen, Tallinn, St. Petersburg, Helsinki, Visby.

ROYAL VIKING QUEEN
(Royal Viking) Jul.-Aug. (13 days): Thames River, Oslo, Stockholm, Tallinn, St. Petersburg, Riga, Szczecin, through Kiel Canal, Amsterdam (terminates).

SEABOURN PRIDE
(Seabourn) Jul. -Aug, (14 days): Amsterdam, through Kiel Canal, Luebeck, Stockholm, Tallinn, St. Petersburg, Heksinki, Copenhagen (terminates).

SONG OF FLOWER
(Seven Seas) Jul. -Aug. (11 days): Amsterdam, through Kiel Canal, Copenhagen, Gdynia, Visby, Riga, Tallinn, St. Petersburg, Helsinki, Stockholm (terminates).

STATENDAM
(Holland America) Jul.-Aug, (13 days): Oslo, Stockholm, Helsinki, St. Petersburg, Warnemuende, Copenhagen, Amsterdam (terminates).

Nynashamn
ANNA KARENNIA
(Baltic Express) year round (1-4 days): St Petersburg; or Kiel

St. Petersburg
AURORA II
(Classical) Jul.-Aug. (8 days): Helsinki, Tallinn, Stockholm, Riga, Klaipeda, Gdansk, Copenhagen (terminates).

Southampton
ROYAL PRINCESS
(Princess) Jul. Aug. (13 days): Hamburg, Stockholm, Helsinki, St. Petersburg, Copenhagen, Amsterdam, Le Havre.

SEA PRINCESS
(P & O) Aug. (14 days): Hamburg, through Kiel Canal, Stockholm, St. Petersburg, Helsinki, Visby, Gdynia, Copenhagen, Kristiansand.

Stockholm
AURORA I
(Classical) Jul.-Aug. (7 days): Visby, Riga, Tallinn, Helsinki, St Petersburg (terminates).

RENAISSANCE V
(Renaissance) Jul.-Aug. (14 days): Mariehamn, Helsinki, St. Petersburg, Tallinn, Visby, Gdynia, Ronne, Luebeck, Copenhagen (terminates).

SONG OF FLOWER
(Seven Seas) Jul.-Aug. (11 days): Helsinki, St. Petersburg, Tallinn, Riga, Visby, Gdynia, Copenhagen, through Kiel Canal, Amsterdam, London (terminates).

Travemuende
BERLIN
(Peter Deilmann Reederei) Jul. (10 days): Riga, Tallinn, St. Petersburg, Helsinki, Klaipeda, Gdynia, Kaliningrad, Sassnitz; or (11 days): Sassnitz, Kalmar, Stockholm, Helsinki, St. Petersburg, Riga, Klaipeda, Kaliningrad, Warnemuende; or Aug. (11-12 Days): Stockholm, Helsinki, St. Petersburg, Tallinn, Riga, Kaliningrad, Gdynia, Copenhagen.

British Isles & Ireland

Aberdeen- Greenock
AURORA
(Classical) May- Jun. (5 days): Lerwich, Kirkwall (Orkney Is.), Isles of Skye/Lewis, Isle of Mull, Iona.

Copenhagen
ROYAL VIKING QUEEN
(Royal Viking) Jul. (13 days): Edinburgh, Invergordon, Kirkwall (Orkney Is.): Stornoway, Galway, Cork, Waterford, Dublin, Plymouth, Thames River, London (terminates).

Hamburg
VISTAFJORD
(Cunard/NAC) Aug. (14 days): London, Invergordon, Lerwick, Shetland Is., Portree, Donegal, Galway, Cobh, Dublin, Waterford, Falmouth, Dover.

Harwich
SUN VIKING
(Royal Caribbean) Aug. (12 days): Le Havre, Plymouth, Cork, Dublin, Liverpool, Glasgow, Inverness, Leith, Amsterdam.

Kiel
ODESSA
(Transocean/Marquest) Aug.-Sep. (12 days): Bergen, Leith, Invergordon, Kirkwall (Orkney Is.), Stornoway, Oban, Dublin, Waterford, Portsmouth, Bremerhaven (terminates).

Lisbon
CROWN ODYSSEY
(Royal) Sep.-Oct. (12 days): Pauillac (Bordeaux), Le Havre, Southampton, Waterford, Dublin, Glasgow, Holyhead, London (terminates).

Liverpool
AZERBAYDZHAN
(CTC) Oct, (2 days): Cobh, Southampton (terminates).

London
AZERBAYDZHAN
(CTC) Sep. (4 days): Le Havre, St. Peter Port, Cobh, Liverpool (terminates).

CROWN ODYSSEY
(Royal) Sep.-Oct. (12-13 days): Holyhead, Greenock, Glasgow, Dublin Waterford, Southampton, Le Havre, Pauillac (Bordeaux), Lisbon (terminates).

Oban
HEBRIDEAN PRINCESS
(Hebridean Island) Jul.-Nov. (7 days): Sound of Kerrera, Castlebay, Isle of Barra, St. Kilda Is., Stornoway, Inverewe, Torridon, Plockton, Kyle of Lochalsh, Sound of Mull; or through Firth of Lorne, Eigg Is., Canna Is., Isle of Skye, Muck, Iona, Colonsay, Islay, through Firth of Lorne; or

Crinan, Gigha, Staffa, Dunvegan, Torridon, Tobermory, Salen, Sound of
Sleat, Kyle of Lochalsh, Inverewe.

Reykjavik
COLUMBUS CARAVELLE

(Transocean/MarQuest) Jul. (10 days): Thorlakshofn, Heimaey, Hofn,
Torshavn, Lerwick, Shetland Is., Kirkwall (Orkney Is.), Stornoway, Invergordon, London (terminates).

Greenland & Iceland

London
COLUMBUS CARAVELLE

(Transocean/ MarQuest) Jul.-Aug. (10 days): Invergordon, Stornoway,
Kirkwall (Orkney Is.), Lerwick, Shetland Is., Vestmanna, Hofn, Heimaey,
Thorlakshofn, Reykjavik (terminates).

Reykjavik
COLUMBUS CARAVELLE

(Transocean/MarQuest) Aug.-Sep. (11 days): Thorlakshofn, Heimaey,
Julianehab, Godthab, Jakobshaven, Sondre, Stromfjord (terminates).

Sondre Stromfjord
COLUMBUS CARAVELLE

(Transocean/MarQuest) Aug. (11 days): Jakobshaven, Godthab, Julianehab, Heimaey, Thorlanshofn, Reykjavik (terminates).

North Sea & English Channel

Amsterdam
ROYAL VIKING QUEEN

(Royal Viking) Aug, (13 days): Edinburgh, Invergordon, Kirkwall (Orkney Is.), Stornoway, Galway, Cork, Waterford, Dublin, Plymouth, Thames
River, London (terminates).

Bordeaux
SEABOURN PRIDE

(Seabourn) May-Jun. (10 days): La Pallice, Nantes, St. Malo, Rouen,
London (terminates).

Copenhagen
RENAISSANCE IV & V

(Renaissance) Aug.-Oct. (14 days): through Kiel Canal, Amsterdam, Zeebrugge, Guernsey, through Strait of Belle Isle, Bordeaux, La Coruna,
Oporto, Lisbon, Motril, Alicante, Barcelona (terminates).

SEABOURN PRIDE

(Seabourne) Jun, Jul. (14 days): Helsinki, St. Petersburg, Tallinn, Stockholm, Ronne, Luebeck, through Kiel Canal, Amsterdam, London (terminates).

Harwich
SUN VIKING
(Royal Caribbean) Jul. -Sep. (12 days): Leith, Oslo, Copenhagen, Warnemuende, through Kiel Canal, Amsterdam, Zeebrugge, Le Havre.

Keil
EUROPA
(Hapag-Lloyd Kreutzfahrten) Sep. (4 days): Copenhagen, Kristiansand, Bremerhaven (terminates).

London
CROWN ODYSSEY
(Royal) Jun. (12 days): Le Havre, Southampton, Dublin, Kirkwall (Orkney Is.), Edinburgh, Amsterdam, Zeebrugge.
ROYAL VIKING QUEEN
(Royal Viking) Aug, (13 days): Thames River, Paris, Seine River, St. Malo, Oporto, Lisbon, Seville, through Strait of Gibraltar, Valencia (terminates).
SEABOURN PRIDE
(Seabourn) Jun. (14 days): Caen, Cherbourg, Jersey, St. Malo, Oporto, Lisbon, Seville, through Strait of Gibraltar, Valencia (terminates).
SONG OF FLOWER
(Seven Seas) Jul. (12 days): Edinburgh, Inverness, Lerwick, Shetland Is., Olden, Trondheim, Kristiansund, Molde, Geiranger, Bergen, Amsterdam.

Nassau
ODESSA
(Transocean/MarQuest) Apr. (20 days): Baltimore, Chesapeake & Delaware Canal, Philadelphia, New York (terminates).

Southhampton
QUEEN ELIZABETH 2
(Cunard) Oct. (3 days): Cherbourg, Brest.
ROYAL PRINCESS
(Princess) Aug.-Sep. (13 days): Le Havre, Zeebrugge, Dublin, Glasgow, Reykjavik, New York, Horta, Ponta Delgaga, LaCoruna, Portsmouth, Bremershaven (terminates).

Norway & Arctic Region

Amsterdam
DAPHNE
(Costa) Jul. (14 days): Bergen, Gravdal (Lofoten Is.), Ny Alesund, Longyearbyen, Honningvag, Tromso, Alesund; or (9 days): London, Ler-

wick, Shetland Is., Alesund, Olden, Sundane, Flam, Vik; or Aug. (12 days): London, Bergen, Andalsnes, Hammerfest, Honningsvag, Geranger, Flam, Vik.

ENRICO COSTA

(Costa) Jul.-Aug. (7 days): Nordfjordeid, Olden, Vik, Flam, Bergen, London.

Bergen

KONG HAROLD/HAROLD JARL/RAGENVALD JARL/LOFOTEN/NARVIK/NORDLYS/ RICHARD WIRTH/NORD NORGE/MIDNASTSOL/KONGO-LAV/VESTERAALENT/NORDVIK

(Bergen) year round Jul.-Dec. (6 days): Floro, Maloy, Torvik, Alesund, Molde, Kristiansund, Trondheim, Rorvik, Bronnoysund, Sandnessjoen, Nesna, Ornes, Bodo, Stamsund, Svolvaer, Stokmarknes, Sortland, Risoyhamn, Harstad, Finnsnes, Tromso, Skjervoy, Oksfjord, Hammerfest, Havoysund, Honningsvag, Kjollefjord, Mehamn, Berlevag, Batsfjord, Vardo, Vadso, Kirknes.

Bodo

POLARIS

(Special Expeditions) Aug. (9 days): Lofoten Is., Tromso, Fugloya, Bjorn Oya (Bear Is.), Spitsbergen, Longyearbyen (terminates).

Bremerhaven

EUROPA

(Hapag-Lloyd Kreutzfahrten) Jul. Aug. (20 days); Kirkwall (Orkney Is.), Reykjavik, Heimaey, Spitsbergen, Honningsvag, Tromso, Hellesylt, Geiranger, Bergen, Lysefjord; or Aug. (15 days): Romsdalsfjord, Kolde, Trondheim, Trinithaven, Mollerhaven, Tromso, Gravdal (Lofoten Is.), Flam, Gudvangen, Bergen, Hamburg (terminates).

LEV TOLSTOY

(Transocean/MarQuest) Aug. (7 days): Ulvik, Eidfjord, Fjaerland, Balestrand, Stryn, Olden, Bergen, Kiel (terminates); or Sep. (6 days): Ulvik, Eidsfjord, Bergen, Sand, Sauda.

ODESSA

(Transocean/MarQuest) Jul.-Aug. (18 days): Kirkwall (Orkney Is.), Reyjavik, Heimaey, Spitsbergen, Honningsvag, Tromso, Hellesylt, Geiranger, Bergen, Lysefjord or Aug. (11 days): Molde, Andalsnes, Svartisen, Gravdal (Lofoten Is.), Honningsvag, Tromso, Hellesylt, Geiranger, Bergen.

Copenhagen

ROYAL VIKING SUN

(Royal Viking) Aug. (12 days): Hellesylt, Geiranger, Trondheim, Honningsvag, crossing Arctic Circle, Molde, Flam, Gudvangen, Bergen, London (teminates).

SEABOURN PRIDE

(Seabourn) Jul.-Aug. (14 days): Oslo, Flam, Gudvangen, Kristiansund, Tromso, Bodo, Hellesylt, Geiranger, Bognes, Stavanger, London (terminates).

Harwich

SUN VIKING

(Royal Caribbean) Jul.-Aug. (12 days): Flam, Gudvangen, Honningsvag, Tromso, Hellesylt, Geiranger, Bergen, Stavanger, Kristiansund.

Kiel

VISTAFJORD

(Cunard/Nac) Aug. (15 days): Stavanger, Molde, Andalsnes, Magdalena Bay, Longyearbyen, North Cape, Hammerfest, Trondheim, Hellesylt, Geirangen, Bergen, Hamburg (terminates).

London

BLACK PRINCE

(Fred Olsen) Jul. (17 days): Bergen, Gravdal (Lofoten Is.), Murmansk, Honningsvag, Alta, Alesund, Bergen, Jondal; or Jul.-Aug. (14 days); Stavanger, Bergen, Hellesylt, Geiranger, Fjaerland, Balestrand, Bergen.

CROWN ODYSSEY

(Royal) Jun.-Jul. (12-13 days): Flam, Gudvangen, Molde, crossing Arctic Circle, Lofoten Is., Honningsvag, North Cape, Trondheim, Hellesylt, Geiranger, Bergen.

CRYSTAL HARMONY

(Crystal) Jul. (14 days): Bergen, Flam, Gudvangen, Hellesylt, Geirangen, Trondheim, Svartisen Glacier, Murmansk, Honningsvag, North Cape, Tromso, Oslo, Copenhagen (terminates).

ROYAL VIKING SUN

(Royal Viking) Aug. (12 days): Bergen, Flam, Gudvangen, Molde, crossing Arctic Circle, Honningvag, Trondheim, Hellesylt, Geiranger, Copenhagen (terminates).

SEABOURN PRIDE

(Seabourn) Jul.-Aug. (14 days): Stavanger, Bergen, Hellesylt, Geiranger Fjord, crossing Arctic Circle, Svolvaer, Tromso, Kristiansund, Flam, Gudvangen, through Skagerrak, Oslo, Copenhagen (terminates).

Longyearbyen

POLARIS

(Special Expeditions) Jul. (9 days): Spitzbergen, Bjorn Oya (Bear Is.), Fugloya, Tromso, Lofoten Is., Bodo (terminates); or Aug. (13 days): add Rost, Geiranger Fjord, Sognefjord, Bergen (terminates).

Southampton
CANBERRA
(P & O) May- Aug. (13-22 days): Hardangerfjord, Angalsnes, Narvin, Spitzbergen Fjords, Trondheim, Hellesylt, Geiranger, Bergen.
QUEEN ELIZABETH 2
(Cunard) Jul. (9 days): Bergen, Hammerfest, North Cape, Hellesylt, Geranger, Stavanger.
ROYAL PRINCESS
(Princess) Jul. (13 days): Oslo, Hellesylt, Gudvangen Bergen.
SEA PRINCESS
(P&O) Jul. (14 days): Eidfjord, Olden, Alesund, Trondheim, Honningsvag, North Cape, Tromso, Flam, Gudvangen, Bergen.

Tromso
SEABOURN PRIDE
(Seabourne) Jul.-Aug. (7 days): Kristiansund, Flam, Gudvangen, through Skagerrak, Oslo, Copenhagen (terminates).

Scandinavia

Amsterdam
DAPHNE
(Costa) Aug.-Sep. (12 days): London, Copenhagen, St. Petersburg, Helsinki, Stockholm, Kiel; or (14 days): add Oslo, Tallinn, Cuxhaven.

Copenhagen
CROWN ODYSSEY
(Royal) Aug.-Sep. (13 days): Oslo, Stockholm, Helsinki, St. Petersburg, Warnrmuende, through Kiel Canal, Amsterdam, London (terminates).

Hamburg
EUROPA
(Hapag-Lloyd Kreutzfahrten) Aug.-Sep. (21 days): Olden, Molde, Andalsnes, Hellesylt, Geiranger, Bergen, Kiel, Riga, St. Petersburg, Helsinki, Tallinn, Stockholm, Goynia, Bornholm, Copenhagen, Aarhus, Kiel (terminates).

London
BLACK PRINCE
(Fred Olsen) Aug. (12 days): Bergen, Molde, Olden, Jondal, Oslo, Copenhagen, Holtenau, Brunsbuettel, Hamburg, Southampton (terminates),
CROWN ODYSSEY
(Royal) Aug. (13 days): Amsterdam, through Kiel Canal, Warnemuende, St, Petersburg, Helsinki, Stockholm, Oslo, Copenhagen (terminates).

Travemuende
BERLIN
(Peter Deilmann Reederei) Aug.-Sep. (10 days): Copenhagen, Nyborg, Aalborg, Gothenburg, Oslo, Jondal, Lerwick, Shetland Is., Edinburgh (terminates). Bratislava.

SOUTH PACIFIC, HAWAII & AUSTRALIA

Alotau-Madang
MELANESIAN DISCOVERER
(Melanesian Tourist Service) Year round (7 days): Kitava Is., Kiriwini, Kaileuna Is., D'Entrecasteaux Is., Esa'Ala, Solomon Sea, Kaibola, Finschafen, Siassi Is., Umboi Is.

Ambunti-Madang
MELANESIAN DISCOVERER
(Melanesian Tourist Service) Year round (5 days):Sepik River, Korogo, Kanganaman Village, Timbunke, Angoram, Manam or Bosa Is.

Auckland-Sydney
ISLAND PRINCESS
(Princess) Dec.-Feb. (14 days): Bay of Islands, Tauranga, Wellington, Christchurch, Dunedin, Milford Sound, Hobart, Melbourne.

Auckland
CRYSTAL HARMONY
(Crystal) Mar. (12 days): Wellington, Picton, Milford Sound, Hobart, Melbourne, Sydney (terminates)

MARCO POLO
(Orient) Feb.-Mar. (14 days) Nuku'Alofa, Suva, Yasawa-I-Rara, Port Vila, Noumea, Bay of Islands; or Mar.-Apr. (7 days): Tauranga, Napier, Picton, Milford Sound, Dunedin, Christchurch (terminates).

ROYAL ODYSSEY
(Royal) Feb.-Mar. (28 days): Wellington, Christchurch, Dunedin, Milford Sound, Hobart, Melbourne, Sydney, Brisbane, Whitsunday Is., Great Barrier Reef, Darwin, Bali, crossing Equator, Singapore (terminates).

Bali
CLUB MED 2
(Club Med) Apr.-May (7 days): Probolinggo, Bawean, Semerang, Lumbo, Banga Is., Singapore (terminates).

EXPLORER
(Abercrombie & Kent) Jun.-Jul. (17 days): Obi Is., Manodo, Sulawesi, Towale, Torajaland, Ujang Pandang, Sandakan, Kota Kinabalu, Brunei Dar es Salam, Sarawak, Bako Nat. Park, Kuching.

FRONTIER SPIRIT
(SeaQuest) Jul. (14 days): Lembar, Lombok Is., Komodo Is., Bone Rate, Tukanbesi, Banda Is., Agats, Merauke, Thursday Is., Port Moresby (terminates).

SEA GODDESS II
(Cunard Sea Goddess) Dec. (14 days): Komodo Is., Larantuka (Flores), Darwin, Thursday Is., Cape York, Lizard, Cooktown, Whitsunday Is., Orpheus Is., Cairns (terminates)

Bali-Cairns

SEABOURN SPIRIT
(Seabourn) Jan. Feb. (14 days): Komodo Is.,Waingapu, Seba, Darwin, Bathurst Is., Thursday Is., Lizard Is., Cooktown, Port Douglas.

Buenos Aires

ROYAL VIKING SUN
(Royal Viking) Jan.-Mar (28 days): Punta Arenas, Puerto Montt, Easter Is., Pitcairn, Papette, Bora Bora, Rarotonga, crossing Int. Date Line, Bay of Islands, Auckland, Christchurch, Dunedin, Hobart, Sydney (terminates).

Cairns

REEF ESCAPE
(Captain Cook) Jul-Dec. Wed (4 days): Hinchinbrook Is., Dunk Is,.Great Barrier Reef; or (7 days): Sat add Cooktown, Lizard Is.

CUNARD CROWN MONARCH
(Cunard Crown) Year round (10 days): Samurai, Townsville, Cid Harbour, Whitsunday Pass, Great Barrier Reef, Whitsunday Is., Sydney (terminates); or Jun.(14 days): Vila Honaria Rabul, Madang,Samarai.

MARCO POLO
(Orient) Apr.-May (15 days): Great Barrier Reef, Thursday Is. Arafura Sea, Darwin, Larantuka (Flores), Komodo Is., Bali, Semerang, Singapore (terminates).

SEA GODDESS II
(Cunard Sea Goddess) Dec.-Jan. (14 days): Lizard Is., Rabaul, Trobriand Is., Deboyne Lagoon, Port Douglas, Townsville Whitsunday Is.; or Whitsunday Is., Townsville, Port Douglass, Lizard Is., Darwin, Larantuka (Flores), Komodo Is.,Bali (terminates).

Christchurch

MARCO POLO
(Orient) Feb.-Apr. (7 days): Dunedin, Milford Sound, Picton, Napier, Tauranga, Auckland (terminates); or Apr. (14 days): Picton, Napier, Tauranga, Auckland, Bay of Islands, Noumea, Cairns (terminates).

Caldera
EUROPA
(Hapag-Lloyd Kreutzfahrten) Jan.-Feb. (31 days): Puerto Quetzal, Acapulco, Puerto Vallarta, Nuku Hiva Is., Fakarava Atol, Papeete, Niue Is., Neiafu, Niku'Alofa, Suva, Port Vila, Noumea (terminates).

Darwin
CUNARD CROWN MONARCH
(Cunard Crown) Apr.-May (14 days): Samarai, Cairns, Townsville, Cid Harbour, Whitsunday Pass, Great Barrier Reef, Whitsunday Is., Brisbane, Sydney (terminates).
EXPLORER
(Abercrombie & Kent) Aug. (17 days): Arnhem Land, Wessel Is., Gove Pen., Port Moresby, Louisiade Arch., Trobriand Is., Wide Bay, Brisbane, Rabaul. Treasury Is., Lumbaria/Kennedy Is., Rennel Is., Santa Ana Is., Palmerston, Cook Is., Aitutaki East New Britain Is.

Easter Island
EXPLORER
(Abercrombie & Kent) Mar.; Oct. (13 days): Ducie Is., Henderson Is., Pitcairn Is., Mangreva, Marotiri, Rapa, Raivaevae, Papeete, Sala y Gomez Is., Alejandro Selkirk Is., Robinson Crusoe Is., Valparaiso..

Guam
CLUB MED 2
(Club Med) Sep.-Oct. (8 days): Ulithi, Palau, Ngulu; or Oct. (3 days): Saipan, Tinian.

Hong Kong
ROTTERDAM
(Holland America) Oct.-Nov. (31 days): Singapore, crossing Equator, Bali, Darwin, Port Vila, Suva, Vava'U, crossing Intl. Date Line, Pago Pago, Christmas Is., Honolulu, Los Angeles (terminates).
ROYAL ODYSSEY
(Royal) Jan. (28 days): Canton, Danang, Kota Kinabalu, Brunei, Kuantan, Singapore, crossing Equator, Bali, Darwin, Great Barrier Reef, Whitsunday Is., Brisbane, Sydney (terminates).

Honiara
FRONTIER SPIRIT
(Seaquest) Jul.-Aug. (10 days): Woodlark Is., Kiriwina Is., Tufi, Esa'Ala (Normanby Is.), Samaria, Port Moresby (terminates).

Honolulu
CONSTITUTION
(American Hawaii) Sat Jul.-Dec. (7 days): Nawliwili (Kauai), Kahului (Maui), Kona.
CROWN ODYSSEY
(Royal) Jan. (16 days): Lahaina (Maui), Nawiliwili (Kauai), Ensenada (terminates).
FAIR PRINCESS
(Princess) Oct.-Nov. (11 days): Kauai, Lahaina, Hilo, Christmas Is., Bora Bora, Moorea Is., Papeete (terminates).
GOLDEN PRINCESS
(Princess) Apr. (11 days): Canton, Da Nang, Kota, Kinabalu, Brunei, Kuantan, Singapore, crossing Equator, Bali, Darwin, Great Barrier Reef, Whitsunday Is., Brisbane, Sydney (terminates).
INDEPENDENCE
(American Hawaii) Sat Jul.-Dec. (7 days): Hilo, Kona, Nawilwili (Kauai), Kahului (Maui).

Lautoka (Fiji)
BLUE LAGOON
(Cruises) Jul.-Dec. (3 days) Every day, Yasawa Is., Nabukeru Bay & Village, Sawa-I-Lau Lagoon, Nanuya Lai Lai; or,Mondays and Thur, Yasawa Is., Yasawa-I-Rara, Nabukeru Bay & Village,

Liverpool
AZERBAYDZHAN
(CTC) Oct.-Dec. (51 days): Cobh, Southampton, Las Palmas, Dakar, St. Helena Is.,Cape Town, Port Louis (Mauritius), Colombo, Singapore, Freemantle, Melbourne, Sydney (terminates).

Los Angeles
CROWN ODYSSEY
(Royal) Jan. (16 days): Ensenada, Kahului (Maui), Lahaina (Maui), Hilo, Honolulu, Nawiliwili (Kauai).
CRYSTAL HARMONY
(Crystal) Feb.-Mar. (21 days): Ensenada, Honolulu, Lahaina, Bora Bora, Rarotonga, crossing Intl. Date line, Bay of Islands, Auckland (terminates)
CUNARD CROWN MONARCH
(Cunard Crown) Oct.-Nov. (28 days): Ensenada, Kona, Honolulu, Tarawa, Suva, Vila, Nomea, Sydney (terminates).
QUEEN ELIZABETH 2
(Cunard) Jan.-Feb. (22 Days): Ensenada, Lahaina, Honolulu, Suva, Aukland, Milford Sound, Melbourne, Sydney (terminates).

PACIFIC PRINCESS
(Princess) Nov.-Dec. (14 days): Honolulu, Lahaina, Christmas Is., Bora Bora, Papeete (terminates).

STATENDAM
(Holland America) Jan.-Feb. (21 days): Kona, Honolulu, Christmas Is., crossing Equator, Pago Pago, crossing Intl. Date Line, Suva, Port Vila, Cairns (terminates)

VISTAFJORD
(Cunard/Nac) Jan.-Mar. (30 days): Lahaina, Kona, Pago Pago, Rarotonga, Papeete, Moorea Is., Bora Bora, Honolulu, Hilo.

Mackay

ROYLEN ENDEAVOR
(Roylen) Mondays Oct.-Mar. (4 days): Brampton Is., Hamilton Is., Great Barrier Reef, Whitsunday Is.

Madang

MELANESIAN DISCOVERER
(Melanesian Tourist Service) Jul.-Oct. (5 days): Manam or Boisa Is., Sepic River, Angoram, Timbunke, Kanganaman Village, Korogo, Ambunti (terminates); or Siassi Is., Umboi Is., Finchhafen, Solomon Sea, Tufi, Kirwan Is., Kitava Is., Alotau (terminates).

Noumea

EUROPA
(Hapag-Lloyd Kreutzfahrten) Feb.-Mar. (20 days): Bay of Islands, Kawau, Auckland, Wellington, Lytelton, Port Chalmers, Milford Sound, Hobart, Sydney (terminates).

CLUB MED 2
(Club Med) Dec.-Feb. 4 days): Isle of Pines, Hienghene; or Ouvea, Port Vila; or Feb. (7 days): Espiritu, Pentecost, Port Vila, Aneityum, Isle of Pines.

Nuku'Alofa

ODESSA
(Transocean/MarQuest) Feb.-Mar. (20 days): Suva, Savasavu, Apia, Pago Pago, Christmas Is., Hilo, Kahului, Long Beach, Ensenada (terminates)

Papeete

EXPLORER
(Abercrombie & Kent) Apr.-May; Sep.-Oct. (12-17 days) Rangiroa, Takaroa, Nuku Hiva (Marquessas), Ua Pou/Ua huka, Hiva Oa, Fatu Hiva, Fakarava, Moorea, Raiatea, Bora Bora, Penrhyn Is., Manihiki Is., Rakahanga, Pukapuka,

EUROPA

(Hapag-Lloyd Kreutzfahrten) Jan.-Feb. (12 days): Niue Is., Neiafu, Niku'Alofa, Suva, Port Vila, Noumea (terminates).

FAIR PRINCESS

(Princess) Oct.-Nov. (11 days): Moorea Is., Bora Bora, Christmas Is., Hilo, Lahaina (Maui), Kauai, Honolulu (terminates).

FRONTIER SPIRIT

(SeaQuest) Jul. ((10 days): Sanarai, Esa'Ala (Normanby Is.), Kiriwina Is., Woodlark Is., Honiara (terminates); or Aug. (14 days): Thursday Is., Merauke, Agats, Banda Is., Bone Rate, Komodo Is., Lembar, Lombok Is., Bali (terminates).

ISLAND PRINCESS

(Princess) Feb.-Mar. (14 days): Moorea Is., Bora Bora, Christmas Is., Honolulu, Los Angeles (terminates).

PACIFIC PRINCESS

(Princess) Dec. (17 days): Morea, Bora Bora, Pago Pago, crossing Intl. Date Line, Suva, Bay of Islands, Tauranga, Auckland, Sydney (terminates); or Feb.-Mar. (14 days): Moorea, Bora Bora, Christmas Is., Honolulu, Los Angeles (terminates).

Port Moresby

VISTAFJORD

(Cunard/NAC) Feb.-Mar. (15 days): Moorea Is., Bora Bora, Honolulu, Hilo, Los Angeles (terminates).

WIND SONG

(Windstar) Sat year round (7 days): Huahine, Bora Bora, Raiatea, Moorea.

Singapore

BELORUSSIA

(CTC) Dec. (16 days): Port Kelang, Jakarta, Bali, Darwin, Townsville, Brisbane, Sydney (terminates).

CLUB MED 2

(Club Med) Apr.-May (7 days): Bankga Is., Semerang, Bowean, Probolinggo, Bali.

EXPLORER

(Abercrombie & Kent) Feb.-Mar. (14 days): Medan, Lake Toba, Sibolgoa, Sumatra, Nias Is., Bukittingi, Krakatoa, Seribu Is.

ISLAND PRINCESS

(Princess) Dec. (14 days): Bali, Port Moresby, Great Barrier Reef, Brisbane, Sydney (terminates).

ROTTERDAM

(Holland America) Oct.-Nov. (27 days): crossing Equator, Bali, Port Darwin, Port Vila, Suva, Vava'U, crossing Intl. Date Line, Pago Pago, Christmas Is., Honolulu, Los Angeles (terminates).

ROYAL ODYSSEY

(Royal) Jan.-Feb. (28 days): crossing Equator, Bali, Darwin, Great Barrier Reef, Whitsunday Is., Brisbane, Sydney, (terminates).

Sydney
BYLORUSSIA

(CTC) Jan. (7-11 days): Boulasi, Port Vila, Lifou Is., Noumea, Isle of Pines, Woodin Canal.

CRYSTAL HARMONY

(Crystal) Mar. 13 days): Brisbane, Whitsunday Is., Cairns, Bali, Singapore (terminates).

CUNARD CROWN MONARCH

(Cunard Crown) Nov.-Apr. (11 days): Noumea, Isle of Pines, Tana, Vila, Honiara, Cairns (terminates); or Jan. (14 days): Melbourne, Milford Sound, Lyttleton, Wellington, Auckland; or Mar.-Apr. (14 days): Vila, Yasawa, Suva, Tana, Isles of Pines, Noumea.

FAIRSTAR

(P & O Holidays) Oct. (13 days): Boulari-Havannnah Passage, Vila, Suva, Dravuni Is., Noumea, Ile Quen; or Oct. (6 days): Suva, Yasawa, Champagne Bay, Vila Mystery Is., Noumea; or Nov.-Jan. (10-14 days): Milford Sound, Dunedin, Christchurch, Wellington, Auckland, Bay of Islands, Boulari-Havannah Passage, Champagne Bay, Port Vila, Suva, Dravuni Is., Noumea, Ile Quen, Yasawa-I-Rara, Mystery Is.

ISLAND PRINCESS

(Princess) Dec. (14 days): Melbourne, Hobart, Milford Sound, Dunedin, Christchurch, Wellington, Tauranga, Bay of Islands, Auckland (terminates); or Feb. (13 days): Auckland, Suva, crossing Intl. Date Line, Pago Pago, Bora Bora, Moorea Is., Papeete (terminates).

ROYAL ODYSSEY

(Royal) Jan.-Feb. (12 days): Melbourne, Hobart, Milford Sound, Dunedin, Christchurch, Wellington, Auckland (terminates).

Timbunke
MELANESIAN DISCOVERER

(Melanesian Tourist Serv.) Jan.-Nov. (4 days): Kaminimbit, Sepik River.

Valparaiso
EXPLORER

(Abercrombie & Kent) Mar.-Oct. (12-20 days): Robinson Crusoe Is., Selkirk Is., Sala y Gomez, Easter Is., Apia,Wallis Is., Funafuti, Majuro, Maloelap Atoll, Pohnpei, Oroluk, Truk, Pulap Satawal, Ifalik, Woleai, Sorol, Ulithi, Yap, Ambon Is., Seram Is., Misool Is., Waigeo Is., Manokwari

Is., Biak Is., Iriian Jaya, Jayapura, Wewak, Madang, Vitu Is., Tingwong Is., Kavieng, Rabual, Trobriand Is. PNG, Alcester Is, Deboyne Is, Port Moresby, Asmat, Aru Is., Kur & Kaimer Is., Bandas Is., Jakarta, Semerang Madura, Paternoster Is., Komodo is., Sumba Is., Savu Is., Kupang, Kalabahi, Gunung Api Is., Ambon Is., Banda Is., Kai Is., Aru Is., Asmat, , Rorotonga, Raiatea, Bora Bora, Moorea, Papeete, Raivaevae, Rapa, Matotiri, Mangareva, Pitcairn Is., Henderson Is., Ducie Is.

Valparaiso
ODESSA
(Transocean/ MarQuest) Jan.-Feb. (23 days): Rapa Is., Pitcairn Is,. Papeete, Huahine, Raiatea, Bora Bora, Avarua (Rarotonga) Neiafu, Nuku'Alofa (terminates)

Yokohama
ASUKA
(NYK) Jan.-Feb. (35 days): Guam, Cairns, Hamilton Is., Brisbane, Sydney, Lyttelton, Auckland, Noumea, Guam, or as 3 day cruise to first Guam.

CRYSTAL HARMONY
(Crystal) Apr. (15 days): Toyko, Midway Is., Nawiliwili, Honolulu, Los Angeles (terminates).

Vancouver
FAIR PRINCESS
(Princess) Sep.-Oct. (9 days): Moorea Is., Bora Bora, Christmas Is., Honolulu, Los Angeles (terminates).

ROTTERDAM
(Holland America) Sep.-Nov. (58 days): Seattle, Ketchican, Hakodate, Vladivostok, Pusan, Xingang, Okinawa, Hong Kong, Singapore, Bali, Darwin, Port Vila, Fiji, Suva, Tonga, Christmas Is., Honolulu, Los Angeles (terminates).

TRANSATLANTIC
Eastbound

Baltimore-Southampton
QUEEN ELIZABETH 2
(Cunard) Oct.-Nov. (5 days) New York.

Buenos Aires
ISLAND PRINCESS
(Princess) Nov.-Dec.; Apr.-May. (19 days): Montevideo, Rio de Janeiro, Recife, Dakar, Casablanca, Gibraltar, Barcelona (terminates).

Ft, Lauderdale
ROYAL VIKING QUEEN
(Royal Viking) Nov.-Dec.; Apr. (13-14 days): Fort Lauderdale, Virgin Gorda, Martinique, Funchal, Monte Carlo (terminates).
VISTAFJORD
(Cunard) Apr. (13 days): Funchal, Casablanca, Malaga, Barcelona (terminates).
WORLD RENAISSANCE
(Epirotiki) Mar.-Apr. (21 Days): Nassau, Puerto Plata, St. Thomas, St. Kitts, Nevis, Martinique, Grenada, Barbados, Tenirife, Casablanca, Gibraltar, Nice (terminates).

New York
CRYSTAL HARMONY
(Crystal) Aug.-Sep; May (8-16 days): Honfleur, London, De Brugge, La Havre, Falmouth, Waterford, Reykjvik, Halifax, Newport.

New York-Southampton
QUEEN ELIZABETH 2
(Cunard) Jul.; Dec. (5 days) Southampton, New York.

Westbound

Barcelona
CRYSTAL HARMONY
(Crystal) Nov. (10 days): Malaga, Funchal, Barbados (terminates).
ROYAL VIKING SUN
(Royal Viking) Oct.-Nov; Apr. (10 days): Hamilton, Ft. Lauderdale (terminates)
SONG OF NORWAY
(Royal Caribbean) Nov. (10 days).Gibraltar, San Juan (terminates).

Cork
SILVER CLOUD
(Silversea) Sep. (8 days): Cork, New York. ???
SEABOURN PRIDE
(Seabourn) Mar.-Apr. (11 days): Ponta Delgada, Lisbon (terminates).

Funchal
SEA GODDESS I
(Cunard Sea Goddess): Oct.-Nov. (9 days) St. Barts, St. Thomas (terminates).

Las Palmas
RADISSON DIAMOND
(Diamond) May-Jun. (9 days): San Juan (terminates); or Nov. (11 days): Lisbon (terminates).

Lisbon
CLUB MED 1
(Club Med) Nov.; Apr. (16-17 days): Cadiz, Casablanca, Lanzarote, Los Palmas, Martinique (terminates)

STATENDAM
(Holland America) Oct. (10 days): Ponta Delgada, Hamilton, Ft Lauderdale (terminates).

VISTAFJORD
(Cunard) Nov.-Dec. (15 days): Funchal, Santa Cruz de Tenerife, Barbados, Martinique, Tortola, St. Thomas, Fort Lauderdale (terminates).

Piraeus
CROWN ODYSSEY
(Royal) No.-Dec.; Apr. (21-24 days): Civitavecchia, Nice, Barcelona, Palma de Mallorca, Gibralter, Casablanca, Funchal, Santa Cruz de Tenerife, Barbados, Martinique, St. Thomas, San Juan, Cadiz, Malaga, Tangier, Lanzarote, Los Palmas, Lisbon (terminates)

WORLD RENAISSANCE
(Epirotiki) Nov.-Dec, (21 days): Genoa, Casablanca, Tenerife, Guadeloupe, St. Barts, St. Maarten, San Juan, Puerto Plata, Ft. Lauderdale (terminates).

INSIDE INFORMATION ON 29 POPULAR CRUISE PORTS

Want to know more about the port you'll be leaving from or arriving at?

The following section provides information about 29 major ports and their passenger ship terminals around the world.

You'll find out where each terminal is located, transportation and parking information, major cruise lines that dock there, and the climate of the area.

Bring a copy of these maps with you and you won't miss the boat.

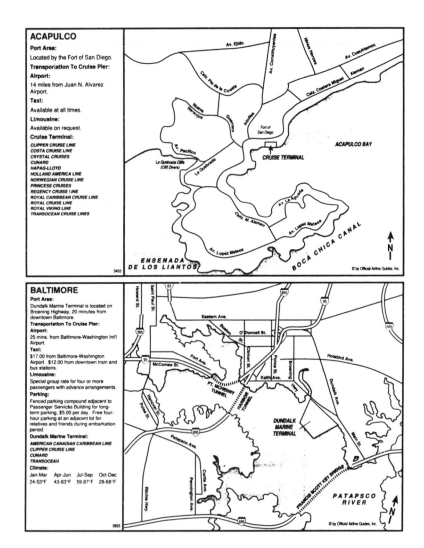

ACAPULCO

Port Area:
Located by the Fort of San Diego.

Transportation To Cruise Pier:

Airport:
14 miles from Juan N. Alvarez Airport.

Taxi:
Available at all times.

Limousine:
Available on request.

Cruise Terminal:
CLIPPER CRUISE LINE
COSTA CRUISE LINE
CRYSTAL CRUISES
CUNARD
HAPAG-LLOYD
HOLLAND AMERICA LINE
NORWEGIAN CRUISE LINE
PRINCESS CRUISES
REGENCY CRUISE LINE
ROYAL CARIBBEAN CRUISE LINE
ROYAL CRUISE LINE
ROYAL VIKING LINE
TRANSOCEAN CRUISE LINES

BALTIMORE

Port Area:
Dundalk Marine Terminal is located on Broening Highway, 20 minutes from downtown Baltimore.

Transportation To Cruise Pier:

Airport:
25 mins. from Baltimore-Washington Int'l Airport.

Taxi:
$17.00 from Baltimore-Washington Airport. $12.00 from downtown train and bus stations.

Limousine:
Special group rate for four or more passengers with advance arrangements.

Parking:
Fenced parking compound adjacent to Passenger Services Building for long-term parking, $5.00 per day. Free four-hour parking at an adjacent lot for relatives and friends during embarkation period.

Dundalk Marine Terminal:
AMERICAN CANADIAN CARIBBEAN LINE
CLIPPER CRUISE LINE
CUNARD
TRANSOCEAN

Climate:

Jan-Mar	Apr-Jun	Jul-Sep	Oct-Dec
24-53°F	43-83°F	59-87°F	28-68°F

BOSTON

Port Area:

Black Falcon Cruise Terminal is located in South Boston off Northern Avenue and Summer Street.

Transportation To Cruise Pier:

Taxi:

15 minutes from Logan Int'l Airport, $10.00. 10 minutes from downtown hotels, $8.00.

Bus:

Charter buses run from pier to South Station, where one can transfer to public transportation to the airport or downtown locations.

Parking:

Short or long-term secured parking is available across the street from the terminal at minimal cost.

Black Falcon Cruise Terminal:

CLIPPER CRUISE LINE
CRYSTAL CRUISES
CUNARD
P & O CRUISES
PRINCESS CRUISES
ROYAL CRUISE LINE
SEABOURN CRUISE LINE

Climate:

Jan-Mar	Apr-Jun	Jul-Sep	Oct-Dec
23-45°F	41-77°F	57-82°F	27-63°F

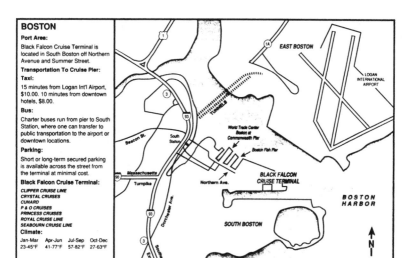

GENOA

Port Area:

Located in the historical center of the city.

Transportation to Cruise Pier:

Airport:

4.5 miles from Cristoforo Colombo Airport.

Rail:

The Piazza Principe Railway Station is within walking distance from the port area.

Taxi:

Taxi stands are located at the Piazza Principe Railway Station and at the Piazza Di Negro.

Cruise Pier:

COSTA CRUISE LINE
CUNARD
EPIROTIKI LINES
GRANDI VIAGGI
GRIMALDI SIOSA CRUISES
HAPAG-LLOYD
HOLLAND AMERICA LINE
P&O CRUISES
PETER DEILMANN
ROYAL CARIBBEAN CRUISES
ROYAL CRUISE LINE
STARLAURO CRUISES

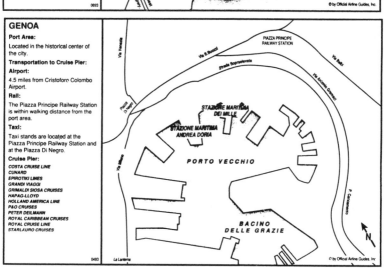

HONG KONG

Port Area:

Located on the southwestern edge of the Kowloon peninsula.

Transportation to Cruise Pier:

Airport:

20 minutes from Hong Kong Intl. Airport.

Taxi:

Taxis are numerous and readily available.

Bus:

Double-decker buses cover most parts of the territory.

Minibus:

Yellow with a red stripe, pick up passengers and let them off anywhere except regular bus stops and restricted areas.

Cruise Pier:

PEARL CRUISES
PRINCESS CRUISES
ROYAL CRUISE LINE
SEAQUEST CRUISES
SEVEN SEAS CRUISE LINE

Climate:

Jan-Mar	Apr-Jun	Jul-Sep	Oct-Dec
47-78°F	65-90°F	72-94°F	54-87°F

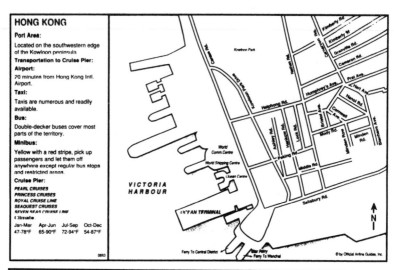

HONOLULU

Port Area:

Located at Mamala Bay.

Transportation to Cruise Pier:

Airport:

2.5 miles from Honolulu Intl Airport.

Limousine/Taxi:

Available from airport.

Car:

Nimitz Hwy. to Ala Moana Blvd.

Parking:

Short term parking available, $1.00 per hr. No long term parking available.

Cruise Piers 8-11:

AMERICAN HAWAII CRUISES
CRYSTAL CRUISES
CUNARD/NAC
HOLLAND AMERICA LINE
P & O CRUISES
PRINCESS CRUISES
ROYAL CRUISE LINE
ROYAL VIKING LINE

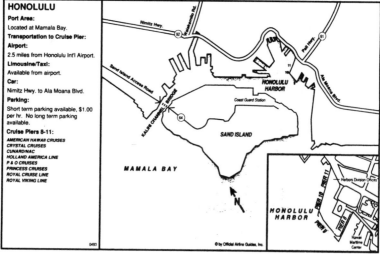

JUNEAU

Port Area:
Located in the downtown area of Juneau. Auke Bay Ferry Terminal is located 14 miles northwest of port area.

Transportation to Cruise Pier:

Airport:
8 miles from Juneau Airport.

Bus:
Downtown bus service is available from airport to major downtown points.

Taxi:
Point to point and charter hire available in Juneau.

Cruise Terminal:
ALASKA SIGHTSEEING/CRUISE WEST
CLASSICAL CRUISES
CLIPPER CRUISE LINE

Climate:

Jan-Mar	Apr-Jun	Jul-Sep	Oct-Dec
17-38°F	31-61°F	42-64°F	27-47°F

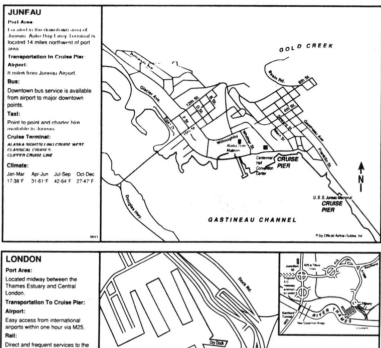

LONDON

Port Area:
Located midway between the Thames Estuary and Central London.

Transportation To Cruise Pier:

Airport:
Easy access from international airports within one hour via M25.

Rail:
Direct and frequent services to the City of London.

Car:
Dual carriageway connection to M25 11 km/7 miles.

Parking :
£3.95 per day.

International Cruise Pier:
CTC LINES
CUNARD
HAPAG-LLOYD
PRINCESS CRUISES
ROYAL CARIBBEAN CRUISES
ROYAL CRUISE LINE
ROYAL VIKING LINE
SEABOURN CRUISE LINE
TRANSOCEAN CRUISE LINES

Climate:

Jan-Mar	Apr-Jun	Jul-Sep	Oct-Dec
36-52°F	39-70°F	52-73°F	36-57°F

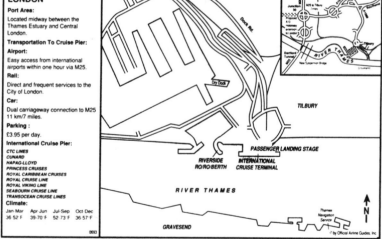

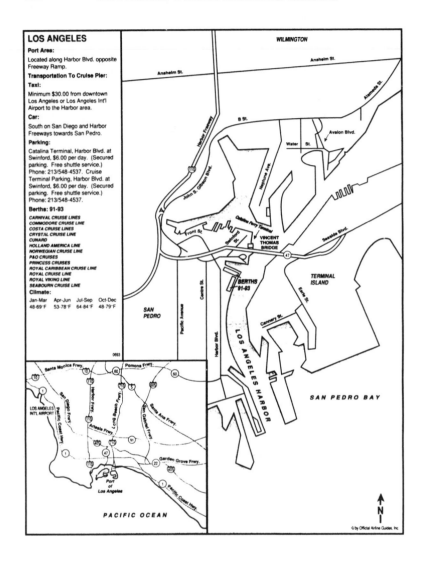

LOS ANGELES

Port Area:
Located along Harbor Blvd. opposite
Freeway Ramp.

Transportation To Cruise Pier:

Taxi:
Minimum $30.00 from downtown
Los Angeles or Los Angeles Int'l
Airport to the Harbor area.

Car:
South on San Diego and Harbor
Freeways towards San Pedro.

Parking:
Catalina Terminal, Harbor Blvd. at
Swinford, $6.00 per day. (Secured
parking. Free shuttle service.)
Phone: 213/548-4537. Cruise
Terminal Parking, Harbor Blvd. at
Swinford, $6.00 per day. (Secured
parking. Free shuttle service.)
Phone: 213/548-4537.

Berths: 91-93
CARNIVAL CRUISE LINES
COMMODORE CRUISE LINE
COSTA CRUISE LINES
CRYSTAL CRUISE LINE
CUNARD
HOLLAND AMERICA LINE
NORWEGIAN CRUISE LINE
P&O CRUISES
PRINCESS CRUISES
ROYAL CARIBBEAN CRUISE LINE
ROYAL CRUISE LINE
ROYAL VIKING LINE
SEABOURN CRUISE LINE

Climate:

Jan-Mar	Apr-Jun	Jul-Sep	Oct-Dec
48-69°F	53-78°F	64-84°F	48-79°F

WILMINGTON

SAN PEDRO

SAN PEDRO BAY

LOS ANGELES HARBOR

TERMINAL ISLAND

BERTHS 91-93

VINCENT THOMAS BRIDGE

PACIFIC OCEAN

Port of Los Angeles

LOS ANGELES INTL AIRPORT

N

© by Official Airline Guides, Inc

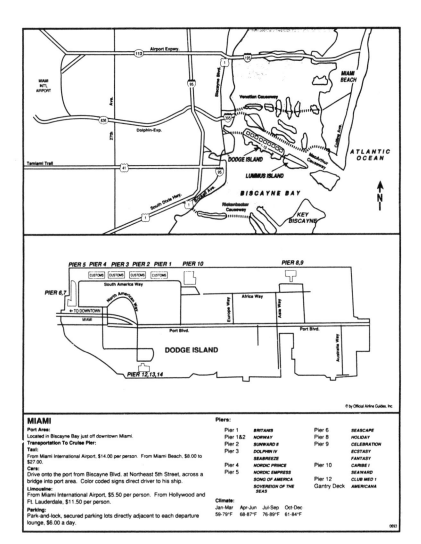

© by Official Airline Guides, Inc.

MIAMI

Port Area:
Located in Biscayne Bay just off downtown Miami.

Transportation To Cruise Pier:

Taxi:
From Miami International Airport, $14.00 per person. From Miami Beach, $8.00 to $27.00.

Cars:
Drive onto the port from Biscayne Blvd. at Northeast 5th Street, across a bridge into port area. Color coded signs direct driver to his ship.

Limousine:
From Miami International Airport, $5.50 per person. From Hollywood and Ft. Lauderdale, $11.50 per person.

Parking:
Park-and-lock, secured parking lots directly adjacent to each departure lounge, $6.00 a day.

Piers:

Pier 1	*BRITANIS*	Pier 6	*SEASCAPE*
Pier 1&2	*NORWAY*	Pier 8	*HOLIDAY*
Pier 2	*SUNWARD II*	Pier 9	*CELEBRATION*
Pier 3	*DOLPHIN IV*		*ECSTASY*
	SEABREEZE		*FANTASY*
Pier 4	*NORDIC PRINCE*	Pier 10	*CARIBE I*
Pier 5	*NORDIC EMPRESS*		*SEAWARD*
	SOVEREIGN OF THE	Pier 12	*CLUB MED I*
	SEAS	Gantry Deck	*AMERICANA*
	SONG OF AMERICA		

Climate:

Jan-Mar	Apr-Jun	Jul-Sep	Oct-Dec
59-79°F	68-87°F	76-89°F	61-84°F

0693

NASSAU

Port Area:

Located in downtown area on the island of New Providence.

Transportation To Cruise Pier:

Airport:

12 miles from Nassau Int'l Airport.

Limousine/Taxi:

Can pick-up and discharge passengers at the berths.

Cruise Pier:

AMERICAN CANADIAN CARIBBEAN LINE
CARNIVAL CRUISE LINES
CELEBRITY CRUISES
COMMODORE CRUISE LINE
CUNARD
DOLPHIN CRUISE LINE
FANTASY CRUISES
HAPAG LLOYD
HOLLAND AMERICA LINE
MAJESTY CRUISE LINE
NORWEGIAN CRUISE LINES
PREMIER CRUISE LINES
PRINCESS CRUISES
ROYAL CARIBBEAN CRUISES
ROYAL CRUISE LINE
SUN LINE CRUISES

Climate:

Jan-Mar	Apr-Jun	Jul-Sep	Oct-Dec
57-81°F	68-86°F	72-90°F	66-88°F

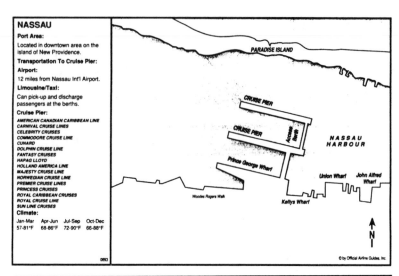

NEW ORLEANS

Port Area:

Located near Poydras, Julia and Robin Streets.

Transportation To Cruise Pier:

Airport:

New Orleans International Airport, 16 miles from downtown hotels and piers.

Limousine:

40 minutes from New Orleans International Airport to the International Cruise Ship Terminal, $21.00 (1-3 persons).

Parking:

Short or long-term parking facilities are available in nearby World Trade Center.

International Cruise Terminal:

COMMODORE CRUISE LINE.
DELTA QUEEN STEAMBOAT CO.

Climate:

Jan-Mar	Apr-Jun	Jul-Sep	Oct-Dec
43-71°F	59-90°F	70-91°F	45-79°F

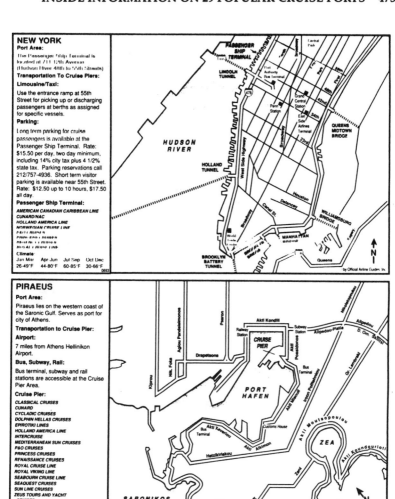

NEW YORK

Port Area:

The Passenger Ship Terminal is located at 711 12th Avenue (Hudson River 48th to 52th Streets)

Transportation To Cruise Piers:

Limousine/Taxi:

Use the entrance ramp at 55th Street for picking up or discharging passengers at berths as assigned for specific vessels.

Parking:

Long term parking for cruise passengers is available at the Passenger Ship Terminal. Rate: $15.50 per day, two day minimum, including 14% city tax plus 4 1/2% state tax. Parking reservations call 212/757-4936. Short term visitor parking is available near 55th Street. Rate: $12.50 up to 10 hours, $17.50 all day.

Passenger Ship Terminal:

AMERICAN CANADIAN CARIBBEAN LINE
CUNARD-NAC
HOLLAND AMERICA LINE
NORWEGIAN CRUISE LINE
P&O CRUISES
PRINCESS CRUISES
ROYAL CRUISE LINE

Climate

Jan-Mar	Apr-Jun	Jul-Sep	Oct-Dec
26-49°F	44-80°F	60-85°F	30-66°F

PIRAEUS

Port Area:

Piraeus lies on the western coast of the Saronic Gulf. Serves as port for city of Athens.

Transportation to Cruise Pier:

Airport:

7 miles from Athens Hellinikon Airport.

Bus, Subway, Rail:

Bus terminal, subway and rail stations are accessible at the Cruise Pier Area.

Cruise Pier:

CLASSICAL CRUISES
CUNARD
CYCLADIC CRUISES
DOLPHIN HELLAS CRUISES
EPIROTIKI LINES
HOLLAND AMERICA LINE
INTERCRUISE
MEDITERRANEAN SUN CRUISES
P&O CRUISES
PRINCESS CRUISES
RENAISSANCE CRUISES
ROYAL CRUISE LINE
ROYAL VIKING LINE
SEABOURN CRUISE LINE
SEAQUEST CRUISES
SUN LINE CRUISES
ZEUS TOURS AND YACHT CRUISES

PORT CANAVERAL

Port Area:

Located between Cape Canaveral Air Force Station and the City of Cape Canaveral.

Transportation To Cruise Pier:

Airport:

45 minute drive via expressway from Orlando International Airport. 40 minute drive from Melbourne Regional Airport.

Taxi:

Service is available.

Bus/Limousine:

Available on prearranged basis.

Parking:

Long-term outdoor parking handled by Port Authority. Passengers drive vehicles to terminals into secured parking, $5.00 per day. Visitor parking scattered throughout port.

Car Rental:

Hertz Rent-A-Car located in Cruise Terminal #3 on Mondays and Fridays, when ship is in port.

Cruise Terminals:

CARNIVAL CRUISE LINES
PREMIER CRUISE LINES

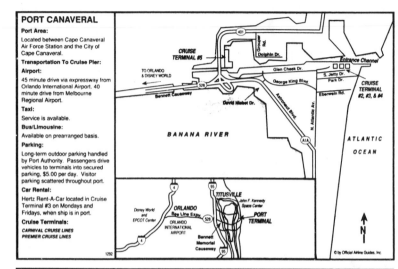

PORT EVERGLADES

Port Area:

Located on southern edge of Ft. Lauderdale and north of Hollywood, FL.

Transportation To Cruise Pier:

Airport:

Less than 1 mile from Ft. Lauderdale-Hollywood International Airport. 25 miles from Miami International Airport.

Taxi:

Available. Fares subject to change.

Limousine:

Service available from Ft. Lauderdale-Hollywood International Airport, Miami International Airport and local hotels.

Parking:

Long term parking for cruise passengers handled by Port Authority. Outdoor/Indoor storage for passengers cars, $6.00 per day. Visitor parking nearby.

Car Rental:

All major car rental companies.

Cruise Piers:

CELEBRITY CRUISES
CRYSTAL CRUISES
CUNARD·NAC
DISCOVERY CRUISES
HOLLAND AMERICA LINE
NORWEGIAN CRUISE LINE
PREMIER CRUISE LINE
PRINCESS CRUISES
ROYAL VIKING LINE
SEABOURN CRUISES
SEASCAPE
SUN LINE CRUISES

Climate:

Jan-Mar	Apr-Jun	Jul-Sep	Oct-Dec
59-79°F	68-87°F	76-89°F	61-84°F

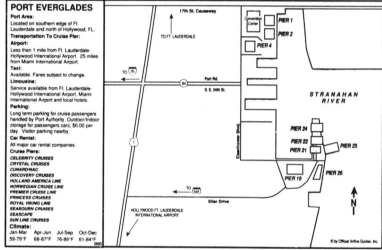

RIO DE JANEIRO

Port Area:

Located in the downtown area of Rio de Janeiro.

Transportation To Cruise Pier:

Airport:

7.5 miles from Rio de Janeiro Intl. Airport.

.7 miles from Santos Dumont Airport.

Rail:

The Barão de Maua Railroad Station is less than 2 miles away from the port area.

Bus:

The Mariano Procopio Bus Station is across the street from the port area.

The Menezes Cortes Bus Terminal is 1/2 mile away from the port area.

Cruise Pier:

CLIPPER CRUISE LINES
CUNARD
HAPAG-LLOYD
PRINCESS CRUISES
ROYAL VIKING LINE
SUN LINE CRUISES
TRANSOCEAN CRUISE LINES

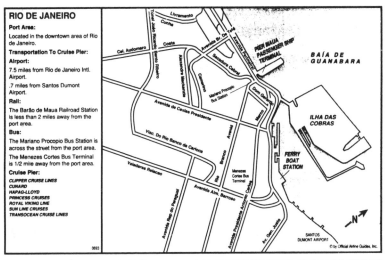

ST. PETERSBURG

Port Area:

Located near downtown St. Petersburg off Interstate 275, Exit 9 (S. Bay Drive).

Transportation To Cruise Pier:

Airport:

35 minutes from Tampa International Airport. 20 minutes from St. Petersburg-Clearwater Airport.

Taxi:

(1 to 4 persons) $25.00 from Tampa International Airport and $14.00 from St. Petersburg-Clearwater Airport.

Limousine:

$9.25 per person from Tampa International and St. Petersburg-Clearwater Airport.

Parking:

Long-term parking adjacent and across the street from the Port Terminal, $25.00 per week.

Cruise Pier:

ODESSA AMERICA CRUISE

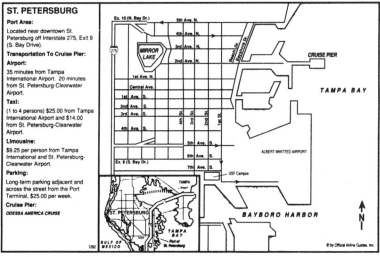

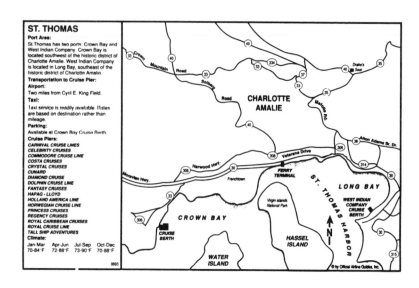

ST. THOMAS

Port Area:
St Thomas has two ports: Crown Bay and West Indian Company. Crown Bay is located southwest of the historic district of Charlotte Amalie. West Indian Company is located in Long Bay, southeast of the historic district of Charlotte Amalie.

Transportation to Cruise Pier:

Airport:
Two miles from Cyril E. King Field.

Taxi:
Taxi service is readily available. Rates are based on destination rather than mileage.

Parking:
Available at Crown Bay Cruise Berth.

Cruise Piers:
CARNIVAL CRUISE LINES
CELEBRITY CRUISES
COMMODORE CRUISE LINE
COSTA CRUISES
CRYSTAL CRUISES
CUNARD
DIAMOND CRUISE
DOLPHIN CRUISE LINE
FANTASY CRUISES
HAPAG - LLOYD
HOLLAND AMERICA LINE
NORWEGIAN CRUISE LINE
PRINCESS CRUISES
REGENCY CRUISES
ROYAL CARIBBEAN CRUISES
ROYAL CRUISE LINE
TALL SHIP ADVENTURES

Climate:

Jan-Mar	Apr-Jun	Jul-Sep	Oct-Dec
70-84°F	72-88°F	73-90°F	70-88°F

GOLDEN ODYSSEY, Royal Cruise Line

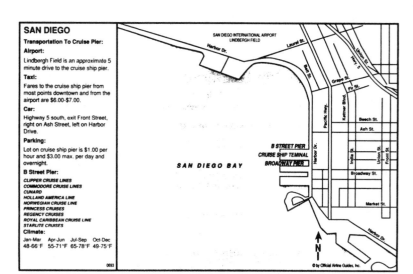

SAN DIEGO

Transportation To Cruise Pier:

Airport:

Lindbergh Field is an approximate 5 minute drive to the cruise ship pier.

Taxi:

Fares to the cruise ship pier from most points downtown and from the airport are $6.00-$7.00.

Car:

Highway 5 south, exit Front Street, right on Ash Street, left on Harbor Drive.

Parking:

Lot on cruise ship pier is $1.00 per hour and $3.00 max. per day and overnight.

B Street Pier:

CLIPPER CRUISE LINES
COMMODORE CRUISE LINES
CUNARD
HOLLAND AMERICA LINE
NORWEGIAN CRUISE LINE
PRINCESS CRUISES
REGENCY CRUISES
ROYAL CARIBBEAN CRUISE LINE
STARLITE CRUISES

Climate:

Jan-Mar	Apr-Jun	Jul-Sep	Oct-Dec
48-66°F	55-71°F	65-78°F	49-75°F

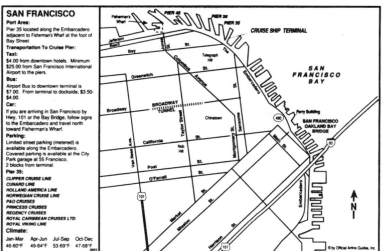

SAN FRANCISCO

Port Area:

Pier 35 located along the Embarcadero adjacent to Fisherman's Wharf at the foot of Bay Street.

Transportation To Cruise Pier:

Taxi:

$4.00 from downtown hotels. Minimum $25.00 from San Francisco International Airport to the piers.

Bus:

Airport Bus to downtown terminal is $7.00. From terminal to dockside, $3.50-$4.00.

Car:

If you are arriving in San Francisco by Hwy. 101 or the Bay Bridge, follow signs to the Embarcadero and travel north toward Fisherman's Wharf.

Parking:

Limited street parking (metered) is available along the Embarcadero. Covered parking is available at the City Park garage at 55 Francisco, 2 blocks from terminal.

Pier 35:

CLIPPER CRUISE LINE
CUNARD LINE
HOLLAND AMERICA LINE
NORWEGIAN CRUISE LINE
P&O CRUISES
PRINCESS CRUISES
REGENCY CRUISES
ROYAL CARIBBEAN CRUISES LTD.
ROYAL VIKING LINE

Climate:

Jan-Mar	Apr-Jun	Jul-Sep	Oct-Dec
46-60°F	49-64°F	53-69°F	47-68°F

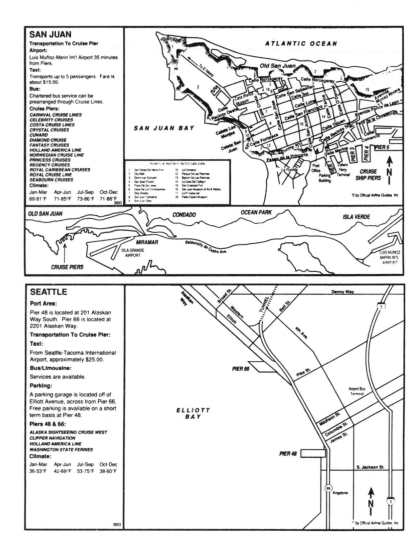

SINGAPORE

Port Area:
The Singapore Cruise Centre is located at the World Trade Complex. The Complex is at the outskirts of the central business district and is easily accessible to all parts of Singapore.

Transportation to Cruise Pier:

Airport:
25 minutes from Singapore Changi Airport.

Taxi:
Taxi bays are conveniently located near the pier area.

Bus:
Direct transfer to/from the airport.

Parking:
Covered and open car parks are available within the World Trade Centre Building and Maritime Square Car Park.

Cruise Pier:
CTC LINES
CUNARD
HAPAG-LLOYD
HOLLAND AMERICA LINE
P&O CRUISES
PEARL CRUISES
PRINCESS CRUISES
RENAISSANCE CRUISES
ROYAL CRUISE LINE
ROYAL VIKING LINE
SEABOURN CRUISE LINE
SEVEN SEAS CRUISE LINE

Climate:

Jan-Mar	Apr-Jun	Jul-Sep	Oct-Dec
73-87°F	75-88°F	75-87°F	74-87°F

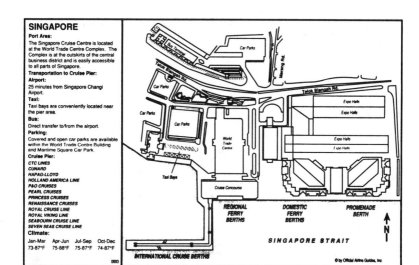

0693

© by Official Airline Guides, Inc

SYDNEY

Port Area:
Circular Quay is located in Sydney Cove between Harbour Bridge and the Sydney Opera House.

Transportation To Cruise Pier:

Airport:
10 km/6.2 mi from Kingsford Smith Airport.

Bus/Train/Ferry:
Accessible by bus, train or ferry.

Cruise Pier:
CTC LINES
PRINCESS CRUISES
ROYAL CRUISE LINE
STARLAURO CRUISES

Climate:

Jan-Mar	Apr-Jun	Jul-Sep	Oct-Dec
63-78°F	48-71°F	46-67°F	56-77°F

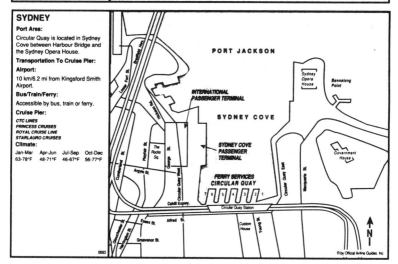

0693

© by Official Airline Guides, Inc

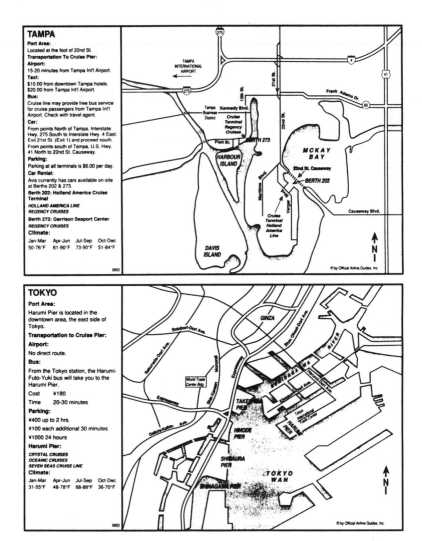

TAMPA

Port Area:
Located at the foot of 22nd St.

Transportation To Cruise Pier:

Airport:
15-20 minutes from Tampa Int'l Airport.

Taxi:
$10.00 from downtown Tampa hotels.
$20.00 from Tampa Int'l Airport.

Bus:
Cruise line may provide free bus service
for cruise passengers from Tampa Int'l
Airport. Check with travel agent.

Car:
From points North of Tampa, Interstate
Hwy. 275 South to Interstate Hwy. 4 East.
Exit 21st St. (Exit 1) and proceed south.
From points south of Tampa, U.S. Hwy.
41 North to 22nd St. Causeway.

Parking:
Parking at all terminals is $6.00 per day.

Car Rental:
Avis currently has cars available on-site
at Berths 202 & 273.

**Berth 202: Holland America Cruise
Terminal**
HOLLAND AMERICA LINE
REGENCY CRUISES

Berth 273: Garrison Seaport Center
REGENCY CRUISES

Climate:

Jan-Mar	Apr-Jun	Jul-Sep	Oct-Dec
50-76°F	61-90°F	73-90°F	51-84°F

0693

TOKYO

Port Area:
Harumi Pier is located in the
downtown area, the east side of
Tokyo.

Transportation to Cruise Pier:

Airport:
No direct route.

Bus:
From the Tokyo station, the Harumi-
Futo-Yuki bus will take you to the
Harumi Pier.

Cost	¥180
Time	20-30 minutes

Parking:
¥400 up to 2 hrs.
¥100 each additional 30 minutes
¥1000 24 hours

Harumi Pier:
CRYSTAL CRUISES
OCEANIC CRUISES
SEVEN SEAS CRUISE LINE

Climate:

Jan-Mar	Apr-Jun	Jul-Sep	Oct-Dec
31-55°F	48-78°F	68-88°F	36-70°F

0693

VANCOUVER

Port Area:

Ballantyne Terminal is located close to Canada Place, 1/2 mile (1.5 kilometres) from downtown Vancouver. Canada Place Cruise Ship Terminal is located in downtown Vancouver.

Transportation To Cruise Pier:

Airport:

25 minutes from Vancouver International Airport.

Taxi:

Approx. $25.00 from Airport to Canada Place Cruise Ship Terminal or to Ballantyne Terminal.

Bus:

Airporter Bus from Airport to Canada Place.

Parking:

Advance Parking - 604/681-1123; Complimentary Shuttle to and from cruise ship terminals.

Canada Place Parking - Citipark 604/684-2251

Canada Place Cruise Pier:

COSTA CRUISE LINES
CUNARD
HOLLAND AMERICA LINE
PRINCESS CRUISES
REGENCY CRUISES
ROYAL CARIBBEAN CRUISE LINE
ROYAL CRUISE LINE
WORLD EXPLORER CRUISES

Climate:

Jan-Mar	Apr-Jun	Jul-Sep	Oct-Dec
32-48°F	41-66°F	50-72°F	34-57°F

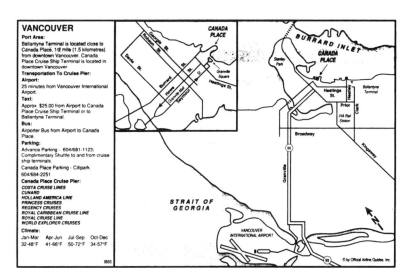

VENICE

Port Area:

Located on the southwestern edge of Venice.

Transportation To Cruise Pier:

Airport:

8 Miles from Marco Polo Airport. 25 Miles from Treviso Airport.

Rail:

St. Lucia Station is minutes away from port area.

Parking:

Parking is available at Isola del Tronchette and at Piazzale Roma.

Cruise Pier:

COSTA CRUISE LINES
CTC CRUISE LINES
CUNARD
EPIROTIKI LINES
INTERCRUISE
OCEAN CRUISE LINES
PRINCESS CRUISES
ROYAL CARIBBEAN CRUISES
ROYAL CRUISE LINE
ROYAL VIKING LINE
SEABOURN CRUISE LINE
SWAN HELLENIC CRUISES

VIDEO AND PRINT RESOURCES

This section offers video and print resources to further help you find an exciting cruise. Many of the publications are designed for passengers; but some are written for agents, who perhaps will let you study them for current information.

Videos are the best way to get an accurate idea of what specific ships are like, without getting on board ahead of time. Consider ordering videos about the ships and destinations you are interested in to help make a wise decision.

PRINT RESOURCES

ABC Passenger Shipping Guide, published by Reed Travel Group, Church Street, Dunstable, Bedfordshire, LU5 4HB, United Kingdom. Phone: (0582) 600111, Fax: (0582) 695230. Extensive listings of ferry services worldwide.

Aware Traveler's Directory, published by Travel Aware, 7658 Royston Street, Annandale, Virginia 22003-3637; 703-354-6600; $99.95. More than 1,400 names and addresses of travel services and organizations in more than 100 categories worldwide, including cruises.

Agent's Cruise Monthly, published by World Ocean & Cruise Liner Society, P.O. Box 92, Stamford CT 06904; 203-329-

2787. Annual subscription $40 for CLIA members, $60 for non-CLIA members.

Choose to Cruise...The Best Vacation Value, published by Cruise Lines International Association, 500 Fifth Avenue, Suite 1407, New York, NY 10110; 212-921-0066; pocket size, four pages, *free*. This informative, brochure provides a compelling value comparison of cruising vs. land-based vacations. Obtain by sending a stamped, self-addressed envelope (29 cents postage) to CLIA.

CLIA Cruise Manual, published by Cruise Lines International Association, 500 Fifth Avenue, Suite 1407, New York, NY 10100; 212-921-0066; over 600 pages, $50 for CLIA affiliates and $75 for non-CLIA affiliates. The manual is published mainly for the travel agency community as a reference source for CLIA's Member Cruise Lines. This annually updated, clearly organized, comprehensive volume reflects suggestions made by travel agents. Send check or money order to Cruise Lines International Association (add $4.00 for postage and handling) or call to order with Visa, MasterCard or American Express.

Cruise Digest, P.O. Box 886 FDR Station, New York, NY 10150. Bi-monthly newspaper published by International Cruise Passenger Association.

Cruise Industry Annual, by Nissen-Lie Communications, 441 Lexington Avenue, Suite 1209A, New York, NY 10017; 212-986-1025; 300 pages, $450. Profiles on 53 cruise lines operating in the North American market, 74 cruise ports in the United States, the Caribbean, Bermuda and Mexico, and 35 shipyards worldwide. Listings of more than 1,000 industry suppliers and service companies. Statistics and industry forecasts not available elsewhere. Issue-oriented articles by industry executives and researchers.

Cruise Industry News, Nissen-Lie Communications, 441 Lexington Avenue, Suite 1209A, New York, NY 10017; 212-986-1025. Twice a month, six pages, $495 a year. Subscribed to by top management at nearly all the cruise lines, overseas owners and holding companies, shipyards, port and tourism officials, financial institutions and supply and service companies.

Cruise Magazine, 37 Gulf Breeze Parkway, Gulf Breeze, FL 32561. Glossy magazine published eight times a year. Features on ship lines and cruising in general, with cruise schedules for three month period.

Cruise Travel, 990 Grove Street, Evanston, IL 60201; 708-491-6440. Subscription price $18.00. Color magazine with feature articles about ships and cruising; six issues per year.

Cruise Views, published by Orban Communications, Inc., 60 East 42nd Street, Suite 905, New York, NY 10165; 212-867-7470. Bi-monthly travel agency magazine. News, charts and how-to-sell features by cruise experts.

Ford's Travel Guides, 19448 Londelius Street, Northridge, CA 91324; 818-701-7414. Selected ship profile data. Consolidated sailing schedules. Separate freighter edition. $14.95 per copy.

Garth's Profile of Ships, by Garth Peterson; Cruising With Garth, P.O. Box 34697, Omaha, Nebraska 68134; 402-571-0995; 200 pages $45. Updates are $25 including one in January and one in July. Profiles of more than 200 ships with factual information on the vessels and ratings. The book comes in a three ring binder.

Maritime Services Directory, published by Aegis Publications, 5394 Linda Vista Road, Suite A, San Diego, CA 92110; 619-294-8630; $85.00 + $4.00 shipping and handling. Extensive listings of maritime vendors, services, associations, and port authorities.

Ocean and Cruise News, published by World Ocean & Cruise Liner Society, P.O. Box 92, Stamford, CT 06904; 203-329-2787. Single issue price $2.50. Newsletter published 12 times per year. Profiles of "ship of the month" and other features.

Also, check out magazines and newsletters such as *Audubon, Caribbean Travel & Life, Conde Nast Traveler, Ecotravelar, Natural History, Outside, Sierra, Smithsonian, The Educated Traveler*, (Dobbs Ferry, NY 10522) *The Natural Traveler, Travel & Leisure*, and *Travel* (Box 728, Glen Cove, NY 11542).

SHIPS NAMED AND RENAMED

Does it seem like you've been on this ship before? Perhaps you have. Ship names often change when they go from one cruise line to another. Here is a list of some of the changes.

PRESENT	FORMER
Abel Tasman	Nils Holgersson
Achille Lauro	Wilhelm Ruys
Aegean Dolphin	Narcis
Alouette	Mars
Amazing Grace	Pharos
American Adventure	Marconi, Costa Riveria
Amerikanis	Kenya Castle
Anna Karenina	Braemar
Aquanaut Explorer	Campeche Seal
Azur	Eagle
Baltic Star	Birger Jarl
Berlin Princess	Mahsuri
Britanis	Monterey, Matsonia, Lurline
Caledonian Star	North Star
Caribe I	Olympia
Carnivale	Empress of Britain
Columbus Caravelle	Sally Caravelle
Constitution	Oceanic Constitution
Coral Star	Global Star

CostaAllegra	Alexandria
CostaMarina	Alex Johnson, Italia
CostaRiviera	Marconi
Crown Diver	Princess of the Waves
Cunard Princess	Cunard Conquest
Daphne	Port of Melbourne
Dawn Princess	Fairwind,Sylvania
Dolphin IV	Ithaca
Enchanted Isle	Monarch Star, Veendam, Bermuda Star, Argentina
Enchanted Seas	Queen of Bermuda, Canada Star, Libertie, Volendam
EnricoCosta	Provance
Explorer	Lindblad Explorer, Society Explorer
Fair Princess	Corinthia, Fairsea
Fantome	Flying Cloud
Festival	Wellamo
Festivale	Transvaal Castle, Vaal
FiestaMarina	Empress of Britain, Carnivale
Flotel Orellana	Flotel Francisco
Flying Cloud	Oiseau des Isles
Galapagos Explorer	Attica,Andrea Mantegna
Glacier Seas	Thunder Bay
Golden Princess	Birka Queen, Sunward, Royal Viking Sky
Hebridean Princess	Columbia
Horizon II	Ex Abrubto
Ilich	Scandia
Independence	Oceanic Independence
Island Princess	Island Venture
Jason	Eros
Kareliya	Leonid Brezhnev
Karneval	Svea
King of Scandinavia	DanaGloria
Kristina Regina	Borea
La Palma	La Perla
Liberte	De Fehntzer

Majestic	*Spirit of London, Sun Princess*
Marco Polo	*Alexander Pushkin*
Mardi Gras	*Empress of Canada*
Meridian	*Galileo*
Mermoz	*Jean Mermoz*
Monterey	*Free State Mariner*
Nord Estonia	*Dana Regina*
Norway	*France*
OceanBreeze	*Azure Seas, Calypso, Southern Cross*
Oceanic	*Oceanic*
Oceanos	*Jean Laborde*
Ocean Pearl	*Finlandia, Finnstar, Pearl of Scandinavia*
Ocean Princess	*Italia*
Odysseus	*Aqua Marine*
Pacific Princess	*Sea Venture*
Pallas Athena	*Princess Carla, Carla Costa, Flandre*
Pegasus	*Sundancer*
Polaris	*Oresund*
Polynesia	*Argus*
Prince of Scandinavia	*Tor Britania*
Quad City Queen	*Mississippi Belle*
Regal Empress	*Cariber*
Regent Rainbow	*Santa Rosa*
Regent Sea	*Great Rivers Explorer, Gripsholm, Navarino, Rhapsody, Royal Odyssey, Shalom*
Regent Spirit	*Constellation*
Regent Star	*Statendam, Rhapsody*
Regent Sun	*Hanseatic Doric, Royal Odyssey*
Rembrandt Van Rijn	*Ursula II*
Rio Amazonas	*Arias*
Royal Odyssey	*Royal Viking Sea*
Royal Pacific	*Empress of Australia, Empress*

Sea Bird	Majesty Explorer
SeaBreeze	Frederico C., Royale
Sea Cloud	Hussar
Sea Pricess	Kungsholm
Seawind Crown	Vasco de Gama
Sir Francis Drake	Godewind
Sky Princess	Fairsky
Song of Flower	Explorer
Spice Islander	Coral Cat
Spirit of Alaska	Pacific NW Explorer
Spirit of Discovery	Columbia
Spirit of Glacier Bay	New Shoreham, Glacier Bay Explorer
Star Odyssey	Royal Viking Star, Westward
Star Princess	Fair Majesty
Stella Oceanis	Aphrodite
Stella Maris	Bremerhaven
Stella Solaris	Campoge
Sunward	Royal Viking Sky
Terra Australia	Savannah
Triton	Sunward II, Cunard Adventurer
Universe	Atlantic
Victoria	Dunnottar Castle
Victorian Empress	Colonial Explorer, Pilgrim Belle
Viking Princess	II Matar
Viking Serenade	Scandinavia, Stardancer
Westerdam	Homeric
Westward	Royal Viking Star
World Renaissance	Homeric Renaissance
Yankee Clipper	Cressida, Pioneer

About the authors:

SHIRLEY LINDE

Shirley Linde is a best-selling author. She has written for many major national magazines, is well-known for her appearances on radio and television, and is author or coauthor of 30 books, including *Dr. Atkins' Superenergy Diet* (Bantam), *The Whole Health Catalogue* (Rawson), *No More Sleepless Nights* (Wiley), *The Charleston Program* (Greentree Press), *Healthy Homes in a Toxic Environment* (Wiley), and *No More Back Pain* (Pharos). Linde is vice president of the North American Travel Journalists Association, has been on the executive board of both the National Association of Science Writers and the American Medical Writers Association, a member of the American Society of Journalists and Authors and the International Food, Wine & Travel Writers Association. She has served as a public relations consultant to hospitals, universities, medical associations, government agencies and corporations. She has a PhD., has received many writing awards and is listed in Who's Who in America, the World's Who's Who of Women, and Foremost Women of the Twentieth Century. She lives in Florida.

LEA LANE

Lea Lane has written over 150 articles on travel. She was managing editor of *Travel Smart* and *Travel Smart for Business* newsletters, and is a contributing editor of *Hotel & Motel Management*, and guidebooks including *Star Service, Birn-*

baum *United States*, and *Zagatsurveys*. She writes for *The New York Times*, *The Miami Herald*, *Newsweek*, *Ms.*, *Washingtonian*, and *Gannett Suburban Newspapers*, and Prodigy on-line system, and was a regular guest expert on The Travel Channel. She has been a consultant for the country's top corporations, and has trained over a thousand people to write more clearly. Her book, *Steps to Better Writing* (St. Martins), is used by schools and businesses; she has also written two produced plays, and was executive producer and scriptwriter of interactive video productions for the Department of Defense. Lea Lane is a member of the North American Travel Writers Association, and the International Food, Wine & Travel Writers Association. She lives in New York and has lived in, worked in, visited or cruised to over 80 countries.

INDEX

Index of Ship Lines and Ship Names

Index of Destination Cities

The World's Most Exciting Cruises on Tape

A video preview of your vacation!

The World's Most Exciting Cruises on Tape brings the most exciting destinations, cruises, and yacht charters right into your living room. These professionally produced videos offer you a "visual tour," letting you plan and preview your cruise vacation.

All the video selections you choose will be custom duplicated onto a single high-quality <u>re-usable</u> video cassette that's yours to keep. The video selections are only $7.00 each plus postage and handling.

BONUS OFFER: Buy 4 or more, get an additional video FREE!*

Cruises:

Code	Cruise	Title
653	Abercrombie & Kent	*Luxury Barging*
626	Alaska Sightseeing Cruise West	*Experience Alaska*
679	American Hawaii Cruises	*The Magic, Mystery & Romance*
784	Bergen Line	*Silja Line: The New Generation*
785	Bergen Line	*Norwegian Coastal Voyage*
824	Carnival Cruises	*Fun Ship Cruising*
524	Celebrity Cruises	*The Meridian*
626	Clipper Adventure Cruises	*In the Spirit of Adventure*
786	Coasting Schooner	*Heritage*
787	Delta Queen Steamboat	*Legend of Steamboatin'*
788	Diamond Cruises	*Radisson Diamond*
789	Dolphin Cruiseline	*Royal Majesty*
790	Epirotiki Line	*Greece and Greek Isles*
567	Holland America	*Art of Cruising*
716	Holland America	*Inside Passage*
649	Holland America	*MS Westerdam*
717	Holland America	*Nieuw Amsterdam*
647	Holland America	*Panama Canal*
550	Holland America	*Westours-Alaska*
656	Ivaran Lines	*MS Americana*
527	KD River Cruises	*Rhine Impressions*
768	Norwegian Cruise	*Dreamward/Windward*
776	Norwegian Cruise	*Dreamward/Windward Alaska*
585	Norwegian Cruise	*SS Norway*
791	P&O (Fairstar/Captain Cook)	
629	Premier Cruise Line	*The Big Red Boat*
738	Princess Cruises	*Alaska*
630	Regency Cruises	*The Regency Difference*
646	Renaissance Cruises	*The Seychelles: Last Paradise on Earth*
631	Royal Caribbean	*The Sun Viking: Alaska*
792	Royal Caribbean	*Bahamas Nordic Empress*
793	Royal Caribbean	*Baja Mexico Serenade*
632	Royal Caribbean	*Bermuda*
794	Royal Caribbean	*Southern Caribbean*
795	Royal Caribbean	*Sovereign Seas*
796	Royal Caribbean	*Majesty of the Seas*
633	Royal Viking	*Royal Viking Queen*
770	Royal Viking	*Royal Viking Sun*
747	Special Expeditions	*Alaska*
628	Special Expeditions	*Among the Great Whales*
745	St. Lawrence Cruises	*Romancing the River*
587	Star Clippers	*The Tall Ships*
634	Sun Line Cruises	*Stella Solaris, Stella Oceanis, & Stella Maris*
797	Tall Ship Adventures	*Sir Francis Drake*
654	Temptress Cruises	*Adventures that Fit Your Nature*
524	The Moorings	*Sailing Vacations*
798	Windjammer Barefoot Cruises	
648	Windstar Cruises	*180 Degrees from Ordinary*
637	World Explorer Cruises	*Cultural Cruises of Alaska*
860	Yankee Schooner Cruises	*Schooner Roseway*

Destinations:

Videos featured below were produced by or in cooperation with the area tourist boards.

731	Anguilla	*Tranquility Wrapped in Blue*	
606	Australia	*Australia: Discover It!*	
684	Bahamas	*We Are the Bahamas*	
565	Barbados	*Take a Closer Look*	
528	Bermuda	*Bermuda: Life in a Day*	
780	Bonaire	*The Natural Choice*	
603	Brazil-Varig Brazilian Airlines	*Worlds of Brazil*	
590	British Virgin Islands	*Nature's Little Secret*	
657	China	*China*	
610	Costa Rica	*Imagination*	
530	Curacao	*Breakaway from the Everyday*	
736	Denmark	*Denmark: A Danish Symphony*	
652	Dominica	*Nature Island*	
540	Fiji	*Fiji Islands*	
666	Hong Kong	*Behind the Mask*	
611	Ireland	*The Emerald Isle*	
671	Israel-El Al Israel Airlines	*Milk & Honey Vacations*	
746	Israel	*It Could Only Be Israel*	
735	Lana'i	*7th Day Island*	
595	Martinique	*La Martinique*	

516	Maui	*There's Nothing Like It*	
638	Mexico	*Colonial Cities of Mexico*	
832	New Caledonia	*Viva La Difference*	
721	New Guinea - Air Nuigini	*Land of the Unexpected*	
613	New Zealand	*New Zealand on My Mind*	
617	Portugal - TAP Air Portugal	*Invitation to Portugal*	
534	Puerto Rico	*Shining Star of the Caribbean*	
615	Scandinavia	*Scandinavia: Only One Place Like It*	
616	South Africa	*Animal Land*	
582	St. Kitts & Nevis	*Secret of the Carribean*	
663	St. Lucia	*Images of St. Lucia*	
767	St. Lucia	*Live the Dream*	
686	Tahiti	*Tahiti and Her Islands*	
622	Trinidad & Tobago	*Discover a World*	
584	U.S. Virgin Islands	*Follow a Rainbow*	
670	Vanuatu-Air Vanuatu	*The Timeless Islands*	
525	Zambia	*Zambia: The Real Africa*	

ORDER NOW TOLL FREE: 1-800-822-4604

To order your Cruises On Tape Videos, credit card customers order Toll Free ... Call 1-800-822-4604. Or mail coupon to the address below indicating which videos you'd like by writing in the order number(s) below. Each Video you choose (each box filled in below) is $7, plus a one-time $4.75 postage & handling charge. (Ex. If you fill in 3 numbers below, that is $21, plus $4.75 for a total of $25.75). Tax is included.

Take advantage of our BONUS OFFER: Buy 4 or more, get an additional video FREE!*

Name _____	Number of Videos selected _____
Address _____	Multiply times $7 each _____
City_____ State_____ Zip_____	Add $4.75 for Postage/Handling __$4.75__
Tel. _____	Int'l. orders: add $15.75 _____
☐ Check ☐ Visa ☐ Mastercard ☐ Amex Expires (mo./year) [____]	Total Enclosed: _____

Card Number: __ __ __ __ __ __ __ __ __ __ __ __ __ __ __ __

Please send me the following videos: [___][___][___][___]

If you ordered 4 or more above, write the # of your *FREE VIDEO here: [___]

SEND TO:
Publisher's Video Group
P.O. Box 5293
Pittsfield, MA 01203-5293
or FAX 413-637-4343

94-05-32